BEN
JONSON

Inigo Jones's design for the Queen's dress as Chloris in 'Chloridia'

BEN
JONSON

Edited by C. H. HERFORD
and PERCY SIMPSON

VOLUMES I & II
The Man and his Work

The Second Volume

OXFORD
At the Clarendon Press

Oxford University Press, Amen House, London E.C.4
Glasgow   New York   Toronto   Melbourne   Wellington
Bombay   Calcutta   Madras   Karachi   Cape Town   Ibadan
Geoffrey Cumberlege Publisher to the UNIVERSITY

FIRST EDITION 1925
REPRINTED LITHOGRAPHICALLY IN GREAT BRITAIN AT THE
UNIVERSITY PRESS, OXFORD, FROM CORRECTED SHEETS OF
THE FIRST EDITION
1954

# CONTENTS

VOLUME II

INTRODUCTIONS TO THE PLAYS (*continued*)

	PAGE
SEJANUS HIS FALL	1
EASTWARD HO!	29
VOLPONE	47
THE SILENT WOMAN	67
THE ALCHEMIST	85
Appendix VI: Bruno's *Candelaio*	109
CATILINE HIS CONSPIRACY	111
BARTHOLOMEW FAIR	129
Appendix VII: Lantern Leatherhead and Inigo Jones	146
THE DEVIL IS AN ASS	149
THE STAPLE OF NEWS	167
THE NEW INN	187
Appendix VIII: *The New Inn* and Fletcher's *Love's Pilgrimage*	198
THE MAGNETIC LADY	201

	PAGE
THE SAD SHEPHERD	211
Appendix IX: The Additions to 'The Spanish Tragedy'	235
MASQUES AND ENTERTAINMENTS	247
THE POEMS	335
THE ENGLISH GRAMMAR	415
THE DISCOVERIES	437
INDEX	453

LIST OF ILLUSTRATIONS

VOLUME II

INIGO JONES'S DESIGN FOR THE QUEEN'S DRESS AS CHLORIS IN 'CHLORIDIA'. *Frontispiece*

INIGO JONES'S DESIGN FOR A NYMPH IN 'CHLORIDIA'. *To face page* 249

INIGO JONES'S DESIGN FOR THE 'FIRST FACE OF THE SCENE' IN THE MASQUE OF 'OBERON'.
Between pages 284, 285

INIGO JONES'S DESIGN FOR THE PALACE IN THE MASQUE OF 'OBERON'. *Between pages* 286, 287

INIGO JONES'S DESIGN FOR THE FIRST SCENE IN 'CHLORIDIA'. *Between pages* 334, 335

INTRODUCTION TO
'SEJANUS HIS FALL'

SEJANUS HIS FALL

IN the 'Apologetical Dialogue' to the *Poetaster*, Jonson had announced that he meant now to abandon Comedy, whose Muse had proved 'so ominous' to him, and to try

>If *Tragœdie* haue a more kind aspect.

But his audience were not to imagine that his experiment in tragedy was merely a bid for popularity. He would be satisfied if but one understanding spirit approved:

>So he judicious be; He shall b' alone
>A Theatre vnto me.

He could not indeed conceal an assurance that the tragedy on which he was already perhaps spending half his nights and all his days would 'strike the eare of time', and compel his countrymen in spite of themselves to wonder and despair. But it was in itself a lonely inspiration, irrelevant to the noisy rivalries of the day which had provoked so much of his comic work, and only to be rightly carried out if they could be put aside and forgotten. And so he breaks off with a sudden impatience in which the bitter flavour of old scorn still qualifies the new-found fervour of the tragic poet—

Leaue me. There's something come into my thought,
That must, and shall be sung, high, and aloofe,
Safe from the wolues black iaw, and the dull asses hoofe.

These powerful lines are the true prologue to *Sejanus*. Their best commentary is the remark of the law-student Manningham, in his diary (under date February 12, 1603), that 'ben Jonson the poet nowe lives upon one Townsend and scornes the world'.

One qualification, however, has to be made to this account. In his address 'To the Readers' of the first Quarto, 1605, Jonson informed them that 'a second Pen' had 'had good share' in the play as originally composed; 'in place of which

I haue rather chosen, to put weaker (and no doubt less
pleasing) of mine own, then to defraud so happy a *Genius*
of his right, by my lothed vsurpation'. Which are the
substituted passages? Whose was the second pen? The
first problem seems to be insoluble. Jonson's minute and
deliberate art is more than a match for our critical methods;
the sutures of his patchwork evade our scrutiny. As to
the second, there is also no explicit evidence. The older
critics assumed without question that 'the happy genius'
whose verses Jonson rejected was Shakespeare. Gifford,
on equally indefinite grounds, declared for Fletcher. But
probability rather points to Chapman. None of his fellow
dramatists, in the first place, could be compared with this
veteran in scholarly equipment, and few in genius; and no
other could have contributed to *Sejanus* work which in the
Jonsonian virtues—'truth of Argument, dignity of Persons,
grauity and height of Elocution, fulnesse and frequencie of
Sentence'—so well matched his own. The nearest contemporary parallels to these Roman tragedies of Jonson's are
the tragedies drawn by Chapman during the next few years
from the recent history of France. We know, moreover, (1)
that the play in its original form excited displeasure in
high quarters, and that Jonson, as he told Drummond, was
'called before the Council for his *Sejanus*,[1] and accused
both of Popery and of Treason' by Lord Northampton.
(2) Although the passages which occasioned these proceedings
were no doubt excised in the first printed text, one, at least,
was left, perhaps by oversight, in the Quarto, and was altered
only in the Folio. Thus in III. 302-10 Silius was made to
say, in the final version,

> so soone, all best turnes,
> With doubtfull Princes, turne deepe iniuries
> In estimation, when they greater rise,
> Then can be answer'd. Benefits, with you,

[1] It is not absolutely certain, from Drummond's phrase, that
Northampton's charge of 'popery and treason' was made on the
occasion when Jonson was called before the Council for *Sejanus*, or, if
it was, that the charge was based upon the play.

Are of no longer pleasure, then you can
With ease restore them; that transcended once,
Your studies are not how to thanke, but kill.
It is your nature, to haue all men slaues
To you, but you acknowledging to none.

These lines doubtless sufficed to prove Silius 'Caesar's foe', but they would hardly have provided a handle for a charge of treason against their author. In the Quarto, however, the opening lines read:

so soone, all best Turnes,
With *Princes*, do conuert to iniuries.[1]

The ensuing lines were thus originally, with far greater force, intended to reflect upon 'princes' at large.[2] Now Chapman, alone among the greater dramatists of the day, strikes this note of republican sentiment in the famous passage of *The Gentleman Usher* quoted long since by Swinburne as 'so far as I know, the first direct protest against the principle of monarchy to be found in our poetical or dramatic literature':

And whats a Prince? Had all beene vertuous men,
There neuer had beene Prince vpon the earth,
And so no subiect; all men had beene Princes.[3]

The lines of Chapman prefixed to *Sejanus* indicate that he and Jonson had been defended from the enemies of poetry and of poets by the intervention of the Lord Chamberlain Suffolk, perhaps in connexion with this very play. These circumstances have been discussed in the 'Life'.

Neither Jonson nor Chapman, if he it was, was new to that branch of the drama whose 'kinder aspect' they now in common sought to invoke. Jonson was known as a writer of tragedy of secondary rank, before he sprang into fame as the author of the first great Comedy of Humours. Beside the *Page of Plymouth* in conjunction with Dekker,

---

[1] Quarto, sig. F 3 verso.
[2] It may be added that the repetition of *turn* in the Folio version is most naturally explained as an oversight due to the alterations of the phrase.
[3] Quarto, 1606, sig. I 3.

and the additions to *The Spanish Tragedy*, he had written the lost *Richard Crookback* (June, 1602), and had plotted a tragedy (1597), which in the course of 1598 Chapman put into dialogue. This may have been the *Fall of Mortimer*, of which the plot and a fragment of the first scene were included in the 1640 Folio, and have sometimes been identified with the 'play of Mortimer' mentioned by Henslowe in 1602.[1] In any case the *Fall of Mortimer* offers an interesting parallel. There too he represented the career of a favourite raised from small beginnings to exalted power by royal confidence, and then, at the height of his insolent security, suddenly struck down. This also was a subject not easily reconciled with 'the strict laws of time' (i. e. the limitation to a single day), for the violation of which he apologizes to the readers of *Sejanus*. On the other hand he intended in *Mortimer* to provide a chorus,—the absence of which he also excuses,—a chorus loosely enough adapted, it is true, to classical precedent, for it consists of at least three several bodies—'ladies', 'courtiers', 'country-justices and their wives', who intervene respectively after the first, second, and third acts. The emphasis which Jonson lays, in the preface to *Sejanus*, upon the difficulties of 'a proper *Chorus*, whose Habite, and Moodes are such, . . . as not any, whome I haue seene since the *Auntients*, (no not they who haue most presently affected Lawes) haue yet come in the way off' suggests that he had himself tried the experiment and found it unsatisfactory.[2] The plot of *Mortimer* may very well represent that experiment. In any case, we have in *Sejanus* the work of one who, with all his classical predilections, meant to follow the ancients 'as Guides, not Commanders' (*Discoveries*, Folio, p. 89). He was writing for the stage, and his sound if not impeccable stage-instinct told him how

[1] Dr. Greg's discussion (*Henslowe's Diary*, ii. 188) seems decisive against this.
[2] Jonson says advisedly 'a *proper* chorus'. For the words 'Mu. chorus', added at the end of the first four acts, show that he intended some kind of choric performance—probably a dance with music—to do duty perforce for the impracticable chorus of the Greeks.

an Elizabethan audience would have been likely to receive a modern *Prometheus* or *Persae*. He knew that all the 'ould state, and splendour' of such plays would not have atoned for their bareness and simplicity of outline and slowness of movement. For he was himself, in these very points of instinctive taste, a true if not altogether confessed Elizabethan; he relished, if he did not frankly approve, the crowded incident, the complex and intricate plot-economy of the popular drama. *Sejanus*, accordingly, while far more solidly built upon classical learning than any previous English play, pays a very distant homage to classical technique. It is certain that Jonson, for reasons which he had justified to himself, and intended to justify to his readers, deliberately infringed the principles of that technique; but 'Vulcan' unhappily intervened and destroyed those 'Obseruations vpon *Horace, his Art of Poetry*' from which we should have learned so much.[1] The 'law of time' is, as has been said, openly set aside. The action covers an historical period of eight years, and of dramatic time, at the lowest computation, several months. A prodigious crowd of persons take part. The *dramatis personae* outnumber those of *Julius Caesar* or *Antony and Cleopatra*, and being less clearly individualized and less harmoniously grouped, they seem even more numerous than they really are. Horace had deprecated violent death upon the stage: Jonson makes Silius stab himself in the open court, and that without any definite warrant from his authority. And Sejanus, an unscrupulous intriguer from first to last, might have been modelled by the hand of a rebel against the classical drama instead of by its champion, so sharply does he conflict with the tragic hero either of Aristotle or of the Attic stage.

II

But if Jonson set aside the canons of antique tragedy, it was in the name of a more thoroughgoing fidelity to

[1] 'To the Readers', sig. ¶ 2. Compare 'An Execration upon Vulcan' (*Underwoods*, xliii. 89, 90).

antiquity itself. 'Truth of *Argument*', 'integrity in the *Story*',—these he meant in a sense and to a degree which no one before him in the English drama had attempted. His Elizabethan joy in sheer abundance and multiplicity— so openly displayed in his Comedies without exception— was here fortified by the scholar's meticulous particularity in rendering historic facts. Both instincts concurred in relaxing his allegiance to the classical ideal in tragedy. The conflict must, however, have been keen. It was not new, for the combination of Elizabethan stage-instinct, historic erudition, and classicist doctrine was bound to produce it; but this combination had always been rare, and had certainly never occurred in a mind where all three elements were so potent and so well matched as in Jonson's. The Renascence, which revealed the antique drama, and its noble commentary, the *Poetics* of Aristotle, had also brought into more vivid proximity antiquity as a whole, with its wealth of tragic and heroic story, told with incomparable art and fascinating abundance of detail. The histories of Caesar and Pompey and Cleopatra were more refractory to the severe scheme of Senecan tragedy than the legends of Oedipus and Agamemnon, Dido and Medea. In Italy and France, indeed, antique scheme held its ground with even increased stringency, completely unaffected by the allurements of a complex historic plot. The passion for literary imitations entirely subdued the nascent interest in historic fidelity; Caesar was presented not in his habit as he lived, but as Euripides or Seneca would have painted him. Trissino's *Sophonisba* and Jodelle's *Cléopatre* are as academic as any of the contemporary *Didos* or *Antigones*. In England, on the other hand, the Senecan tradition was less confidently accepted and applied even on the exclusive private stages of the universities and Inns of Court; while on the popular stage it made no headway at all until its most sensational ingredients had been artfully fused with the native tradition by Kyd. The first tragedy, *Gorboduc*, is an extraordinary example of the concessions which the national temperament forced even upon writers with a pronounced bias for antique form. And for thirty years afterwards, the national History remained a field in which the native stagecraft and the native taste asserted themselves unchecked. While Tragedy and Comedy made rapid advances towards a real unity of action, thanks largely to the compact Italian novels on which they were so often founded, the 'History' had no unity but a reign, and no limits but the proportion of its sensational happenings which could be compressed into three hours. Even when, in the nineties, the advance in structural coherence and form became general all along the line, it made its way more slowly, and by more uncertain steps, in the 'History' than elsewhere. Shakespeare himself, to whom a really formless drama was from the first impossible, yet allows himself far greater structural liberties in the Histories than in any other branch of his plays. And when, at the beginning of the new century, he turned from England to Rome, it was to write dramas which were no longer 'Histories' even in name. In the Roman plays he evolved a true historical drama, structurally organic, yet sufficiently free and plastic to represent the complexity and movement of a great historic action. The structural mastery of the Roman plays is the more remarkable since he was here handling sources with far closer fidelity than before. In *Julius Caesar* above all, essential historicity was achieved without detriment to the most pellucid simplicity of structure. And when Jonson sat down to write *Sejanus*, *Julius Caesar* was still one of the resounding successes of the day.

It is certain that *Julius Caesar* counted for much more than Jonson would have acknowledged, or was aware of, in the making of *Sejanus*. He planned his work, no doubt, in conscious and even disdainful emulation. The splendid Roman triumph won by the man of small Latin and less Greek, who 'wanted art', was a challenge to his conscious superiority both in art and learning. He had himself openly derided, if we may trust his report in the *Discoveries*, a slip in the fluent language of Shakespeare's play.[1] But Jonson's emulation was itself a tribute. His attempt to outdo *Julius Caesar* rested in large part upon imitation. Shakespeare had led the way in historic drama founded upon the great portraits in the ancient historians reproduced in detail. Jonson did the same, only drawing upon more sources, and reading them at first hand. Shakespeare represented a famous Roman conspiracy, ending in the ruin of the conspirators. Jonson meant to show what could be made of another Roman conspiracy by a poet who had access to the greatest of Roman historians and could render Tacitus in language as authentic and hardly less sinewy. In *Julius Caesar* the creative or re-creative processes of Shakespeare are relatively unobtrusive. The matter is clarified and ennobled, but not completely transfigured, like the matter of *Hamlet* or *Othello*. Caesar himself is, in Shakespeare, almost a failure. It is hard to lay a finger on the point at which the divinity steals into his 'god-like' Romans. There is no romantic heightening of stature, no hint of legendary glamour, hardly any deliberate and palpable invention. Much of the alchemy consists in a mere sifting and straining away of disturbing elements, of confusing and insignificant incident, of vague or redundant traits, of the baser and poorer kinds of prose. It is not inexplicable that Jonson should have seen in *Julius Caesar* the loose brilliance of an amateur. He overlooked the miracles which even the unobtrusive touches of Shakespeare effect in that simplest of his masterpieces.

[1] Caesar did never wrong but with just cause.
The phrase is represented in our texts by the quite unexceptionable:
Know, Caesar doth not wrong; nor without cause
Will he be satisfied—

Jonson's version may caricature the original defect, but it is unlikely that his criticism was wholly without ground. On the other hand, Shakespeare may have written something like what Jonson says, and have later amended it, perhaps in consequence of this very criticism, No unfriendly animus could be inferred from that. But the correction had in this case been made for many years, as Jonson must have known, and it would remain noteworthy that he should ignore the fact.

III

The fullest and most authoritative account of the story of Sejanus is the narrative of Tacitus in the fourth and fifth books of the *Annals*. This is the principal source of Jonson's play. It was, however, unfortunately not available for the last three years of Sejanus' career, told in the lost portion of the fifth book. For these years in particular, but also as a subsidiary source throughout, he used the account in Dion's *Roman History* (lvii. 22—lviii. 12), drawing also some telling phrases and traits of character from the collection of anecdotes which Suetonius called his 'Life' of Tiberius. The details of the catastrophe and of the frenzied popular vengeance which followed he took from Juvenal's powerful sketch in the Tenth *Satire* (ll. 54-113), and from Seneca (*de Tranquillitate*, c. 11). This rich material Jonson handled not only, as was to be expected, with the security of a scholar, but with a dramaturgical mastery which, after his last three comedies, was very much less a matter of course. Justice has even now hardly been done to the extent and value of Jonson's creative work upon his sources. *Sejanus* is popularly regarded as, in Hazlitt's unfortunate phrase, an 'ancient mosaic' of 'translated bits'. Even were it so, to have evolved out of the combined and assorted bits so powerful a picture would argue no mean art. But, in fact, the proportion of matter translated or closely paraphrased amounts at the utmost to a quarter of the whole. Narrative sources do not as a rule yield drama on these easy terms. Apart from the interspersed speeches and conversations, most of which he substantially incorporated, Jonson has to frame dialogue for most of his persons on the basis of a mere mention of their meeting, or a summary indication of their aims, policy, and character. When his authorities are silent, he interprets and expounds their silence with much freedom; introducing, for instance, persons on occasions when they are not stated to have been present. More than this, he has sometimes deliberately modified the historical sequence of events, and with it, once or twice at least, their complexion and significance. He has, to this extent, rewritten the script of history, as well as filled in its lacunas. The cases which bear directly upon the plot may be noticed at the outset.

(1) Tacitus represents Sejanus' intrigue with the wife of Drusus as an act of vengeance for the blow he had publicly received from the prince, and therefore, of course, as subsequent to it.[1] Jonson's Sejanus, when we first encounter him, is already preparing, by his intermediary Eudemus, to corrupt her (I. 178-90), and this simply in order to gain access to the secrets of her husband with a view to his destruction.

> Prosper it, PALLAS, thou, that betterst wit,
> For VENVS hath the smallest share in it.
> (I. 383-4.)

The public insult follows, at the end of the act.

(2) In Tacitus, the attack upon the sons of Germanicus, their mother Agrippina, and her partisans Silius and Sabinus, is a more gradual process, with several clearly marked phases. The boys are introduced to the Senate after the death of Drusus, with every mark of favour, by Tiberius himself;[2] it was only in the following year (A.D. 24) that a proposal of the pontiff to offer the same prayers for them and the emperor roused the latter's dangerous jealousy. 'Vexed beyond measure', he took the Senate roundly to task, and the fate of the boys and of their mother, though still delayed, was sealed. Of this mood of Tiberius Sejanus now took advantage to urge the destruction of their party. Silius, accordingly, and Sabinus are marked for doom, and the accusation of the first-named immediately follows. Jonson compresses this and in some degree alters the connexion of events. The ruin of Silius is part of the vast scheme of vengeance conceived by Sejanus after the insult received from Drusus; it is announced to Tiberius

---

[1] *Ann.* iv. 3. Dion makes Sejanus himself the aggressor.
[2] *Ann.* iv. 8.

and accepted by him, even before the death of Drusus is known (II. 188 fol.): and Silius is accused at the same meeting of the Senate in which Tiberius introduces and recommends the children of Germanicus (III. 156).

(3) In Tacitus the accusation of Cremutius Cordus has no connexion with that of Silius, and follows it a year later (in A. D. 25).[1] Jonson makes it immediately follow the death of Silius, at the same meeting of the Senate (III. 315)

To a different category belong Jonson's additions to the recorded facts. These are never arbitrary, and usually they show the keenest insight into the situation. Thus Domitius Afer is introduced as the accuser of Silius and Cremutius. In Tacitus Afer figures first two years later[2] as the accuser of Claudia Pulchra. But the Tacitean description of him as a man 'eager to become notorious by any sort of deed' makes Jonson's anticipation dramatically apt and plausible in a high degree.

More important is the use made of the imposing figure of Arruntius. This implacable critic and denouncer of tyranny is not mentioned by Tacitus, Dion, or Suetonius during the career of Sejanus. Tacitus' references to him elsewhere, besides giving brief but vivid indications of his character (especially in *Annals* i. 13), show that he lived through that period hated by Sejanus as well as afterwards by his successor Marco, 'not for any fault, but as one who could not tolerate gross iniquities'.[3] On the basis of these slight indications Jonson has fashioned the Arruntius who plays so impressive a part in this tragedy. For this Jonsonian Arruntius is something more than the vehement and caustic opposition leader whom Tacitus' sketch allows us to divine. He is the voice and exponent of the irrepressible critic and censor in Jonson himself. Such an exponent Jonson needed. The classical chorus he had unwillingly dispensed with; the Elizabethan Fool he had scornfully banished; but he could not yet dispense in

---

[1] *Ann.* iv. 34-5.   [2] *Ann.* iv. 52.   [3] *Ann.* vi. 48.

tragedy, any more than in comedy, with the author's proxy on the stage.[1]

If Jonson the censor provided a spokesman for himself at some cost to historic fidelity, the inborn Elizabethan Jonson allowed some of the sensational suggestions of the plot free play, against the warrant of the classic rules. The words of Tacitus at least lead us to suppose that the suicide of Silius took place elsewhere than in the open court; that is, than on the stage.[2] Jonson in the teeth of Horace chose to make it happen there, to the immense advantage of the whole scene which issues in this tragic climax. The gain is less clear, and the historic foundation still less solid, in the great scene of Sejanus' arrest. It does not appear that in reality any actual physical violence was offered to him until he was being dragged from the Senate-house to the prison. When the terrible closing sentences of the imperial Letter at length threw off the mask, a yell of execration burst from the senators; but his friends and kindred were present in strong force, and fear was still as potent as rage; so that Regulus, dreading opposition, dropped formalities and, on the strength of a single voice, ordered Sejanus to be carried off to prison. And then, at last, when all danger was palpably at an end, the suppressed fury of the Senate found full vent. Jonson imagines the scene somewhat otherwise. Certainly he gives no idea of the united clamour of abuse; his senators sit 'amaz'd, and silent'. But one of Sejanus' foes, and the most formidable of all, who was not even present at his surrender, Jonson allows to anticipate this violence. 'Am I call'd?' Sejanus has asked, half-bewildered

---

[1] That so bold and unsparing a critic of the Government should go unscathed when so many other less conspicuous supporters of the house of Germanicus were struck down, demanded, for dramatic purposes, an explanation. Jonson accordingly makes Sejanus slightingly dispose of him as one who 'only talkes' (II. 299), and may thus be left alone, like Sabinus, till his fate is ripe; all the more because to spare such an assailant would argue justice, not malice, in the punishment of the rest (III. 497-501). This hardly accords with the estimate of him formed, according to *Annales*, i. 13, by Augustus as well as Tiberius, and evidently endorsed by Tacitus himself, as a man no less daring than capable.

[2] *Ann.* iv. 19.

at the unwonted sound of a command. ' I, thou', Macro bursts out,

> Thou insolent monster, art bid stand.
> . . . .
> Come downe *Typhœus* . . . thus I . . .
> Kicke vp thy heeles in ayre, teare off thy robe,
> Play with thy beard, and nostrills. Thus 'tis fit,
> (And no man take compassion of thy state)
> To use th' ingratefull viper, tread his braines
> Into the earth. (V. 705-17.)

With few and trifling exceptions such as these the plot of *Sejanus* is built with severe conformity to the historical record. With the reserves indicated, the history is incorporated in the play, and the play contains no incident not derived from the history. It is naturally otherwise with the actual dialogue. Largely as Jonson has availed himself of the fragments of talk recorded in his sources, by far the greater part of the dialogue is based upon brief indications and general descriptions, or the mere hint supplied by the situation. Two long colloquies are in the main paraphrases from Tacitus: the crucial speech in which Sejanus asks his master's permission to marry Livia, with Tiberius' reply,[1] and Cremutius Cordus' speech in his own defence.[2] Even here, however, there are masterly touches of Jonson's own, such as the ominous 'H'mh' which escapes Tiberius at the first hint of the favourite's audacious demand.

Among the scenes founded upon descriptions are Sejanus' earlier colloquy with Tiberius (II. 163 fol.), and the memorable Letter—*verbosa et grandis epistola*—from Capreae, which closed his career. The former has no further basis than a sentence of Suetonius (*Tib.* c. 55), which states that Tiberius had promoted Sejanus to power solely that he may be his agent in disposing of the children of Germanicus; and a paragraph of Tacitus which describes Sejanus' machinations against Agrippina. For the Letter Jonson had, besides Juvenal's famous phrase, only Dion's graphic but quite general description: 'The letter was long, and

---

[1] III. 516-76; *Ann.* iv. 39-40.   [2] III. 407-60; *Ann.* iv. 34-5.

contained nothing decisive against Sejanus, but first something on another matter, then a slight reprehension of him, then something different, than something further against him. And at the close he ordered two senators of his party to be punished, and Sejanus himself to be put under arrest.'[1] From these hints, supplemented by the few extant specimens of other imperial communications to the Senate, Jonson composed the masterly utterance of pusillanimous malignity which in an instant annihilates the apparently all-powerful favourite. He can hardly have been unconscious of the analogy in situation between this scene and Antony's wonderful *tour de force* in *Julius Caesar*; and if he contemplated his own performance with some equanimity he was not altogether without excuse. Antony's oration is a superb piece of poetical eloquence, perfectly imagined for the effect to be produced, and almost as moving to the modern reader, who knows its purpose, as to the Roman mob. But precisely because it is a piece of consummate acting— however genuine the personal grief which underlay it—it cannot take the impress of the mind and character of the speaker, the crowning glory of dramatic oratory, as do, for instance, Othello's speech to the Senate or Volumnia's in the camp. The Letter of Tiberius is not less subtly calculated than Antony's speech to compass its purpose of ruining a party without prematurely alarming it; but we follow in it also step by step the workings of the old emperor's slow, timid and insidious brain, as he hints and qualifies, suggests a fault, then hurriedly effaces it with a compliment, condemns all ungrateful favourites and protests that Sejanus is not meant—on whom nevertheless it would be well to keep an eye.

IV

Closely as Sejanus is modelled upon history, none of Jonson's dramas is more Jonsonian in conception and execution. If he alters little in his historical materials, it is partly

[1] Dion, lviii. 10.

because history in some important points played as it were into his hands, providing both a kind of action and a prevailing quality of character singularly suited to his genius and to his art. The advance in coherence upon any of the Humour plays, after the first, is enormous; upon *Every Man in his Humour* itself, it is considerable. He was entering in fact upon a new phase of his art. The immense constructive grip soon to be shown in *Volpone* and *The Alchemist* is already approached, as their dramatic situation is anticipated. In the history of Sejanus Jonson found the prototype of the motif which he was twice again to handle and with yet greater mastery—a pair of consummately bad men in league against society, which they mercilessly exploit; until some false move turns the alliance into a mortal if undeclared struggle for supremacy, in which one or both fall. The inferior in station—Sejanus, Mosca, Face—is, at least at the outset, the superior in craft, but two of the three suffer a more disastrous overthrow. And the catastrophe has this peculiarity, which we may venture to call Jonsonian, that, overwhelming as it is when it comes, it is not a climax, long prepared for and foreseen, but a sudden fall brought about by a slight disturbance of the equilibrium of huge opposed forces, like the last throw of the dice which decides an almost even game. In the deadly last tussle of Volpone and Mosca the servant finally goes under; in that of Face and Subtle, the master; but, with a little readjustment of the circumstances Mosca would have emerged a magnifico instead of a galley-slave, and Face have found himself in the Fleet instead of being restored to place and favour. In the tremendous world-duel of Sejanus and Tiberius the apparent equipoise is yet more complete, as the ensuing ruin is even more abysmal. Rome looks on, hating and fearing both, and impartially ready to fall upon whichever first stumbles. The boundless imperial power, which could at any moment have crushed the force it had created, is checked, and comes near being checkmated, by the personal spell which enables Sejanus to paralyse the emperor's sleepless mistrust and inexhaustible duplicity, so that, as Tacitus says, the man who was impenetrable to all others became open to him. Sejanus accordingly spreads his toils with impunity, until, in a fit of the amazing blindness which sometimes betrays these tamers of wild beasts, he seeks alliance with the imperial house. Tiberius dissembles and temporizes, but appoints Macro to watch him, and Sejanus' career seems to be closed. But a rare opportunity, adroitly seized, saves him; he rescues Tiberius at the farm of Spelunca (IV. 48) and instantly recovers his ground. The emperor remains in permanent seclusion at Capreae, leaving the favourite free scope at Rome; and supreme power seems already within his reach. But the reports sent to Capreae grow more and more menacing, and Tiberius, at length genuinely alarmed, resolves to crush Sejanus. Even now, however, fear paralyses his hand; he dares not strike until the dictator is completely off his guard. Hence the succession of cunningly ambiguous letters, which quietly undermine the assurance and fidelity of his supporters, without arousing the least suspicion in their chief; and the final masterstroke of the Letter itself. Instantly the fabric of Sejanus' power collapses. His body is torn to shreds, the whole man annihilated. The swiftness and completeness of the 'Fall' stands in dramatic contrast to the long undecisive poise of the scales of fortune which preceded. Such a career was congenial to the ways of Jonson's imagination. Slow and prolonged movement, with its uncertain and fluctuating poise, appealed to his grim liking for holding the hearer in suspense, and checking or deluding his expectation. Sejanus' brief recovery of his foothold on the slippery ground has its counterpart in the momentary triumph of Mosca. And his fall was no less congenial, as has just been said, to Jonson's love for sudden, complete, and irrevocable catastrophes. Even the physical brutalities which marked it cannot have been aesthetically distasteful to the future author of *Volpone*. One cannot but contrast with the reticence of Shakespeare in this matter the zest with which Jonson writes out (from Juvenal) sanguinary details of the popular vengeance on his body, and accentuates the more savage circumstances of his arrest.

V

The characters, like the plot, of *Sejanus* show few traces of deliberate departure from the historical data. Here too this subject was on the whole highly favourable to his range and quality of dramatic power. Romantic passion, fresh and ardent youth, children, noble women—all of them uncongenial to his art—were either of subordinate importance, or wholly wanting. Such examples of them as his story offered he is too apt to degrade. His Agrippina is an eloquent woman incessantly inveighing against the tyrant; but she has only this one mood: Jonson does not show us, like Tacitus, her pathetic desolation (*Ann.* iv. 53); even her anger, as he renders it, flashes out in no such annihilating strokes as her single sentence in Tacitus when she finds Tiberius sacrificing to his father: ' It befits not the same man to sacrifice to the divine Augustus and to persecute his posterity.'[1] Agrippina's sons are but lay figures; even Drusus, Sejanus' first assailant and first victim, flashes into distinctness only for a moment (I. 571-86). The pathetic story of the slaughter of Sejanus' children, is less moving in the *ad captandum* rhetoric of Jonson's ' Nuntius ' (V. 869-89) than in the austere recital of Tacitus (*Ann.* v. 9).

The case is different with the much larger group of characters who neither provoke nor are intended to provoke pity, but contribute, actively or passively, to the atmosphere of scorn and hate which pervades the play. The enemies of Sejanus and his agent—the old irreconcilables of vanquished Liberty, and the minions of the new régime— belong to satire rather than to tragedy. The grand figure of Arruntius, as has been already indicated, resumes the

[1] *Ann.* i. 52.

Asper-Crites-Horace of the Humour comedies. He cannot indeed play a like triumphant part. The throng of would-be wits and futile courtiers is replaced here by a colossus of make-believe, armed with irresistible powers. Arruntius has no function but that of a chorus, who speaks daggers but uses none, and is unheeded and for the most part unheard by those for whom they are meant; but the virtue of old Rome breaks out in his indignant or ironical comments, an excellent foil to the more than 'Greek' duplicity of his great opponent.

In Eudemus and Livia we seem to return for a moment to the familiar theme of his comedies—the Jonsonian satire of Court ladies and professional charlatans. Yet, with all respect to Dryden, Jonson's first distinguished critic, his description of this scene as itself comedy 'unnaturally mixed', in 'this oleo of a play', with tragedy,[1] is surely beside the mark. No doubt some lines and speeches would not have been out of place in *Cynthia's Revels* or *Every Man out of his Humour*, just as Lear's 'levelling' outburst might occur in a satire on the abuses of fashion. The test of 'comic mixture' is whether the potentially comic material is applied to actually comic effect. And surely this light talk of washes and dentifrice in the course of arranging the details of Drusus's murder, far from interrupting or 'relieving' the tragic action, adds to its horror. The thoughts and occupations of Livia are, if we will, an 'oleo', an 'unnatural mixture' of frivolity and crime. But the fact only exposes the cynical effrontery of this contriver of harms, and deepens our sense of pitiless powers determining the issues of the struggle. And this effect, whatever else it be, is not 'comic'. Livia has to the full the hard inner consistency of Jonson's criminal types in general. Different matters engage her, but her mood is always the same. She pursues her course with the dull uniformity of a machine, undeflected by love or fear (as she truly says),[2]—a kind of automatic Lady Macbeth, incapable of her inrushes of

---

[1] *Essay of Dramatic Poesy*, ed. Ker, p. 60.   [2] II. 47.

pathetic appeal ('Had he not resembled my father as he slept') as of her tragic remorse. It was not along these lines that the author of *Sejanus* sought to take the kingdom of tragedy by storm. Whatever effect he aimed at in tragedy it was not the purifying pity excited by the fatal errors of a noble nature. Of this kind of ' error' there is no trace in his tragedies. His criminals have no complexity of moral nature; they just do their kind, like beasts of prey. If their actions seem inconsistent, it is because they fluctuate between different ways of achieving the same bad end. The overthrow of such men, however cruel in its circumstances, necessarily misses the effect of the finest tragedy. If it is simply a due requital of their misdeeds, tragic pity is excluded by satisfaction that justice is done. The only element of proximate tragedy open in such a case lies in the fatal illusions in which even the astutest criminal may be entangled by the very triumph of his plots. When, through such fatal misreading of the men he is dealing with, he is suddenly hurled from power, the clearest recognition that he deserves his lot cannot check some stirring of the thrill with which we see any man overwhelmed by forces he had inadvertently provoked. For this approach to tragedy the character of Sejanus, as presented by Tacitus, Dion, and Suetonius, offered an undoubted opening. Astute as he appears, he is in the end palpably overmatched in cunning, and Tacitus even professes to ascribe not to his craft, ' for in that he was outdone ', but to a divine interposition, his extraordinary ascendancy over Tiberius.[1] After the withdrawal of the emperor, at his persuasion, to Capreae he feels secure. Jonson, without introducing any point definitely new, has heightened the impression of illusory self-confidence. The Tacitean Sejanus is a political adventurer who shrinks from nothing in the struggle for power: Jonson's Sejanus is, with all this, an artist in crime, ambitious of renown for unheard-of prodigies of wickedness. His colossal brag belongs to the Marlowesque phase of tragedy; such

[1] *Ann.* iv. 1.

a speech as this looks back to Barabas as well as forward to Volpone:

> Adultery? it is the lightest ill,
> I will commit. A race of wicked acts
> Shall flow out of my anger, and o're-spread
> The worlds wide face, which no posterity
> Shall e're approoue, nor yet keepe silent: Things,
> That for their cunning, close, and cruell marke,
> Thy father would wish his; and shall (perhaps)
> Carry the empty name, but we the prize.[1]

At moments he has touches of the sublimity of Tamburlaine, but with a delirious ecstasy which marks the newly aggrandized, as at the opening of the fifth act, when to discerning eyes his doom is already impending:

> Swell, swell, my ioyes: . . .
> I did not liue, till now; this my first hower:
> . . . . Great, and high,
> The world knowes only two, that's *Rome*, and I.
> My roofe receiues me not; 'tis aire I tread;
> And, at each step, I feele my' aduanced head
> Knocke out a starre in heau'n![2]

If we are ever reminded of the more human criminals of Shakespeare, it is in moments of half-pitiful disdain for the helpless victims he has doomed. His

> Thou lost thy selfe, childe DRVSVS, when thou thought'st
> Thou could'st out-skip my vengeance: or out-stand
> The power I had to crush thee into ayre,—[3]

strikes the same chord as Richard's 'Simple plain Clarence!' and Macbeth's 'Thou wast born of woman!' When the omens begin to hint disaster, Sejanus braves it out; and even when his domestic statue of Fortune turns her face from him during the sacrifice, Jonson makes him demean himself as one who has not received divine honour for nothing. The wild unreason of this scene approaches the grotesque, but it is in admirable keeping with the fatuity which fatally crosses the astute policy of the Jonsonian Sejanus.

[1] *Sejanus*, II. 150-7.   [2] V. 1-9.   [3] II. 143-5.

> I, . . .
> That have been titled, and ador'd a god,
> Yea, sacrific'd vnto, my selfe, in *Rome*,
> No lesse then IOVE: and I be brought, to doe
> A peeuish giglot rites?[1]

The man whose head was thus turned by the monstrous honours paid him was likely, after all, to commit some fatal oversight in the deadly game. It is plain that, deceived by the unique ascendancy he had so easily won, Sejanus supposed he could play as he would upon the emperor's mind. It is equally plain that he under-estimated both the astuteness and the susceptibilities of his antagonist. 'Dull, heauie Caesar!' he bursts out, when Tiberius has left him (III. 586), apparently about to follow his interested counsel of retirement to Capreae. And Tiberius' parting words have been full of gracious regard for his 'carefull Sejanus'. None the less, his trust in the careful Sejanus has been irrecoverably shaken. From this moment Tiberius' apparently undiminished kindliness to him conceals a jealous and watchful scrutiny. His withdrawal to the remote island increased Sejanus' peril as well as his power. Tiberius interfered less in Roman affairs, but his occasional interpositions were more dangerous—desperate strokes of a timid and cruel man against invisible foes—while Sejanus purchased his increased command of resources and greater freedom of action at the price of losing his chief safeguard, the ascendancy of his personality over the despot's will. He became stronger to assail, weaker to resist. Unnerved for a moment by the disastrous omens, and still more by the secret arrival of his arch-foe Macro, he confronts his fate with sublime assurance,—

> *Rome*, *Senate*, people, all the world haue seene
> IOVE, but my equall; CAESAR, but my second;
> (V. 263-4.)

and falls an instant prey to the ready assurances of Macro:

> Fortune, be mine againe; thou hast satisfied
> For thy suspected loyaltie. (V. 366-7.)

[1] *Sejanus*, V. 203-6.

And then he turns with an outward burst of scorn, as near sublimity as anything in Jonson, to denounce the 'vain' and 'vile' passion of fear, that had beguiled him, and the whole heaven of signs and prodigies:

> When I doe feare againe, let me be strooke
> With forked fire, and vnpittyed die:
> Who feares, is worthy of calamitie. (v. 397–9.)

With all his old arrogant demeanour he attends the fatal meeting of the Senate, cuts short the familiarities he had for a moment encouraged, and accepts the servile fawnings of Senators once more eager for his 'lord-like nod'.

Two points in Sejanus' story seem chiefly to have interested Jonson's imagination; the sudden fall, as already noticed, and his blind arrogance. What he felt to be tragic in the story of Sejanus was in part that which the whole medieval world understood by tragedy, and the authors of the *Mirror for Magistrates* still exemplified in their tragic tales,—the sudden passage from prosperity to adversity. But this elementary tragedy was heightened, for Jonson's classical instinct, by the 'insolence' which precedes and provokes his fall. Arrogance was an emotion which Jonson profoundly understood, and he found utterance for it in verse of unusual splendour and intensity. It is in these moments of insolent assurance that Sejanus is as a poetic creation most imposing. When the blow has actually fallen his lofty spirit instantly gives way, and with it disappears also the vigour of Jonson's poetry. His few feeble and halting protests are taken almost literally from the poor narrative of Dion; in the tragedy, as in the history, calamity merely undoes him, leaves him nerveless and effete; a victim, ready bound and dumb, for the physical destruction soon to follow; but calls up no semblance of loftier manhood out of the depths of overthrow, nor any faintest throb of the tragic cry.

As Sejanus is not himself a genuinely tragic figure, so Tiberius belongs to tragedy only in virtue of the dooms he inflicts and the terror he excites. He is drawn even more predominantly from the outside than Sejanus; and as he has no soliloquies we never hear the lonely thoughts of this brooding and fanatical recluse. The powers of tyrannic rule had never been painted with more ruthless power than in this play ; but Jonson made no attempt to emphasize— perhaps he hardly heard or heeded—the note of inward torment which makes this monster of cruelty and lust pitiable as well as appalling, even in the stern and vindictive record of Tacitus. Tiberius at Capreae, as there portrayed, is not only the crafty despot, striking down foe after foe with calculating malignity from an unassailed vantage-ground ; he is the cowardly and superstitious criminal whose worst acts are impelled by a frenzy of fear, and whose accumulated crimes, if they do not haunt and torment his imagination, wreak on him a not less tormenting paralysis of will. 'What to write to you, at this time, may the gods undo me worse than I feel myself daily undone, if I know:' this desperate opening of an imperial Letter to the Senate, reported by both Tacitus and Suetonius, flashes a strange, involuntary light upon the inner mind of the despot, else so astutely veiled.[1] It is characteristic of Jonson's temper and of his art that he found no place in his minutely studied portraiture of Tiberius for this poignant touch of nature. He borrowed indeed the less expressive phrase in the sentence, but transferred it to a letter written under totally different conditions,—the tissue of calculated phrases which sealed the fate of Sejanus, where it takes the character of its context, and appears not as an involuntary ejaculation but as a piece of studied craft.[2] And it is the crafty Tiberius, the profound dissembler, that Jonson has almost exclusively given us. But this trait lay wholly within Jonson's compass, and he exposes it with all his patient and searching industry,—' mining his way ', as Hazlitt says, ' like a mole, and throwing the rich earth on the surface in prodigious quantities '. He has added little that is specifically his own, less than in the case of Sejanus; but the

[1] Tacitus, *Ann.* vi. 6 ; Suetonius, *Tib.* c. 67.
[2] The words are embodied in the Letter.

masterly portrait that he had before him needed no further touch, and Tiberius, the central theme with Tacitus, was for Jonson subordinate in importance to his upstart favourite. His Tiberius is rather displayed than revealed; the man, as the world saw him, and as his chosen intimate saw him, is drawn in elaborate detail; but what he fundamentally was, Jonson does not show us; the ultimate recesses of his soul are not probed. He exhibits, without tediously emphasizing them, the expressive oddities of manner, the perplexed and hesitating speech,[1] the habitual silences, the laconic commands. And the audience doubtless had before them, in the actor (probably Burbage) who personated him, some imitation more or less effective of that blotched face with its uncanny amiability, those appalling eyes, large and protuberant, and credited with power to see into the dark,[2] those long locks falling in most un-Roman fashion over his neck.[3]

Far as the character of Tiberius falls below the great tragic creations of Shakespeare, it has points of superiority to its nearest analogue in his Roman plays—the character of Julius Caesar. The Caesar who is declared to be 'the foremost man of all the world', and 'mighty yet' after his death, is inadequately represented by the Caesar we see. The magnificence of the poetry in which he expounds and vindicates his character ('We are two lions littered in one day,'—'I am constant as the northern star') does not diminish our sense of psychological disparity. From this defect the Jonsonian Tiberius (with whatever help from his source) is certainly free. His Tiberius, less complex than the Tacitean original, is perhaps the most complex character he ever drew. · But this Tiberius is psychologically unassailable; no hint of native grandeur provokes us to resent the eternal atmosphere of artifice. Duplicity is the element in which he lives, and he appears to be created to live in that element.

[1] As 'And now we better thinke—,' ''Tis thought—' in III. 629, 647; 'We reflect not, in this, on SEIANVS, notwithstanding, if you keepe an eye vpon him—,' v, at the close of the Letter.
[2] For example, 'our night-ey'd TIBERIVS' (IV. 363).
[3] Suetonius, *Tib.* c. 68.

The feigning of such men is as full of character as their frankness, and Jonson must be allowed the merit of having, where tradition failed him, imitated to the life the specifically Tiberian duplicity. Such a passage was, as we have seen, the Letter to the Senate.

Sejanus can never be a popular play. Even when Jonson died, at the height of his poetic renown, audiences thought it 'irksome', and it is a tribute to Jonson's prestige that we should be told they

prizde more
Honest *Iago*, or the jealous Moore.[1]

His sacrifice of the unity of time, whether or not it destroys the play's title to be 'a true poem', did very little to 'preserve popular delight'. On the contrary, by removing all check upon Jonson's prolix fidelity to the slow involutions of history it hindered the success which a concentrated action might have won. In any case Jonson failed to make his Rome as lucid and expressive as his London. The vast company of persons who cross the boards is imperfectly grouped and organized; most of them are slightly drawn.

On the whole, *Sejanus* is the tragedy of a satirist—of one who felt and saw more intensely the vices and follies than the sorrows of men, and who, with boundless power of scorn, was poorly endowed in pity. He could draw the plotting of bad men, their savage vengeance, their ruinous fall; he could draw the fatuities and mishaps of fools; but the delusions which jangle and overthrow a noble nature lay beyond his sphere. Jonsonian tragedy suffers from an inner poverty in the humanities of the heart,—analogous to the wilful bareness of style which masks the poetic core of the tragedy of Ibsen. But the imagination is nevertheless impressed by this sombre fabric of verdureless flint and granite, too arid and savage to leave any coign of vantage for sympathy.

[1] Leonard Digges, 1640.

INTRODUCTION TO
'EASTWARD HO!'

EASTWARD HO!

I

Eastward Ho has, in strictness, no title to be included, as a whole, in an edition of the works of Jonson. He certainly did not write it all; and it is equally certain that he had little if anything to do with shaping the plot and devising the characters. But it is no less certain that he contributed something to it. And its connexion with a famous and (if we may trust his own account of it as reported by Drummond) heroic episode in his life invests this play with a sort of personal interest for the student of Jonson which none even of his wholly authentic works altogether matches. However small his portion in the play, it was considerable enough to amount, in his eyes, to joint-authorship, and to involve the honourable obligation to share penalties as well as payment with his fellow-authors. To prison accordingly Jonson voluntarily went, apparently towards the close of 1604, to join Chapman and Marston, and that though, he tells us, he had no part in the particular passages which led to their arrest.

Of the circumstances which led to this co-operation we know nothing. Chapman was a good friend, but Marston had very recently been his bitter assailant and the victim of his retributive lash. The fact is, however, confirmed by the title-pages of the three quarto editions, in all of which the play is stated to have been 'made by Geo: Chapman. Ben: Ionson. Ioh: Marston'. The piece had been played at the Blackfriars by the Children of the Revels. It was published in September, 1605, by William Aspley. Notwithstanding the multiple authorship, the play presents an appearance of singular wholeness and unity. It is in fact one of the best made of Elizabethan comedies. Its clearcut strength and simplicity of structure was rarely, if ever, approached by any one of its three authors elsewhere. Of the disparities of technique so rarely absent from work by several hands in common, it has less than many a piece entirely shaped by one; and the attempt to distribute the play among the three reported authors has not hitherto advanced beyond the plausible assignment to one or other of them, here and there, of a scene, a passage of dialogue, or a speech.

II

The main subject strikes back to a type of plot characteristic of the early or middle years of Elizabeth's reign rather than of its close. In spite of elaborate and ingenious developments at certain points, it is impossible to mistake the simple and severe outlines of the Prodigal Son story first dramatized in the interest of educational discipline by the austere schoolmasters of the sixteenth century. In the 'Glass' of this Parable, between 1525 and 1575, Palgrave, Ingeland, Gascoigne, and more than one anonymous writer, had sought to show the Unchaste, or the Disobedient, Child, or the Nice Wanton, his image. But the dramatic capacities of the story were at least as considerable as its didactic force; and it is not surprising that it should have been taken up, in the very culminating moment of the English drama—in the very years of *Hamlet*, of *Othello*, of *Lear*—by three dramatists of genius, all without the slightest leaning to Puritanism. Naturally, atmosphere and scene were wholly changed. To the audiences which thronged Blackfriars or the Globe, the fortunes good and ill of schoolboys or university students would have made little appeal. It was an academic audience, in a Cambridge college hall, which had applauded, a year or two before, the sorry progresses of university prodigals to, and from, Parnassus. But unless spiced with some sensational relish, like the story of Faustus, the comedy and tragedy of academic life won no hold upon the playgoing London public. What was most distinctive in them was unfamiliar, and what was familiar inevitably fell short in zest of the subtler villanies and rogueries of Italy and London. And for some years past, when *Eastward Ho* was produced, the rich drama of London life had been assuming its natural place on the London stage. Jonson had himself given an immense impetus to this movement, if he did not actually originate it. Shakespeare's incomparable Eastcheap scenes perhaps preceded *Every Man in his Humour*; but London proper, the London of burgesses, householders and shopkeepers, appears only as background to his genial Bohemia of aristocrats and vagabonds—a merchant to be robbed, a hostess to be fleeced, a sheriff to be outwitted. Jonson had at least as keen an eye for Bohemia, but he drew with impartial zest the humours of 'philistine' and bourgeois London, and the striking change in scene and temper in *The Merry Wives* may owe something to his example. A sympathetic study of the citizen was not to be expected of the playwrights whose profitable operations the City corporation repeatedly did its best to suppress or curtail. The citizen on the stage had been habitually at least touched with ridicule, and Jonson and Shakespeare, if they did not start the practice, entirely fell in with it. Their citizens, when merely intended as samples of the political futility of the many-headed beast, are always touched with some foible; they are doting husbands, like Deliro and Albus, or jealous ones, like Kitely and Ford, or over-anxious and gullible fathers, like Kno'well.

Dekker thus showed some freshness of mind when in *The Shoemakers' Holiday* (acted in 1599) he created the genial craftsman Simon Eyre. This portrait is the nearest anticipation we have to the homely, peremptory, but tender-hearted goldsmith, Master Touchstone.

III

Touchstone is a citizen in the strictest sense. He is not a whit raised above his order; but he has all the thrifty virtues of the honest tradesman, and they are honoured and vindicated in him, instead of being derided. Even his scorn for the stage is portrayed without reserve or irony; while the scapegrace Quicksilver overflows with scraps of plays—of plays, it is true, which were ridiculed by the dramatists themselves. Yet Touchstone is saved by a score of picturesque and humorous touches from being a mere moral type. Homely as he is, he has irony at command, and the severity of the judge is crossed in him by the relish for a jest, for the 'encounter with the counter', which distinguishes the merry Justice of Jonson's first Humour comedy. His tag 'Work upon that now' happily marks him off from the mere purveyor of moral platitudes. His morality comes from him in pithy figures of speech and 'wholesome thrifty sentences' steeped in character.

The good apprentice and son-in-law, Goulding, is in more danger than his master of being a mere moral lay figure. The School dramatists had long since relieved the good scholar from the disparagement which attaches to the elder brother in the Parable; just as they had frequently deprived the Prodigal himself of forgiveness and made him an unqualified foil to his blameless and discreet comrade. Gascoigne, who, among those who had handled the story in England, deals out the sternest measure to the Prodigal, directly associated the virtuous scholars with the Nemesis which befalls their quondam companions. None of the three authors of our play was likely to be influenced either by the ethics of the Gospel or by those of Calvin; but all had an eye for an effective situation; and in effect by judiciously blending the sterner and the milder traditions of the subject they have both given Goulding a role of much dramatic strength, and made him personally more attractive, in spite of much unction, than it has usually been given to the descendants of the 'elder brother' to be. It is an excellent touch that his distinctions—even the dazzling one of 'Master Alderman's deputy', which makes it his office to judge his former comrade—come to him unsought: while his final stratagem for bringing about the pardon of the culprits, by procuring his own arrest for debt, carries virtue to a point of self-devotion which almost brings us round once more into the Christian atmosphere of the Parable, as it were by way of the Antipodes. But the character is somewhat outside the Elizabethan beat, and is nowhere in the play, we think, managed with perfect security and ease. A nice scrutiny may perhaps even detect some hesitation or inconsistency in the language put into his mouth. The good apprentice who delivers his copybook sentiments with so much unctuous propriety in the scene with Mildred (II. i) can stand up to Quicksilver with phrases as terse and racy as his own (I. i).

Mildred is still more slightly drawn; she clearly did not interest the writers, and she leaves the reader cold. Her discretion and good sense are wholly without charm; she is no 'gracious silence', like Hero or Virginia, but a wooden piece of respectability whose pulse never quickens with passion or with virginal fear, a seventeenth-century exemplar of the 'unco guid'.

Far better, and obviously more within the scope of the writers, are the 'wicked' pair, Quicksilver and Gertrude. Gertrude, in particular, is drawn with extraordinary verve and visible gusto. The City wives and daughters, and their aspirations after intercourse or alliance with courtly society, were stock subjects in the first decade of the seventeenth century; but it may be doubted whether their aspirations are anywhere else painted with so much vivacity and force. Jonson's Chloes and Fallaces themselves are tame compared with this Jacobean parallel to Goethe's Philine, whose life is a mere acting out of the prompting of her volatile brain and her wanton blood. 'I did but my kinde, I,' she declares, with sufficient accuracy, at the close (V. i); 'he was a Knight and I was fit to be a Lady.'

Quicksilver, as his name indicates, is intended to be a rogue—like Autolycus—of mercurial temperament. But the traditional lines of the story demanded that he should be also something of a dupe. The Prodigal who falls into bad company and is cheated of all he has is crossed in him with the cunning and astute knave, and the divergence of characters is not always kept within the limits of a natural consistency. At the outset he appears a swaggering 'vnthrift', a 'crackling Bauin' deluded by the 'Gallants that weare socks and cleane linnen, and call me kinde coozen *Francke*, good coozen *Francke*, for they know my Father; and, by gods lidde shall I not trust 'hem? not trust?' He is a gentleman born, and, as his birth demands, will be idle and drunk (I. i). In the next act, in Security's house, he appears an abler and more formidable person, a successful cozener of others (II. ii), with a manner of speech more elaborate, rhetorical and reflective, even touched at moments with poetic afflatus, as in his meditations on the hazards of the mercantile marine: 'What are these Shippes, but Tennis Balles for the windes to play withall? Tost from one waue to another?' It is he who takes a leading part in cheating Gertrude and Securitie, and who, when the money is lost in the Thames, produces a recipe for blanching copper so cunningly that it shall endure all proofs but the test (IV. i). His repentance, like so many Elizabethan repentances—even in Shakespeare—is very sudden, slightly grounded and brief. In IV. i we hear the sententious and lyric Quicksilver of the first scene with Securitie utter his conviction that his desperate game is lost, in lines which might pass for a bit of 'English Seneca'.

> I know not what to doe, my wicked hopes
> Are, with this Tempest, torne vp by the rootes.
> O, which way shall I bend my desperate steppes,
> In which vnsufferable Shame and Miserie
> Will not attend them?

Sixty lines later we find him, completely recovered from his despair, replying with a jest to the inquiries of Seagull and Petronel and rallying the knight on his 'vnknightly faintnesse': 'I hope I haue some tricks, in this braine of mine, shall not let vs perish' (IV. i). His final 'conversion' in the prison, founded perhaps on the historical example of Hatton, is not made dramatically plausible, and could not have been made so without a degree of psychological refinement which is not among the virtues of this rapidly written play.

Of the other characters Mistress Touchstone is a highly finished comic study of the citizen's wife, both subtler and more lifelike than Jonson's cognate women. Jonson's hard satire almost always excludes sympathy; but the authors of *Eastward Ho* have contrived to make this foolish woman's fatuity piteous as well as laughable, as she struggles to find an accommodation between her motherly devotion to her 'lady-daughter' and her bourgeois sense of her own inferior station. When Gertrude, in her last straits, but still defiant, hurls at her the culminating insult, 'By this light, I thinke hee is not my legitimate Father', provoking a protest even from the hardened Syndefie, Mistress Touchstone has no thought but grief for her 'ladyship's' lost gentility. 'Nay, nay, let her eene alone. Let her Ladishippe grieue me still, with her bitter taunts and termes. I haue not dole inough to see her in this miserable case, I? without her Veluet gownes, without Ribbands, without Iewels, without French-wires, or Cheat-bread, or Quailes, or a little Dog, or a Gentleman Vsher, or any thing indeed, that's fit for a Lady' (v. i).

The usurer, Securitie, with his wife and daughter, Winifred and Syndefie, form an only less finished group. Even the lawyer Bramble, and the jailor Wolf, who holds them to be of the best religion who pay fees best (v. iii), are much more than lay figures. The intrigue of which Securitie and his wife are the victims is the most palpable addition made to the materials of the Prodigal-story.

IV

We may now approach the question of the shares of the three poets in their joint work. The data of authentic fact are as follows: (1) Jonson's statement to Drummond, already quoted, to the effect that he, Chapman, and Marston 'had written it amongst them'; (2) the appearance of these three names on the title-page of the first edition; (3) Jonson's implication, in an extant letter to the Earl of Salisbury, that he was not the author of the passages in the play at which offence had been taken: ('If others have transgress'd, let not me bee entitled to they^re Follyes'). To this may be added the explicit assertion of Chapman, in a letter not dated but clearly referring to the same emergency, that their (his and Jonson's) 'chief offences are but two clawses, and both of them not our owne'. In other words, that the incriminating passages addressed to Scots and knights were due to Marston.

Apart from these passages, however, which are of little concern to the modern student of drama, the known facts give us little help in distributing shares in the play. Much of it is not specially characteristic of any one of the three writers. Its admirable plot is built, as has been said, with a combined simplicity, lucidity, and strength of which none of the three was obviously capable. Jonson, by far the most powerful plotter of the three, was certainly capable of its strength. But neither he nor Chapman, the second in power, showed any care for the strong simplicity of which the ancient drama, more familiar to these two than to any of their fellows, might have given them a relish. Both were prodigals, too lavish of their immense resources to be content with the choice but temperate fare of *Eastward Ho*. The question of Marston's share in the plot-making may be for the moment reserved.

The three poets are obviously distinguished by pronounced differences in cast of invention, *ethos*, and general mentality, reflected in technique and style. Jonson is marked off from Marston by his more massive sentence-building, his less vivacious and impulsive movement in dialogue, his more pregnant reflection; from Chapman by his more orderly and formal habit of mind, and the absence, which naturally followed, of those fine but incongruous kindlings and exultations of phrase to which the high aspiring spirit of the elder poet was prone.

In the genius of Chapman, again, there ran a vein of ethical dignity, of epic imagination, of romance, and of whimsical bizarrerie. He loved daring and fantastic combinations; half a dozen years before, he had produced, in *The Blind Beggar of Alexandra*, a play which in the wildness of its suppositions goes beyond all Elizabethan parallel. At the date of *Eastward Ho* he was already the author, also, of *All Fools*; but neither this nor any other of his extant plays moves in the atmosphere of bourgeois manners and sentiment from which, in fact, something grandiose, even heroic, in his fundamental make of mind probably always estranged him.

Marston, too, whose high vaulting ambition was only fitfully sustained by genuine dramatic power, cultivated a vein of extravagant and daring invention appropriate enough to the lurid vocabulary in which he clothed it, and which had recently brought upon him the sarcasms of the *Poetaster*. By the date, however, of *Eastward Ho*, that sharp medicine had wrought a notable effect on the patient, assisted doubtless by his reconciliation with the physician. He had become master of a dialogue style strikingly vivacious, rapid and colloquial though rarely overweighted with thought. Italy, his mother's native land, furnished the scene and the atmosphere of the fantastic and sanguinary intrigues in which, even in comedy, he is most at home. No one used the motif of disguise, in particular, with more persistence than the author of *Antonio and Mellida*, *The Malcontent*, and *The Fawn*. In one comedy only did Marston deal with the life of bourgeois London, in *The Dutch Courtesan* (published in 1605), in many ways the best product of his spasmodic and fitful powers. Widely as it differs in plot and personnel from our play, it is in certain points more cognate to it than any earlier or contemporary play of either Jonson or Chapman. One of the foulest-minded playwrights of his time, Marston could pose, quite sincerely, as an austere guardian of morality, put forth edifying or warning examples, and call upon his audience to 'look upon this picture or on that' in the interest of honest manners. So it was with *The Dutch Courtesan*; the full scope of which he himself in the 'Fabulae Argumentum' defines to be: 'The difference between the love of a courtesan and a wife.' Between Franceschina, Freewill's abandoned mistress, and Beatrice, his bride, there is a contrast as edifying and even more unqualified than that which divided the good and bad apprentice, the modest and the wanton daughter, of our play. And the lines with which Touchstone closes the second scene might have served with little change to introduce the action of the *Courtesan*:

This match shal on, for I intend to prooue
Which thriues the best, the meane or loftie loue.

Marston's characteristic ἀναισχυντία thus goes along with an unusually emphatic note of bourgeois morality. He is also a bold purloiner of Shakespearian phrases. *Hamlet* in particular, the great dramatic event of the year or two before our play, seems to have obsessed his imagination.

V

It may be conjectured, then, that the idea of a play with an edifying moral, and founded upon what may be called 'this-picture-and-that' situations, was struck out by Marston. Possibly the Prodigal Son story was commended as the ground-work of the plot by its simplicity and breadth, in a case where a common understanding among three writers of unlike habits of mind had to be maintained. How does the case stand with the new motives and characters introduced into the story? We have to distinguish plot-elements, characters, and style; and it is obvious that plot-elements, originated by one of the three, may have been executed by another; that more than one of them, in the same way, may have contributed to the exposition of the same character; and that of all the ingredients of the play, the actual writing, the style and manner, has the best chance of bearing the impress of the writer.

Plot-elements.

The original developments of the plot are chiefly:

1. *Securitie and his household.* The 'harlot', Syndefie, may be held to be involved in the Prodigal story. But the devising of the scenes in which she occurs may be plausibly ascribed to the author of *The Dutch Courtesan.*

2. *The trick played upon Securitie*, by making him take part in the abduction of his own wife under the belief that she is Bramble's, and then propose to deceive Bramble by disguising her in his own wife's dress, is in the same vein of humour as the central device of Chapman's *All Fools*, where Gostanzo, the real victim of the deceit, assists, with huge gusto, in making game, as he thinks, of Mark Antonio. Compare especially the situation in which Securitie hardly contains his laughter at the delusion of Bramble III. iii) with the similar guffaws of Gostanzo (*A. F.* IV. i). Note the abruptness with which this motive is introduced in Petronel's speech in III. ii,

> Thankes, my deare *Gossip*. I must now impart
> To your approued loue, a louing secret—

where there is an equally abrupt change from compact and matter-of-fact prose to expansive and flowing verse,—marking without doubt the transition to another hand, probably Chapman's.

3. *The voyage and shipwreck.* The invention and diffuse picturesque treatment indicate Chapman, whose mind had much epic quality. Note the lively interest with which the varying fortunes of the several wrecked persons are painted, —as it were so many companions of Ulysses.

4. *Quicksilver's device for replacing the lost money.* It is obvious to suspect here the hand of the future poet of *The Alchemist.*

5. *The denouement.* 'This day shalbe sacred to *Mercy*, & the mirth of this *Encounter* in the *Counter.*'—Touchstone's program, and the scene in which it is faithfully carried

out, recall the genial close of *Every Man in his Humour*, where Justice Clement, in his own house, indulges his easy good nature and his uproarious humour at the same time. And there are traces, here also, of the retarding or counter-movements which so often add complexity and suspense to Jonson's finales. Gertrude's persistent 'repetition' of her offensive speeches comes dangerously near being a repetition of the offence. More significant is Securitie's recurrence to the jealous suspicion of his wife which he has already (at the end of IV. i) emphatically abandoned. 'Villaine, and Monster that I was,' he there exclaims, on hearing Winifred's report: '... Talke not of it I beseech thee, I am ashamed to imagine it; I will home, I will home, and euery morning on my knees aske thee hartely forgiueness.' In spite of this we find him in V. v harking back to the old conviction. ' I say any thing sir, what you'll ha me say. Would I were no Cuckold.' To which his wife retorts: 'Cuckold, husband? why, I thinke this wearing of Yellow has infected you.' There is a precise parallel to this in the history of the relations of old Kitely and his wife, as they appear in the Quarto of Jonson's play (V. i). There too, Thorello, even after his wife's suspicious conduct has been cleared up, cannot so easily get rid of his suspicions—it is precisely his 'humour' to entertain them,—and recurs to them (V. iii). Even the same pun (yellows—jealous) had there too been turned to account :

'But brother *Thorello*, and sister,' says Prospero (Well-bred), 'you haue a spice of the yealous yet both of you, (in your hose I meane,) come do not dwell vpon your anger so much, lets all be smoth foreheaded once agayne.
Tho. He playes upon my forehead, brother *Giulliano*, I pray you tell me one thing I shall ask you : is my fore-heade any thing rougher then it was wont to be?
Gui. Rougher? Your forehead is smoth enough man.
Tho. Why should he then say? be smoth foreheaded, Vnlesse he iested at the smothnesse of it?
And that may be; for horne is very smoth;

. . . .

Tell me *Biancha*, do not you play the woman with me?
　Bi. Whats that sweet hart?
　Tho. Dissemble?'

And presently he announces that he is 'not iealous, but resolued I haue the faythfulst wife in *Italie*'.[1]

Touchstone here plays the part of Clement as the general reconciler, and he occasionally recalls him very closely. Thus, after Thorello has announced his final abandonment of jealousy, Clement proceeds: 'Why thats well, come then: what say you, are all agreed? doth none stand out?' To which Prospero replies: 'None but this gentleman' (Lorenzo). Similarly Touchstone, after hearing Gertrude's confession, inquires: 'What is else wanting, to make our Harmony full?' Nay, his rallying tirade to Securitie upon the consolations of cuckoldry at the end of V. v is surely an upcrop of the Clement-vein of uproarious humour in the sober goldsmith.

Characters.

To Marston would thus belong the first outline, at least, of Touchstone; of Goulding and Quicksilver; Gertrude and Mildred.

Style.

The writing in large tracts of the play is not sufficiently distinctive to be ascribed confidently to any one of the three. But in certain passages the characteristics of each emerge.

1. Jonson. III. i. Petronel, Quicksilver, and Securitie here speak in a dialect strikingly unlike that given to them (probably by Marston) in the previous scene (II. iii). Securitie's invitation to breakfast is given in these terms (II. iii, *ad fin.*):

　Secur. If you will not sup from your Knight Madam, let

---

[1] This little episode was smoothed out in the Folio version. That Jonson, if it was he, repeated it in substance in 1605 adds to the probability that the revision of *Every Man in his Humour* is of later date.

me entreate your Ladiship to sup at my house with him. . . .

Pet. What a Medcine is this? well maister *Securitie*, you are new married as well as I; I hope you are bound as well: we must honour our young wiues you know.

Their talk after their breakfast (III. i) is in this fashion:

Petr. Thankes for our feastlike Breakefast good Maister *Securitie*, I am sory, (by reason of my instant haste to so long a voyage as *Virginia*,) I am without meanes, by any kinde amends, to show how affectionatly I take your kindnesse, and to confirme by some worthy ceremonie a perpetuall league of friendship betwixt us.

Sec. Excellent Knight; let this be a token betwixt vs of inuiolable friendship. . . .

2. Marston. III. ii (up to the entrance of Touchstone, Goulding, and Mildred). This scene, with its rapid succession of motives and swift by-play, is a good example of Marston's work. Within the hundred lines we have: (1) the Coachman grumbling at the fuss made about citizens riding out of town; (2) Hamlet, the running footman, calling the coach; (3) Potkin abusing Hamlet; (4) Syndefie summoning Potkin; (5) Mrs. Fond and Mrs. Gazer discussing the coming show; (6) Gertrude greeted by the onlookers, and making private inquiries of her mother; (7) the mother pleading on behalf of the running footman; (8) Petronel taking leave of Gertrude; (9) Quicksilver announcing that Mildred and Goulding are to be married that morning, to Gertrude and her mother's indignation, in the very paroxysms of which Gertrude glances off, with a 'but sirra *Frank Quicksilver*' to remind the latter (10) of their old relations, with a final snatch of Ophelia's song.

3. Chapman. IV. i (the entrance of Quicksilver). Quicksilver's repentance in the tragic vein is sharply marked off in style from his later mood of abject piety. That these are separated by a scene in which, without any explanation or transition, he appears continuing his nefarious courses, doubtless marks an imperfect congruity in the plans of the several collaborators.

The prose dialogue between Winifred and the Drawer is, in a lesser degree, distinguished from the staple texture of the play by frequent touches of lofty sentiment or expression; as in the Drawer's 'Comfort your selfe; That power that preserued you from death: can likewise defend you from infamie, howsoeuer you deserue it'. And Winifred's reply to his question: 'Unhappy that I am, I was.'

The opening of II. ii, where Securitie is introduced, marks a notable and sudden ascent in dignity and height of style. 'My house is as 'twere the Caue, where the yong Out-lawe hoords the stolne vayles of his occupation; And here when he will reuell it in his prodigal similitude... I am Securitie it selfe, my name is *Securitie*, the famous Vsurer.' And Quicksilver's: 'Come old *Securitie*, thou father of destruction: th' indented Sheepeskinne is burn'd wherein I was wrapt, and I am now loose, to get more children of perdition into thy vsurous Bonds.' Still more striking is his subsequent speech, 'I shallbee a Marchaunt for-sooth' (II. ii). The same lofty tone marks the answering speeches of Syndefie, 'Well *Francke*, well; the Seas you say are vncertaine' and 'But hee's worse then a Prentise that does it', and Securitie's further comments. This intellectual colloquy, held in such a house, can owe nothing to the pen, or to the invention, of Marston. Nor is it in Jonson's way. Chapman seems to have taken less pains to accommodate himself to the common design than the others; and there are signs that his work had to be at certain points hastily brought into line with the rest.

It will be seen that the attempt to analyse out the shares of the three reputed authors in the play yields no very far-reaching results. In this Introduction the problem is dealt with on broad critical grounds. Other evidence, bibliographical, textual, and stylistic, bearing upon it will be adduced in the Commentary. While the analysis may claim to make certain that all three did actually participate in it, the proportion of features, whether of invention or of technique, which can be called distinctive is comparatively small. In other words, *Eastward Ho* must be regarded as one of the more remarkable among the known examples of successful collaboration. For not merely is the fact of collaboration to an extraordinary degree successfully concealed, but the alliance appears to have elicited a result superior in some features to the independent work, single handed, of any of the three.

INTRODUCTION TO

'VOLPONE'

VOLPONE

I

Volpone, the amazing product of five weeks' labour, was most probably written during the first months of 1606.[1] It was acted shortly after its completion by the King's Men at the Globe; and later on, perhaps in the autumn term of the same year, with great 'love and acceptance' before the two Universities. Early in 1607-8[2] Jonson published it in quarto, with a stately and pregnant dedicatory address, the most important document we possess of his notions in criticism, and of his mind about his own art in this early phase of his career.

With *Volpone* Jonson returned, in his own view at least, to comedy. But it was to comedy widely different from all previous work of his own in that kind, and rather hard to accommodate not merely to the elastic Elizabethan notions of comic art, but (what Jonson cared much more for) to 'the strict rigour of' ancient '*comick* law'. In the sternness of the catastrophe, as Jonson felt, it approached tragedy. And in its whole conception and conduct, in the lurid atmosphere which pervades it from beginning to end, in the appalling

[1] The allusions in II. i to 'another' young lion 'whelped in the Tower', 'three porcpisces seene, aboue the bridge', and 'a whale discouer'd, in the riuer as high as *Woolwich*', are very explicit, and the two latter, in any case, can only refer to the incidents which Stow thought it worth while to record under January 19, 'and a few days later', 1606, in terms almost identical with Jonson's. Peregrine, who reports these wonders, says that he left London on the very day of the appearance of the whale, and that this was 'seven weeks' before. We are not bound to take this reckoning as exact, but it would be quite in the manner of Jonson's realism to identify the supposed date of the action with the actual date of the performance. In this case, the piece must have been played about the middle of March (allowing a week from January 19 for Stow's 'a few days later'); in any case before the 25th, if we are to rely upon the date '1605' of the Quarto title-page. See also Holt in *Modern Language Notes*, xx. 6.

[2] The dedicatory epistle is dated in the Quarto: '*From my house in the Black-Friars this* 11 *of February*, 1607.'

and menacing character of the principal movers of the plot, it approaches, not indeed the profound and human-hearted tragedies of Shakespeare, but, very obviously and significantly, his own grandiose and terrible tragedy of two years before. *Sejanus* opened up to him that new technique in drama of which *Volpone* was to be the finest fruit.[1] History, in the great example of Sejanus' career and fall, brought home to him anew the immense value of a continuous and close-knitted plot, with terror and scorn for its ruling motives; it perhaps impressed him also, anew, with the wealth, in dramatic material of this kind, of the records of imperial Rome, still unexplored and unexploited by his dramatic contemporaries.

Among Roman institutions thus capable of yielding terror and scorn, yet rich too in the grim and sardonic comedy which suited Jonson's present mood, that of legacy-hunting (*captatio*) stood in the front rank. The Roman *captator* who presented his fortune to the legatee in the expectation of a more than corresponding reward, and the prospective legatee who played maliciously on the greed of rival candidates for his bequests, might seem to be ready-made sources for Jonsonian comedy, so aptly do they fall into his standing categories of the cheated and the cheat. His earlier comedy had 'sported' with the comparatively naïve follies and pretensions of his day. His later applied its more elaborate technique to organized humbug and corruption,—alchemy, the news-staple, Bartholomew Fair. The Roman institution of legacy-hunting provided an example of organized humbug better fitted perhaps to call into play the energies of Jonson's comic satire than any of these,—save in the one respect that it was un-English, and that his powerful realism was thus deprived of one of its sustaining sources. On the other hand, like the career of Sejanus, the institution of legacy-hunting was illuminated by a mass of ancient literature; for the scholar the satire of the first and second centuries had left brilliant and incisive pictures of this vice of the

[1] See pp. 17-18.

early empire, the *captator* was derided by Horace, Juvenal, and Pliny;[1] he provided the theme of an amusing episode in Petronius' *Satiricon*; and, in particular, his appetences and mortifications, and the strategy on both sides evolved in this conflict of base interests, provided the material for some of the wittiest of Lucian's *Dialogues of the Dead*.

It was on this strategical aspect of legacy-hunting, with its rich development of make-believe, of criminal invention and resource, that Jonson fastened. He found especially in Lucian amusing pictures of the legator who meets game with counter-game, the laugh being regularly with him, not with his persecutors.[2] Thus in *Pluto and Mercury*, an old man, Eucrates, with no children, but fifty thousand *captatores*, plays upon their hopes, feigning death when he is actually in the best of health. Pluto orders that he shall be restored to youth, while the *captatores* are forced, instead of becoming his heirs, to go to Hades before him. In another case, a *captator*, Callidemidas, tries to hasten matters by poisoning Ptoeodorus, the expected legator, but accidentally takes the poison himself. Similarly Cnemon leaves his fortune to Hermolaus, expecting to be made his heir; unluckily he is himself killed by accident before his time. Terpsion complains loudly in the underworld of the hardship of having to die at thirty, when old Thucritos, whom he had besieged with gifts, has lived beyond ninety. While in the *Simylus* we are introduced to one, Polystratos, who has lived for thirty years on the gifts of his expectant heirs.[3]

A more ambitious but scarcely more effective use of the legacy-hunting motive was made by Petronius, the *arbiter elegantiarum* of Nero's Court. Petronius, as little as Jonson, was a mere observer; and he put into his book the same gifts of ingenious combination and piquant elaboration which, applied to the entertainment of Nero, had made his fortune and were to cost him his life. The 'Supper of Trimalchio',

[1] E.g. Horace, *Epp.* i. 1. 77; Juvenal, iii. 129; Pliny, *Epp.* ii. 20; iv. 2. 2.
[2] Cf. *Mod. Phil.* ii. 238 f.; *Modern Language Notes*, xxi. 113 f.
[3] Lucian, Νεκρικοὶ διάλογοι, v–ix.

the most famous of all the extant scenes, is a little masterpiece of Aristophanic invention. The story of the adventures of Eumolpus at Croton is less effective, partly because it is more fragmentary; but we easily trace the outline of an even more audaciously fashioned plot. Eumolpus, a white-haired poet, with a *rusé* countenance and a past career of successful dissimulation, is the arch-strategist of the company. Wrecked off the south coast of Italy, he and his comrades escape with difficulty to the shore. A bailiff informs them that they are in the neigbourhood of Croton. On their inquiring the character and pursuits of the inhabitants, 'Gentlemen,' puts in the bailiff, 'if you are men of business, change your purpose and seek other means of support. But if you are men of wit and refinement, able to keep up a fraudulent pretence, you are come to a regular El Dorado. For in this city learning gets no reward, eloquence has no place, grave and honest manners avail nothing, but the whole population is divided into two classes, *aut captantur aut captant;*—legacy-hunters and their prey. In this city no one rears children, since whoever has heirs of his own is excluded from all feasts and games, refused all the conveniences of life and hides his head among the outcasts of society. Whereas bachelors with no near kin are advanced to the highest honours.... You are entering a town which is like a pestilence-stricken plain, filled with nothing else but crows and corpses, the tearing and the torn' (§ 116). Eumolpus accordingly proceeds to pose as a hapless old man who has just lost his son, and has left his native place in order to avoid being daily harrowed by the sight of his son's friends and burial-place. In the shipwreck he has just lost all his equipment, but he owns vast estates and hosts of slaves in Africa. It is further arranged that he is to cough violently, to talk of gold and silver, complain of the miserable yield of his estates, to sit every day at his accounts, and make a new will every month (§ 117). Thus prepared, Eumolpus and his party enter Croton and presently fall in with a throng of *captatores*, who, on hearing their story, immediately vie with one another in heaping their wealth upon Eumolpus and entreating his favour (§ 124). Eumolpus and his companions plunge into wild licence and luxury. Only one incident need be specified. An aged and 'honourable' matron, Philomela, in her youth an adept at legacy-hunting, introduces her children, a clever boy and girl, to Eumolpus for this purpose. The issue of the adventure cannot clearly be made out from the extant fragments.

It will be seen that neither Lucian nor Petronius can be said to have provided the plot of *Volpone*. But to one or both Jonson doubtless owed the fundamental situation of the legator who makes game of the legacy-hunters, and a few details of the execution.

II

In choosing such a subject as this Jonson, then, necessarily abandoned one of his surest holds upon the play-going public, his powerful presentment of the London life at their doors. In Jacobean London similar concoctions of greed, cunning, and credulity were not perhaps much less rife than in imperial Rome; but this particular variety of them was not yet at home there. Yet the very unfamiliarity of this 'folly' touched the vein of a Jacobean audience at another point. If they enjoyed seeing London gallants and prentices, country simpletons and City wives, made sport of, they were at least as accessible to the romantic fascination of strange or exotic crime. This kind of interest, however, would have been much deadened had the plot been laid in a vanished society, known only to the learned and by books. Jonson therefore took a most politic step in transferring his *mise en scène* from ancient Rome—already of ill augury for the audiences of *Poetaster* and *Sejanus*—to modern Italy. For the Jacobeans Italy was the classic contemporary land of sensational evil-doing. Among Italian cities Venice, with Florence as the city of Machiavel, stood in the front rank for this sinister repute. Shylock was but one, and hardly the most consummate, of those whom the stage had shown plotting monstrous things by the Rialto. To make the Fox a Venetian grandee was thus to give him and his story the best chance of being at once piquant and plausible. English foibles do not indeed wholly escape the lash; but Sir Politick and his lady are introduced only as eccentric English visitors at the house of the Venetian grandee. If the scene, then, is laid in Venice, 'Venice' is no longer merely a transparent cloak for London, as the 'Florence' of the original *Every Man in his Humour* had been, and as the 'Rome' of the *Poetaster* in great part was. But neither does it mean precisely 'Venice' in the literal and realist sense which Jonson attached to 'London' in the revised play. There is no evidence or probability that Jonson had discovered a Venetian Eucrates or Eumolpus. He had merely transferred to a modern *milieu* a situation imagined in the spirit of imperial Rome, and under the stimulus of the renewed and close occupation with its historic records from which he had but recently emerged. The element of scholarly and literary reminiscence in Jonson's mind, so harmoniously allied with his powerful realism in *Every Man in his Humour*, here gains a decided predominance. The cunning slave and boastful soldier of ancient comedy had done little more than give a cue to the observant eye which elicited a Brainworm and a Bobadill from the Elizabethan throng. But Volpone bears the clear stamp of his purely literary origin; the antique satiric stuff is everywhere visible, and the intense intellectual elaboration it has undergone has been carried out in comparative detachment from actualities. The result is work certainly wanting in the fresh charm of the earlier piece; even repellent by reason of the remote, abstruse, and at times scarcely human, types of criminality among which we move. Yet for all its strangeness, it attains, in the grip of Jonson's mind, an amazing imaginative veracity, which has made its sinister outlines only less ineffaceable in the English memory than the more splendid and passionate creations of Shakespeare.

If *Volpone* marks a wide departure from the realism he had earlier enjoined upon the comic dramatist, it violates still more strikingly his second demand, that comedy should 'sport with human follies', not with 'crimes'. If Jonson ever 'sports' here, it is in the sombre and lurid fashion of his own 'sporting Kyd'. There is folly enough, to be sure; but it is the formidable and menacing folly of men who have capacity and resource and absolutely no scruples, and whether such men commit follies or crimes is merely a question of occasion and circumstance. All the principal persons are capable of any crime; they are gamblers playing desperately for high stakes, and when they see their advantage, Corbaccio plays his son's inheritance, and Corvino his wife's honour. The moral repulsion, however, with which they so powerfully affect us is less due to the actual crimes and vices they perpetrate than to the impression of unlimited possibilities of evil which they convey. The air is heavy and fetid with moral disease; a passing breath of freshness and purity just stirs it when Celia and Bonario go by, but the relief is faint and ineffectual, and the total impression is not sensibly mitigated even by the catastrophe which attests that 'there is force in the decrees of Venice' to punish even these iniquities.

Never before had Jonson painted with so much power humanity denuded of every germ of goodness. Of moralizing there is not a trace, but the moral accent is none the less pervading and intense, like a continuous burden accompanying all the variations of the music, never distinctly or separately heard, but qualifying the value of every note. To this intensity of moral accent neither Petronius nor Lucian, it need hardly be said, contributed or could contribute anything whatever. Juvenal, whose temper was kindred, contributed little more. Jonson understood the lighter arts too, and was already winning by his Masques—his *Masque of Blackness* had been produced but a few months before—a better title than any of his literary contemporaries to be called the 'arbiter elegantiarum' of the Court of James. But those gracious artifices of the Christmas candlelight were only the *parerga* of a great and strenuous artist, for whom his art was a weapon, and whose writing, more than any other of his time, was inspired by the indignation which makes silence hard. The indignation which inspired *Volpone* was, it is true, not the purely ethical passion of the Hebrew prophet, or even of Juvenal; it is, on the evidence of his own eloquent Preface, stirred as much by the degradation into which the glorious name of poetry had fallen, as by the rampancy of vice. And that degradation was itself in part purely literary; a matter of bad style, —'such impropriety of phrase, such plenty of *solœcismes*, such dearth of sense, so bold *prolepse's*, so rackt *metaphor's*'; —and who shall say that the stylistic audacities of *King Lear* and *Macbeth*, neither of them many months old, were not in Jonson's mind when he wrote these words? But the deeper ground of that degradation and of his anger lay in the gross neglect by contemporary poets of the lofty function prescribed for the poet by antiquity, to be a moral educator of mankind; and in their imperviousness to the high doctrine received from the same source, that no man can become a 'good Poet, without first being a good man'. 'The too-much licence of *Poetasters*, in this time, hath much deform'd their Mistris'; and, whatever we may think of the critical perception which discerned, on the morrow of *Hamlet* and *Othello*, no compensatory accesses of glory about her 'deformed' shape, *Volpone* remains a magnificent vindication, among other things, of the office even of the 'comic' poet 'to imitate iustice, and instruct to life', as Jonson understood these things.

III

Happily, he understood them as a poet, and carried them out, fundamentally, under the conditions of poetry. The desire to hold up a terrifying example is subordinated to a passion, hardly apparent before *Sejanus*, and even there far less rigorously carried out, for complex and intricate but perfectly organic plot. The ground-work is laid with great care. Volpone is no unknown foreign adventurer, like Petronius' Eumolpus, but a grandee of Venice whose rank and position are beyond dispute. He is not all impostor. He is really wealthy, and really childless, as he professes. His imposture starts from a foundation of assured respectability. The consideration he enjoys facilitates his fraud and enables him to carry it to further lengths with impunity; it delays his detection, and when detected, it softens the rigour of the law, in favour of one who is ' by bloud, and ranke a gentleman ' (V. xii. 117). In this case at least, Jonson unhesitatingly blunted his 'moral' in order to benefit his plot. On the other hand, he has perhaps given his moral scorn for this 'Venetian gentleman' too free a rein to be wholly true to the part. He has given him the highest degree of the subtle craft, and the calculated cruelty, for which the patrician government of Venice was famous; but nothing of the high-bred courtesy in speech and manner which prevailed in Venetian society, and which Shakespeare had just rendered so excellently in *Othello*, and rather less excellently earlier in *The Merchant of Venice*. Volpone is no mere amateur in roguery, but a professional virtuoso exulting in his virtuosity. The artist in him is even stronger than the wealth-hunter or the voluptuary. He is not merely, like Overreach, a grasping man of brains, who cheats with professional coolness for definite practical ends; on the contrary, he takes a huge delight in the tricks he plays for their own sake, glorying

> More in the cunning purchase of my wealth,
> Then in the glad possession,

and carries them out when he has everything to lose and nothing to gain. His room, crowded with the costly offerings of his dupes, is a sort of private box from which he watches unobserved the sordid comedy of contending greeds. In the intervals of these performances he finds diversion in another yet more hideous spectacle,—the contortions of a dwarf, a eunuch, a hermaphrodite, whose splayed or stunted ditties are made, with horrible ingenuity, to reflect their several deformities. But Volpone is too inveterate an artist to be content with the role of the looker-on. Like Nero, he leaps upon the stage, recites, assumes characters, compels the plot to move as he wishes. If Nero's colossal caprices have any parallel in literature, it is in the lurid imagery with which the brain of Volpone invests his vices and his crimes. The morning hymn to gold, with which he first opens his lips in our hearing, transfigures avarice with the glamour of religion and idealism; the sordid taint of usury, the prosaic associations of commerce, fall away from this man who boasts:

> I wound no earth with plow-shares; fat no beasts
> To feede the shambles; . . .
> I blow no subtill glasse; expose no ships
> To threatnings of the furrow-faced sea;
> I turne no moneys, in the publike banke.[1]

And when the supposed bedridden and impotent old man, throwing off the mask, leaps from his couch before the hapless Celia, he seems for a moment to have discarded with his senility the grossness and brutality of his mind; he is not the Faun gloating over his victim, but the young Antinoos whom he once played

> For entertainement of the great VALOYS,

ravishing his lady's ear with Catullian song and besieging her imagination with visions of fabulous opulence and magnificence,—

> A diamant, would have bought LOLLIA PAVLINA,
> When she came in, like star-light, hid with iewels,
> That were the spoiles of prouinces; take these,
> And weare, and loose 'hem: yet remaines an eare-ring
> To purchase them againe, and this whole state. . . .
> Thy bathes shall be the juyce of iuly-flowres,
> Spirit of roses, and of violets,
> The milk of vnicornes, and panthers breath
> Gather'd in bagges, and mixt with *cretan* wines.[2]

[1] I. i. 34-39. [2] III. vii. 194-215.

Volpone is a consummate actor; it is his misfortune that he is liable to be carried away by the zest of his part. He owes his final ruin less to rash and hasty unmaskings, such as this, than to the audacious adventures he undertakes with the mask on. His passion for taking part, as it were, in his own play, and moving it on towards the consummation he desires, is the mainspring by which the whole action is brought to the consummation he does not desire. The bent grows upon him visibly, and is carried out to more and more extravagant lengths. The monstrous jest of the commandatore (v. v–ix) would be incredible had it not been preceded by the gay adventure of the mountebank, as that would be had it not been prepared for by the farce of the sick room. With each fresh success his temper grows more sanguine, his humour more wanton; he cannot bear his fortune soberly. 'I must ha' my crotchets! and my *conundrums*!'[1] ... till at last he makes a snare for his own neck and runs his head into it wilfully. The dramatist Cumberland objected to this final mad freak of Volpone's as 'the weak part of the plot'. But this is to demand, as the eighteenth century was too prone to do, that the persons of a drama should never act contrary to a reasonable view of their own interests. The Elizabethans retained no such illusion; and Jonson had the peculiarly keen eye common in men of his vehement temperament and critical brain for the fatuities of the overweening. The collapse of Volpone's astuteness in the delirious joy of his wanton triumph is imagined with an irony yet more Greek than Elizabethan. While the supposed 'commandatore' is gaily mocking the victims he has disinherited, the spectator knows that Mosca, the pretended heir, is quietly preparing, behind the scenes, to ruin the pretended testator. And it is only by the desperate shift of stripping off his own mask that Volpone is able to checkmate the superior cunning of his formidable parasite, and send him to a doom yet sterner than his own.

[1] v. xi. 16.

IV

Neither this wonderfully contrived catastrophe nor the quondam ally whom he compels to share it owes much to any earlier model. The hideous sketch of Encolpius, who at Croton acts as servant to Eumolpus, has but the vaguest resemblance to Mosca. Nor has he much affinity with the ordinary parasite of classic comedy. We must look for an analogy rather to that more potent and terrible 'parasite' of history, whose 'fall' had so recently occupied Jonson's imagination. With certain obvious qualifications, Mosca is a Sejanus of private life. In the history of Sejanus Jonson found the fundamental situation of his two greatest comedies. The league of two able villains, master and servant, ending in a deadly struggle between them, was a theme of immense dramatic possibilities new to the English stage. The finale of *Sejanus* by no means equals in constructive mastery the unsurpassed catastrophes of *Volpone* and *The Alchemist*; but this was not altogether Jonson's fault; and some of the most impressive effects of the two later plays are foreshadowed, within the limits imposed by the historic facts, in the earlier. Like the Letter of Tiberius, the final confession of Volpone abruptly closes the career and life of the quondam 'parasite' at the moment when his triumph seems complete. But Jonson was now free to 'punish vice', and bent upon punishing it, without reserve; the master therefore, unlike Tiberius, shares, with slight modification, the servant's doom. In *The Alchemist*, where this primitive zeal was allowed less ample scope, the issue of the duel was still further and more ingeniously varied; it being here the 'parasite' who gets the upper hand, by a yet more daring and unexpected stroke.

Mosca has thus hardly a closer relation than Sejanus to the parasite of classic comedy, though the title is expressly applied to both. Jonson felt this, and has adroitly forestalled criticism by making Mosca himself, in an incisive soliloquy, explain his points of superiority to the ordinary breeds of the creature. Volpone's all-powerful familiar will not be confounded with the hungry professional 'diners-out' who

> haue your bare towne-arte,
> To know, who's fit to feede 'hem;

and vend their scraps of news for a precarious invitation, to jest for a dinner, at the risk of summary expulsion if the jest should not please.[1] As little will he be mistaken for one of the low cringing companions—

> With their court-dog-tricks, that can fawne, and fleere,
> Make their reuennue out of legs, and faces,
> Echo my-Lord, and lick away a moath.

If his position and authority distinguish him from the vulgar parasite in the literal sense, his brilliant capacity equally distinguishes him from the professional jester. His 'mystery' is a liberal art, exacting great wits and worthy of them, the

> fine, elegant rascall, that can rise,
> And stoope (almost together) like an arrow;
> Shoot through the aire, as nimbly as a starre;
> Turne short, as doth a swallow; and be here,
> And there, and here, and yonder, all at once;
> Present to any humour, all occasion;
> And change a visor, swifter, then a thought!
> This is the creature, had the art borne with him;
> Toiles not to learne it, but doth practise it
> Out of most excellent nature: and such sparkes,
> Are the true Parasites, others but their *Zani's*.[2]

Mosca, like his master, has something of the artist's joy in his feats, and is carried away no less by the zest of the game. With all his astuteness he falls, in the wantonness of success, into a blunder which, in conjunction with Volpone's final escapade, involves the final ruin of the fortunes of both.

[1] Eupolis, Κόλακες, fr. 1 (ed. Meineke):
εἶτ᾽ ἐπὶ δεῖπνον ἐρχόμεσθ᾽ ἄλλυδις ἄλλος ἡμῶν
μᾶζαν ἐπ᾽ ἀλλόφυλον, οὗ δεῖ χαρίεντα πολλὰ
τὸν κόλακ᾽ εὐθέως λέγειν, ἢ φέρεται θύραζε.

[2] III. i.

> I feare, I shall begin to grow in loue
> With my deare selfe, and my most prosp'rous parts,
> They doe so spring, and burgeon ; I can feele
> A whimsey i' my bloud: (I know not how)
> Successe hath made me wanton. I could skip
> Out of my skin, now, like a subtill snake,
> I am so limber.

It is in this reckless, 'limber' mood that, with obvious intention on Jonson's part, he encounters Bonario, the son whom Corbaccio is about to disinherit in Volpone's favour. The amazing audacity of his next move, the communication to Bonario of his father's design, coupled with the fatal consequences for himself which actually accrue from it, has led some sober critics to accuse Jonson of having brought about a situation he required (Bonario's presence in the gallery when Celia is attacked), without troubling to provide a sufficient motive.[1] But it is in Mosca's character to take great risks ; from first to last he is playing a dangerous game, and at this very moment he is elated by success. But he is not wantonly courting danger. He has a definite plan, and it is not the fruit of a sudden impulse on the appearance of Bonario. 'Who's this?' he says to himself on seeing him enter, 'The person I was bound to seeke' (III. ii. 1). Mosca's own subsequent explanations of his motives to Corbaccio and then to Voltore (III. ix) are naturally seasoned to their palate. But it is not difficult to detect the real policy, now frustrated, which had dictated his act. Corbaccio was attached to his son, and corrupt as he is, had at first demurred to the project of disinheriting him. It is Mosca's cue to prevent any recurrence of these dangerous scruples, and he takes the course which he expects will promptly and violently alienate father and son. What he meant to happen is substantially what he tells Corbaccio *has* happened, with a climax which Corbaccio's tardy arrival prevented. Bonario was to break out in rage against his father and threaten his life ; Mosca would then intervene to save him.

[1] J. A. Symonds, *Ben Jonson*, p. 86.

securing thereby the gratitude and confidence of the old man for himself and the legacy for his chief.[1] There were several openings for failure in this calculation; as there were in the calculations of Iago and of Richard. But it was sufficiently well grounded to be adopted by an able and daring man; and the circumstance which upsets it, the premature arrival of Corvino and Celia, is provided with a motive admirably in keeping with Corvino's character, and yet so extravagant in its vileness that even the depraved imagination of Mosca could not be expected to foresee or reckon with it.[2]

V

The three dupes are drawn in less detail but with a no less incisive and powerful hand. They stand clearly and unmistakably apart, but not because they differ a jot in the quality or degree of their rapacity. Raven, crow, vulture, they represent but a narrow class even among birds of prey. They differ in their circumstances, not in their bent. Voltore, the knowing advocate, is as blinded by greed and as easily gulled as the dull and deaf Corbaccio, and executes volte-faces when the cause requires it as shamefully as Corvino. Wonderfully as the adventures of the three are invented and discriminated, one cannot but contrast with the unrelieved monotone of their decadent and criminal corruption the picturesque diversity of the clients of Subtle and Face. Both the strong ethical bias which animated Jonson in *Volpone*, and the comparative absence of realistic stimulus and suggestion, contributed to this effect. In no other of the comedies are the persons so sharply distinguished as bad or good. The rank and uniform depravity of the rogues and dupes is set off by the white innocence of Celia and Bonario, who to tell the truth are, as characters, almost

---

[1] This seems more likely than to suppose, with M. Castelain (*Ben Jonson*, p. 303), that Mosca reckons on Bonario *killing* his father. For, warned as he was, it was probable that he would do this, if at all, before the old man had completed the transfer of his inheritance; and then where was Mosca's advantage?

[2] III. vii. 4, 5 : '. . . did ere man haste so, for his hornes? A courtier would ply it so, for a place.'

as insipid as they are innocent. Even the *avocatori* fall apart into two corresponding groups,—the three abstract and colourless administrators of justice, and the 'fourth', who seeks to temper its rigour to a possible son-in-law. Of the proper and normal material of comedy, extravagancies and absurdities, there is, in the main plot, nothing. Its nearest approach to humour lies in the horrible simulations of the ludicrous effected by the misshapen creatures of Volpone's household.

One exception there is, however, to the otherwise unbroken predominance of dull virtue and revolting vice—the by-plot of Sir Politick Would-be. A breath of lighter and more wholesome air from the old Humour-comedies enters with this quaintly refreshing personage and his associates; and it is significant that Jonson recovers the normal temper of his comedy precisely where he is reverting to his normal topics, when he turns from the Venetians of his erudite invention to the English of his familiar experience, the eccentrics whose humours were to be studied from the life in Fleet Street and Westminster. Sir Politick and his lady are, in truth, as alien to the spirit of the play as they appear to be to the usages of Venice; foreigners full of naïve curiosity and enterprise, who thrust themselves into dangerous entanglement with an affair which they do not in the least comprehend and on which they have not the least effect. The peculiar humour of the picture depends in large part on the contrast between their fussy and officious interference and their irrelevance; humour which was not to be had, if their absurd contortions had had any bearing upon, or inner relation to, the main theme. Jonson had painted in Puntarvolo the absurdities of English travellers at home; his Venetian scene here provided an opening hard to resist for exhibiting the fantastic tricks they played in the foreign cities of their resort, and nowhere more extravagantly than in Venice. Cumberland and others have demurred to their 'loose connexion with the plot', and justly enough if perfect plot-building means that every person contributes definitely to the progress and evolution of the action. But in that case what function remains in drama for the fussy, inefficient people who only blunder round about the real business without affecting it, important buzzing flies upon the engine wheel? A most effective comic role would in that case have no legitimate place in comedy. Jonson had from the first dealt largely in pretentious inefficiencies, and the exposure of this kind of comic irrelevance was in truth a part of his finished technique. Master Stephen and Master Matthew may in a sense be said to set the plot of *Every Man in his Humour* in motion, but through its remaining course the humour of Stephen, in particular, lies precisely in his uncomprehending irrelevance. For the rest, without belonging to the highest rank of Jonson's comic characters, Sir Politick is a pleasant variation of his 'projector' type, and Lady Would-be an admirable specimen of the seventeenth-century bluestocking, more comic in herself and employed to more genuinely comic purpose than the Collegiate Ladies of the next play, which her merciless loquacity at the expense of Volpone in another way anticipates.

INTRODUCTION TO
'THE SILENT WOMAN'

THE SILENT WOMAN

I

Epicoene, or The Silent Woman was probably the work of 1609. It was first acted in 1609 by the Children of the Revels, and entered for publication in the Stationers' Register on September 20 of 1610.[1] Quarto editions dated 1609 and 1612 have been alleged to exist;[2] but the first extant version is that of the Folio, in 1616. This, however, is attested by Jonson's express statement to have differed in no point from the original text. 'There is not a line, or syllable in it changed from the simplicity of the first Copy.'[3] Of the circumstances of the first performance nothing definite is known. The Prologue indicates that the stern flagellant of vice and folly was, in this play, with relaxed brows deliberately seeking to amuse. He no longer hectors his audience; he hardly even instructs them. Instead of haughtily summoning them to turn from the 'ill customs' of the popular stage to his own austerer art, he promises them a multifarious banquet contrived to please 'not the cookes taste, but the guests', where every one from the knights and ladies to the waiting-wench and the daughter of Whitefriars will find the dishes that suit them. And instead of inveighing at the popular writers who pandered to the corrupt popular taste, he now reflects, gravely, upon the too fastidious sect of writers:

> That, onely, for particular likings care,
> And will taste nothing that is populare.

[1] The year is given in the Folio. Mr. Fleay has argued (*Biog. Chron.* I. 374) that this is Old Style, and the true date early in 1610.
[2] Whalley mentions one in 1609; Gifford, stating that he has been unable to discover this, adds that the first that has 'fallen in his way' is one of 1612. Neither is now known.
[3] Dedicatory epistle to Sir Francis Stuart.

Notwithstanding this engaging appeal it would seem that the play was not altogether well received. Drummond's story of the satirical verses found on the stage after the first performance, to the effect that the play was well called *The Silent Woman* since there was never one man to say plaudite to it, must rest upon Jonson's report, and cannot be disregarded; and the dedication to Sir Francis Stuart is most naturally understood, notwithstanding the scornful protest of Gifford, as an appeal to the scholarly old sailor's unbiased judgement from the 'hatred', 'iniquity', and 'contumely' which perverse interpretation of the play had procured him in certain quarters. Some indeed it had 'pleased'; but clearly it had gravely displeased others. As clearly, the displeasure was due to the supposed personal application of one or more of this motley crowd of comic characters. That Morose, in particular, the main butt of the fun, had an 'original' was confidently insinuated; and Dryden, sixty years later, was 'assured from divers persons that Ben Jonson was actually acquainted with such a man, one altogether as ridiculous as he is here represented'.[1] Against such imputation Jonson lodged an emphatic protest, when it was already too late, in the second so-called Prologue:

> If any, yet, will (with particular slight
> Of application) wrest what he doth write;
> And that he meant or him, or her, will say:
> They make a libell, which he made a play;

a marginal note of Jonson's informing us that the protest was 'Occasion'd by some persons impertinent exception'. It is not surprising that a dramatist who had formerly made comedy so formidable a sledge-hammer for the correction of his fellows was not at once taken at his word when he

---

[1] *Essay of Dramatic Poesy* (ed. Ker), p. 74. Cf. also vol. i, Appendix I, p. 188, where it is recorded that 'my lord B.' took the poet into the country at Christmas, and that he wrote *The Silent Woman* upon a 'new character' he found there, and my lord made him 'a noble present upon reading the first act to him'. A character, like Morose, if he existed at all, would naturally live in the seclusion of the country; to transfer him to town life would heighten the comic possibilities of the character, and further recall Libanius.

uttered these emphatic protests. The modern critic will do well not to dismiss these denials as mere bluff. But it remains a question whether Jonson was very unwilling that persons whom he disliked should be 'identified' with ridiculous figures in his plays not principally 'meant' for them; and further, whether he always refrained from giving the cue to this process by some suggestive label. To this small extent we may accept Mr. Fleay's association of Daw with Sir John Harington. Harington cannot possibly be 'identified' with Daw. The attempt to establish common traits comes to extremely little.[1] But it is hard to believe that Jonson called Daw 'Sir John' without some malicious desire that the rival epigrammatist should be discovered in his sorry knight, whom he could still honestly deny to be 'meant' for him.

And whatever private offence *The Silent Woman* may have given, it fulfils in an unexpected degree the hopes doubtfully raised, one surmises, in its first audience by the un-Jonsonian intimation, already quoted, that the dramatic banquet had been prepared, 'not to please the cookes tastes, but the guests'. Not that the Cook, even now, did any sensible violence to his own tastes. But he chose his dishes in the main from those which the severe and popular palate alike approved; and, without forgoing his own nicely regulated methods of preparation, disarmed criticism by the undeniable relish of the result. In plot-structure, in the unities of time and place, *The Silent Woman* is not a whit less strictly ordered than *Volpone*. The action, though one of the most elaborate in our drama, occupies some twelve hours, from morning till nightfall.[2] It is carried on,

---

[1] There is, for instance, no analogy between Daw's summary disposal of the classics and Harington's admirable and pointed eulogies in *Brief Apology for Poetry*. Thus Virgil, for Daw, is one who 'talks ... of dunging of land, and bees'. The whole purport of the allusion in the *Apology* to the Georgics is to point out how topics in themselves unattractive, like these, become delightful in Virgil's verse. Cf. the whole pleasant passage in Gregory Smith, *Elizabethan Critical Essays*, ii. 206 f.

[2] At the opening of the play Clerimont is dressing; in III. v it is still

if not, as Dryden said, in two places, yet in five, all closely adjacent.[1] And in coherence and compactness it even surpasses *Volpone*. On the other hand, Jonson marked his descent from the austere heights on which he had there moved to something like genial familiarity with his audience by the use, throughout the play, of prose. Never since *Every Man in his Humour* had he been so willing simply to amuse. The satirist had not sheathed his rapier, nor altogether laid his bludgeon by, and the critic still provides that his audience shall laugh, if at all, 'according to the rules'; but he lays himself out more unreservedly than even in the first great comedy to ensure that at any rate they shall laugh.

II

Much, however, had happened on the Comic stage during the eleven or twelve years which had elapsed since *Every Man in his Humour* was planned. The pretention there made (even if not yet explicitly announced) to show the right way in comedy was, under the then conditions, not wholly unjustified. But the dazzling apparition of plays like *As You Like It, Much Ado, Twelfth Night, The Merry Wives*, not to speak of the great semi-historical comedy of *King Henry IV*, put another complexion upon the matter. All were in full vogue, and most of them contained things that Jonson's masters of the Old Comedy, Plautus or Aristophanes, would themselves have enjoyed. Jonson might even discover in them occasional indications that his own dramatic seed had not fallen on

'afore noone'; in IV. iv we are told, 'This is but a day, and 'tis well worne too now'; in IV. v, 'If I do it not yet afore night, as neere as 'tis'.
[1] Clerimont's lodgings (Act I); Daw's lodgings (II. iii. iv); Mrs. Otter's house (III. i–iii); a lane near Morose's house (II. vi); Morose's house, the remainder. Miss Henry points out (p. lxv) that these are all close together. Epicoene is 'lodged i' the next street' to Morose (I. ii) and 'in the house where Sir IOHN DAW lyes' (ibid.); while Morose's house 'is but ouer the way, hard by' from Mrs. Otter's (III. iii). If our view that *Every Man in his Humour* was revised in 1612 is right, the present play is the first of Jonson's in which the scene was openly laid in London.

barren ground. Master Slender was little more than a 'country Gull' in the country, a Master Stephen at home. Pistol, again, Malvolio, Aguecheek, and the pseudo-Falstaff of *The Merry Wives*, though in no sense borrowed from or suggested by Jonson, might be called brilliant experiments or variations in the Humour Comedy;—Jonsonian examples of men 'in their Humours', and buffeted, by more or less robustious Jonsonian methods, out of them. To pass from the Falstaff of Eastcheap to the Falstaff of Windsor is in some sense to pass from Shakespearean to Jonsonian comedy. The comparison can indeed but make more palpable Shakespeare's immeasurably richer and subtler psychology, not to speak of the charm, the ease, the *entrain* which were his alone. This more brilliant and genial presentation of themes conceived somewhat in his own manner was not perhaps likely to excite immediate emulation in the haughty younger writer to whom the compliment was paid. There immediately followed, moreover, the estrangement of the Stage Quarrel, and Jonson's abandonment of comedy; when he returned to it with *Volpone*, it was in a kind the most remote conceivable from the gaiety of Shakespeare. But the great and lasting success of this masterpiece did much to assuage the sternness of his attitude, as a man of letters, towards the world. Certainly, the *unus contra mundum* temper of the later Humour plays never recurs. And the advance in geniality marked by the *Alchemist*, when compared with *Volpone*, otherwise so closely akin to it, is patent. It is certain, in any case, that when, in 1609, he again appeared in comedy, he had fully recovered the capacity and disposition for pure fun that he had shown in his first comedy. One of the signs of this more genial temper is his tacit recognition that his great rival's work, if it 'wanted art', at least provided excellent raw material. The 'duel' of Daw and La Foole (IV. v) is palpably built on that of Aguecheek and Viola. The charm of Viola's half-pathetic feminine embarrassment was not within Jonson's capacity, nor probably to his mind. But the situation of persons caught in the toils of their own strategy was intrinsically Jonsonian. And the pretentious yet thin-blooded Sir Andrew was imagined, as already noticed, quite in his vein. He accordingly replaces the shrinking girl by a second variety of the effeminate knight—reducing the scene thereby from romantic to purely satiric comedy, for the two duellists are both cowards, differing only in the manner of their cowardice; Daw 'a whiniling dastard', La Foole 'a braue heroique coward, . . . afraid in a great looke, and a stout accent'.

In other respects *The Silent Woman* attaches itself to *Every Man in his Humour* more closely than to any of the intervening Comedies. Youth, adventure, and enterprise had there triumphed over middle-aged timidity and caution; but in the succeeding comedies the genial spirit of youth shares the honours of the game with the stern spirit of law. Young Ovid in the *Poetaster* is touched with the zest of Jonson's lingering romance; but he is less the hero than the sagacious Horace; while the implacable Asper of *Every Man out of his Humour* is there the chosen exponent of Jonson's deliberate mind. But in *Epicoene* there is an abrupt reversion to the *gaudeamus igitur* note of the opening comedy. It is the day of the young men once more and more decisively than ever, and Dauphine carries out, with more concentration and to a more drastic issue, the duel of youth with crabbed age initiated by Edward Kno'well.

In neither of the old men of the earlier comedy, indeed, is the 'crabbedness' of age rendered with so sharp an emphasis as in the hero of *Epicoene*. They are admirably real and human; Morose is drawn with a violence of caricature none the less foreign to high comedy that it is inspired by exuberant fun and not by bitter animosity. The best that is to be said for his farcical horror of noise is that it goes well with his surly self-centred antagonism to the world at large, and especially to the most joyous and noisy section of it. Shakespeare, eight or nine years before, had handled a kindred theme, and that in the same play from which

Jonson, as we have seen, was to borrow suggestion in the present drama. The baiting of the surly Morose, who abhors revelry, has a parallel in the baiting of Malvolio for his puritan rigour towards the lovers of cakes and ale. The story of Malvolio is itself somewhat Jonsonian in conception. And the specific 'Humour' of Malvolio has a nearer relation to that of Morose than to any of Jonson's earlier Humours. It would be rash to say that Jonson owed anything to the rich comedy of Malvolio.[1] It remains interesting that both poets should have dwelt upon a type of comic situation even faintly symbolical of the larger antagonism of mind and temper which was so fast defining itself in the life of the English people.

III

The main plot is an adroit combination of two Greek jests or practical jokes; both variations on the stock comic motive of the man induced to marry by false pretences. In the one a quiet-loving recluse is led to marry an exhaustibly loquacious woman under the pretence that she is 'silent'; in the other an old voluptuary is proxy-wedded to a boy. The first was taken from a source which had already furnished some incidental fun in the preceding play, *Volpone*, III. iv, the well-known 'declamation' of the Greek sophist Libanius, on the surly man who had married a talkative wife.[2] The deluded husband is represented seeking a remedy for his evil state by an appeal to the courts. He implores the judges to permit him to end a life which his wife's tongue has rendered no longer worth living. By the counsel of a friend he had been beguiled into marrying. The uproar of the wedding festivities, already a severe trial, had been merely a prelude to the discovery that the wife he had taken for her excellent voice and few words had an

---

[1] A slight point of contact is, that Morose too is treated like a madman.
[2] Libanius, 314–90 A.D. His works, Greek text with a Latin translation, were printed in Paris in 1606; but the use of this declamation in *Volpone* shows that Jonson's acquaintance with them did not begin then, as suggested by Koeppel (*Quellen-studien*, p. 9).

exceptional gift of speech and an insatiable thirst for knowledge. The second trick was taken from the *Casina* of Plautus, itself founded upon a Greek original. A vicious old man, Lysidamus, having designs upon the person of his female slave, Casina, arranges to marry her to a creature of his own, Olympio. His wife discovers his design, and contrives to substitute for Casina a fellow-slave Chalinus, whereupon Lysidamus and Olympio suffer an ignominious exposure.

The amusing oration of Libanius offered but slender stuff for drama. The *Casina* story provided a genuine dramatic intrigue, but one in which the denouement alone had any comic quality. By substituting Libanius' farcical misogyne for Plautus' elderly profligate, Jonson gives the whole plot a gaiety and humour which the *Casina* exhibits only incidentally. But he at the same time incurred the proverbial consequences of tacking slighter to more substantial material, and the wealth of comic detail he has lavished on it by no means effaced the disparity. The common criticism of the plot to the effect that it is a coherent and logical development of an absurd supposition expresses the facts accurately enough. And the inconsistency was no mere result of a capricious choice of subject; it was grounded in deep-seated contrarieties in Jonson's own artistic nature, where the bent of a great realist for truth and nature never overcame the satirist's and humorist's weakness for fantastic caricature.

The handling of Morose himself exhibits the disparity of aim. On his character the whole plot hinges; and Jonson has obviously sought to give it more substance and credibility. He has developed the qualities of temperament which, even in Libanius, are ultimately responsible for the sufferings inflicted upon the enemy of noise. The Greek *Morosus* is an unsociable but harmless person, who marries simply for the sake of a quiet life, and when that hope is frustrated has no resource but suicide. Jonson's Morose is a more aggressive, if not a more formidable, type of the surly man: it is spite against his nephew that induces him to imperil his quiet life by marriage; his plot, as well as the nephew's more artfully laid counter-plot, is inspired by his active malice, not by his horror of noise. Jonson had palpably remembered his last great comedy, and infused something of the malignity of Volpone, and something of his situation, into this generally gayer and more innocent world. Morose is indeed a feeble ineffective Volpone, his match in nothing but ill will, with no astute confederate by his side, and hopelessly out-played by his imagined victim. Rich and childless, like Volpone, he has not even Volpone's excuse for cheating his heir, for the nephew is no 'captator', but the legitimate inheritor. His horror of noise itself is capable of being overcome or forgotten in the zest of vindictive rage; and Morose insensibly warms to the work of cursing the guilty barber, under the stimulus of the eloquent Truewit, until he breaks off with a sudden: 'Good sir, no more. I forgot my selfe.'[1] With great skill too, Jonson avoids throwing the stress of the plot upon its weakest point by making Morose not merely marry primarily to spite his nephew, but resolve definitely upon the marriage in a sudden access of fury, which blinds him to the extreme hazard of marriage with a woman whose 'silence' has no better guarantee than her capacity, when she chooses, to hold her tongue. Nothing in the play is more admirably contrived than the happy blunder of Truewit, whose naïve dissuasions from marriage threaten to baulk the whole scheme, but actually cut away every obstacle and precipitate Morose headlong upon his fateful career. Nothing will serve but that he must be married that very day. 'This night I will get an heire, and thrust him out of my bloud like a stranger.'[2]

With all this, however, the farcical horror-of-noise-motive could not be dispensed with, nor softened. If Morose's marriage could be explained without it, his desperate desire, at any cost, to be released from the marriage bond demanded

[1] III. v.   [2] II. v.

the retention of this trait in all its extravagance. And Jonson has responded to this demand of his plot with unmistakable gusto. In these exuberant and laughable scenes, where Morose is brought before us conversing with his servants in dumb show, or walking the streets 'with a huge turbant of night-caps on his head, buckled ouer his eares',[1] we forget the sternly faithful portrayer of the follies of the time in the riotous humour of the caricaturist. If Morose was entitled to stand in the category of 'men'—the proper subjects, for Jonson, of Comedy—and was not rather a new and far from plausible variety of those 'monsters' which he bade her taboo, the bounds which divided him from these were perilously narrow.

In one point, however, Jonson has brought Morose decidedly nearer to human nature than his Attic prototype. Lysidamus in his desperate straits, as one hopelessly wedded to a talkative wife, proposes to hang himself. This solution, though sufficiently in keeping with the farcical conception of the whole *jeu d'esprit*, would have seemed gratuitous in the highest degree to a Jacobean audience, familiar with other and more agreeable recipes for the management of uncongenial wives. Morose might have tamed his shrew, or have killed her with kindness; or he might have bought her off, paid 'anything', in fact, 'for a quiet life'; but suicide meant paying a high price without enjoying the goods, an obviously unpractical mode of doing business. In transferring the solution to the region of bargaining and *quid pro quo* Jonson was true to the national character of his audience. To carry this through, however, implied, of course, that the marriage should be capable of being annulled. The *Casina* plot enabled Jonson to effect this in a novel and wholly unexpected way. The substitution of a boy had the advantage for the purposes of comedy, and especially of Jonsonian comedy, over any other of the possible grounds for divorce, that it involved neither amorous passion nor medical technicalities, and that it was, in its very

[1] I. i.

nature, absolutely final and beyond dispute. It may be added that no other plea for annulment admitted of being made good on the very day of the marriage, and thus within the limits of time required. 'Had Morose been content to postpone his divorce even to the morrow of his marriage Dauphine's whole intrigue would have broken down. As it is, Morose's farcical impatience for release, and Dauphine's well-founded eagerness to secure the ransom before Morose discovers the nature of his marriage, are admirably contrived to second one another. It needs, however, the united strength of both motives to make plausible the prodigious rapidity with which the solution is brought about. The technical resources employed in knitting close the texture of the plot are immense; but the one farcical motive runs like a thread of cheaper material through the whole fabric, vitiating in a measure Jonson's most brilliant combinations.

IV

Dryden, in his famous 'examen' of this play, which he took to be the most perfect of all English, nay of all modern, comedies (an opinion shared it would seem by his rival Shadwell, and by Mr. Pepys[1]), expressed a special admiration of this denouement. ' For the λύσις, or untying of it, 'tis so admirable that when it is done no one of the audience would think the poet could have missed it; and yet it was concealed so much before the last scene, that any other way would sooner have entered into your thoughts.'[2] Dryden here assumed without question a doctrine still hotly debated among dramatic critics—that a secret vital to the action of a play may legitimately be kept from the audience. Yet it had little support in Elizabethan technique. To the frank and genial technique of Shakespeare this secretive and mysterious method is almost entirely foreign: the most

[1] Pepys, September 19, 1668: 'To the King's Playhouse, and there saw "The Silent Woman"; the best comedy I think that ever was wrote; and sitting by Shadwell the poet, he was big with admiration of it.'
[2] *Essay of Dramatic Poesy*, p. 6 (ed. Ker).

signal example of it occurs where so much else in the technique bears witness to alien influence, in *The Winter's Tale*. But even there, only a dull audience could have been surprised when the 'statue' of Hermione descended from its pedestal warm and alive; so transparent is the demeanour of Paulina. To play tricks with his audience, to cheat and baffle them, was far more in keeping with Jonson's temper; we have seen how he loved to hold his catastrophe in suspense. But even he never before or afterwards devised a cheat so colossal and so perfectly sustained. Dryden's admiration for it cannot be shared without reserve. The sudden and simple solution of an apparently impossible problem produces a pleasant kind of surprise; but if we have reason to think that the problem was not fairly proposed, the pleasure is crossed with a certain mortification like that of the victims of Columbus's well-known feat with the egg. A shade of such mortification has probably always qualified the pleasure naturally produced by Jonson's denouement. Very possibly it is reflected in the bad temper ascribed to the audience which experienced this rebuff for the first time. The denouement would in fact be more effective if it were less surprising,—if the audience were in a position, as persons in the secret, to enjoy the surprise of Clerimont, the favoured friend, and Truewit, the archplotter and connoisseur in womankind. Half the humour of Truewit's pretensions is lost by the tardiness of the discovery. No one, for instance, new to the plot would appreciate the archness of the recluse student Dauphine's request to Truewit for enlightenment upon the nature of women: 'How cam'st thou to studie these creatures so exactly? I would thou would'st make me a proficient. TRV. Yes, but you must leaue to liue i' your chamber then a month together vpon AMADIS *de Gaule*, or *Don Qvixote*, as you are wont; and come abroad'... (IV. i). And the confession by Daw and La Foole of their relations with Epicoene (V. i) similarly fails of the effect which comes to it when the plot is known.

V

If Jonson did not completely overcome the inherent defects of his plot, we cannot but recognize, with Dryden, the profusion of comic invention which he lavished upon it. The main agent of the intrigue, and its victim, are surpassed in vivacity and truth, as dramatic creations, by eight or nine other figures; hardly a single person in the piece is insignificant. And the art with which, while pursuing their own ends, they are all drawn into the main plot, and made willing or involuntary instruments in its consummation, marks an advance in technique even upon *Volpone*. The last act of *The Fox* is in thorough keeping with the first four, but it is not their indispensable climax like the fifth act of *Epicoene*. Daw and La Foole, Truewit and Cutbeard, Otter and his princess, and the Ladies Collegiate, all contribute their particular pang to the 'variety and changes' of Morose's 'torment'; but all have an independent dramatic value. They are mostly loquacious; but their loquacity is of several different orders. The two gulls are only less excellent specimens of the lively chattering variety of the species than are Stephen and Matthew of the 'melancholy' section; and Daw's 'as I hope to finish Tacitus' may be matched with the soldierly asseverations of Bobadill which are Stephen's despair. Truewit is a Brainworm with a formidable virtuosity of speech added to his other efficiencies, and a subtler irony is manifested in his fate. We laugh when Brainworm the arch-plotter is entangled in his own devices; but there is finer comedy in the situation of the omniscient Truewit, who, after playing a brilliant game with his friends as pawns, discovers at the close that he himself has been a pawn in a yet deeper game played by his friend. The Otters, drawn in Jonson's broadest vernacular manner, approach burlesque; but the loud-tongued 'Amazon', who allows her 'captain' husband half a crown a week and four pair of stockings a year, acquires an added zest as a living example to the hapless Morose of the terrors of marriage: 'I have perceiu'd the effect of it, too late, in madame OTTER' (IV. iv). In the Ladies Collegiate who take possession of the young wife, and instruct her, as they think, in the proper management of her husband, Jonson has brought into the crowded field yet another powerful deterrent from the married state. Memories of Aristophanic satire upon women's clubs and leagues may have contributed something to these scenes; but 'colleges' of this kind were known to Jacobean as to Elizabethan London; 'an order betweene courtiers, and country-madames, that liue from their husbands; and giue entertainement to all the *Wits*, and *Braueries* o' the time.'[1] Jonson succeeds better with his bold, than with his modest, women; and the three 'Collegiates' are vigorously drawn. As so often, however, he is content to discriminate by merely external traits the members of a group who have the same general function in a play. Haughty, Centaure, and Mavis differ psychologically even less than Voltore, Corvino, and Corbaccio. They are all jealous, all rail at one another, and all make love to Dauphine; it is only that one woos him with a jewel, another 'cautiously', and the third with an 'Italian riddle'.

The wealth of comic motive and comic character in *Epicoene*, its lively and veracious painting of manners, and the admirable precision of its plot-building, must always entitle it to a high rank among comedies. What prevents our reckoning it among the masterpieces of comedy is not so much the absurdity as the insignificance of its main motive. The traditional criticism that this motive is 'farcical' expresses only a part of the truth. Farce may be an ingredient in great comedy. Molière, who found farce in possession of the comic stage, never wholly turned his back on it; as one of his best recent exponents has

---

[1] I. i. Truewit describes this as 'a new foundation here i' the towne'. But Nashe, in *Christ's Tears* (*Works*, ii. 151) had alluded to similar 'foundations' as already familiar: 'A great office is not so gainefull as the principalship of a Colledge of Curtizans.'

said, he 'continued to mingle an element of farce, in cunningly calculated doses, with his loftiest conceptions'.[1] And he had, like Shakespeare, the art of giving value, by brilliant and profound character-painting, to incident in itself whimsical or extravagant without sacrificing any of its natural comic quality; so that these 'doses' of farce betray themselves only to the coolest analysis, and then rather as an atmosphere of irrational gaiety somehow communicated, like a seasoning, to the whole than as a definitely alien ingredient. In this power Jonson, with all his prodigal wit and talent, fell far short of the master with whom he most challenges comparison. The *Malade Imaginaire* touches farce at half a dozen points, yet, while we watch or read it, the plot unfolds itself with an air of magical coherence, and we forget to ask how Argan comes to put up with this amazing Toinette, or not to penetrate her disguise. But Jonson does not create this illusive reality; the extravagance of the Morose-motive asserts itself as a distinct unassimilated element in spite of the wealth of comic matter in which it is embedded. More than this, Morose, real or not, is at any rate an uninteresting and unimportant person: whether we take him as a man of grotesquely sensitive nerves or as the peevish egoist, he remains from first to last limited as a comic creation to a narrow section of the field of possibilities to which these characteristics open. His egoism is petty and vulgar spite, too mean to be laughable; a naked contemptible thing, devoid of that vesture of specious and plausible illusion which makes Sir Willoughby supreme food for the Comic Spirit; devoid even of the illogical extravagance of animosity which places Alceste within, and Timon not far without, the borders of comedy. Morose has sometimes been compared with these famous misanthropes, but he has as little of their sublime unreason as of their idealism. He is no victim of disillusion; and his venom is a thin, acrid fluid, which discharges itself in vengeance upon the particular person who has offended him,

[1] Eugène Rigal, *Molière*, ii. 307.

not the potent virus which floods the brain with universal hatred of mankind. The comparison with Alceste is wholly out of the question. The comparison with the victim of nerves, Argan, no doubt lies nearer. But even this comparison, in spite of the vastly greater profusion of comic detail lavished upon him, Morose cannot really support. Argan is not merely more amusing and more true, he is more typical; he touches life and experience at more points, and at points of more interest and significance. He is, like Morose, a man of nerves, and even exhibits as one of his symptoms Morose's horror of noise. But at the root of his 'imaginary' maladies lies the real malady which Toinette wittily calls the *maladie de la médicine*. His naïve faith in whatever wears the medical garb, or issues from the apothecary's laboratory, founded as it is in the futile fear of death, is a human and natural eccentricity, and therefore in itself proper stuff for comedy; while Morose's distemper merely gives occasion to comedy without being itself comic at all.

INTRODUCTION TO 'THE ALCHEMIST'

THE ALCHEMIST

I

The Alchemist was first published in quarto, in 1612. Four years later it was included in the first Folio edition of Jonson's works. The title-page of the Folio states the play to have been 'acted in the yeare 1610. By the Kings Maiesties Seruants'; and this was undoubtedly the date of its first performance, and also of its composition. It was entered in the Stationers' Register on October 3 of that year, and internal evidence shows that it had been written during the preceding weeks. Several passages imply that the action is itself supposed to take place in this very year, 1610.[1] During this summer and autumn (from July 12 to November 22) the plague raged in London, and Jonson astutely contrived to give his attack upon the crying scandal of alchemy a direct bearing upon the sensation of the hour. The plot is directly founded upon this visitation, Lovewit having quitted his house (Subtle's 'studio') for fear of the 'sickness' which now is 'hot'. The prospective audience for which he wrote would be largely composed of persons whose empty houses had for months not long before offered asylums as secure as Lovewit's for the operations of sorcerers and harlots. They would follow with peculiar zest adventures which might equally have befallen themselves. The denouement, brought about by Lovewit's return to the city before he is expected, implies a date for the supposed action at a time when the plague had somewhat abated but was by no means past. 'O, feare not him,' says Face (I. i);

[1] Dame Pliant is said by Drugger to be 'But nineteene, at the most' (II. vi. 31); and she herself implies that she was born in 1591:
Neuer, sin' *eighty-eight* could I abide 'hem,
And that was some three yeere afore I was borne, in truth.
(IV. iv. 29, 30).

While there dyes one, a weeke,
O' the plague, hee's safe, from thinking toward *London*.

Jonson, writing while the plague was still virulent, could only roughly forecast the date required, from the precedent of previous visitations. It would seem from certain indications that he chose a day towards the end of October;[1] and since the plague habitually declined as the October chills came on, this was a very plausible calculation. To all appearances it was fulfilled. The actual performance of the play would naturally be impossible until the plague had so far subsided that the theatres could be reopened; and Jonson thus doubtless anticipated a performance some time in November, two or three weeks after the imaginary date. There is no reason to suppose that it was played later than he expected.[2]

II

The Alchemist is the most signal triumph of Jonson's difficult and original dramatic art. *Volpone* and *Epicoene*, both with surpassing excellences of their own, have yet the air, when viewed from the vantage-ground of their successor, of experiments or essays towards an ideal of drama which neither completely achieved. Their extraordinary effect was not gained without some straining of the stuff, some departure from the rigour of the comic law. *Volpone*, with its accesses of sublimity and its gleams of pathos, had pressed hard upon the threshold of tragedy; *Epicoene*, with

---

[1] Subtle, in III. ii. 129-30, reckons that the brethren will have to wait 'some fifteene dayes' before 'the *Magisterium* will be perfected'. This, Ananias reckons, means 'about the second day, of the third weeke, In the ninth month'. Mr. Hathaway (ed. p. 14), makes it probable that the months are to be reckoned from March; so that this date would be November 16th, and the date of the action November 1st. In the final scene Ananias declared that the elders' money was paid in 'Vpon the second day of the fourth weeke, In the eight month' (v. v. 103-4). This would be October 23rd. If either indication is to be taken literally, it is rather the first. But too much honour need not be done to Ananias's accuracy. The two dates may be taken as fixing the supposed day of the action in the last days of October.

[2] Mr. Hathaway without warrant takes for granted that the supposed date of the action was the anticipated date of the performance (p. 13).

its ineradicable triviality of motive, decidedly crossed the threshold of farce. Both were somewhat factitious and unreal; invented, and betraying their inventedness. All the genius of the execution could not conceal, in either play, a nucleus of alien matter; the joyless laughter of the Neronian Court, the scholastic jests of decadent Athens, refused to be entirely assimilated to Elizabethan humanity. But in *The Alchemist* Jonson fell upon a theme which allowed him to gratify his propensity for the grandiose and the recondite in crime and folly without passing beyond the Jacobean England of his day or the teeming and squalid London at his door. The profession of alchemy was perhaps the fittest subject then to be found in Europe for such comedy as his. No other vulgar roguery of the day crowned its impudent brow with so imposing a nimbus of superhuman pretensions, or gathered about it a robe so marvellously inwrought with the subtle erudition, the daring experiment, the mystic speculation, of the past. The alchemist stood with one foot in the region of the prodigious, which allured Jonson's burly and vehement imagination, while the other was planted firmly on that ground of current human nature and everyday experience which satisfied his Humanist taste. The audiences which had 'graced monsters' would find something congenial in a figure which nevertheless belonged without question to the category of 'men',

such as *Comœdie* would chuse,
When she would shew an Image of the times.

The alchemist of Jonson's time had as assured a place in English society as the alchemist of Chaucer's. Two hundred and fifty years had passed by, 'medieval' had become 'modern' England; but this singularly 'medieval' figure, as we are apt to regard it, had in no way relaxed his grip upon the modern world. He was a survival, if we will, but he survived among new conditions fully as favourable to him as the old, and he accommodated himself to them with at least equal skill. The sixteenth century, in some aspects an age of *Aufklärung*, had perhaps started as many superstitions as it destroyed, and fortified as many as it sapped. The Protestant reformation revived some forms of spiritual faith, but it quickened every form of demonology, and turned the belief in witchcraft, in particular, from a sporadic disease into a national epidemic. Luther believed in the devil as passionately as he believed in God, and diabolic assault was for the devout Protestant a nearer peril, as the divine grace was a nearer hope. Alchemy was less affected by the religious revolutions of the age than by its eager scientific curiosity, its ingenious experimental art, its Utopian economics. The prospect of generating gold from baser metals, which gave alchemic practices their tenacious hold upon the mass of men, lost none of its attractions in an age of eager enterprise, among men easily lured to the desert by the mirage of an El Dorado. The rapid increase in the standard of luxury which the Renascence everywhere promoted, the demand for social display in furniture, pottery, gold and silver plate, multiplied the incentives to the discovery of new avenues to wealth; while the influx of gold in fabulous sums from the Indies into the coffers of Spain drove prices steadily up throughout Western Europe, and added a double incentive to the average citizen's normal appetite for gain. The prospect, as it seemed, of swift and easy enrichment concurred with the practical urgency of dearer living. Sovereigns openly or furtively encouraged these useful adjuncts to a needy exchequer; even the papacy, which up to 1500 had condemned alchemy, tolerated the publication of an alchemic treatise in that year at Rome itself. The workshop of the goldsmith, in particular, easily became a laboratory in which the secret of gold-making was furtively pursued, and was liable to be credited with such practices where they did not exist.[1]

[1] The goldsmith Güstenhover of Strasburg was reported by his workmen to the Emperor Rudolf, in 1603, to have made gold, and was imprisoned because he failed to reveal the secret he did not possess (K. C. Schmieder, *Geschichte der Alchemie*, Halle, 1832, p. 331).

Experimenters in other materials for other purposes applied the clues they won by the way to the engrossing search for gold. The great potter Palissy dealt in alchemy, and with such success that he was able to furnish his countrymen with an 'unfailing recipe' for multiplying their treasures.[1] The zest of scientific curiosity is rarely untouched by the greed of gain; while, on the other hand, the thrusting-on of the grosser instinct was continually blended with the afflatus of the finer. When the alchemist Denys Zachaire went to Paris, in 1539, he found there no less than a hundred 'gold-makers'. 'They formed', he tells, 'a hermetic union' which met daily; but all their proceedings were futile. 'Every one assumed the air of uncommon knowledge, but what he wanted was to listen to the others.'[2] Very early in Elizabeth's reign repeated offers were made by enterprising pretenders of this type to manufacture gold for her. And she more than dallied wiih the prospect. We are able to follow, in the extensive correspondence still extant at Hatfield and elsewhere, her protracted dealings with Cornelius de Lanney, who after undertaking in 1565 to produce 50,000 marks a year, and being allowed to experiment in Somerset House, failed and was consigned in 1567 to the Tower, where he continued his experiments, still without success, and probably died.[3]

Until far into the seventeenth century the search for gold was carried on with all seriousness by a line of acute and patient inquirers. In the midst of these efforts to solve an impossible problem, the real problems of chemistry gradually disengaged themselves. And even with their own problem they sometimes attained an illusion of success specious enough to convince trained and sceptical onlookers.

[1] 'Récepte véritable par laquelle tous les hommes de la France pourront apprendre à multiplier leurs trésors' (Schmieder, *u. s.* p. 295).
[2] Schmieder, p. 272.
[3] *Dom. State Papers, Eliz.*, xxxvi. 12; xl. 28, 53; xlii. 30. Other offers of the kind are referred to in ib. lxxiv. 66; ccxxxix. 76; ccxlv. 130; ccxlvii. 36, 72; ccl. 9; ccli. 57, 58; ccliv. 46; cclxxi. 103. For the Tower as a place where prisoners might be employed 'to make gold for the state', cf. *Alch.* IV. vii. 79-82.

Nay, even the modern historian of alchemy is persuaded by the remarkable account of the Scottish alchemist Alexander Seton, whose conversion of lead into gold at Köln in 1604 staggered the narrator, a sceptic, doctor of medicine and of laws, and professor at Freiburg.[1] And to-day, when gold has actually been made in the laboratory from another metal, modern physical chemistry has fulfilled the dreams, if it has not justified the methods, of the old alchemists.

And alchemy, which thus flattered or fell in with so much else in the activities of this complex epoch, harmonized in a very remarkable way with some of its daring and brilliant guesses about the nature of the physical world and of Life at large. The idea of a common substance pervading the diversities of the elements gave a philosophic plausibility to the problem of deriving one metal from another which conferred a higher status upon the most vulgar practitioner. In vain Paracelsus vindicated the 'divine science' of alchemy, which has but one end—to extract the quintessence of things—against the 'false disciples' who took its end to be the making of gold and silver. The higher speculations reacted upon the lower. And alchemy profited, as a persuasive creed, by biological analogies which modern chemistry was austerely to disregard. Subtle silences the uninstructed scepticism of Surly by comparing the production of gold from an alien substance to the hatching of the chick from the egg.[2] So the sulphur and mercury were conceived as the 'husband' and the 'wife', from whose union emerged gold, 'the child'. But 'analogies' of this kind, while they tended to confirm the reality of the alchemic process, left its marvel unimpaired; so that the art benefited by the twofold associations of a mystery and an illuminating example; and the alchemist enjoyed the prestige simultaneously of the sacrosanct priest and the philosophic discoverer. He

---

[1] See the story of Seton in the narrative of Dr. Johann Wolfgang Dienheim, *De universa medicina*, Strasburg, 1610 (Schmieder, p. 325 f.).
[2] *Alchem.* II. iii. 131-6.

was a divine, in his fashion, and the efficacy of his work even depended, like the priest's, upon his moral state. Unchastity might frustrate the operations of the laboratory;[1] while their success, it was sometimes thought, hung, like the event of prayer or good resolution, less upon the quality of his 'works' than upon vouchsafed 'grace'.[2]

But the way was short and easy from the sublime pretensions of a Paracelsus to the sordid cunning of the charlatan, who covered his nakedness with this imposing vesture of philosophic theory. To the charlatan, too, one form of profitable fraud was as good as another; and the professional alchemist was probably more often than not an adept also in other magic crafts which attracted other varieties of dupe into the number of his clientele. He understood astrology, almanac-making, and the choice of lucky times and places; he had potions and images which infused love into the heart of an unresponsive mistress, or did a successful rival to death; sometimes, like Dee and Kelly, he had spirits at his beck and call, and charms for exorcising them. Of the famous pair just mentioned the chief member, Dee, died two years before the date of *The Alchemist*; both must have been well known by repute to Jonson. And another, who combined alchemy with astrology, medicine, necromancy, and other crafts, Dr. Simon Forman (1552–1611), was at the height of his reputation when Jonson wrote.

III

A social malady thus intricately involved both in the weaknesses and in the strength of the sixteenth century was not likely to escape reflection in the brilliant mirror of its art. The reflection was commonly pitiless enough. The alchemist, as represented in literature, profited little by the

[1] Cf. Kelly's poem in Ashmole's *Theatrum-Chemicum*.
[2] Ib. All you that faire philosophers would be,
The more you work the more you lose and spoil.
No my friends, it is not vaunting words
Nor mighty oaths that gain the sacred skill;
It is obtained by *grace* and not by swords.

grain of subtle speculation embedded in his farrago of nonsense; he did not get the benefit of his hint of philosophy, as the practitioners of other, less sordid, kinds of magic in some sense did of their reputed access to the spirit world and mysterious potency over human lives. In the hands of poets like Tasso and Spenser the enchanter, however diabolic his aims and origin, became an imposing and formidable power; in the hands of Shakespeare, almost simultaneously with *The Alchemist*, he became the most majestic symbol in literature of a benignly interposing providence. But the alchemist habitually figures as an impostor of the grossest kind. Ariosto, whose *Negromante* (1520) gave the cue for much later handling of the type, is as remorseless, though not so solemn, in its exposure as Jonson himself. His Master Jachelino is 'philosopher, alchemist, physician, astrologer, magician and exorciser of spirits', all in one, though hardly able to read or write. But 'folly is abundant in the world', and this impudent quack thrives on a legion of dupes. Bruno's Cencio, in the *Candelaio*, is drawn in less detail and employed on less equivocal business, but he is a knave of the same complexion. And Lyly's 'Alchemist' in *Gallathea*, though only a secondary figure, is painted in the same shade.

Jonson's Subtle, therefore, though by far the most elaborate and powerful of these dramatic alchemists, had a well-established tradition behind him. It remains to ask what he owed to these antecedents. Ariosto and Lyly may be put aside at once. The *Negromante* he is very unlikely to have known; the *Gallathea* he doubtless knew, but it was too slight to teach him anything. The case of the *Candelaio* is more plausible; it has interesting points of likeness, and a critic of weight has described it roundly as 'the source' of *The Alchemist*.[1]

This claim must nevertheless, we think, be dismissed. Internal and external evidence alike make it very doubtful whether the *Candelaio* was even known to Jonson at all. Pub-

[1] Professor C. G. Child, in the New York *Nation*, July 28, 1904.

lished at Paris in 1582, the *Candelaio* was still untranslated.[1] Jonson even in 1619, according to Drummond (*Conv.* iv), did not understand Italian, and though the Parabosco verses, which he seems to have translated, may qualify Drummond's contemptuous negation, he nowhere shows any interest in Italian literature.[2] Bruno's short visit to England in 1583-5 has been credited with important literary results, but it is likely that the impression he made was slight, evanescent, and, so far as it remained, unfavourable.[3] His fellow-countryman Florio, who met him in London, was afterwards well known to Shakespeare and Jonson. That Bruno's untranslated comedy should be lent or described or translated to Jonson by Florio is undeniably conceivable. But the filament of possible connexion is extremely slender, and the chances, even in the case of a scholar of erudition so vast and so curious as his, are altogether against it. The claim to complete originality made in the motto prefixed to the Folio reprint,

petere inde coronam,
Vnde priùs nulli velarint tempora Musæ

is, moreover, tolerably good evidence that Jonson had never heard of any earlier play, at all resembling his own, from which his own was in any degree derived.[4]

[1] A summary of the plot is given below in Appendix VI.
[2] His remarks to Drummond on Italian literature consist of a criticism on the *Pastor Fido* (translated in 1591), and round abuse of Petrarch as the author of the sonneteering movement.
[3] His glaring deficiencies in taste and tact, and his daring originality in speculation, alike barred his way to recognition in the cultured but unphilosophic mid-Elizabethan society. An allusion by an Oxford undergraduate who heard him lecture in the schools is the only known reference to him by any English contemporary. Of all his writings earlier or later, the formidable and grandiose *Spaccio della Bestia Trionfante* which he dedicated to Sidney has alone left an unmistakable trace upon later literature, and that (save, possibly, in the Mutability cantos of *The Faerie Queene*) only after half a century in the *Coelum Britannicum* of Carew (1634). He is barely and slightingly mentioned by Bacon and by Burton as a system-monger, a Copernican, and an atheist. The case is convincingly put by Professor Elton in *Modern Studies*, p. 334.
[4] This motto, with its specific claim to originality, was substituted in the Folio for the motto of the Quarto, a conventional appeal to an

A direct connexion with *The Alchemist* could be established only by internal evidence of a very unequivocal kind. But this is hardly forthcoming. Any dramatic exposure of alchemy was bound to satirize its dupes; and with Jonson it was equally inevitable that the dupes should be set off, and the rogues exposed, by a more knowing spirit. The resemblances between the *Candelaio* and *The Alchemist* hardly go beyond this common ground, and Jonson's way of handling these features is altogether his own, and in close keeping with his procedure elsewhere. Subtle, Face, and Dol are an improved version of the earlier partnership of Volpone and Mosca; they occupy the centre of the picture and are the main instruments of the plot; Scaramure, Cencio, Sanguino, and Lucia form no such league, and are only incidentally and in part accomplices. Sanguino and Face resemble one another[1] only as one arch-trickster resembles another; Lucia has only her voice in common with Dol. To say that Scaramure the magician and Cencio the alchemist are 'unified' in Subtle is gratuitous; they were already 'unified' in versatile practitioners, like Forman, whom Jonson had before his eyes; moreover Subtle is not, in relation to the love affairs of his clients, a magician, like Scaramure or Forman, at all, but a brothel-keeper. Nor does the 'unification' of the two imbeciles Bonifacio and

audience 'fit tho' few'. The change was probably occasioned by the appearance, in the interim, of N. Tomkis's *Albumazar*, first acted before James I at Trinity College, Cambridge, March 9, 1614. The only point of contact between the plays is that there is an astrologer in both. But Dryden in a prologue for the revival of *Albumazar* at the Duke of York's theatre in Lincoln's Inn Fields in February, 1668, chose somewhat unscrupulously to declare that 'Subtle was got by our Albumazar'.

[1] The butler's personation of 'Captain Face' no doubt recalls Sanguino's disguise as 'Captain Palma'. But the resemblance is only external. Palma is the dignified head of the constabulary and Sanguino uses his authority to arrest quasi-disturbers of the peace; 'Captain Face' is a purely Bohemian potentate,

the most autentique dealer
I' these commodities. The *Superintendant*
To all the queinter traffiquers, in towne,

and the reference to him at once convinces Surly that he is among knaves (II. iii. 302-4).

Bartholomeo carry us far towards the magnificent Sir Epicure Mammon. There were Bartholomeos and Bonifacios enough in Jonson's England; and the frugal 'candlemaker', who grudges the money for a single mistress and tries to compel her love by an 'image', cannot have furnished even an ingredient towards the composition of this knight, whose imagination is aflame with visions of the prodigal opulence of Roman vice and the teeming seraglio of Solomon. The sceptical Surly no doubt bears some resemblance to Gian Bernardo; he even ridiculed alchemy, at one point, in very similar terms; but the story of the gold hidden in the coals, which they both retail, was a venerable weapon of the lay critic, and accessible to Jonson in no more recondite source than the *Canon's Yeoman's Tale*. The clue to Surly is rather to be found in Bonario, the inconvenient honest man of *Volpone*. Jonson's sceptic is also a man of honour, in his less romantic key, who safeguards the imperilled virtue of Dame Pliant, as Bonario delivers the hapless Celia, and has no thought of making terms with the confederates. Whereas Bruno's sceptic is himself a confederate, takes part in the discomfiture of the chief dupe, and makes love against her will to the dupe's wife when she is left in his charge. Bernardo is an astute person who knows how to turn both the fooleries and knaveries of other people to his own account; Surly is more honest than penetrating, is silenced in argument by Subtle, and fobbed of his fiancée by Face. The distinction is not ill pointed by the contrasted comments of the alchemists in the two plays after the first keen encounter of their wits. 'Truly,' says Cencio to himself, 'if Bartholomeo had this man's brains, I should cast my nets vainly on this ground'.[1] 'O *Monsieur Caution*, that will not be gull'd' is the disdainful verdict of Subtle.[2] The resemblances between *The Alchemist* and *Candelaio* thus reduce themselves to features which can be explained from Jonson's own well-defined procedure in satiric comedy. The characters, whether of

[1] *Candelaio*, I. ii. (ed. Lagarde, p. 30).   [2] *Alchem.* II. iv. 15.

knaves, dupes, or sceptic, are almost as diverse as possible within the limits of these generic attributes ; the intrigue is altogether different. Bruno's comedy cannot be regarded as Jonson's ' source ', even in the most extended sense of this much-abused term ; that it even gave him the ' suggestion ', in Professor Schelling's more guarded phrase, is a conjecture which naturally cannot be disproved, but which we do not require. In the early years of the seventeenth century, in the days of the ' Rosy Cross ', of Dr. Forman, when the career of Dee and Kelly was still recent, the idea of applying the method of *Volpone* to the exposure of this kindred modern scourge was not very remote. It certainly lay nearer than the idea of *Volpone* itself.

IV

There is no doubt, on the other hand, that Jonson took over from Plautus the device of making his rogues carry on their practices in another person's house without the knowledge of the owner, whose unexpected return provides an effective and legitimate *deus ex machina* at the close. The hero, indeed, of the *Mostellaria* is the son of the owner, and otherwise bears no resemblance to Subtle ; but the cunning slave Tranio is evidently remembered in the position and later fortunes of the ' butler ' Face. Like Face he confronts his master, induces him by a terrifying story not to enter the house, and is finally exposed, but escapes punishment.

There are traces too, as might be expected, of Erasmus's dialogue *De Alcumista*, doubtless familiar to Jonson from his schooldays. Erasmus deals with the elementary situation of a gold-maker's relations with a well-meaning patron, his successive deceits and ruses, detection in debauchery, and final pardon. There can be no parallel between this simple novelette of alchemy, and the vast, complex, but powerfully integrated drama of Jonson. But there are several interesting points of contact.[1]

[1] These are indicated in the following summary of the dialogue.

V

But none of these, or some other slighter obligations, affect the thoroughly modern and Jacobean character of the play. In sheer realism of subject *The Alchemist* thus stands apart from all Jonson's previous comedies. Plautine types no longer shimmer through the Elizabethan trappings; Face is not, like Brainworm, a local and modern version of the astute slave, nor Mammon, or Subtle, of the covetous *senex*. Nay, Jonson has emphasized with a severity even beyond his wont the realist aspect of his theme. *The Alchemist* comes nearer than even *The Silent Woman* to a complete observance of the so-called unities of time and place; from first to last the scene changes only from the room in a house to the adjacent street, and vice versa; and the supposed duration of the action hardly exceeds that of the performance. Nay, as we saw, Jonson deliberately turned to account, for the purposes of the stage, the very calamity which had closed it. The cautious Lovewits of actual London had scarcely ventured back to town when

---

Balbinus, a grave and discreet person in the ordinary affairs of life (II. iii. 280, 281), is won over by a knave who agrees to work at his expense, dividing the profits equally, though he wished them all to go to his patron (II. ii. 105, IV. i. 122–4). Money paid for instruments is spent in debauchery, but a furnace is built. Failure follows; it is due to the fuel being of oak, instead of beech or hazel (II. ii. 22–3). A second failure is caused by defects in the glass vessels. A third attempt is likely to be more prosperous if an offering of gold is made to our Lady of Walsingham; the alchemist is dispatched with it (IV. v. 92–6). Still there is failure. He cannot make it out, but, following a cue given by Balbinus' question, he remembers with contrition that he has once or twice forgotten to say the Ave Maria. Presently he comes to Balbinus in a fright and says the courtiers have detected the work. Balbinus is scared, for the offence is capital. It is not death the impostor fears, but perpetual imprisonment in some tower, where he will have to make gold all his life for his captors (IV. vii. 79–82, i. 152–4). Money is given him to bribe the courtiers. After twelve months of this, the alchemist is detected in an intrigue with a courtier's wife and has a narrow escape. Balbinus takes him to task, telling him 'Sin hinders the work; only the pure can handle it' (II. ii. 97–9 and *passim*). The man confesses, and Balbinus pardons him, giving him travelling expenses to avoid an exposure (V. v. 68–71). The whole sketch is an interesting comment on Jonson.

the audience of the Globe was laughing at the confusion caused by the return of their stage counterpart.

The same insistent realism, with one significant exception, marks the treatment throughout. The *Volpone* type obviously reappears in its structure, but adapted to the demands of a livelier actuality, and of a more genial conception of comic orthodoxy. Volpone yields nothing in knavery to Subtle, but Subtle is despoiled of the explicit poetry which breaks in lurid flashes from the Fox; he comes before us, not chanting an exultant morning hymn to his shrined treasure, 'the world's soul and mine', but exchanging volleys of uncompromising Billingsgate with his partner in iniquity.[1] And this sordid impostor of the north is at bottom far more intelligible than the Venetian patrician. Volpone, so securely incorporated, by his rank and status, with the very body of the Venetian polity, is yet felt to be the alien he is; and Jonson, beyond dubbing with a Venetian title and quality the literary plant he had stuck in the Venetian earth, was at no very great pains to produce the illusion of natural growth. Subtle is bound by no such ties of ostensible community to the society he preys upon, and his operations are far more deeply ingrained with sham; but we are made, none the less, to see that this creature had a natural history, that he is a growth of the soil,—a fungus-growth rooted in the greed and hunger of London. In words of Carlylean flavour and pungency Jonson tells us what his naked root was like:

> At *pie-corner*,
> ·Taking your meale of steeme in, from cookes stalls,
> Where, like the father of hunger, you did walke
> Piteously costiue, with your pinch'd-horne-nose,
> And your complexion, of the *romane* wash,
> Stuck full of black, and melancholique wormes.

And Subtle remains to the end sordid in his making and

---

[1] The altercation which so effectively opens *The Alchemist* has a parallel, as Gifford pointed out, in the quarrel of the slaves Grumio and Tranio at the beginning of the *Mostellaria*; the Spanish scene between Surly, Subtle, and Face, in the 'Carthaginian' scene of *Poenulus*, where Milphio 'interprets' the Punic conversation of Hanno and Agorastocles.

spending of money. His present fortune depends on a lucky chance, and he plays his part with the seriousness of one who was hungry yesterday and knows that he may be hungry to-morrow. He has the cunning of the opulent magnifico without his vein of fiendish romance. Volpone's freaks of insolent bravado here become the routine of a cheating trade. He plays the mountebank in a fit of exuberant caprice, Subtle in the sober way of business. The alchemist has indeed his philosophy too, and can expound it in lofty phrases and support it by arguments which silence the sceptic Surly and give pause even to our easy modern scorn for alchemy. Jonson has not been content, like Bruno, to put merely the hocus-pocus verbiage which imposed upon the mob into the mouth of the impostor he sought to confront. Less out of generosity than out of the thoroughgoing candour of the scholar, he allows him the benefit of the best answer which the wisdom of alchemistic speculation could provide. A practitioner whose methods with the public were subjected to so annihilating an exposure might be allowed to score an intellectual victory over a layman with little risk. But Subtle's philosophy, his phrases, and his arguments are not, in any intimate sense, his own; they are not, like Volpone's, tinged with the humours of an individual mind and temper. They are merely the common property of his bogus order, stock weapons which he handles according to the rules of a conventional sword-craft,—the trade practices of the alchemist quack. Even his sensuality is of a lower deep. Volpone makes base love to a noble woman, Mammon to a base woman whom he thinks noble: Subtle makes base love to Dol Common or Dame Pliant as occasion serves or the 'longest cut at night' decides, and if another man has been before him, it is 'only one man more'.

Face is much more nearly related to Mosca than Subtle to Volpone. But he is far from being a replica. The fabric of make-believe which he sustains is several degrees more complicated and various. Mosca is a real parasite dependent upon a real patron; Face plays alchemist's drudge, as he plays the 'Captain', the joint business in which, at least, he is the more masterful partner and has the larger stake. The energetic opening scene, where the two rogues vie in tearing away the last ragged vesture of each other's self-respect, makes us vividly aware of the natural history of Face no less than of Subtle; Mosca is the parasite of the books and of Roman satire; but Jeremy, the enterprising butler, accomplished in all the varieties of backstair pilfering, who compounds with a conjurer for the use of his master's empty house on the terms of equal profits and a bonus in the shape of 'quarreling dimensions' and 'rules to cheat at horse-race, cock-pit, cards', must have been instantly accepted as a London rascal true to type.

If Face is a Mosca of more shifts and better luck, the third member of the 'indenture tripartite' has no equivalent in the earlier play. The female rogue, paramour and partner of the chief contriver of the harms, was, however, a figure not unknown to Jonson; and in the same qualified sense in which Sejanus may be called a prototype of Face, Livia, his confederate in the death of Drusus, may be called a prototype of Dol. But Livia plays only a passing part, while Dol is an indispensable member of the 'house',—indispensable to the precious pair whose game she plays and whose dangerous feuds she quells, indispensable to the intrigue which she complicates and enriches, indispensable above all to the satire, to the flavour of which her presence adds an ironical pungency not to be otherwise obtained. Even the business of catering for the lust of clients illustrates less drastically the pretension of the alchemist to 'holy living' than do the sordid lotteries and altercations of Subtle and Face for the possession of their common mistress. As a character Dol falls short of being a masterpiece, but she stands in the front rank of Jonson's women, and may be counted one of the best 'Dol Commons' in our literature. Falstaff's mistress, whom Jonson perhaps had in mind, is of course a mere sketch.

VI

The dupes of *The Alchemist* show an even greater versatility and fecundity of invention than the rogues. In comparison Corvino, Corbaccio, and Voltore appear of a somewhat dull uniformity; servants of evil clothed in the livery, slightly diversified, of the same vice. But Dapper and Drugger, Ananias and Wholesome, Sir Epicure and Dame Pliant and the Angry Boy, do not even want altogether the same things, and so far as they do, they resemble one another only as the motley crowd of customers who frequent the same shop. The difference arises in part from the situation. Only a more or less limited circle of private friends or privileged strangers could speculate with much likelihood on the testamentary favours of a Volpone; whereas Subtle kept open shop, like any other itinerant quack, for all comers, and high and low flocked in. But there was also a difference of temper and method. Jonson was now drawing from the life, from the London he knew by heart, not from the fabricated Petronian-Venice of a scholar's indignant dreams. The *saeva indignatio* which ignores everything in its victims but the vice of which it makes them incarnate embodiments, has not altogether subsided; but it is qualified by livelier observation and a more flexible comic spirit. The clients of Volpone are even more knave than gull, those of Subtle are more gull than knave. Poor Dapper with his gingerbread gag and his luckless quest of the 'Fairy Queen', suffers worse things than he deserves —a draggled knight of romance decoyed upon the 'famous Voyage'. In the admirable character of Drugger, on the other hand, Jonson has exemplified the side of alchemy which commended it to the plain, prosaic philistine who wanted to insure his business, or to steal a march upon trade-rivals by more 'scientific' methods than theirs. And the scholar's ridicule for pseudo-science is here compounded with the ridicule of a man of shrewd sense for the dabblers in science who try to make learning do the work of mother-wit, and book knowledge take the place of practice. To this extent Jonson went along with Shakespeare's scorn of academies in *Love's Labour's Lost*. Master Stephen, possessed of a hawk and wanting 'nothing but a book to keep it by', suffers this second kind of ridicule only; Drugger, proposing to plan his shop 'by necromancy', and Kastril, eager to qualify for the company of the other Angry Boys by learning how to take the altitude of a quarrel (III. iv), suffer both. They are less innocently amusing creatures than Stephen ; but the infusion of gull in their composition, if slighter, is intrinsically of a deeper dye. They are pedants of a bogus craft.

The Puritan dupes, Ananias and Wholesome, on the other hand, mark a new departure. Jonson, as a professed Catholic during the previous ten or eleven years, can never have felt any attraction to the 'saints' of the Reformation ; but this was his first undisguised exposure of Puritan foibles on the pillory of the stage. In this sense *The Alchemist* foreshadowed *Bartholomew Fair*. His attitude to Puritanism was indeed not unlike his attitude to alchemy. Both were, for him, social pests, offensive by their hypocritical pretensions and their masquerade of hollow and questionable learning. He treats the two Puritans indeed with a palpably deeper contempt than any of the other dupes, or even than the Alchemist himself. The debates with Subtle are insidiously contrived to exhibit the similarity of their aims and his. The philosophers' stone is a more effective and certain way of getting that advantage which the Puritan sought through the cumbrous machinery of 'long-winded exercises' and inconvenient dress ; and Subtle's praise of it thus naturally takes the form of an ironical recital of the Puritan practices with which the stone will enable them to dispense. When Ananias introduces himself as 'a faithfull Brother' (II. v. 7), and Subtle affects to understand by this a devotee of alchemy, the two professions at once assume the air of parallel fraternities. And Jonson's erudite humour is thoroughly in its element

The Alchemist

when he is pitting the two professional jargons against each other, as in the second scene of Act III. From this motley throng the figure of Sir Epicure Mammon stands apart and aloof. He belongs not merely, and not so much, to a different social rank as to a different order of imagination. The realism of Jonson's method, elsewhere in this play so pervading and to all appearance so sedulously preserved, here gives way to a personage who belongs to the London of Jonson and James I by about as good a right as Marlowe's Faustus to Wittenberg. The sinister romance of Volpone, the hint of poetry in his worship of gold, the god, is resumed and heightened in Sir Epicure's magnificent dreams. Jonson is here for once Marlowesque, but in a kind unborrowed and his own. Mammon is a Faustus of the senses, captivated by the dreams of exploring the utmost possibilities of recondite and exquisite sensation, as Faustus by the dream of boundless knowledge and power. The sordid Mephistophiles of the laboratory never fulfils his bond, but Mammon has already taken possession of his kingdom, and feasts full at the orgies his imagination provides. Volpone's imagination is an instrument of his cunning and cruel brain, employed to discover new ways of exploiting and deluding others; Mammon's only forges dazzling illusions for himself. Both are 'magnificent in sin'; even their lust is aristocratic and demands a noble prey; but while Volpone almost secures the noblest and chastest lady in Venice, Mammon hails a harlot as a princess, and discovers in the common mistress of Subtle and Face not only the Austrian lip and the Medicean forehead, but an air

> That sparkles a diuinitie, beyond
> An earthly beautie!

VII

Little need be said of the three characters who in various degrees and ways contribute to bring about the denouement, and who, though all at one point or other victims of the imposture, yet stand apart from the main body of the Alchemist's dupes. Dame Pliant is in every sense the least important. In his desire to make her character expressive of her name, Jonson has really made her of 'no character at all'. Even Pope, however, would not have regarded her as like 'most women'; she is little more than a passive and serviceable abstraction—a ball whose various movements serve to exhibit the quality of the players and mark the progress of the game—projected by the Angry Boy, saved by Surly, struggled for by Surly and Face, and finally secured by Lovewit. It is in this last stage of her fortunes that she at length counts decisively in the plot, when her person and her money serve to buy off the Nemesis which threatens the chief rogue, and bring about one of those amazing revulsions with which Jonson was somewhat too fond of baffling his hearers' expectations. Her part in the plot somewhat resembles that of Celia; but Jonson has this time taken care that, as a character in a comedy, she shall not excite any tragic pity. Unfortunately, in denuding her of this improper kind of interest, he has made her too unsubstantial to be even matter for mirth.

Surly, too, is drawn with the curious air of grudging ill will which so often marks Jonson's presentment of the well-meaning in his later work, as if in reaction from the too immaculate virtue and too unqualified triumphs of the earlier Crites, Asper, or Horace. If his function in the plot connects him with Asper, his name associates him with Morose, and the one man who sees through and exposes the imposture is as effectually denuded of heroic quality as Dame Pliant is of pathos. He is beaten in argument by Subtle; more than all, when on the verge of triumphantly establishing his case, carrying out his just vengeance, and reaping his modest reward, he is checkmated by Lovewit's *volte-face*, and involved in the general discomfiture of the rogues and dupes. Surly corresponds to Bonario in *Volpone*, as Dame Pliant to Celia. No change better illustrates the more purely comic ideal consistently pursued by Jonson in the present play. Bonario's rescue of Celia is a wooden imitation of the chivalry and the pathos of romance: the rescue of Pliant by Surly is denuded of romance to the last shred:

> You are,
> They say, a widdow, rich; and I am a batcheler,
> Worth nought: Your fortunes may make me a man,
> As mine ha' preseru'd you a woman. Thinke vpon it,
> And whether, I have deseru'd you, or no. *Pli.* I will, sir.[1]

Surly at this point appears, like Bonario, to have the game in his hands. Subtle, like Volpone, is for the moment dumbfounded, but Face, like Mosca, promptly recovers the lost ground, and enlists the whole band of dupes against the one shrewd man.

Their triumph is instantly, but as it proved delusively, frustrated by the appearance of Lovewit, and Surly is set free to open the eyes of the dupes and bring them, eager for revenge, to besiege the closed doors of the den. Righteous Nemesis at the hands of an indignant mob allied with offended justice appears to impend, and an issue too sanguinary for comedy to be inevitable. It is Lovewit, once more, who at a stroke reverses the situation. Jonson was bent upon avoiding the lofty retributive air by which in *Volpone* he had established his abhorrence of vice at some cost to the 'rigour of the comic law'; and he has contrived the denouement with great skill for this end. Lovewit is as far as possible from resembling the ideal vindicator of virtue. He comes with an authoritative air; but the *deus ex machina* proceeds to strike a bargain with the principal culprit for the lion's share of the spoils. He effects a revolution in the plot in virtue merely of a temper too easy and humorous seriously to resent wrongs even when they concern himself, and ready for a jest to overlook a multitude of sins. 'I loue a teeming wit, as I loue my nourish-

[1] IV. vi. 11-15.

ment', he declares, in the spirit of the merry Justice who similarly presides over the issues of *Every Man in his Humour*; and indeed his only concern, when he hears of the mysterious doings in his house, is as to the 'nature' of the 'device' which his witty knave may have contrived. Once more, as in his earliest comedy, Jonson places the direction of the catastrophe in the hands of a lover of jest, 'a jovy boy', 'not hide-bound', whose easy geniality proves a ready solvent for menacing tragic harms. And once more the witty trickster comes off unscathed, while the fools and dupes suffer. Certainly the solution is here less easy to accept. *Every Man in his Humour* is concerned with fatuities and misunderstandings, not with crimes; even Brainworm's mischief is harmless and honest. The triumph of Face stands on a different footing. If the comic dramatist were bound to punish all his characters in proportion to their demerits, it would be indefensible. But even when he deals with crimes, his proper method is not that of the criminal judge. His weapon, even there, is ridicule, not bloodshed. And whether the object of ridicule be a criminal or a fool, the ridicule may easily depend upon the impunity of other and far worse offenders. George Dandin would obviously not be the telling example he is of the folly of marrying above one's rank, if his wife and her lover remained less absolutely master of the situation. And the withering humiliation of Subtle, as he and Dol escape, baffled and penniless, through the back window of their laboratory, is made more poignant by the parting sarcasms of the triumphant Face :

                  All I can doe
Is to helpe you ouer the wall, o' the back-side;
Or lend you a sheet, to saue your veluet gowne,
   DOL.
.   .   .   .   SVBTLE,
Let's know where you set vp next; I'll send you
A customer, now and then, for old acquaintance:
What new course ha' you?

It is Subtle, not Face, the Alchemist, not his butler-confederate, who is the subject of the comedy, and the mark of its satire; and when the frauds and delusions of alchemy are finally paraded with ironical mockery by the incomparable rascal who had taken a chief part in them, we are entitled to say, with Face himself, that ' 'twas decorum'; it is in keeping with the ends of comedy. It was the union in this play to a hardly paralleled degree, of comic 'decorum' with freedom of movement and richness of invention, which won the famous praise of Coleridge, when he classed it with *Oedipus Tyrannus* and *Tom Jones*, as examples of the ' three best plots in literature '.

APPENDIX VI

BRUNO'S 'CANDELAIO'

The *Candelaio*, written at Paris in 1582, is an Italian comedy of humours directed against three characteristic follies of the time. Bonifacio, an infatuated elderly profligate, finding 'nature' insufficient to procure the favours of the courtesan Vittoria, calls in the aid of 'art', and is duly instructed by the magician Sacramure how to compel her love by means of a waxen image. Bartholomeo, the dupe of alchemy, serves two equally uncompliant mistresses, Argentaria and Aurelia, under the direction of a second impostor, Cencio. Mamphurio, finally, is a pedant, with more than the prolixity of Holofernes and none of his wit. The plot by which all three are humiliated is the work partly of Vittoria, in league with Bonifacio's young, beautiful, and justly vindictive wife Karubina, partly of the shrewd painter, Giovanni Bernardo, as champion of sceptical common sense and also, not without reward, of Karubina; but chiefly of the irresponsible mischief-maker Sanguino. Bonifacio is induced to visit Vittoria disguised in Bernardo's hood and beard; but encounters, instead, his own wife in Vittoria's dress; escaping from her vengeance, he is first confronted by the painter whom he has impersonated, and then delivered over into the custody of the pretended Captain, to be released only after abject apology to his wife, by the prearranged intervention of Scaramure, whose 'explanation' of the failure of his image the poor dupe willingly accepts. Bartholomeo, a degree less fatuous, discovers his betrayal by the alchemist, and resents it with an energy which leads, likewise, to his mock arrest of Sanguino. Then Mamphurio, variously fleeced and beaten, finds himself at last in the same quarters; unlike the others, however, he has learnt nothing, and invites the applause of the public, in the Epilogue, with all his sins of pedantry full-blown as ever.

This comedy, though written with Bruno's usual spirited exuberance and constructed with considerable skill, is not a work of first-rate importance. The characters and the situations are in general of the type current in the Italian comedy of the century from Ariosto onwards; and the handling and style show neither originality nor mastery proportioned to the prodigious fanfaronnade—two dedications, detailed argument, 'antiprologo', 'proprologo', 'Bidello',—with which the 'Achademico di nulla Achademia' ushered it in. Bruno had not the temper of the artist; his vein flowed with an impetuous vehemence hardly compatible with precision and delicacy of outline. Of the loftier elements of his character little enough filtered unmistakably through into the boisterous, hard, and sometimes cruel humour of the *Candelaio*. But it is not necessary to know the other writings of this Rabelaisian prophet of the Renascence to discover that the *Candelaio* was a weapon, and not the meanest, in the lifelong battle which was to end, for him, in 1600, at the stake in Rome.[1] His 'Candlemaker', as he hints in the second dedication, was to illuminate some dark places in the earth; to expose the purveyors of sham knowledge who encumbered the way of philosophy. Bruno's alchemist and magician are drawn with an art not palpably more serious though certainly less accomplished than Ariosto's; but where Ariosto found a good comic subject, Bruno sought an object of satire under comic forms.

[1] One scene in the *Candelaio* (v. 22 f.) is obviously modelled on the famous chapter of Rabelais, the marriage-dialogue of Pantagruel and Panurge.

INTRODUCTION TO

'CATILINE HIS CONSPIRACY'

CATILINE HIS CONSPIRACY

I

Catiline his Conspiracy, a tragedy, was acted by the King's men in 1611. The first two acts went well, the third was tolerated, but the long oration of Cicero in the fourth provoked the impatience of the pit, and the play was damned. Jonson, conscious of the high literary merit of the piece and imperfectly alive as usual to the mere playgoer's point of view, published a quarto edition of it in the course of the same year, with a preface of concentrated scorn addressed 'To the Ordinary Reader', followed by a laconic appeal 'to the Reader extraordinary'. That appeal was enforced, in yet more emphatic terms, in the Folio dedication to William Earl of Pembroke, the Lord Chamberlain: 'Posteritie may pay your benefit the honor, & thanks: when it shall know, that you dare, in these Iig-giuen times, to countenance a legitimate Poeme. I must call it so, against all noise of opinion: from whose crude, and ayrie reports, I appeale, to that great and singular faculty of iudgement in your Lordship, able to vindicate truth from error.' *Catiline* was the latest of the plays to be included in the Folio edition of 1616. The subsequent history of the piece tended, on the whole, to justify Jonson's estimate. After the Restoration, in particular, it enjoyed a decided popularity. When Langbaine wrote, at the end of the century, it was 'still in vogue' and 'always presented with success'.

The subject, unlike that of *Sejanus*, was not new to the English stage. The conspiracy of Catiline enjoyed a kind of precedence, only rivalled by that of Brutus, among the historic conspiracies of the ancient world. The incomparable eminence of its principal victim would in any case have graven the latter subject deep in the memory of after times. But to the Renascence scholar Cicero, the principal frustrator of Catiline's plot, was a hardly less illustrious figure than Caesar; and the classical orations published by him as a monument of his fortunate consulship made the name of Catiline henceforth inseparable from his own. A play on *Catiline's Conspiracie* was written by Stephen Gosson in his youth, and exempted by him, in 1579, from his general censure upon the plays of his time.[1] Two of Jonson's own contemporaries and fellow-workers, Wilson and Chettle, produced a *Catiline* in the year of *Every Man in his Humour*. Both these are lost, but it is highly unlikely that Jonson owed anything whatever to either. His only source was the ancient authorities, and its only precedent was his own *Sejanus*.

II

Like *Sejanus*, *Catiline* was designed to be a 'Tragedy'. How far removed Jonson's ideal of Tragedy was from any ancient example, *Sejanus* shows, and *Catiline* in almost every respect not less. Once more, a stage crowded with characters (there are over thirty persons not counting supernumeraries), a plot of crowded incident and intricate movement, and scenes in which tragic dignity and pathos are replaced by satire or genre painting, show how tenaciously the Elizabethan in him resisted, in these matters, all the demands of classical 'simplicity'. Horace's precepts and Seneca's example alike once more go by the board.

In two respects, however, Jonson has reverted, in *Catiline*, to a classical or Senecan technique: the Chorus and the Prologue. The Chorus between the Acts was the most striking distinction between Seneca and the native tragedy of the Elizabethans. It obviously impressed the early classicizers, and was imitated, awkwardly enough, by the authors of *Gorboduc*. Later classicizers, as Daniel in his *Cleopatra* and *Philotas*, and Alexander, introduced the Chorus as an indispensable apanage of orthodox tragedy, but showed no comprehension whatever of its dramatic value.

[1] *The School of Abuse,* 1579, p. 23.

In the popular drama it never struck root, and the occasional introduction of a 'Chorus' illustrates only the Elizabethan ingenuity in adapting alien material to the radically different conditions of their own stage. By far the most brilliant and elaborate example of this, Shakespeare's *Henry V*, provoked, as we know, a captious reproof from Jonson. Shakespeare's 'Chorus', identified with the Prologue, is not an actor, but the author in disguise, and speaks with his knowledge and authority. And Jonson must have seen further double evidence of 'want of art' in a playwright who first required his audience to 'cross the seas' between act and act, and then misused the classical Chorus to 'waft them' over. But the notion that the business of a Chorus was to interpret or give needed information was well established in the popular mind when Jonson wrote. 'You are as good as a chorus, my lord,' was Ophelia's well-known comment on Hamlet's far from Senecan remarks at the Play.

Jonson himself, when once more calling into use this antique device, ignored this heresy as a matter of course. His four choric odes, though certainly more pedestrian than Shakespeare's winged speeches, were meant to be lyrics, possibly to be sung.[1] And the 'Chorus' is not the author in disguise, fond as Jonson was of providing a mouthpiece for his own views, but (as Horace demands) an actor, representing a member of the loyal and right-minded public of Rome, genuinely concerned for the welfare of the city and ready to pray to the gods on its behalf, but without any special information or intelligence, and thus a prey, like the multitude, to fluctuating hopes and fears. So in the alarmed and perplexed outburst at the close of Act III, on the first disclosure of the conspiracy:

>   What is it, heauens, you prepare
>   With so much swiftnesse?

and of Act IV when the issue is still uncertain.

---

[1] In the Quarto *Sejanus* the acts are followed by the words 'Mu. Chorus', which probably indicates that Jonson originally meant to have music between the acts.

For the rest this Jonsonian Chorus utters not ill the probable mind of the Roman *boni* about the spread of luxury (Act I), and the need of a strong and wise rule (Act II). Yet Shakespeare has contrived to achieve the purpose of the classical chorus, to support the good cause, or what he and all his audience held to be such; and may thus claim, as so often, to be, with all his incidental heresy, more truly classical than Jonson. For his Choruses are not merely sources of authoritative information, but the voice of England, the 'little body with a mighty heart', as the choruses of the *Persae* were the voice of Greece.

Besides the Senecan Chorus, Jonson equipped *Catiline* with a Senecan Prologue. In introducing Sylla's ghost as an infernal patron and authorizer of the crimes of Catiline, Jonson clearly imitated the *Thyestes* of Seneca, where the spirit of Tantalus performs a like function. It was an unfortunate departure from the method of his earlier tragedy. Sejanus's criminal career was not felt to need such sanction or incentive. Jonson was borrowing a device which had meaning and truth only where the belief in transmitted fate prevailed. In Jacobean England it was an anachronism. But Jonson refused to learn from the profounder psychology of Shakespeare, and therefore failed to profit by his more psychological technique. Whatever supernatural agency may have to do with the action of *Hamlet* or *Macbeth*, its mode of operation is entirely natural, the simple 'soliciting' of one person in the drama by another.

III

Apart from these not wholly fortunate indulgences of his Senecan classicism, *Catiline* accords in method very closely with its predecessor. As in *Sejanus*, Jonson sought to present an historical event with as much fidelity, subject to the conditions of tragic drama, as the extant materials allowed. The result is, once more, by no means justly described as a 'mosaic' of translated bits. Only a small part of the material was presented in even approximately dramatic form. The speech of Catiline to the conspirators, and those of Caesar and Cato in the final debate in the Senate, given by Sallust, the four speeches of Cicero, and some incidental scraps of dialogue, this was nearly all that Jonson found ready to hand. Apart from the speech of Cicero in the fourth act (ll. 64 fol.), which no doubt reproduces with too much indulgence the copiousness of the original (*In Catilinam I*), he cannot be said to have abused his command of the classical sources, or his gift of turning them into strong and racy, if not often choicely felicitous, vernacular. But the 'ordinary' playgoer justly declined to accept these merits as compensation for dramatic defects. For the rest, Jonson is never servilely dependent upon his source even when actually paraphrasing a speech. He curtails the ample rhetoric of Cicero's published speech, much of it probably introduced in the process of revision. The more pregnant phrases, on the contrary, he interprets and expands.[1] A telling detail here and there (like the breastplate which

'peeres aboue his gowne
To tell the people, in what danger he was)[2]

belongs to a different occasion. The poet in him steps without effort into the place of the translator; far from flagging under the sudden stress, his wit and invention, even his command of phrase and of rhythm, seem to awaken to new vigour. Catiline points, for instance, to the engrossing of the powers of the commonwealth in the hands of a few; Jonson translates this plain prose affirmation into a grandiose figure, and the 'few' become

The giants of the state, that doe, by turnes,
Enioy her, and defile her.[3]

---

[1] It is to be remembered that Sallust, like his master Thucydides, professes to reproduce only the substance of the speeches he reports: 'tum ... huiusmodi verba locutus est' is his standing formula.
[2] IV. 91, 92.
[3] I. 359, 360.

Catiline's concise and general summary of the riotous luxury of these 'few', in the later part of his speech, touched a yet more kindred vein in Jonson, and he overflows in picturesque detail in the manner of Sir Epicure Mammon. Thus the compact substance of a single sentence: 'Cum tabulas signa toreumata emunt, nova diruunt, alia aedificant, postremo omnibus modis pecuniam trahunt vexant, tamen summa lubidine divitias suas vincere nequeunt,'[1] is unfolded in twenty verses, themselves, it is true, charged with other classical material, but full of colour and animation:

They buy rare *Atticke* statues, *Tyrian* hangings,
Ephesian pictures, and *Corinthian* plate,
Attalicke garments, and now, new-found gemmes,
Since POMPEY went for *Asia*, which they purchase
At price of *prouinces!* . . .
Their ancient habitations they neglect,
And set vp new; then, if the eccho like not
In such a roome, they pluck downe those, build newer,
Alter them too . . .[2]

Then Catiline contrasts with this profusion his own and his comrades' situation, in terms of the same pregnant brevity: 'At nobis est domi inopia, foris aes alienum . . .' How Elizabethan is Jonson's way of making the transition:

We, all this while, like calme benum'd Spectators,
Sit, till our seates do cracke; and doe not heare
The thundring ruins: whilst, at home, our wants,
Abroad, our debts, doe vrge us . . .[3]

This first speech, based in general upon Sallust, does not completely satisfy Catiline's followers; and their tentative queries and requests for specific details provoke him to an outburst which is in substance wholly Jonson's own, while its expression and manner, where they are not purely Elizabethan, are of Seneca, not of Sallust:

How, friends!
Thinke you, that I would bid you, grasp the winde?
Or call you to th' embracing of a cloud? .

[1] Sallust, *Catiline*, c. 20. [2] I. 405-16. [3] Ibid. 425-8.

> Put your knowne valures on so deare a businesse,
> And haue no other second then the danger,
> No other gyrlond then the losse? Become
> Your owne assurances.[1]

The speeches of Caesar and Cato (V. 442-92, 513-61) are without these exuberances. They are composed throughout in the unadorned manner historically characteristic of the speakers. Caesar's speech is much shorter than in Sallust, being shorn of the historical allusions and legal technicalities, frequently gaining much in nervous simplicity thereby. Jonson has evidently aimed at a manner approaching the elegant concision of Caesar's own writings; and it may perhaps be allowed that his version of Caesar's speech is more Caesarian in style than Sallust's. In Cato's speech Jonson has yet more obviously intended to suggest the traditional blunt and homely vigour of the original; while Sallust, as elsewhere, hardly modulates the uniform tenor of his quasi-Thucydidean style. Compare the opening sentences. The Sallustian Cato states his opinion, decidedly indeed, but yet with some ceremonious elaboration: 'Longe alia mihi mens est, patres conscripti, cum res atque pericula nostra considero et cum sententias nonnullorum ipse mecum reputo. Illi mihi disseruisse videntur de poena eorum, qui patriae parentibus, aris atque focis suis bellum paravere; res autem monet cavere ab illis magis quam quid in illos statuamus consultare.' Jonson's Cato opens his case in a more Catonian vein than this. Cicero has requested him to speak his 'sentence'.

> CAT.   This it is.
> You here dispute, on kinds of punishment,
> And stand consulting, what you should decree
> 'Gainst those, of whom, you rather should beware.

Sallust's Cato ends by pointing to the urgency of the crisis, which left no room for correcting an erroneous decision, if once taken, and making a formal motion for the death of the convicted persons: 'Whereas by the evil counsel of

[1] Ibid. 450-6.

certain criminal citizens the State has been brought into supreme danger, and they by the evidence of T. Volturcius and the legates of the Allobroges have been convicted and have confessed, ... let them, as having confessed and as having been convicted of a capital charge, be punished as the custom of our forefathers prescribes.' This is impressive; but it might have closed the speech of any other orator who was of the same mind. Jonson's Cato sums up in these strong and pithy lines:

If there had beene but time, and place, for you,
To haue repair'd this fault, you should haue made it;
It should haue beene your punishment, to' haue felt
Your tardie error: but necessitie,
Now, bids me say, let 'hem not liue an houre,
If you mean *Rome* should liue a day. I haue done.

Dramatic rewriting of this kind sufficiently exempts Jonson from any charge of 'servility' to his sources. It is just to recognize that his Cato and his Catiline are, as dramatic personages, still more forcibly and vividly presented than they are in Sallust. But Jonson had here the advantage of a groundwork of actual speech already provided. A different type and order of dramatic faculty was involved where, as in the case of Sempronia, Curius, Fulvia, a character was merely portrayed in general terms. The portrait of Sempronia [1] is one of Sallust's most finished and effective sketches; but it did not go far towards the brilliant delineation of her in Jonson's second act. It is contained in a dozen lines which may be here rendered for comparison. 'Among the feminine allies of Catiline was Sempronia, already the author of many crimes of masculine daring. She was a woman of good family, well favoured in person, fortunate in her husband and children; skilled in letters both Greek and Latin, and a more elegant performer in music and dance than becomes an honest woman, with many other accomplishments serviceable to wantonness. But she valued everything above decorum and modesty;

[1] *Catiline*, c. 25.

whether she was less tender to her purse or to her reputation, were hard to decide; . . . She had often, ere this, betrayed her faith, forsworn her trust, been privy to murder; she had had sudden alternations of wealth and poverty. But her intellect was by no means contemptible; she had a gift of verse, of humour, of talk by turns grave, tender, and impudent; and altogether abundance of wit and charm.' This portrait has certainly lost nothing in being translated into the dialogue and by-play of Jonson's scene; nor does the dramatic version with all its vivacity and resource add any new trait. But his skill and humour within these self-imposed limits are as admirable as in any of the Comedies. Sempronia's intellectual accomplishment, for instance, is hit off by the open-mouthed wonder of Fulvia's woman, Galla; and the position of the past-mistress of culture and crime, with the prestige of her Greek and of her good birth, taking part on equal terms with political conspirators, is vividly conveyed in her scornful denunciation of the upstart, Cicero:

And, we must glorifie,
A mushrome? one of yesterday? a fine speaker?
'Cause he has suck'd at *Athens*? and aduance him,
To our owne losse? No, FVLVIA. There are they
Can speake *greeke* too, if need were. CAESAR, and I,
Haue sat vpon him.[1]

Not less admirable in its coarse, strong, Jonsonian fashion, is the elaboration, from still slighter materials, of Fulvia, culminating in the disclosure scene—the crucial moment of the play.

IV

The eight years which had elapsed since the production of *Sejanus* had seen the consummation of Jonson's comic art, and brought him a notable increase of prestige. He had given three masterpieces to the public stage. At Court his position as the first of masque-writers was assured by a

[1] II. 135-40.

long series of triumphs. Neither the greater maturity of his art, however, nor his more assured position, has left any palpable trace upon the second of his extant tragedies when compared with the first. Nor have the achievements of others. *Othello*, *King Lear*, *Macbeth*, as well as, in his special sphere of Roman history, *Coriolanus* and *Antony and Cleopatra*, had all appeared in the interim; but Jonson neither learnt nor forgot. Whether *Catiline* is better or worse than *Sejanus* may be a debatable point;[1] that it is constructed upon identical principles, and informed with the same characteristic and peculiar conception of tragic art, can hardly be disputed. Were we ignorant of their relative priority, internal evidence would fail altogether to determine it. Once more he found his tragic subject in a conspiracy, and a Roman conspiracy. Once more he wove into the texture of his plot and dialogue all the extant historical material. Once more, in the process of giving dramatic shape to this material, he neglected all sources or springs of tragic effect save those derived from the spectacle of boundless wickedness armed with formidable power. In *Catiline* as in *Sejanus*, Jonson appears wholly inaccessible to the attraction of the profound 'humanity' and psychology of Shakespearian tragedy. If *Julius Caesar* is often recalled, it is because Jonson has so pointedly adopted a different course in his treatment of similar situations. The meeting of his conspirators by night in Catiline's house in the first act outwardly recalls the nocturnal assemblage at the house of Brutus. A passing allusion to the day just dawning in the east may even remind us of one of Shakespeare's charming bits of by-play in the same scene. While the two leaders converse apart, Cinna and the rest discuss with easy good breeding an indifferent matter, the point at which the sun will rise. They are Roman gentlemen as well as conspirators. But Jonson disdains this

---

[1] It is put below the earlier play by the majority of critics, with whom the present editors concur, but is preferred by Swinburne and by Sir A. W. Ward.

beautiful yet appropriate irrelevance. His conspirators are conspirators out and out: this self-controlled detachment is not for them; if they observe nature at all it is under the obsession of the vast political issue impending; for them 'it is a morning full of fate', that

> riseth slowly, as her sollen carre
> Had all the weights of sleepe, and death hung at it!

And these Jonsonian conspirators are drawn with a relentless insistence on every ferocious trait. No hint of hesitation or of protest retards the hideous ceremony of the oathtaking; the one discordant note in the proceedings is the instinctive shrinking of the 'somewhat modest' page. They include no single estimable figure, though their savagery and fatuity are of different degrees.

V

Catiline himself, ostensibly the central figure of the tragedy, is hardly a tragic character. Less terrible, with all his ferocity, than Tiberius, he is also far less profoundly and subtly drawn. He has imagination, and plots out the future disposal of the resources of the world with the magnificent abandon of Sir Epicure Mammon. His speeches are rhetorically powerful, more particularly when they are not paraphrased from Sallust; but, like so much else in Jonson, they only exhibit with great variety and frequent splendour of expression a hard monotony of mood. He has no conflict, no light and shade; his anarchic fury rages undisturbed and undisguised, checked by no impulse of friendship or affection, humanized by no gleam of ideal purpose. The historical Catiline, according to his great enemy, Cicero, had such 'gleams'. There was 'much in him which indicated, not indeed clearly, but in outline, a virtuous ideal'.[1] Jonson's Cicero does not go so far; he

---
[1] Cicero, *Pro Caelio*, § 13 'Habuit enim ille ... permulta maximarum non expressa signa sed adumbrata virtutum'. The context is an elaborately balanced character-sketch, pitting Catiline's good qualities against his vices.

allows him only 'excellent gifts of ... nature'[1] which he had abused. And Jonson's Catiline hardly affects to have any more specious aim than to assert the claim of the have-nots against those who have—a claim, moreover, here presented in its least persuasive form, as the revolt of a needy and debased aristocracy against the state at large. Far from showing us the genesis and growth of Catiline's aims, Jonson cuts the knot by his fantastic apparition of the ghost of Sylla 'sent from the Stygian sound' to infect the world like a pestilence and take possession of the soul of Catiline:

> PLVTO be at thy councells; and into
> Thy darker bosome enter SYLLA's spirit;
> All that was mine, and bad, thy brest inherit.[2]

It was a natural but unfortunate result of Jonson's method that Catiline, after the first act, ceases to be the principal person in the drama of which he is the nominal hero. Cicero scores a fresh triumph over Catiline by half effacing him in Jonson's play. Shakespeare would probably have reported the drift of his speech in twenty lines, or even in a phrase or two, as he does on a later occasion in *Julius Caesar*;[3] to Jonson the possession of so ample and indubitable an historical document as the Catilinarian orations was an irresistible bait, and he flooded the later acts with Cicero's eloquence, even in the original too voluble for our taste and hardly relieved by a faint note of ridicule here and there, which Jonson was too devout a humanist unreservedly to indulge in Tragedy, and too inbred an exponent of 'humours' altogether to suppress.

Catiline's withdrawal from Rome still further removes him from the centre of interest, and Jonson's adherence to the 'unity of place', though by no means pedantically rigid, yet forbade a complete shifting of the scene in the later stages of the drama to the camp at Faesulae. It is thus but a brief glimpse of Catiline in person that is afforded

[1] IV. 120.   [2] I. 16-18.   [3] *Julius Caesar*, I. ii. 282-3.

us in the last act;[1] and his last stand and death are described for us in a passage as nearly sublime probably as Jonson ever wrote, yet dramatically not in perfect keeping either with the character of Catiline or with that of the narrator. There is beyond question in Catiline's end a grandeur which was very far from denoting his life; but it is the grandeur of epic rather than of drama; the sublimity of a desperate and prodigal heroism, uttered and utterable only with the sword, and passing to extinction fitly with no last cry of confession or despair, but in the marble silence of Medusa's victims:

> And as, in that rebellion 'gainst the gods,
> MINERVA holding forth MEDVSA's head,
> One of the gyant brethren felt himselfe
> Grow marble at the killing sight, and now,
> Almost made stone, began t' inquire, what flint,
> What rocke it was, that crept through all his limmes.
> And, ere he could thinke more, was that he fear'd;
> So CATILINE, at the sight of *Rome* in vs,
> Became his tombe.[2]

In keeping with this epic climax are the grandiose visionary figures who move in the background,—the Furies who preside over the close of Catiline's career as they had inspired its commencement,

> Circling the place, and trembling to see men
> Doe more, then they,—

and Piety, slinking sadly from the field,

> Grieu'd for that side, that, in so bad a cause,
> They knew not, what a crime their valour was.[3]

The conflict-interest, always so strong in Jonson, thus has its full share in the shaping of the play. His second tragedy is substantially a duel between Cicero and Catiline, as his first was a duel between Tiberius and Sejanus. He occupies us with the game, accentuates incidents which prolong it by putting the combatants more nearly on equal

---

[1] v. 367–419.
[2] v. 672–80. The passage is borrowed from the *Gigantomachia* of Claudian, ll. 91–101.   [3] v. 650–4.

terms, and keeps us by a steady succession of hints aware how much better matched they were than either supposed. Each side plays into the hands of the enemy by unreasonable confidence or supineness. Cicero urges Catiline to retire instead of arresting him; Lentulus entrusts his dispatches to the Allobroges, who betray them to Cicero.

The combat itself, if inferior to that of the earlier play in psychological interest, has a richer social and political import, and both sides gain impressiveness, and therefore aesthetic value, in virtue of the masses of opinion, and desire, which they represent and express. The seething discontent which found its organ in Catiline was in its nature sorry and disreputable enough; but to be the head even of a party of anarchists was to stand above the solitary egoist of crime. To that extent his fate excites feelings distinct from those with which we witness the doom of an Edmund or a Sejanus. He is not tragic, but something akin to the elemental pity with which, in tragedy, we watch the ruin of momentous and significant things, infuses itself into the spectacle of his 'brave bad death'.

VI

Of the other characters, if we except a single group, none are individualized with much power. Caesar's dangerous game is lucidly set forth, but the player is a shadow. Cethegus, with his wealth of Senecan phraseology, his scorn for other people's methods of assassination, and his churlish contempt for feminine conspirators; Lentulus, with his fatuous dreams of kingship and his easy credulity, are types, but little more. The women, on the other hand, particularly Fulvia and Sempronia, are among Jonson's best achievements in this kind. His insight into certain types of womanhood was extraordinarily keen, but it was the insight of an intellectual analyst and satirical observer. Dryden was not altogether wrong in regarding the brilliant scenes between the fashionable harlots, and between Fulvia and Curius,[1] as akin to his comedy. But he was wrong in condemning the result as merely an 'unnatural mixture' —an 'oleo'—of comic and tragic effects.[2] Every line of these vivacious dialogues has its purpose and value in the evolution of the plot. Sempronia, the queen—a little *passée*—of an intellectual Bohemia; Curius, the masterful *roué*, alternately storming and wheedling at the unwonted resistance of his mistress; Fulvia, haughtily inaccessible to threats and prayers, but captured at once by the prospect of being in a political secret, and then betraying it the more readily because her more brilliant female friend is in it too, —of such slight but sufficient materials is the tissue woven which brings the schemes of Catiline to naught. The temper of Jonson's comedy is, in truth, not so remote from the temper of such tragedy as his that the transition from the one to the other is difficult or startling. If his comedy is poor in laughter, his tragedy is poor in passion and in tears. There runs through both a vein of cruelty, of scorn, vindictive and retributive, inflicting upon follies and upon crimes a Nemesis which only differs in degree. His tragedies, rioting as they do in the most hideous excesses of Roman corruption and relieved by scarcely a single noble or spiritual figure, oppress us by the monotonous prevalence of evil, but they do not appal us, like *King Lear*, with a sense of its ruthless might; still less with the suggestion such as some critics discover there, of an omnipotent malignity controlling the issues of life. Jonson's criminals are of a deeper dye than Shakespeare's, but his way of dealing with them indicates, if it can be said to indicate any philosophical judgement about life at all, only a burly confidence that sense and judgement will in the long run prevail over savagery and fanaticism, and crimes, like 'humours', be, sooner or later, mulcted in the proper penalties. This limitation of artistic quality removed some

---

[1] Act II.
[2] *Essay of Dramatic Poesy*, ed. Ker, pp. 60, 61. Dryden includes in his censure the scene between Livia and Eudemus in *Sejanus*, II. 54-88.

phenomena from his field which at once harrow and uplift the reader of Shakespeare's tragedies. A Cordelia, a Desdemona, were beyond the sphere of his art, probably beyond the sphere of his interest and sympathy. He is not vexed by the problem of such fates as theirs; but neither does he give us, as they do, the lofty encouragement and consolation which the revelation in poetry of the supreme possibilities of human nature affords.

INTRODUCTION TO
'BARTHOLOMEW FAIR'

BARTHOLOMEW FAIR

Bartholomew Fair was first printed in 1631.[1] It opens the series of plays issued in the second volume of the Folio, which, in its complete form, bears the date 1640.[2]

The date and circumstances of the first performance of this play are known with unusual precision, the 'Articles of Agreement' in the Induction stating it to have taken place on the 'one and thirtieth day of *Octob.* 1614', at the Hope Theatre on the Bankside. The title-page adds the information that it was acted by the Lady Elizabeth's servants. On the following day (November 1), it was performed at Court with a Prologue to the King. By the public at least, it was received with great applause. The lively satire of Puritans had probably as large a share in its success on the stage they disparaged, as its brilliant rendering of the amenities of the famous London fair. But with the growth of the Puritan power in the City, the brandishing of this insulting trophy became an enterprise of increasing peril, and soon after 1620 the play, at least in its complete form, disappeared from the stage. After the Restoration it was promptly brought out of hiding, and its polemical salt now helped to preserve a piece which flagrantly contravened in many points the new tendencies of the drama. Even so, however, it did not universally please. On September 7,

---

[1] In Richard Meighen's title-page prefixed to this play, *The Staple of News*, and *The Devil is an Ass* in the Folio of 1640 the title is so printed. But in Allot's title-page of 1631 and in the running title the first word appears, throughout the play, as 'Bartholmew', and this as well as 'Bartlemew' were current pronunciations.

[2] The complicated problems relating to the second volume of the Folio will be discussed in the critical introduction. For the purpose of the present introduction it will suffice to note that the present play, *The Staple of News*, and *The Divel is an Ass* (in that order) were printed together in 1631, and issued as a separate volume. They were then included with the remainder of the second volume in the issue of 1640, the new title-page bearing that date being prefixed.

1661, Pepys saw the first performance, 'with the puppet show, acted today, which had not been then for forty years, (it being so satirical against Puritanism they durst not till now, which is strange they should already dare to do it, and the King to countenance it), but I do never a whit like it the better for the puppets, but rather the worse'. In *Catiline* Jonson had made a last attempt to provide the play-going public with tragedy after his own mind; and the public by an overwhelming majority had made it plain that his mind, in this matter, was not theirs. He had bitterly resented the rebuff, and appealed to the judgement of the reading public, with surly assurances of its incompetence to judge. The three intervening years had completely allayed his rancour, or at least brought it under complete control. In the great world at least, *Catiline* had only enhanced its author's fame, and the continued favour of the 'extraordinary reader' made indulgence easier towards the weaker vessels.[1] The series of his Christmas masques at Court had continued uninterrupted, save for the Christmas of 1612-13 after the death of the Prince of Wales, when no masques at all were performed there, and when Jonson himself was abroad. On December 27, 1613, his *Challenge at Tilt*, and on the 29th his *Irish Masque*, contributed to celebrate the inauspicious marriage of Somerset to the Countess of Essex; the latter was so well liked that it was repeated on January 3. Whatever, in any case, the assuaging influences may have been, in *Bartholomew Fair* the most masterful of playwrights appears once more disposed to meet his unruly audience more than half-way; to give them as much as he in conscience could of what they wanted, instead of as much as they would stomach of what they ought to want; and above all, to resent no man's disapproval. The impersonal severity, the censorious sternness, which make comedies like *Volpone* and even *The Alchemist*

[1] The notion that Jonson suffered a loss of Court favour during the years 1610-13 is an unsupported theory of Mr. Fleay's. See the discussion in Appendix VII on Jonson's relations with Inigo Jones.

but equivocal examples of the comic spirit, have as far as the playgoing public are concerned wholly vanished from *Bartholomew Fair*. The preacher has descended from his pulpit, the censor has stripped off the robes of his authority and of his chartered scorn; he mingles with the people, with the mob of 'ordinary readers' and the vaster mob of the unreading and the cannot-read, takes part in their least refined exhibitions and amusements and, as the chief exhibition of all, pillories for their ridicule the embodiments of the censorious spirit itself. The Induction at once betrays and announces this changed disposition. Instead of branding his public, in an 'armed Prologue', as ignorant enemies of art if they found his play dull, or swearing the play was good 'and if you like't you may', he now makes a genial compact with them to the effect that 'euery person here (shall) haue his or their free-will of censure, to like or dislike at their owne charge, the *Author* hauing now departed with his right'.[1] The play about to be presented is not merely 'sufficient'—the Jonsonian self-assurance will not be quite kept down—but 'merry, and as full of noise, as sport: made to delight all, and to offend none. Prouided they have either the wit, or the honesty to thinke well of themselues'. In conformity with this promise, *Bartholomew Fair* has the air of a kind of saturnalia of the comic muse—a true holiday play in keeping with its holiday theme, the rigours of dramatic art suspended as the routine of daily business is put by. The Fair was a chartered resort for all the gross pleasures and passions of the capital, and these have their full fling in this Smithfield of the stage, the inevitably defective realism of the boards being eked out by the circumstance that the place of performance was 'as durty as *Smithfield*, and as stinking euery whit'.[2] Jonson has indeed carried his observance of what he pleasantly calls the 'speciall *decorum*' of veracity to lengths which modern delicacy finds it difficult to stomach. The scene is, once for all, as he warned his royal audience on the second night,

[1] Induction, sig. A 5. [2] Ibid. sig. A 6.

'a Fair'; and everything in the play took its character, and derived its apology, from that salient fact:

> Such place, such men, such language & such ware,
> You must expect.

Yet we should do Jonson wrong if we supposed that he had really deserted here the fundamental principles of his art. We know, indeed, that he composed an express defence or 'Apologie' for it, which, being prefixed to his version of Horace's *Art of Poetry*, must have dealt with its technical qualities as a drama.[1] The very text of his play indicates how many things happened at the real *Bartlemew* which Jonson refused to admit. He is a humanist still, and even in this sink of humanity, where monstrosities of every kind were the prime attraction, forswears 'monsters', to draw 'men'. With all his desire to give his audience what they want, he postulates that they shall *want* as spectators at a play and not at a bear-baiting or a raree-show. With unusual tact he makes the 'stage-keeper' complain to the audience of these limitations on the part of the poet:

> But for the whole *Play*, will you ha' the truth on't?... it is like to be a very conceited scuruy one, in plaine English. When't comes to the *Fayre*, once: you were e'en as good goe to *Virginia*, for any thing there is of *Smith-field*. Hee has not hit the humors, he do's not know 'hem; hee has not conuers'd with the *Bartholmew*-birds, as they say; hee has ne're a Sword and Buckler man in his *Fayre*, nor a little *Dauy*, to take toll o' the Bawds there, as in my time, nor a *Kind-heart*, if any bodies teeth should chance to ake in his *Play*. Nor a Iugler with a wel-educated Ape.... None o' these fine sights! Nor has he the Canuas cut i' the night, for a Hobby-horseman to creepe in to his she-neighbour.... Nothing![2]

Instead of these popular but undramatic attractions of the show he offers them, with ironical apologies, persons 'such as

---

[1] *Conversations*, v. 82–5. The *Apologie* afterwards perished in Jonson's fire.
[2] Induction, sig. A 4.

comedy would choose' or would not altogether reject,—'a strutting *Horse-courser*, ... a fine oyly *Pig woman* with her *Tapster*, to bid you welcome, ... A wise *Iustice* of *Peace meditant*, in stead of a Iugler, with an Ape. A ciuill *Cutpurse searchant* . . .'—men, in short, and not monsters.[1] And he goes on, in the same vein of good-natured irony, to regret that he cannot accommodate his hearers, as did some of his contemporaries, with the perversions of nature they relish. 'If there bee neuer a *Seruant-monster* i' the *Fayre;* who can helpe it? he sayes; nor a nest of *Antiques*? Hee is loth to make Nature afraid in his *Playes*, like those that beget *Tales, Tempests*, and such like *Drolleries*, to mixe his head with other mens heeles.' It can hardly be doubted that Jonson was here glancing at *The Tempest* and *The Winter's Tale*, whose brilliant success was still recent: both had been chosen for performance at the marriage festivities of the previous year. We need not quarrel with Jonson for not relishing the imaginative loveliness of Shakespeare's romantic comedy. A great creative mind can rarely compete in versatile security of appreciation with the critic whose whole business it is to taste and try. The intellectual energy which went to the making of *The Alchemist* or *Bartholomew Fair* tended to deplete the springs of feeling which *The Tempest* or *The Winter's Tale* might have touched. And the student of our play will not bear Jonson hard if the amazing wealth of knowledge and resource which he has lavished on bodying forth in its very image the sordid humanity of the Fair, left him a little intolerant of the irresponsible poetry of enchanted islands and impossible sea-coasts.

But, besides the devotees of romance—whether in the new style of Shakespeare's latest plays or in the old style of '*Ieronimo* or *Andronicus*',—there was another class of possible spectators to whom Jonson thought fit to give a salutary hint. At the close of the Induction he engages the audience

[1] Ibid. sig. A 5, verso.

neyther in themselues to conceale, nor suffer by them to be concealed any *State-decipherer*, or politique *Pick-locke* of the *Scene*, so solemnly ridiculous, as to search out, who was meant by the *Ginger-bread-woman*, who by the *Hobby-horse-man*, who by the *Costard-monger*, nay, who by their *Wares*. Or that will pretend to affirme (on his own *inspired ignorance*) what *Mirror of Magistrates* is meant by the *Iustice*, what *great Lady* by the *Pigge-woman*, what *conceal'd States-man*, by the *Seller* of *Mouse-trappes*, and so of the rest.

This protest, not made for the first time,[1] must be held decisive against the attempt to identify any person of the drama with originals in Jonson's *milieu*. But it does not require us to suppose that, in drawing the thirty or more figures of the play, Jonson never borrowed a trait from living persons he knew, that he handled them without any reminiscence of the persons they resembled, that he even avoided touches which might recall them to others. Drama and literature, as they were carried on at the Fair, were a kind of natural or ready-made burlesque of the drama and literature of the upper and outer world ; it was hard to draw to the life the master of the puppets or the purveyor of their libretto without some suspicion of reflections upon the manipulators of loftier shows in the City or Court, and Jonson scarcely took great pains to avoid the suspicion. In this sense, and to this degree, it may be allowed to be not unlikely that in Lantern Leatherhead the 'motion-man' Jonson glanced at Inigo Jones, and in Little-wit at his old rival as a masque-maker, Daniel.[2]

It is not superfluous to dwell upon these elaborate prefatory explanations and warnings. Nowhere does Jonson appear more concerned lest the character of his art should be misunderstood than in introducing a work which on the face of it bears so largely the character of a holiday riot of the comic and satiric Muse. If Jonson here relaxed some principles of technique on which he had formerly insisted,

---

[1] See particularly *Every Man out of his Humour*, II. vi, the concluding comments of the 'Grex'.
[2] See Appendix VII.

he had never shown himself a more consummate artist. The shaping and contriving hand has not been less active, but its operations have been less obtrusive and more subtle. The art which conceals art was a difficult gospel for the most masterful and self-conscious of artists to practise; but for once he approaches it. The abstract and scholastic elements of his mind, which had asserted themselves with varying force in all the Humour plays, even in *Every Man in his Humour*, and had made *Every Man out of his Humour* resemble a museum of selected curiosities, are here completely in abeyance, if not, as the sequel showed, completely overcome. Even in the greatest of his plots, in *Volpone* and *The Alchemist* themselves, the method, however admirable, is somewhat too easily descried and formulated. But in the artistry of *Bartholomew Fair* the last trace of artifice has vanished. The lines of cleavage between the tricksters and the dupes, which so largely determine the structure of Jonsonian comedy, are here unusually complicated. The comic harms come about inevitably, as natural incidents of the Fair, without the intervention of a professional contriver called Brainworm or Buffone. Of palpable literary reminiscence in the plot-making there is hardly a trace. Whatever nutriment Jonson has drawn from Plautus has passed into the blood and been converted into nerve and tissue. We have not to do with Plautine cunning slaves and boastful soldiers more or less cleverly disguised, but with unadulterated English roguery and vagabondage, as they grew and throve in the ripe soil of the great London show. The Fair is indeed the true subject of the play, the salient, obsessive, uncircumventable, ubiquitous fact to which all the bewildering multiplicity of persons and interests have relation. There is no hero, no dominant character, no well-defined unity of plot; but the Fair, which has brought all this motley multitude together, and set in motion their legion of appetencies, provides a real unity of theme and tone, analogous in its realist fashion to that imposed by the enchanted woodlands of

Athens or of Arden upon the throngs of incommensurable creatures—fairies, artisans, antique heroes and courtiers, or shepherds of pastoral and of real life—who meet and mingle in its shades. For every class of London citizen it offers some kind of allurement. To some it is a forbidden paradise of ungodly savours and shows, to some an unweeded garden crying for the hoe, to some an unequalled place of business, where rotten goods can be got rid of, and fools exploited, more easily than elsewhere; regular *habitués*, practising their venerable frauds and well-tried recipes for profit or plunder, jostle with novices who have ventured curiously over the threshold of iniquity, with austere reformers in quest of matter for the hurdle or the pillory, with gentle-folks who look on disdainfully at the gross amusements, but still look on. Like the laboratory of Subtle, the Fair lays all sorts and conditions of men under its spell; and the main source of comedy lies in the disasters which befall the adventurous or curious explorers from outside. Although it is in this way the occasion of humour, and some individuals, like Ursula, exhibit a vein of strong, earthy humour themselves, the spirit of the Fair is no more humorous than the spirit of Subtle. As alchemy in Jonson's hands lost all its hint of poetry, and became purely a gross and sordid imposture, so the Fair, where crowds of Londoners doubtless found harmless amusement, loses all suggestion of gaiety, and appears purely hard, grasping, and foul. This was, it may well be, a less baleful monster than the other, though it spread its tentacles farther; but he has painted it with no less force of imagination, and no less amplitude of squalid and unsavoury erudition. No writer of comedy ever understood better than Jonson the humours of money-making and the fantastic tricks induced by the opportunity of making it in unusual quantities and with less than the usual trouble. The petty traffic of the Fair did not admit the intensity and complexity of dramatic effect he had educed from the grandiose operations of the Fox and the Alchemist. But

Jonson lays bare the economics of this sordid and shabby world with a no less curious intimacy. He makes us understand the energy of the economic interests which found their account in the chartered licence of the Fair, and for which the head and front of Puritan offending was that it stood in the way of a thriving trade. He shows us the wrath of the hucksters when Busy denounces 'this Idolatrous Groue of images, this flasket of Idols'—'Here he is, pray you lay hold on his zeale, wee cannot sell a whistle, for him, in tune.'—'A poxe of his *Bedlem* purity. Hee has spoyl'd halfe my ware . . .'[1] He shows us their angry disdain for the unprofitable abstemiousness even of those who did not denounce: 'What aile they *Vrs*?' asks Knock-hum, of the Littlewit party; 'Aile they? they are all sippers, sippers o' the City, they look as they would not drinke off two penn'orth of bottle-ale amongst 'hem'.[2] The whole motley population of hucksters, vagabonds, and swindlers is saturated with the spirit of the place. They are not warped or eccentric individuals, like the 'Humours', more or less at odds with their *milieu*, but the very growth of the soil, impregnated with the rankness of the mould they thrive

> in like the fat weed
> That rots itself in ease on Lethe wharf.

Distinctions of character can be observed among them; there are grades of cunning, shades of rapacity or of malice; but the trait which finally denotes them, and in which all these minor distinctions merge, is the particular business each carries on in the Fair. Knock-hum, the horse-courser, has no speech but the language of horse-coursing; Zekiel Edgworth cuts purses with the precise blend of the virtuosities of the actor and the thief which best meets the conditions of the Fair; Nightingale sings ballads nicely calculated to favour the incidental picker of pockets; Mooncalf, of the weasel shape and the grasshopper

---

[1] Act III, scene vi.   [2] Ibid. scene ii.

thighs, is a trusty henchman of his mighty 'aunt', the pigwoman, and a stickler for the honour of her booth; and the pigwoman herself, a female Falstaff who lards the ground in knots as she goes, and threatens to 'melt away to the first woman, a ribbe againe',[1] is wearing out her youth and prime in the roasting of the famous Bartholomew dish which the world went to the Fair to eat. The visitors to the Fair, still more numerous than the clients of the Alchemist, are no less closely studied from life, and still more representative of the various classes and dispositions of the civic world. Both the dupes and the critics include at least one character which surpasses in keenness of observation and wealth and precision of detail any previous creation of Jonson's in the same kind. Master Bartholomew Cokes is a better 'country gull' than even Master Stephen; Rabbi Busy is a finished picture where Ananias is a lively sketch; and Surly, the honest man *manqué*, cannot be compared in reach and significance with the equally luckless detector of 'enormities', Overdo. The later group are more closely studied, they are richer in characteristic traits and more intimately true to their place and time. Stephen is drawn with crude emphatic strokes, little removed from caricature; Cokes is a subtler and more imaginative study in fatuity. Stephen is like a mechanical toy, always giving off the same calculable effects when the same stimulus recurs; Cokes has the butterfly temperament of the loose-hinged brain, and flutters hither and thither at the beck of every whimsy. 'A pretty little soule, this same Mistris *Little-wit*! would I might marry her,' he exclaims, casually, in her presence and that of his own betrothed.[2] A moment later another kind of romance has caught him in its meshes—the romance of the raree-show; now it is 'The *Fayre, Numps*, the *Fayre*', and Numps has a pretext for his incisive description of his charge's brain: 'he that had the meanes to trauell your head, now, should meet finer sights then any are i' the *Fayre*; and make a finer voyage

---

[1] Act II, scene ii.   [2] Act I, scene v.

on't; to see it all hung with cockle-shels, pebbles, fine wheat-strawes, and here and there a chicken's feather, and a cob-web'. This is the very poetry of the rubbish-heap; and it is admirably translated into drama in the last act, where Cokes finds himself at last perfectly in his element among the puppets; 'I am in loue with the *Actors* already, and I'll be allyed to them presently. (They respect gentlemen, these fellowes) *Hero* shall be my fayring: But, which of my fairings? (Le' me see) i'faith, my *fiddle*! And *Leander* my *fiddle-sticke*: Then *Damon*, my *Drum*; and *Pythias* my *Pipe*, and the ghost of *Dionysius*, my *hobby-horse*. All fitted.'[1] ' The place becomes him, me thinkes,' drily observes his other incisive critic, Grace.[2] This scene is no bad counterpart to that in which Falstaff remembers Justice Shallow at Clement's Inn 'like a man made after supper of a cheese-paring'.[3] Cokes has points of resemblance to Sir Andrew Aguecheek. They are both poor in 'blood'—the spirit of 'heart' or courage—and their deficiency is played on in the same possibly current phrase: ' In his blood?' says Edgworth scornfully, 'hee has not so much to'ard it in his whole body, as will maintaine a good Flea.'[4] But Cokes in one feature is distinguished from all previous gulls of English comedy—he has a tutor. Waspe, whose discomforts and surly humour in the conduct of his charge add so much to the pleasantness of the situation, has no doubt a prototype in the pedagogue of Italian comedy. But the resemblance is purely general. Waspe is drawn with great freshness and zest, and if we are to seek a source for his experiences, literary reminiscence is less probable than acute personal experience. Only a year before he drew these scenes Jonson had returned from his unlucky journey to France as ' governor' to young Ralegh. Young Ralegh, more knave than fool, is as little to be identified with Cokes as Waspe with Jonson; but in several circumstances they

---

[1] Act v, scene iii.   [2] Ibid. scene iv.
[3] *Henry IV, Part II*, III. ii.
[4] Act IV, scene ii. Cf. *Twelfth Night*, III. ii. 65.

recall one another: Ralegh was, in the year of the play, like Cokes, 'nineteen yeere old',[1] and 'now vpon his making and marring'; his education had been unfortunate, though in a different way; and his mother's management was extremely well calculated to suggest the doubt of 'what may happen vnder a womans gouernment' which Waspe insinuates in respect of Cokes's 'natural sister'; finally, Waspe's culminating embarrassment in convoying his charge through the streets of London, and his fear of his 'learning of vile tunes, which he will sing at supper, and in the sermon-times', were hardly described without a vivid remembrance of even more compromising scenes enacted at the governor's expense in the streets of Paris.[2] In all this there may be no literal borrowing; every trait is adapted to its new context; but the adventures of a tutor with an ill-conditioned youth are very feelingly described.

But the main emphasis naturally falls upon those visitors to the Fair who represent the considerable section of London citizens which protested in varying accents and with varying degrees of sincerity against its 'enormities'. The critics of the Fair are not all Puritans. With great dramatic tact Jonson allows us to see plainly enough that persons of breeding differed little in their attitude towards it from the straitest of City wives: they called it ribald, not 'ungodly', but they disdained it as heartily, and their curiosity as often got the better of their disdain. But the 'gentles' as usual are drawn with slight and ineffective touches. Respectability, in the persons of Winwife and Quarlous, overwhelmed by the flood of Ursula's greasiest eloquence, is a topic of much comic possibility, if the respectables had been as powerfully imagined as the pigwoman. Of Grace the best that can be said is that her tragi-comic fortunes in troth and courtship are imagined in the very spirit of the place. It is romance rendered from beginning to end in terms of

[1] Act I, scene iv.
[2] 'At which sport' (a scandalous practical joke played upon Jonson) 'young Raughlies mother delighted much, (saying his father young was so inclined), though the Father abhorred it' (*Conversations*, xiii).

the Fair and its customs. Bargaining and fraud make up all the circumstance of the story. A purchased ward, sold to a foolish suitor, she is about to become his possession when the marriage licence is abstracted by a pickpocket and transferred to one rival, who for a consideration resigns it to the other. As for Grace herself, it can only be said that she is apparently intended to possess charm, and is yet without it. Jonson from first to last never succeeded in drawing a woman at once fascinating, young, and modest. In the mercenary and sordid atmosphere of the Fair, in that Carnival of licensed and unlicensed appetites, her mental features and cold decorum afford a secure but somewhat uninviting oasis—an orderly but rather barren plot cleared in the jungle.

The visit of the Puritan family to this sink of iniquity is, on the other hand, a comic motive of the highest quality, and it is worked out with exuberant power. The family group itself is rich in the germs of drama. The situation of young Littlewit, proctor and furtive author of a puppet play, between a Puritan mother-in-law and the saintly elder who holds a proctor to be a Claw of the Beast, and that she has 'little less then committed abomination' in marrying her daughter to him, is one which in the hands of a dramatist of less drastic methods might have yielded much pleasanter and more human comedy than we find here. Littlewit and his wife are excellent studies in *niaiserie*, but their veracity in some sense detracts from the ends of comedy; they are too unequivocally silly to be in any high degree amusing. The insipidity of empty-headed good nature, which welcomes insult with a fatuous smile and overflows on all occasions with a froth of feeble jokes, was never more tellingly drawn; but we turn with relief from these thin parings of humanity to the solidly based hypocrisy of Dame Purecraft and the saintly glutton Busy. Busy is a full-length portrait, drawn with enormous vivacity and vigour of invention. His demonstration of the legitimacy of eating pig in the Fair, 'so it be eaten with a reformed mouth, with *sobriety*, and humblenesse', and his conclusion 'In the way of comfort to the weake, I will goe, and eat, ... there may be a good vse made of it, too, now I think on't: by the publike eating of Swines flesh, to professe our hate, and loathing of *Iudaisme*, whereof the brethren stand taxed'[1] —are admirable pieces of casuistry. But he cannot sustain the comparison he invites with Tartuffe. Jonson commands the Puritan jargon with his usual scholarly virtuosity, but his satire does not touch the deeper strata of Puritan thought, nor could it well be guessed what school or phase of Puritanism Busy reflects. Like Jonson's hypocrites in general he is not profoundly plausible, and it is significant that he makes no dupes. No Orgon prostrates himself before the holy guest, no Elmire half-listens to his suit; for widow Purecraft knows him to be 'the capitall Knaue of the land'.[2] Overdo, Busy's fellow-censor of the Fair, and fellow-victim of its pains and penalties, the over-zealous collector of 'enormities' who is finally arrested as one himself, is perhaps drawn with a less sure and trenchant hand, but he is a character, like Cokes, while Busy is a caricature, like Stephen. The well-meaning enthusiast whose innocence leads him into traps which every one else escapes; the dupe of every one else's disguise and the victim of his own; who embarks on the 'project' of saving from bad company and poetry that 'civil and honest young man', the pickpocket and chief contriver of harms; who finds himself, with Busy, in the stocks, the unskilfully hypocritical suffering the same punishment, as often, with the inopportunely fanatic, and seasons this homely misfortune with the high Roman philosophy of endurance—this is a conception worthy of high comedy. Admirably invented also is his too faithful henchman Troubleall; the ghost of demented legality fluttering distractedly about the wilderness of Licence, with his hollow cry, 'By whose warrant?' The foibles of legal formalism are excellently hit off when Quarlous in Troubleall's clothes borrows this cry, and the Justice, eager to

---

[1] Act I, scene vi.   [2] Act v, scene ii.

reward such touching devotion, puts his name and seal to the blank charter of fraud.

Jonson was hardly unaware of the profounder bearings of the contrasts and controversies which his satire so powerfully exhibits. But the new temper which was coming into the mind of the English people was not even distantly touched by his rogues in Puritan mask, brilliantly as they are drawn.

To Jonson the gross pleasures of the Fair, culminating in the hideous burlesque of *Hero and Leander*, can have possessed attraction only as a rude but plentiful banquet for the comic spirit; but he involved its critics and its dupes in the same ridicule. To wish that he had represented the profounder protest against the Fair and the life it symbolized, as kindred protests were represented in *Don Quixote* and in the *Misanthrope*, is no doubt to wish not only that Jonson had imagined a greater kind of comedy than his own, but that he had passed beyond the bounds of comedy, in any strict sense, altogether. It is not in this direction, of intellectual subtlety and ethical manysidedness, that Jonson had any temptation to pass those bounds. No character in the whole range of his works suggests, as Quixote and Alceste suggest, that its author saw, in the complexity of life, no sharp antithesis of wisdom and folly, but a dualism of opposed ideals, each having something of eternal reason, and each something of eternal illusion, on its side. *Twelfth Night*, a dozen or more years before, leaves us with the impression that the Puritan problem presented itself somewhat thus to the genial humanity of the mature Shakespeare. *L'Allegro* and *Il Penseroso*, eighteen years later, clearly announce that in the finely balanced nature of the young Milton it also took this form. The great satiric comedy produced nearly midway between them is an amazing example of exuberant comic genius and of original but effective technique. But it is, more emphatically than any other of Jonson's greater plays, of an age, and not for all time.

APPENDIX VII

LANTERN LEATHERHEAD AND INIGO JONES

The strongest evidence of a connexion between Leatherhead and Jones is the saying reported of Selden, that 'Ben Jonson satirically expressed the vain Disputes of Divines, by Inigo Lanthorn, disputing with his puppet in a Bartholomew Fair' (*Table Talk*, sub 'Religion'). But this equally indicates, for Selden knew what he was talking about, and was Jonson's friend, that the satire conveyed through Lantern Leatherhead was partly directed against the vain disputatious divines, and therefore (if at all) only incidentally against Inigo. It is true, as Brotanek urges (*Englische Maskenspiele*, p. 246), that we have no evidence of a quarrel between Jones and Jonson at this early date. But the evidence that we have, though not decisive, favours the view that official alliance between these two great but arrogant artists, each unassailably assured of the supremacy of his own art, was from the first eminently insecure, and that though it may not have been openly broken off before 1616, the rupture was preceded by a period of strained relations, from about 1610 onwards. (See the *Life*, pp. 60-2.) This state of things would more naturally provoke the covert and incidental allusion than the full-length satiric portrait. And such allusions might be made through more than one character of the play. Hence it is not right to say, with Gifford and others, that Jonson's subsequent comparison of Inigo with Overdo in the *Expostulation* 'destroys' the theory of his connexion with Leatherhead; it merely shows that his connexion with the puppet-manager and with the busy 'firking' justice alike, was only incidental. During the two years between Christmas, 1612, and January, 1615, it may be added, with the possible exception of a few months in the middle of 1613, the two men had little or no direct personal intercourse whatever, friendly or otherwise; first Jonson and then Inigo having been on the Continent. Jonson had, however, returned by June 29, 1613, and Inigo cannot be shown to have left before September. Mr. Fleay's theory of a period immediately preceding *Bartholomew Fair* during which Jonson was under a cloud at Court while Jones basked in Court favour, finds no support in the known facts. Jonson's non-participation in the wedding festivities of February, 1613, is explained by his absence in France; and in the following December he was employed to compose two entertainments, the *Challenge at Tilt* and the *Irish Masque*. It is possible, in the same way, that in certain traits of Littlewit Jonson glanced at his old rival Daniel. But the grounds on which Mr. Fleay has confidently 'identified' the two are very slender. His case rests mainly on the two epigrams of Sir John Davies upon 'Dacus'. In Epigram 30 he described 'Dacus' in terms highly suggestive of Littlewit, as one who furnished 'prose speeches' to showmen of various kinds—'the man that keeps the elephants, . . .' and also 'him which puppets represents', who was 'numbered among the poets', and yet 'could never make an English rhyme'. The only part of this which can possibly apply to Daniel is the last sentence; Jonson too declared Daniel to be 'a good honest man . . . but no poet'. In the second epigram, however (No. 45), Davies almost certainly described Daniel—quoting his much-ridiculed phrase 'silent eloquence'. That he inaccurately says this is used of 'his love' (Delia) instead of Rosamond is immaterial. But, as Small has shown (*Stage Quarrel*, p. 193), the same name was often used in epigrams to cover satire upon several different persons; Sir John Harington, in particular, used 'Lynus', almost as a generic term, in no less than thirteen epigrams, and the discrepancy of the greater part of No. 30 with what we know of Daniel supports the view that this Dacus is distinct from the other, which would destroy our principal reason for connecting Daniel with Littlewit. But we will add an argument from another source, not adduced by Mr. Fleay, of as slender substance perhaps as any of his, but not altogether to be overlooked in this highly speculative region. In the Introduction to *Hymenaei* Jonson reflects severely upon some unnamed persons who 'may squemishly crie out, that all endeauour of *learning*, and *sharpnesse* in these transitorie *deuices*, especially where it steps beyond their little, or (let me not wrong 'hem) noe braine at all is superfluous'. Brotanek has shown (*Engl. Mask.*, p. 185) that this is probably a retort upon Daniel's preface to *The Vision of the Twelve Goddesses*, which somewhat disdainfully refers to those who 'would fain have the world to think them very deeply learned in all mysteries whatsoever', and thus strive to show most wit about these 'puntillos of dreams and shews' where 'there needs no exact sufficiency in this kind; for *ludit iste animus, non proficit!*' Jonson, it is true, goes on to express his contentment that 'these fastidious *stomachs* should leaue my full tables, and enioy at home their cleane emptie trenchers, fittest for such ayrie tasts'—terms hardly applicable to Littlewit's production, however suited to Daniel's; but this cannot avail against the cogency of Jonson's phrase *little* or *no brain at all*.

INTRODUCTION TO

'THE DEVIL IS AN ASS'

THE DEVIL IS AN ASS

I

The Diuell is an Asse was first printed in 1631; together with *Bartholomew Faire,* and *The Staple of Newes,* it opened the second volume of the Folio edition of Jonson's works, 1640. For some reason not now apparent this play in this edition was placed after *The Staple of Newes,* its successor. After the printing of the present play in 1631 the further printing of the second volume of the Folio for some reason ceased and was only completed after Jonson's death in 1640, a new title-page with that date being prefixed to the entire volume. There is no reason to suppose that these plays were printed without Jonson's supervision; but it was the supervision of a paralytic, and the text is below the high level of the first volume. An extant letter indicates that he had much to suffer also from the printer.[1]

The play was first performed by the King's men at their Blackfriars Theatre, in the autumn of 1616.[2] We have no record of its reception. But Drummond reports Jonson to have stated, some three years later at Hawthornden, that he had been 'accused upon' the play. Our only hint of the ground of the accusation is contained in his further laconic sentence: '$\Pi\alpha\rho\epsilon\rho\gamma\omega\varsigma$ is discoursed of the Duke of Drownland. The King desyred him to conceal it'.[3] Nothing

[1] 'It is the Lewd Printers fault, that I can send yor Lo^p, no more of my Booke done. I sent you one peice before, the fayre, . . . and now I send you this other morcell, the fine Gentleman that walkes in Towne; the Fiend, but before hee will perfect the rest, I feare, hee will come himselfe to be a part, vnder the title of the absolute knaue, wch he hath play'd wth mee' (Letter to Earl of Newcastle, printed in Appendix II. vol. i, p. 211).
[2] The year is fixed by I. i. 81, the Blackfriars Theatre by I. vi. 31. The theatre was not used in the summer. Many slight indications, collected by W. S. Johnson (Introd. pp. xvii, f.) and Professor Kittredge (*Mod. Phil.*, 1911), go to show that the first performance took place in October or November.
[3] *Conversations,* xvi. 414, 415.

is known of this affair on independent evidence. But it may be inferred that some part of the satire, in the play as originally performed, struck home, that Jonson at the king's request softened or effaced the personal point, real or apparent, and that this revised version is represented by the printed text.

The precise ground of the offence given cannot, therefore, be determined. But the satire, even as it stands, is aimed at abuses so specific and so notoriously rife that it must have fitted many caps. We are far, here, from the broad generic painting of the early Humour plays. The comic material is hardly changed; the old duel of gull and exploiter is renewed; but the stamp of time and place is more deeply impressed, the fatuities and knaveries have the specific brand of Jacobean London, and even of those critical middle years of James's reign in which the play was conceived and composed.[1] The central figures here are the 'projector' and his wealthy dupe; and the 'projector' is an adept in a variety of current methods of rascality, which he successively

[1] The year 1614 marked a crisis in the economic as in the political history of the reign, and the two sets of circumstances were connected. 'The air was full of projects for encouraging national industries' (G. Unwin, *Industrial Organization in the Sixteenth and Seventeenth Centuries*, p. 166), and the Crown in these years had shown itself peculiarly alive to the advantages of these practices by the grant of monopolies, always for a consideration direct or indirect, thus itself in effect becoming a projector. In 1614-15 the Government, after forbidding the export of unfinished cloth (for the benefit of the English finishers), granted a charter to a new company for the export of the finished article (Unwin, *u. s.*, p. 182). In 1616 the Government found itself involved in endless embarrassments as a result of its rash Protection policy. We can understand that a play which in this very year introduced a project in which the Government, however innocently, was to receive a share, touched delicate ground.

The particular project of reclaiming the 'drowned lands' of the Fen counties was only an extravagant caricature of contemporary schemes. The Domestic State Papers of these years testify to the efforts made by the Government to induce the county authorities to maintain or improve the channels which drained the fen-waters. The serious interest of the Crown in the Fen drainage belongs to the next reign. In view of this attitude of Charles, Jonson might naturally be disposed further to temper the satire upon the Duke of Drown land which had already offended James. But it remains sufficiently incisive, and the single text we possess offers no clue whatever to the extent of any changes which Jonson may on either occasion have made.

The Devil is an Ass

turns to account in his dealings with Fitzdottrel. We may distinguish three in particular—(1) bogus speculation; (2) bogus settlement of quarrels by the laws of duelling; (3) sham demoniac possession. But in each case it is plain that satirical exposure of these practices was not the dominant purpose of the play. The abuses connected with duelling, in particular, are merely the occasion for an admirable example of Jonson's humorous invention—the supposed state-office of 'dependencies' (or impending duels), an invention akin to the later 'Staple of News'. While Drummond's report of Jonson's statement, unless he wholly misunderstood it, goes to indicate that the whole topic of the 'Duke of Drown land' was subordinate to the devil-drama; the picture of the shady places of Jacobean society being meant primarily to serve the comic demonstration that 'the devil is an ass'. It is this latter feature, in any case, which gives the play its most individual character in the Jonsonian drama, and constitutes its chief interest in a survey of Jonsonian art.

The title itself appeared to mark a definite change of front. Nine years before, in the proem to *Volpone*, he had loftily derided those 'antique relics of barbarism', those 'ridiculous and exploded follies', the fools and devils of the stage; and the passage had reappeared without qualification in the Folio text published in this very year. How did it come that the man who had then sternly swept the devilries of the stage into the limbo of 'exploded follies' now came forward with a devil-play, executed with all the resources of his mature art?

Jonson was not the man to make any open surrender of principle, or even to confess to a change of policy. But it is clear that, from about 1610, he shows in comedy a growing willingness to relax the severity of his canons, to accommodate himself to popular tastes and make use of popular traditions. *The Alchemist* might be described as a vernacularized *Volpone*—the huge comedy of organized humbug translated into the terms and lingo of London roguery. *Bartholomew Fair* carried the accommodation some degrees farther, hazarding the unity of action itself in the profuse painting of the humours and manners of the Fair. And the process was only carried yet a step farther when Jonson in the present play, swallowing his old contempt, offered his audience another example of the 'ridiculous and exploded', but still feverishly popular, devil play.

For the Jacobean playgoer continued to find in this and other 'relics of barbarism' a satisfaction which his mentor could not ignore and at length found it expedient to recognize. Among the older plays, *Faustus*, though a generation old, was still familiar; Machiavelli's famous story of the fiend Belphegor had been brought on the stage in Haughton's *Devil and his Dame* (*Grim the Collier of Croydon*) so recently as 1600, and was to inspire another devil-play, Wilson's *Belphegor*, so late as the Revolution. Another play, nearly contemporary, *The Merry Devil of Edmonton*, was still, as Jonson half enviously owns, the 'dear delight' of his public. Moreover, at least two new plays of this type had been written and performed during James's reign. Barnes's *The Diuells Charter*, performed in 1606-7, attested the continued vitality of the Faustus legend on which it drew. While only four years before Jonson's play his old rival and enemy, Dekker, had scored a notable success with *If this be not a good play, the Diuell is in't*, a vivacious transcript of the legend of Friar Rush. Far from slighting these incorrigible champions of an obsolete mode, Jonson almost humbly appeals to his audience to judge his piece by the standard of their favourite plays.

II

The devil-dramas of the Renascence normally turn upon a duel between diabolic and human power. In one group the action is provoked, as in Dr. Faustus and Peter Fabel, by the ambition or curiosity of a man; in another it originates, as in Machiavelli's Belphegor, in the enterprise of the infernal world. The issue, again, varies: the devil either triumphs or suffers humiliating defeat. And a favourite variety of this second type is that which represents the devil as not only defeated but stupid, and extracts comic capital from his stupidity.[1] It was to this line of development that Jonson attached himself in his new experiment, and it is not hard to understand his choice.

The 'stupid' devil had flourished in popular belief or make-believe long before he figured on the Renascence stage. Jonson's very title was a proverbial formula, defiant or reassuring as the case might be.

>   Dost thou think
> The devil such an ass as people make him?

says a character in Fletcher's *The Chances* (V. ii).

Two mythic types—even two national mythologies—cross and blend in this figure. The purely terrible diabolus of Jewish and Christian belief is doubled in him with the homely gullible giant of Germanic folk-lore.[2] The devil, baffled and beaten by the Vice, had for centuries provided a gay interlude to the serious or tragic matter of the Mysteries, and Jonson makes Satan expressly recall these exhibitions, which still lingered here and there in England when he first began to write. On the Elizabethan and Jacobean stage, after Faustus, the delight of seeing the devil outwitted carried the day over the thrill of his dreadful triumphs. Fabel in *The Merry Devil of Edmonton* eludes him, and the connoisseurs in devilry introduced by Jonson later in *The Staple of News* dub this devil with express reference to Jonson's Pug in the present play (which they are characteristically made to advertise) 'an asse'.[3] Two other plays bear more directly on Jonson's handling of this type, and demand a brief notice.

In Haughton's *Devil and his Dame* a Renascence jest of

---

[1] How easily these varieties could intermingle was shown when Goethe, by his Prologue in Heaven, made his Faust story originate in Mephistophiles's wager with the Lord; and also when he made Mephistophiles, who is not precisely stupid, nevertheless lose his wager.

[2] 'When we nowadays call the devil *dumm*, a quondam giant is really meant' (Grimm, *Deutsche Mythologie*, tr. Stallybrass, p. 529).

[3] *The Staple of News*, First Intermean.

an outwitted devil is grafted upon the native legend of Grim the Croydon Collier. The Collier merely proves the devil's match. But Machiavelli shows his Belphegor ignominiously routed by the craft and duplicity of women. The *Novella* is in substance merely a satire upon marriage, ingeniously conveyed through the motive of an infernal emissary. Belphegor is sent to report whether wives are really as bad as they are reputed, and returns grievously disillusioned and beguiled. The Belphegor of Haughton's play takes with him an attendant spirit Akercock,[1] who assumes the form and also the character of Robin Goodfellow, and in keeping with that role promotes the marriage of Grim and his Joan, as the Merry Devil does that of Millicent and Mounchesney. His master, on the other hand, as a Spanish grandee, is first cheated into marrying the maid instead of the mistress, and then so completely nonplussed by his wife that he only escapes multiple death with poison and dagger, by abruptly retreating whence he came:

> Hell, I salute thee! now I feel myself
> Rid of a thousand torments. O vile earth,
> Worse for us devils than hell itself for men!

The more recent play of Dekker, *If it Be not good, the Divell is in't*, offers a less decisive example of the stupid devil, but describes with point and humour the shrewd and knowing society of Jacobean England, where even an able devil was bound to be baffled.

Dekker's play belongs to our first type. The opening scene exhibits Pluto and Charon in debate. It is hard times with both, for

> Ghosts come not now thronging to my boat,
> But drop by one and one in,

and the royal table needs replenishing. To meet this embarrassment three fiends are hastily dispatched to earth. Ruffman takes a courtier's disguise, and makes for the Court of young Alphonso of Naples; Grumshall dons a citizen's

---

[1] This probably translates the 'Auerhahn' of the *Faustbuch*, another link between the first great Elizabethan devil-drama and the last.

'treble ruffles' and takes service with a substantial Neapolitan merchant; and Shacklesoul, assuming the 'grave habit' of a friar, seeks the 'friery best famed in Naples for strict orders'. All three at once begin operations, and human nature, taken off its guard, everywhere succumbs. Alphonso forgets his lofty intentions and becomes a monster of lust and tyranny; Barterville, the merchant, begins to practise the 'true City doctrine' of unbridled self-regard; and the spare-living friars fall a prey to the epicurean banquets provided by their demon-cook.[1]

This play, though hasty and loosely put together, like most of Dekker's, and not comparable with Jonson's in literary force, anticipates it in several important points. Here, too, the diabolic emissary operates incognito in the world, for the better supply of damned souls; here, too, he enters the service of the persons he seeks to corrupt. And Dekker feels as acutely as Jonson the incongruity of the methods and manners of the medieval devil in the complex and sophisticated London of the seventeenth century. His devils themselves recognize the change, and adapt themselves with skill and success to the new position of the game. If the Friar is still an evident kinsman of the legendary Rush, it is because the society in which he operates is itself, for English spectators, a legend. His colleagues who practise in the City and the Court are as modern in manners as in garb. The polished urbanity of King Alphonso's guest, the ironical serviceableness of Barterville's clerk, recall the Mephistophiles of Goethe rather than of Marlowe.

But Dekker more than hints also that this modern devildom was outdone in wit. An infernal world which dropped its proper weapons and borrowed those of men necessarily lost much of its terror; it confessed itself outplayed in the game so far, and however formidable the odds, was as likely as not to get the worst in any future encounter. The

---

[1] The relations of this play with the legend of Friar Rush are more expressly dealt with in C. H. Herford's *Literary Relations of England and Germany*, p. 311 f.

fiends of Dekker quite understand this. They no longer enter upon their adventures with the old lighthearted security; they are conscious that mankind can only be mastered by an intelligent study of its methods. Thus, Charon is sometimes cheated of his fare; he proposes to raise it, but Pluto angrily intervenes lest the revised tariff should check imports, and the souls decline to enter hell at all,
> crying out th' are heere
> Worse racked then th'are in tauernes.

III

Jonson's play obviously owes something to these hints of Haughton's and of Dekker's. A hell embarrassed by modern conditions, sending its emissary to take service in the upper world—this fruitful notion he found in his old enemy's work, and applied to it his own immeasurably greater analytic and constructive power. He devised, in particular, a logical catastrophe. Dekker's devils, whatever their misgivings of failure, do in fact succeed. Jonson's, yet more clearly aware of the changed conditions, signally fail to cope with them. The trusted agents of fifty years ago, the venerable Iniquity, the once terrible Vice ' in his long coat shaking his wooden dagger' are become wholly unserviceable against the astuter generation which breeds its own vices as it does its own horses:

> Wee, still striue to breed,
> And reare 'hem vp new ones; but they doe not stand,
> When they come there: they turne 'hem on our hands.
> And it is fear'd they have a stud o' their owne
> Will put downe oures.[1]

The old savage horror, palpably fading in Dekker's play, has wholly vanished in Jonson's; the privileges of the infernal world are gone, it has sunk to the footing of a mere rival state, whose merchandise can be impounded and its citizens put in the Counter or carted to Tyburn. And this

[1] I. i. 105–9.

change of status is symbolized in the fortune of a hero who like Haughton's fiend is definitely outwitted and undone. The devil is in this play too, but the only effect of his being in it is to prove him 'an Ass'. Jonson's stupid devil owes something to both the earlier plays, is in a certain sense their logical outcome; a translation, in any case, of their devilries into Jonsonian terms. It was only as 'an Ass', only as a *stupid* devil, that the devil could be in a Jonsonian play at all. A fearsome fiend could not have taken shape under Jonson's hands; the stupidity which made him a comic figure is his passport into Jonsonian comedy; the badge which marks his fellowship with the great army of gulls who so largely people it. And the comedy of the stupid devil, like the comedy of the gull, culminates with Jonson. He had precursors in both; but just as he first made sheer fatuity laughable in Master Matthew and Master Stephen, so he was the first to give its full value to the simple incompetence of the stupid devil.

Pug, then, has traits which relate him to all the three earlier figures named. Like Grumshall, he takes service with an earthly master; like Robin, he is a boy; while his disposition is an unlucky blend of Belphegor's placidity and Robin's good-nature with a native dullness peculiarly his own. If Belphegor is outwitted, it is as one experienced strategist may be outplayed by another; but Pug is a helpless participant in a game he cannot control—the fly on the engine-wheel. There are some unmistakable reminiscences. Like Belphegor he feels anxiety about his reception on returning from his mission:

>How shall I give my verdict up to Pluto
>Of all these accidents?

asks Belphegor; and Pug almost echoing him:

>What a lost fiend
>Shall I be, on returne?[1]

Both are on the verge of suffering the indignity of execution.

---

[1] v. vi. 4.

Belphegor is saved by the mere expiry of his twelve months' limit:

> All threaten—none shall do it, for my date
> Is now expired, and I must back to hell.

Jonson, with more humour, brings in a *diabolus ex machina*, who saves the unlucky scapegrace out of pure *esprit de corps*:

> But, that I would not such a damn'd dishonor
> Sticke on our state, as that the *diuell* were hang'd;
> And could not saue a body, that he tooke
> From *Tyborne*, but it must come thither againe:
> You should e'en ride.[1]

It must be owned, however, that the natural estrangement between Jonson's art and the obsolete devilry of the stage betrays itself even in this judiciously chosen specimen, and that even his tried skill in making stupidity amusing has not saved the adventures of his stupid devil from being a little dull. Devils were not out of date in the Jacobean world for nothing; Pug's awkwardness in the midst of the changed conditions seems to have checked the abounding verve of his creator also. His nullity is, for dramatic effect, overdone: he is simply forgotten when he is out of sight; he is not even a marplot, but merely a negligible quantity, and when a character's insignificance is carried to this point, the reader is in danger of asking why a character who signifies so little should be there at all.

IV

For the real 'ass', the comic 'hero', whose fatuities actually furnish the comic matter and provoke the comic harms, is not a devil at all, but a purely human simpleton. Fitzdottrel[2] is not the best of Jonson's long line of well-

---

[1] v. vi. 69–73.
[2] Mr. Fleay's attempt to establish a connexion between Fitzdottrel and Sir Edward Coke, one of the ablest men of the day, who had been addressed by Jonson in highly honourable terms some three years before (*Underwoods*, xlvi), fails altogether. It is elaborately discussed by Mr. W. S. Johnson (Introduction, xvi. f.).

born imbeciles or 'country gulls'. But none of his predecessors was so elaborately provided with opportunities of exhibiting his folly. The bookish side of Jonson's imagination, so completely subordinate or submerged in *Bartholomew Fair*, here reasserts itself with renewed vigour. Cokes, in the *Fair*, is just Bartholomew Cokes, Esquire, of Harrow. Fitzdottrel, in comparison with these fresh observed types, smells of the laboratory; he is *made*, and his making is incomplete; his folly is an amalgam of many kinds of foolery which, unlike the ingredients of the complex melancholy of Jaques, cohere doubtfully. Like most of Jonson's foolish squires, he has a passion for wealth and social advancement. But this common trait takes singular forms. He is possessed with the dream of hidden treasure, to be revealed to him by the devil, and at the outset appears as a vulgarized Jacobean Faustus, ready, like Boccaccio's Francesco, to offer his Helen to Mephistophiles as his price, even tho' 'to be a cuckold' is 'the one main mortal thing' he fears.[1] But this infatuated treasure-seeker is also the victim of a boundless intellectual ambition: he has a wit which he credits against all mankind,

> it rauishes him forth,
> Whither it please, to any assembly' or place,
> And would conclude him ruin'd, should hee scape
> One publike meeting, out of the beliefe
> He has of his owne great, and Catholike strengths,
> In arguing, and discourse.[2]

Neither the vulgarized Faustus nor the platform-orator prepares us for the needy and parsimonious squire who is hardly induced to take Pug into his service by the reflection that it will save him £4 a year; nor again, for the patient husband who permits another to exercise his gifts of

---

[1] I. iv–vi from the *Decameron*, iii. 5. Mr. Johnson (Introduction, xlvii) points out that Jonson has greatly altered the circumstances, making Fitzdottrel arrange the 'courting' in the presence of both Wittipol and his wife. We cannot, however, agree in regarding this as a 'blunder' of Jonson's. Fitzdottrel is merely a yet more fatuous person than Francesco. A further incident in the 'courtship', II. ii. vi, is perhaps suggested by another tale of Boccaccio's *Decameron*, iii. 3.

[2] I. iv. 31–6.

'arguing and discourse' upon his own wife for the wager of a cloak. It is only when he appears as the dupe of the great projector Meercraft, and so falls back into the familiar categories of Jonson's art, that Fitzdottrel acquires body and distinct personality.

Meercraft, the principal agent in exploiting his credulity, is the true Mephistophiles of the piece—a cunning human devil who easily supplants the stupid authentic one, and provides at least the illusory prospect of treasure which the other is helpless even to suggest. And even Subtle, the alchemist, is outdone by Meercraft in riotous fertility of terms and schemes; for Subtle's erudition is the common matter of the alchemic faith; while Meercraft is a 'projector' in the fullest sense; his schemes are the mintage of his brain. Even his fertility, however, is hardly a match for Fitzdottrel's appetite; and Jonson has no more admirable gulling scene than that (III. iii) in which Fitzdottrel's reluctant attention is first caught by the lure of the 'Court of Dependencies', and then gradually fanned into an ecstasy of helpless enthusiasm by the recital, one after another, of its fascinating formalities and processes, until every instinct of avarice dissolves, and he answers with gold as fast as Meercraft can invent claims:

    I haue enough on't! for an hundred pieces?
    Yes, for two hundred, vnder-write me, doe.[1]

The further plot of the 'Spanish Lady' carries Fitzdottrel into yet giddier heights of illusion and perversity, from which his fall is abrupt, but sobering. His outburst on coming to his senses, against the whole tribe of promisers and projectors who offered to make him better or happier than he was, is admirably natural:

        I will not think; nor act;
    Nor yet recouer; do not talke to me:
    I'll runne out o' my witts, rather then heare;
    I will be what I am, *Fabian Fitz-dottrel*,
    Though all the world say nay to 't.[2]

---

[1] III. iii. 144–5.   [2] IV. vii. 90–4.

No reader of Jonson is surprised to find that this apparent recovery is not final. His gulls are at bottom beyond cure, his rogues beyond conversion, and full of resource. Under such conditions the game of cheating and being cheated can come to no natural end; and both Jonson's militant temperament and his intellectual and inventive energy prompted him to give it full scope, letting it reach an apparent issue only to start afresh on a new cue. Hence the fifth act, normally devoted to the untying of the knotted threads of the plot, with Jonson often ushers in a new and unexpected complication. In *Volpone* and *Epicoene* this new development is welded with masterly skill into the plot. But this cannot be said of the possession-feigning scenes of the present play (v. iii, viii). The plot of Meercraft and Everill to invalidate Fitzdottrel's deed of feoffment by making him feign possession by a devil has no effect on the issue, the supposed victim's confession of his 'tricks' leaving matters as they were before he thought of them, or even rendering more improbable the calm restoration of his estate ('His land is his') to the man who has sought to recover it by this dastardly incrimination of his wife. Whether or not, as has been suggested, this gratuitous piece of futility was actually added by Jonson as an after-thought, it adds nothing to the power of a play not otherwise very remarkable for coherence. Its importance lies in extraneous circumstances only—in its bearing upon the contemporary scandals of sham possession, fraudulent exorcising, and witch-hunting. To a particularly flagrant example of these Jonson explicitly refers (v. iii. 6–8); 'little *Darrels* tricks' of 1596–1600 were still well remembered. But it is probable Jonson covertly alluded to a much more recent case, that of the boy John Smith of Leicester, whose sham possession had in July, 1616, led to the conviction and execution of nine 'witches' there.[1]

[1] Cf. Professor Kittredge's article 'James I and *The Devil is an Ass*', *Mod. Philology*, 1911. The case is significant in view of the part taken by James, who visited Leicester in August, examined the boy, and obtained his confession, whereupon the judges who had convicted were

That Jonson should display a strong animus against this or any other imposture was of course to be expected from the author of *The Alchemist*. But there are some signs that ethical feeling enters more largely than usual into Jonson's scorn. Stern vindicator of justice as he believed himself to be, he was neither very consistent nor very happy in his attitude as a dramatist towards moral force. The men who circumvent his rogues are rarely very successful as characters unless they have a spice of roguery themselves; and Jonson sometimes has the air of punishing them for their honesty, like Surly, by allowing them to be finally circumvented. The three characters who, in the upshot, appear to be champions of honesty, are drawn with less power and consistency than many less worthy persons; their speech is curiously equivocal and fluctuating; but at their highest they reach the accents of a very noble speech. Manly, less substantial than Surly, is more disinterested, and plays his honest game with more skill and better success. Wittipol, up to the end of the third act, is not easily distinguished from the unscrupulous gallant, Boccaccio's Il Zima, whose exploit he copies. And the lady, too, is up to that point not sharply marked off from her prototype, Francesco's wife. The fourth act compels us to revise our conception of both characters, but not without severely straining our sense of their consistency and coherence. In Mrs. Fitz-dottrel Jonson appears to have intended to draw an honest wife who, in just resentment at the outrage done her by her foolish husband, is willing to go some length in indulging the passion of her admirer. But her passive submission, after the faintest of protests, to the wager, and then her demure acceptance of Wittipol's extremely unreserved ' courtship', at the window (II. vi), do not suggest this

reproved, and the remaining prisoners released. In drastically exposing the fraud Jonson was thus acting in harmony with the king's known opinions. In Justice Eitherside he may, as Professor Kittredge thinks, have glanced at Winch, the Leicester judge. But Eitherside is satirized, if at all, less for his mistaken action in the trial than for the plasticity of mind which prompts his ready conversion.

interpretation, and afford it but the slightest of foothold when it is suggested by her subsequent conduct. We are half inclined to accept her husband's judgement of her as a *niaise* (I. vi. 18), little as he is entitled to pronounce it. The fourth act shows this *niaise* transformed without notice into a woman of lofty ethical power and commanding eloquence. Sudden awakenings of the moral nature have their due place, no doubt, in drama, as they have in the world of psychological experience, which the drama is supposed to reflect. But there was no kind of internal experience in which the psychology of the Elizabethans was more often at fault. And the gravest defect of Jonson as a dramatist, his want of imaginative sympathy with his creations, is nowhere so manifest as when he attempts to exhibit them in growth and movement, to become not their portrait-painter but their historian. *The Devil is an Ass* shows an undiminished freshness of invention and an unexpected capacity of crossing the apparently rigid limits of his artistic domain; and it contains one scene in which Jonson touches the limits of his virtuosity in the language of lyric love. But it betrays, none the less, a more than incipient decadence of constructive power; a decadence accompanied, however, by no corresponding decay of the power of style which was still to cast a fitful splendour over even the worst of his 'dotages', and destined to be interrupted by at least one energetic rally of his virile genius.

INTRODUCTION TO
'THE STAPLE OF NEWS'

THE STAPLE OF NEWS

I

LIKE *Bartholomew Fair*, *The Staple of News* was first printed in 1631. It had been designed for publication some years before, having been entered in the Stationers' Register on April 14, 1626. It was then certainly new. An unmistakable allusion in III. ii. 300, 'Now, at the Coronation', makes it clear that it was performed soon after that event, which occurred on February 2, 1626.[1] We may also assume from the introduction of Mirth, in the Induction, as the 'daughter of *Christmas*, and spirit of *Shrouetide*', that Shrovetide (February 19th) had already begun. It was performed by the King's Men, first on the public stage, then at the Court; being recommended to the audience, in the one case by a vigorous rallying Prologue, in the other by a graceful Sonnet.

How these audiences received it may fairly be gathered from Jonson's curious effort to placate them,—the address 'To the Readers' prefixed to the third act of the printed drama. The allegory and purpose of the author in the great Staple scene of this act were, he complains, 'wholly mistaken, and so sinister an interpretation . . . made, as if the soules of most of the *Spectators* had liu'd in the eyes and eares of these ridiculous Gossips that tattle betweene the *Acts*'.

Jonson had some reason to resent this grudging reception of his play. The ten years that had passed since *The Devil is an Ass* had not in any degree withered or staled his powers; at fifty-three his vein was as rich as it had been at forty. *The Staple of News* was, beyond question, a greater and stronger drama than its immediate predecessor.

[1] Fleay, *Biog. Chr.* i. 384. The date '1625' given on the title-page of the first edition as the year of its first performance is thence to be understood as Old Style.

The Devil is not without some marks of weariness; of the two, it prophesies far more obviously of the decadence which, almost on the morrow of *The Staple*, was to become disastrously clear. His record during the interim suggests flagging interest in the drama, but not decline of dramatic power. The Christmas and Twelfth Night masques produced by him during this period of estrangement from the stage contain some of his happiest and most brilliant inventions, and his services had never been more in request at Court. From about 1620, too, the Court Masque had shown a lively attraction towards the comedy of the regular stage; the rough comic realism of the Antimasque, originally a mere foil to the stately dance and song, was becoming the principal business. Chapman and Fletcher had taken the lead in this innovation; it was clearly popular, and Jonson, little as he loved to accept other men's guidance, had probably no choice but to follow suit. The result was the exuberant comedy of *The Gypsies Metamorphosed*, performed thrice during the summer of 1622; or of the prelude to *Time Vindicated*, where the allegoric motive of Fame, treated in the spirit of serious poetry in *The Masque of Queens*, yields a series of purely comic scenes. To pass from masques like these to regular comedy involved no such violent transition as when in former days he had turned, say, from the *Masque of Blackness*—a tissue of more or less elegant symbolism—to *Volpone*. We know, in fact, that Jonson had, by 1623, at least, returned to drama; 'parcels of a play' having been among the ruins wrought by Vulcan in his library. And if his later masques had assimilated something of the method of comedy, the play with which he now returned to the stage showed, in its turn, traces of the masque-writing of the immediately preceding years. The idea of a 'Staple of News', with the humours of printer, factor, and the rest, had already been sketched in *News from the New World*; the comic parallel of poet and cook in *Neptune's Triumph* is resumed in Lickfinger, who happily combines these callings. The story of the Prodigal and Miser has no such direct connexion with any masque. But its allegoric abstraction and obtrusive moral symbolism palpably, recall the characteristic themes of the Masque proper, the nucleus which all the realist and humorous accretions of the latest variety did not extrude. Never since *Cynthia's Revels* had Jonson so freely admitted to his stage persons who have a symbolic as well as a strictly human value. He is not a whit afraid of his allegory, and mixes it in boldly with the more matter-of-fact business of the piece. No art could make the mixture of elements so discrepant altogether acceptable. But Jonson brought to the problem he had created all the resources of his tried stage-craft and of his rich invention, and the result was a drama which in its least admirable portions shows an astonishing talent for giving abstractions the semblance of life, while in its greatest scenes it falls short of nothing that he had ever done.

Notwithstanding these and similar links with his recent work in other fields, the nucleus of the play allies it unmistakably with the comic masterpieces of the previous decades. A partnership of rogues for exploiting the credulity of the public, the business of the Staple is but one more variation on the business of Volpone's sick chamber, of Subtle's laboratory, and of the great Fair itself. Cymbal is an alchemist of News, who feeds the idle curiosity of his clients with the products of his crucibles; and both he and they are drawn with a relative amenity, corresponding to the less criminal quality of their imposture.

But the *Staple* differed from all these precursors in having in view a quite recent feature of London social life. Alchemy was old-established and deeply rooted; the Fair was immemorial; but systematic 'news-mongering' had been first projected and practised in England only a few years before Jonson wrote.

The outbreak in 1618 of a great war on the Continent, and the ensuing disasters to the throne and fortunes of an English princess, had created throughout the country an interest beyond all precedent in continental news. Already in the summer of 1621 we hear of sheets printed 'every week at least', 'with all manner of news, & a strange stuffe as any we have from Amsterdam'.[1] This free circulation of unauthorized reports of important events, whether 'strange' or authentic, was not likely to be welcome to any Government, and the words just quoted were occasioned by 'a new Proclamation (of July 24, 1621) against lavish and licentious talking in matters of State either at home or abroad'.[2] As Germany was the focus of interest, the Low Countries were the natural mediating agency, and it is clear from the above allusion that Amsterdam was already notorious for the sensational flavour of the 'news' it produced. It is not surprising that the earliest regular newssheet run in London was simply translated from the Dutch.

Two such enterprises, at least, can be distinguished in London from 1622 onwards, each of which contributed traits to Jonson's picture of the Staple, and probably persons to its staff. Both were started by London 'stationers'. These were:

1. *Weekely Nevves from Italie, Germanie, Hungaria, Bohemia, the Palatinate, France, and the Low Countries, Translated out of the Low Dutch Copie.* London. Printed by I. D. for Nicolas Bourne and Thomas Archer, and are to be sold at their shops at the Exchange, and in Popeshead Pallace. (May 23) 1622.

2. *Newes from most parts of Christendom.* September 25, 1622. This was issued by Nathaniel Butter, in co-operation with William Shefford, whose shop, like Archer's, was in Popes-head Alley.

By 1623 there was apparently another, the *Weekly Courants with Paules Seale*, referred to by Jonson in the 'Execration upon Vulcan', ll. 79–81.[3]

Of the 'stationers' who ran these sheets and the editors who collected, arranged, or invented the 'news' little is

---

[1] Chamberlain to Carleton (*State Papers, Domestic*, August 4, 1621).
[2] Rymer's *Foedera*, xviii, p. 314.   [3] See note there.

definitely known. But two figures stand out with some distinctness in the lurid uncertain light of contemporary satire. One is the 'stationer' Nathaniel Butter, joint founder of the second of the news-sheets, and traceable everywhere in the 'butter' allusions of his contemporaries as well as of the present play. 'I would set up a press here in Italy,' says Coxcomb in Fletcher's[1] *Fair Maid of the Inn*, IV. ii (licensed 1626), 'to write all the corantoes for Christendom' (with obvious allusion to the title of Butter's sheet); and he applies to Forobosco to provide him with a docile spirit for the purpose. Forobosco promises him 'the ghost of some lying stationer, a spirit shall look as if butter would not melt in his mouth; a new *Mercurius Gallo-Belgicus*'.

The other was a 'captain', undoubtedly to be identified with an old soldier of the Irish wars, Captain Gainford (or Gainsford), a more redoubtable person, and as terrifying in journalism as in war.[2] Coxcomb, in the scene just

[1] This scene is possibly Jonson's.
[2] The *Irish State Papers*, 1600, No. 80, mention a 'Captain Gainsford' as wounded in a skirmish with Tyrone. They also mention, 1603-6, a 'Francis Gainford', or Gainsforde, who receives a pension of 3*s.* 6*d.* a day. Sir S. Lee in *D. N. B., u. s.*, identifies 'Captain Gainsford' with Thomas Gainsford, a somewhat voluminous writer of the time, and does not notice the reference to Francis Gainsford. We believe that he is right. Francis's name occurs, without addition, in a list where the rank or title is elsewhere added; he was therefore presumably not 'Captain Gainsford'. And Thomas Gainsford's writings not only suggest the vein of exuberant rhodomontade to which the contemporary allusions point, they show that he had actual experience in the Irish wars. Numerous allusions to his participation as an eyewitness in this campaign are scattered through his writings. Thus in his *The Glory of England, or A true description of many excellent prerogatiues and remarkable blessings whereby she Triumpheth ouer all the Nations of the World . . .* (1618), he gives (Book i, chap. xviii) a 'description of Ireland', with several personal reminiscences, e. g. (p. 147) good fishing: 'a Trout . . . taken up in *Tyrone* 46 inches long, and presented to the L. Montioy, then Deputie: you would demand, whether I was *oculatus testis*, and I answer, I eat my part of it, and as I take it both my L. Daueis, and *Sir William Goodolphin* were at the table' (p. 293): 'in our owne Kingdome of *Ireland* . . . I was my selfe an eare-witnesse.' Further, Gainsford wrote the Life of Tyrone, again with emphatic assertions of first-hand knowledge: 'The True Exemplary, and Remarkable History of the Earle of Tirone, . . . Not from the report of others, or collections of Authors, but by him who was an eye witness of his fearefull wretched-

quoted, rejoins to Forobosco's vaunt: 'Oh there was a captain was rare at it.' 'Neer think of him,' retorts Forobosco,

> Though that captaine writ a full hand gallop,
> And wasted indeed more harmlesse paper then
> Ever did laxative Physick,
> Yet wil I make you to outscribble him.

Jonson himself, in the 'Execration', counts the works of this scribbling Captain among the rubbish which Vulcan had better have devoured.

> —Captain *Pamphlets* horse, and foot; that sallie
> Upon th' Exchange still, out of Popes-head-Alley.

And twenty years later, when militant journalism was no longer a lively figure of speech, but an urgent need, a pamphleteer could recall the almost unrivalled feats of nes and finall extirpation.' It is dedicated to the Earl of Clenricard, whom Gainsford says he saw 'knighted . . . in the durty fields before Kinsole. . . . I was in those dayes beholding to your Table and Purse, and in a manner the third Officer of your Regimen.' In the title-page of this and his other books, Gainsford describes himself as 'T. G. Esquire'. But his identity with the Captain Gainsford of the State Papers is further confirmed by the Elegy which 'Captain Tho: Gainsford' contributed to the eighth edition of Sir T. Overbury's *Wife, and Characters*.

Other circumstances in Gainsford's career show that he was marked out to be the first Master of a Staple of News. Thus, even if we discount his profession (*The Glory of England*, Preface, p. 8) that he is about to relate what he had himself 'knowne, as *oculatus testis*, in most countries of Europe', it is probable that he knew enough about many strange lands to furnish forth a plausible 'Newes Letter' about them even had he been less of the born journalist than he evidently was. He was, moreover, already practised in the art of contriving such letters, having published a collection of model epistles of this kind—an early example of the type. This was: *The Secretaries Studie: Containing new familiar Epistles or Directions, for the formall, orderly, and iudicious inditing of Letters* (1616). It is dedicated to a 'Right hopeful Yong Gentleman' at Charterhouse, and evidently written for the benefit of such persons. After giving models of many other types of epistle, he devotes a last section (pp. 104–24) to 'Letters of Newes', under such headings as 'Newes from Constantinople', 'Newes from Malta', 'Newes from Venice', 'Newes from Zidon, and Ierusalem', &c.

It only remains to add that Gainsford was already, in 1618, associated with Nathaniel Butter, having published with him, in that year, his *True and Wonderfull History of Perkin Warbeck*.

It cannot be doubted that this was the scribbling Captain of contemporary satire.

the Captain who heretofore wrote weekly intelligence from *Popes-Head Alley*; who usually took Townes in Cyder, and after his second draught in *Metheglin* still struck in with the Surdes, and in lesse then two Houres operation ordinarily over-runne all the chiefe parts of *Germany*. I never knew any professed sword man but this make *Gazets* his Trade of living'.[1]

It seems certain that this literary Captain died in 1624, the year following Jonson's allusion in the 'Execration'.[2] He was thus dead at the date of the *Staple*.

Nathaniel Butter, then, and 'the Captain' were two familiar and well-remembered figures in the London of 1626. And Jonson has clearly made ample use of at least one of them in *The Staple of News*. In Nathaniel, the Clerk of the Staple, the 'stationer' was of course instantly recognized. But Cymbal, the Master of the Staple, though clearly meant to recall the Captain, is still distinguished from him. For 'the Captain' is said (I. i) to be dead, as Gainsford actually was, and the Captain's loose habits in the provision of news are equally superseded, we are given to understand, in the severely business-like Staple of Cymbal. The countrywoman who would have a groat's-worth of any news, she cares not what, to carry down this Saturday to her vicar, is told to 'haue patience':

It is not now, as when the *Captaine* liu'd.[3]

The days of impromptu news production, we are to understand, are gone by; you now had to wait to be 'fitted' till the correspondents (or 'emissaries') came in from the Exchange or Paul's. Other bad practices of the older newsmongers are corrected, we are told, with Jonsonian irony, under Cymbal's stricter rule; if the news is 'buttered', there is at least no 'buttering over again of antiquated pamphlets'. The old soldier had overdone the thing with his

[1] *Mercurius Anti-Britannicus, or the Second Part of the King's Cabinet* [1645], p. 24.
[2] Chamberlain to Carleton, September 4, 1624 (*State Papers, Domestic, James I*, clxxii. 5): 'The season is sickly, the deaths last week 407; among them . . . Capt. Gainford, the gazette maker.'
[3] I. iv. 17.

headstrong military methods. Jonson evidently has in mind an astuter kind of rascal, who casts his nets wide, employs a battalion of correspondents, clerks, translators, and makes a brave show of superior trustworthiness and authenticity. He is a 'wit', 'a man of fine sounds', a 'tinkling captain', 'grand captain of the Jeerers'; and he is well aware of his superiority to the agents he employs, one half the proceeds of the business being divided, with the same systematic precision, among his underlings, while a 'just moiety' goes to himself.

In all this and much more, the marks of caricature are apparent. We need not suppose the Staple itself to have been an actual institution, and the evidence that it was is mainly derived from Jonson's own vivid scenes. He himself warns us not to accept his picture as literal truth. We 'shew you common follies,' he declares in the Prologue at Court,

and so knowne,
That though they are not truths, th' innocent *Muse*
Hath made so like, as Phant'sie could them state,
Or *Poetry*, without scandall, imitate.

And in the address to the reader prefixed to the third act he repudiates with great emphasis the too liberal and matter-of-fact interpretation put forward by 'most of the *Spectators*', in the spirit of the 'ridiculous Gossips that tattle between the *Acts*. But hee prayes you thus to mend it. To consider the *Newes* here vented, to be none of his *Newes*, or any reasonable mans; but *Newes* made like the times *Newes*, (a weekly cheat to draw mony) and could not be fitter reprehended, then in raising this ridiculous *Office* of the *Staple*, wherein the age may see her owne folly, or hunger and thirst after publish'd pamphlets of *Newes*, set out euery Saturday, but made all at home, and no syllable of truth in them . . . .' The 'Staple' is thus simply a satirical device, an imaginary fabric 'raised' by the poet, and deliberately made 'ridiculous' in order to compel the infatuated public to recognize the folly of its blind hunger and thirst for news by a concrete *reductio ad absurdum*.

This is confirmed by many features of the execution. The very idea of a 'Staple of News' is a felicitous and witty application of the model of the old-established Staples of great national industries, like wool, to the new industry of news-production. And the idea is worked out, as already noticed, on lines familiar to Jonson's comic art. The Staple Office is simply a variant of the Alchemist's Laboratory, devised for the fabrication of news instead of gold, and the exploitation of uncritical curiosity instead of vulgar greed. Like the Aristophanic 'Thinking shop' it sets a grotesque and ludicrous colour upon a rudiment of fact, and this Staple may well be a little nearer to the actual newsmongering of Jonson's London than the *Phrontisterion* was to the dialectic of Socrates. But the invention is made plausible by a variety of devices. The men who work it are chosen, like the imaginary correspondents of the *Tatler* eighty-four years later, from the resorts popularly credited with ready access to news: Fitton the 'court-rat'; Picklock the lawyer; 'Emissary Westminster', with his 'worming brain, and wriggling ingine-head'; Ambler who paces the aisles of Paul's; Nathaniel, the 'decayed stationer', most notorious of the actual newsmongers of the day; Thomas the barber, by profession a member of the most ancient order of newsmongers in the world. But if this Staple had analogies in the industrial sphere, its ancestry belonged to poetic tradition. Literary comparisons emerge unprovoked in the minds of its officials. ''Tis the House of Fame, sir,' declares the Registrar to young Peniboy—

> 'Tis the house of *fame*, Sir,
> Where both the curious, and the negligent;
> The scrupulous, and carelesse; wilde, and stay'd;
> The idle, and laborious; all doe meet,
> To tast the *Cornu copiæ* of her rumors,
> Which she, the mother of sport, pleaseth to scatter
> Among the vulgar.[1]

And the final collapse of the adventure is told, by Tom

[1] III. ii. 115-21.

the barber, in terms which might describe the sudden annihilation of some wizard's den:

> Our *Staple* is all to pieces, quite dissolu'd! ...
> Shiuer'd, as in an earth-quake! heard you not
> The cracke and ruines? we are all blowne vp! ...
> Our *Emissaries, Register, Examiner,*
> Flew into vapor: our graue Governor
> Into a subt'ler ayre.[1]

II

The 'Staple' scenes are, beyond question, the salt of the play. It is in them alone that the claim of this drama to a place in the first rank of Jonson's comedies must rest. They form nevertheless only a brilliant episode; the main drift and purport of the plot are symbolized by the visit of the spendthrift Peniboy and his Lady Pecunia. It is money interest which drives the Staple; its lies are priced and paid for, its clerks pay huge sums for the posts which entitle them even to a small fraction of the profits. In an imitation of our play, Davenant's *News from Plymouth* (licensed 1635), a Staple is founded purely as a pastime by a foolish knight;[2] but Jonson's Staple is built upon money greed, held together by the cash nexus, and collapses upon the failure of funds. But Jonson has chosen to graft upon this financial speculation a story of inferior quality and interest, in which money and its various uses and abuses are the primary theme. It is the customers of the Staple whose fortunes are brought most prominently before us; and the concerns of the prin-

---

[1] v. i. 39–47.
[2] Koeppel, B. *Jonson's Wirkung auf zeitgenossische Dramatiker*, p. 130. Sir Solemn Trifle, Justice of Peace and Custos Rotulorum, with the assistance of a single clerk, provides 'news' for the general benefit from Rome, Florence, and elsewhere: the Prince of Orange is to be Emperor, the Pope is turned Brownist, Antichrist is converted, and so forth. But Trifle is only a practical jester, and Topsail asks, with an amazement which would have been quite unnecessary in Butter's case:

> But what's your end, Sir Trifle?
> Or the delight you take, if there be any,
> In broaching these unpossible untruths?

cipal group of them are developed along lines with which the Staple has very little to do. Young Peniboy, the hero, both as a Jonsonian personage and as a figure in the drama at large, has a complex ancestry. He has some traits in common with freehanded young gallants of the type of Asotus in *Cynthia's Revels*; like Asotus he makes love to a representative of wealth (Argurion, Pecunia), whose allegorical habitually endangers her human value. Like Deliro, Albius, and Littlewit, he is alive to the social value of an attractive wife, and causes her to requite his friend's compliments with kisses, as Asotus disposes of Argurion's jewelled chains and pendants to the Court ladies.[1] But Peniboy is some degrees farther than Asotus from the mere personified Humour; after his first escapades, he develops, learns wisdom, detects and frustrates the plot to which he is expected to fall a victim, and recovers in a quite natural way his father's favour and his own better self—a climax more acceptable to ordinary dramatic instincts than the huge Aristophanic or Lucianic jest of the 'Palinode' in which Asotus and the rest recant their sins. Peniboy is, in short, in spite of the ambiguous humanity of his mistress, a thoroughly human creature; no mere type of Prodigality, but a genuine specimen of the dramatic Prodigal. In England hitherto, the figure of the Prodigal had not, as such, obtained any great vogue on the stage. The London playwrights of Shakespeare's generation were too familiar with the type to find it very interesting, and it was represented, so far as their purses permitted, in the majority of their own order. The pictures of headstrong young men defying the counsels of sage experience which meet us, a generation earlier, in *Lusty Juventus* or *The Disobedient Child*, and Gascoigne's *Glass of Government*, had been drawn by devout or Puritan moralists, in the interest of an austere ideal of family life not widely current among those who either frequented, or purveyed for, the popular stage. Even the abundant and purely mundane examples of loose-living sons and anxious

[1] *Cynthia's Revels*, IV. iii.

fathers offered by Roman comedy were turned to account mainly by Christian Terences of this type, who used them to fill in the missing scenes in the story of the biblical Prodigal, their standing model. In the mature drama the biblical Prodigal survives chiefly in plays of definitely bourgeois cast, like *Eastward Ho*. The Prodigals of classic comedy, too, count for less, even with scholarly dramatists like the authors of the Parnassus plays, than the living types of youthful dissipation before their eyes; and in Jonson's own Know'ell and Wellbred the Plautine free-living son is merely recalled without being obtruded. But beside the free-living son Jonson set the anxious and inquisitive father, still recalling Plautus, but effacing the last trace of biblical reminiscence. The adventures of the elder Know'ell belong to a type of situation which during the next decade won a decided vogue: that of the person in authority watching, unsuspected, the 'tricks', usually more or less 'fantastic', of his subordinate. King Henry chatting incognito with his troopers at Agincourt (1599); the Friar-Duke witnessing unrecognized the self-betrayal of Angelo (*c.* 1603); Duke Hercules, in Marston's *Parasitaster* (printed 1606), following his son Tiberio to the Court of Urbino to watch his conduct disguised as a parasite, are examples in regions of drama utterly remote from one another. An allied variety of this situation represented the watching of an unseen providence rather than of a detective; the persons being here usually father and child. Friscobaldo in Dekker's *Honest Whore* watches tenderly over the hazardous fortunes of his daughter. One may even venture to recall in this connexion the ghostly visitant in *Hamlet* who reappears 'his tardy son to chide'. In the play of *The London Prodigal*, finally (by 1605), this hidden-providence motive is combined, not ineffectively, with a story of the genuine 'prodigal' type. Old Flowerdale is reported to be dead; Young Flowerdale 'comes to his own' and exhibits all the traditional infirmities of the young heir released from constraint. But the father watches over him, relieves his necessities, and finally discloses his identity and receives the Prodigal's repentance. That the corresponding feature of Jonson's play was suggested by *The London Prodigal* can hardly be doubted.[1] Peniboy Canter, like Old Flowerdale, is reported dead, and his supposed will, though of opposite tenor in the two cases,—for Young Flowerdale finds himself disinherited,—plays an equal part in the subsequent evolution of each plot. But the points of resemblance, though decisive for Jonson's knowledge of the older play, do not go very deep, and the whole pathetic story of Luce, in particular, has no counterpart in the latter. It is doubtful whether such a story was not beyond his powers; but in any case his concern here was with satire and comedy, not with pathos; and different fortunes inevitably await Peniboy and his bride. Even Jonsonian comedy, however, did not involve that their story should be as poor in human interest as it is. Young Peniboy is sufficiently alive, and his impulsive good nature gives scope and promise enough of comic entanglements. But the Lady Pecunia, his bride, is merely a symbol, unelusively dressed as a woman, and her abstractness, never wholly forgotten, exerts a paralysing influence upon all the relations in which she has a part. Pecunia, however, 'now a woman, now a money-bag', is only the point at which the abstractness of Jonson's comic scheme emerges most nakedly. His Prodigal story is but a translation, executed with varying success, of an ethical classification into its human equivalents. The Aristotelean triad of Prodigality, Parsimony, and Liberality, was never perhaps more effectively turned into drama, but its scholastic formality is not overcome. The disguised father of *The London Prodigal*, who instigates the unscrupulous designs of his scapegrace son, now appears as the standard of golden mediocrity in the use of wealth, and the mouthpiece of Jonson's weighty wisdom on this fertile topic. Golden mediocrity is a theme more favourable to good sense than to poetry; but the Canter's

---

[1] Cf. Mr. de Winter's scholarly introduction to *The Staple of News* (1905), where the parallels are exhaustively stated. But we cannot follow him in ascribing *The London Prodigal* also to Jonson's hand.

summing up is not inferior in its dignified eloquence to the fierce declamation of Timon against 'this yellow slave':

>   *Pecunia* her selfe,
> Is come to free him fairely, and discharge
> All ties, but those of *Loue*, vnto her person,
> To vse her like a friend, not like a slaue,
> Or like an *Idoll.* Superstition
> Doth violate the Deity it worships:
> No lesse then scorne doth. And beleeve it, *brother*,
> The vse of things is all, and not the *Store*.[1]

III

In this allegorical treatment of Wealth, Jonson clearly, and indeed inevitably, had in mind the satirical comedy in which Aristophanes so trenchantly exposed the naïve illusions of the plain man about riches, and extolled 'Poverty' as the nurse of arts and mother of inventions. Yet the points of contact with the *Plutus* in our play are neither very numerous nor very important. Chremylos, who is good but poor, and being good thinks that he ought to be rich, resembles the Canter chiefly in having a son of an opposite turn of mind. But Blepsidemus is frankly 'bad', and plays a minor part in the action. It is rather in the ideal 'Poverty' (*Penia*) and in the 'Just man' that, if anywhere, we may discover points of possible contact with the Jonsonian 'Canter'. Penia, too, stands, not for destitution, but for the mean or moderate state, distinguished alike from Beggary and from Luxury; 'a life of frugality and attention to business, having nothing that you can spare but also lacking nothing that you want';[2] and she expounds the philosophy of this state as eloquently as he. No one understood better than Jonson the worth of this sober and strenuous 'poverty'; and there is more of the Aristophanic Penia than of Horace in the lines which he had put into the mouth of his own 'Horace' in the *Poetaster*:

[1] v. vi. 19–26.   [2] *Plutus*, ll. 552–3.

> As if the filth of pouertie sunke as deepe
> Into a knowing spirit, as the bane
> Of riches doth, into an ignorant soule.[1]

Under the defective distribution of wealth which marks the existing régime, the 'Just man' is the principal sufferer. He wears, like the Canter, a ragged cloak; and this symptom of his need is symbolically transferred from his shoulders to those of the Sycophant who has thriven upon the misuse of wealth.[2] In the same way Canter, after discomfiting his heir by his unexpected reappearance transfers his rags to the Prodigal. But these resemblances are insignificant at most. Even the figure of Pecunia herself cannot be said to have more in common with that of Plutus than that both are personifications of wealth.[3] Aristophanes had here the advantage of drawing upon a still living mythology; Plutus, like Dionysos, Hermes, and the rest, stood ready to his hand, present to the fancy, and not too remote from the faith, of all his hearers. Jonson had not this advantage; and it is likely that with his sturdy faith in invention and the inexhaustible fertility of 'Nature' he grieved very little at the loss. The traditional forms of myth and folk-lore rarely allured him, resolute stickler as he was for fidelity to history. His Lady Pecunia was not his own device—nearly thirty years earlier Barnfield had composed his *Encomion to the Lady Pecunia* (1598); she bears in every feature the mark of fabricated, not inspired, work, and Jonson's attempt to give her vitality by connecting her with the political sensation of the hour has merely added a second and confusing symbol to the first. For no better reason, apparently, than that Spain was the mistress of the golden El Dorado in the west, and that any allusion to the frustrated Spanish match was sure of applause, Pecunia is made to stand for the Infanta whose hand Prince

---

[1] *Poet.* v. i. 81-3.   [2] *Plutus*, l. 936 f.
[3] She is nearer of kin to the all-attractive Lady Mead, in Langland's *Vision*. To Aristophanes Jonson here also owed little but general hints, in themselves the commonplaces of all the world-old satire upon wealth. Pecunia, like Plutus, is universally needed, and all men flock around her.

Charles, now king, to the delirious joy of the nation had just failed to obtain. She is '*Infanta* of the *Mines*',[1] 'a great Princesse, of mighty power,'[2]—Aurelia Clara Pecunia. Less laboriously vitalized, but more alive, are Pecunia's attendants, Mistress Band, Mistress Statute, and Rose Wax the Chambermaid,—'a good plyant wench, and easie to be wrought'.[3] If the humanity of Pecunia is crushed beneath the symbolism, her attendants, barely touched with the brush, wear their symbolic names as lightly, and with almost as little detriment to their human nature, as any 'Cash' or 'Downright' of his prime.

Old Peniboy, the miser, too, is one of Jonsons best usurers, admirable in his secure and disdainful mastery of the situation while Pecunia remains in his charge, in his final collapse and surrender, even in the burlesque 'trial' of the offending dogs. The idea was no doubt suggested by Aristophanes' *Vespae*, l. 891 f., but, as usual, Jonson has worked it out altogether in his own way. It cannot be claimed, however, that his 'dog-trial' is either as amusing in itself, or at all as proper to the business of the play. In Aristophanes it happily parodies the Athenian passion for lawsuits: and his dog as prosecutor, if more uproariously farcical, is also better farce than the dog-trial, which merely illustrates the derangement of their master. 'All things are subservient to wealth,' declares the Aristophanic Chremylos.[4] 'All this *Nether-world* is yours, you command it, and doe sway it,' Old Peniboy assures Pecunia.[5] The whole action of the *Plutus* might be considered an expansion of this thought; scene after scene exhibits the supreme importance, for all sorts and conditions of men, of the god of wealth. Jonson's play resists so summary a description. But certain scenes, in particular the greater part of Act II, have little closer connexion with the plot than that of illustrating the same fertile common-place. Piedmantle, Fitton, Almanac, Shunfield, Madrigal,

---

[1] Intermean II. [2] I. vi. 46. [3] II. ii. 33-4.
[4] *Plutus*, l. 145 f. [5] Act II. i. 38-9.

hover about the house of the miser 'to see Pecunia', as her suitors and servants. Many of the old 'Humour' types may be recognized in this sorry crew—the Court-politician, the astrologer, the military poltroon, the affected rhymester,[1] but the colours are palpably faded ; Madrigal is not to be compared with Master Matthew, Fitton with Sir Politick, far less Shunfield with Bobadill, while the 'Jeerers' and the 'noble whimsy' of the 'Canters' College', vivaciously enough described, cannot be compared for *vis comica* with his earlier picture of the Lady Collegiates in *Epicoene*. And when, in the last scene, the whole 'covey' of the Jeerers scatters in headlong flight, they exhibit a want of stamina in keeping with their inferiority in poetical substance. It is as if the mighty Jonsonian scorn for shams, working here always near the verge of allegory, and crossing it often in great headstrong lunges and gasconnades, had wreaked itself at parting on this bevy of futile pretenders by exposing them as the hollow phantoms they were—

> a poore, affrighted,
> And guilty race of men, that dare to stand
> No breath of truth : but conscious to themselues
> Of their no-wit, or honesty, ranne routed
> At euery *Panicke* terror themselues bred.[2]

In such passages the rude vehemence of the Jonsonian

---

[1] Madrigal has been supposed by some critics to stand for a living original. The most plausible guess is that of Mr. de Winter (*Staple of News*, p. lv f.), who is confident that he is Wither. In favour of this contention is the fact that Jonson had actually ridiculed Wither in the masque of *Time Vindicated* in January, 1624, just two years before. Some tricks of Wither's seem to be glanced at in Madrigal : his somewhat self-conscious pose as the satirist of 'the time' ('the crowned *Poet* of these our times', I. vi. 81), his prolix and nauseously minute inventory of his mistress's charms in the eulogy on Pecunia (IV. ii). But Madrigal has other traits not proper to Wither. Wither was not very conspicuously a madrigal-writer, still less could it be pretended that he could write nothing but madrigals and had his name thence. Jonson drew his sketch with a lively remembrance of one who had recently provoked him, but we must not 'identify' the two.—Mr. Fleay's declaration that Madrigal 'is, of course, Jonson himself' is apparently based upon Peniboy Junior's reference to him as Horace : 'And *Horace* here' shall read the '*Art* of *Poetry*' (IV. iv. 95). Jonson had shown dislike for the Madrigal, as a light form of verse, in *Epicoene*, II. iii.

[2] V. vi. 2–7.

scorn rises into poetry, and the old Canter, in his beggar's rags, becomes the prophet, as Jonson himself in his best hours had always been, of an ideal order founded upon measure and upon truth. Against this order the buffoon licence of the Jeerers and the organized lying of the Staple are equally grave and equally rampant offences. And behind and underlying both he saw the worship of wealth, inciting the hungry pretenders to their frauds and the newsmongers to their fabrications, and only variously disguised in the miser and the prodigal. Pecunia, the least vital figure in the piece, is thus in some sense its subject, a heroine in her human capacity negligible, barely credible, but as a symbol the source of a universal attraction which gives an inner unity to an otherwise loosely ordered play.

Among other old devices of his dramatic technique which he resumed in this first drama of his later days, was the colloquy of critical comment interposed between the acts. Nothing in the play shows better, however, than the Induction and 'Intermeans' how vastly Jonson's art had progressed since the days when the tedious involution of the action of *Every Man out of his Humour* had paused in order that Cordatus and Mitis might expound and admire. That deep-rooted instinct of his doctrinaire mind to instruct the public what to admire and why was at length mastered, and he tried the more promising path of ironical self-ridicule, with more covert but good-humoured banter of his audience. Mirth, Censure, Expectation, and Tattle are dramatic figures of much vivacity, and their scornful cavils at the play, with its lack of 'Divells' and Fools, their epigrammatic sketches of Pecunia and the Peniboys, and their merciless caricature of the person of Jonson himself, exhibit the flexibility of temper which Jonson's comic manner had now gained, without any sacrifice of his strong and vivid touch.

INTRODUCTION TO 'THE NEW INN'

THE NEW INN

THE comedy of *The New Inn* was first published in 1631, in a single octavo volume, having been entered in the Stationers' Register on April 17th of that year. It was not included in the second volume of the Folio, and was first reprinted in the Third Folio of 1692.[1] The first performance, probably on January 19, 1629,[2] had been disastrous. The actors, if Jonson's angry epithets of two years later do not slander them, had grossly neglected, or even openly derided, their somewhat thankless parts; and a large section of the audience appear to have walked out before the end.[3] Some personal allusion hidden under the seemingly innocent name of the chambermaid, 'Cis', further disturbed the temper of the public, and the play was decisively damned. A second performance before the Court had been intended, and Jonson now appealed, in a new and specially written Epilogue, from the vulgar audience that had trampled upon his pearls, to the choicer and more critical spectators 'aboue the stayres, and past the guard', who would understand their value. This audience would not 'hisse Because the Chamber-

[1] Statements to the contrary rest on error. No known copy of the 'Second' Folio (1631-41) contains this play. Cf. Dr. W. W. Greg, in *A List of Masques, Pageants, &c.*, p. xvii note.

[2] The date depends on Malone's report of an entry in the lost Office-book of the Master of the Revels, stating that the play was licensed on January 19, 1629, and on the assumption, probably correct, that this was the date of the first performance. Cf. Malone in Variorum ed., 1821, i, p. 421.

[3] The statement made by Gifford, and frequently repeated since (Ward, *Hist. Eng. Dram. Lit.* ii. 375; *D. N. B., s.* Jonson), that the play 'was not heard to the end', i.e. that the performance was actually broken off, goes beyond the evidence, as Mr. Tennant (p. xi f.) has shown. But he makes too light of the matter when he argues that the 'hundred fastidious *impertinents*' who rose and left the theatre were merely following an old custom. It is plain from Jonson's vehement and enduring anger that the behaviour, both of these fashionable persons and of the audience at large, expressed a quite unusual degree of hostility to the play; and he knew something of the displeasure of playgoers.

maid was named *Cis*'; but to avoid all risks, he hastily changed her name to Prudence, or Prue.[1]

What the provocation was we can only conjecture; but it is likely that the hissers took the phrase to convey some personal allusion, and certain that this, whatever it may have been, was absolutely irrelevant to the business of the play. In I. i the girl, entering with the momentous proposals of her mistress, is referred to, pleasantly and naturally enough, as 'Secretary Cis'. Some years before, Jonson had made his 'Charis' take counsel with 'Secretarie *Sis*', whether '*Fucus* this Be as good, as was the last' (*Und*. ii. 8); this 'secretary' being presumably also a chambermaid. Upon this slender basis Mr. Fleay (i. 325, 385) erects an elaborate romance. But even if 'Secretarie *Sis*' (or Cis) allude to the same person in the two cases, it by no means follows that the mistress is the same; and whether Charis be Lady Hatton in her ingenuous youth, or Lady Purbeck, to whom Jonson, according to Mr. Fleay's pleasant arrangement, 'transferred' his verses 'at Lady Hatton's request', his 'enigmatic references having been too open', there is not the slightest proof that Lady Purbeck is Lady Frampul. Had she been, Jonson would hardly have been so confident that his allusion to 'Secretary Sis', which, by hypothesis, helped to identify her mistress, would be less offensive at Court than on the popular stage. And Jonson expressly repudiates any significance in the name which, in deference to the unexplained susceptibilities of his popular audience, he had changed.

> For any mystery we there haue found,
> Or magick in the letters, or the sound,

she might have been called Prue at first. She was merely meant for 'a girle of wit' whom her mistress provided with 'a Prouince' (Second Epilogue). The offence seems to have originated in a gratuitous misunderstanding on the part of a section of the audience.

---

[1] 'Cicelie' still remains in the list of persons in I. vi. In some copies the name 'Cis' survives in ll. 22 (stage direction), 25, 29, 32, 46 'Cicely'. In others it is corrected to 'Prue' and 'Prudence'.

But this was of no avail. The play, condemned in more or less emphatic terms by almost all who had seen it, was dead, and the Court appears to have cancelled the proposed performance; it was, in any case, not performed, and the Court Epilogue, in consequence, remained unspoken.

Jonson himself had not witnessed the performance at Blackfriars. Confined to his bed by a second stroke of paralysis, he had awaited the news of its reception with less than his usual self-confidence. The Epilogue he had written for it is almost an apology. With a humility pathetic in so proud a man, he admits that the play may be faulty. But he insists that the blame must be laid only on his sick body. His powers, though soon to succumb, are still intact.

> If you expect more then you had to-night,
>   The maker is sick, and sad. But doe him right,
> He meant to please you: for he sent things fit,
>   In all the numbers, both of sense, and wit,
> If they ha' not miscarried! if they have,
>   All that his faint, & faltering tongue doth craue
> Is, that you not impute it to his braine.
>   That's yet vnhurt, although set round with paine,
> It cannot long hold out. All strength must yield.
>   Yet judgment would the last be, i' the field,
> With a true Poet.

But if Jonson was aware that his play stood in need of defence, its decisive dismissal was not the less mortifying. Three weeks later a piece by his quondam servant and pupil, Richard Brome, was played with brilliant success upon the same boards.[1] Jonson was a loyal and generous chieftain and 'father', but an angry gibe at the audience, for which 'Brome's sweepings' did as well as 'his master's meal', shows that the younger man's glory only added to the poignancy of the elder's defeat.[2] His resentment now broke forth in that

---

[1] *The Love-sick Maid, or the Honour of Young Ladies*, licensed by Herbert, February 9, 1629 (Malone's *Shakespeare*, i. 409). The significance of this play in the present connexion was first appreciated by Mr. Tennant, p. xxv f.

[2] That this phrase is authentic, and must have occurred in the original draft, was first seen by Mr. Fleay. Mr. Tennant prints a manuscript version in the Bodleian (p. xxii f.) which may, as he thinks, resemble

unique blast of lyric scorn, the *Ode to Himself*, begotten, as he explained to the reader of the 1631 edition, of 'The iust indignation the Author tooke at the vulgar censure of his Play'. Of the Ode and the replies and comments which it provoked from foe and friend this is not the place to speak. That he reprinted it after nearly two years (effacing only the unworthy allusion to Brome) testifies to the depth of the wound, and to the undiminished resilience, under provocation, of his self-esteem.

It only remained to appeal to the reader through the press, and this Jonson at length did. He would have disdained to plead with these new judges for a more lenient judgement, but he was willing to assist their imperfect powers of appreciation. He accordingly, with hardly concealed anxiety, provided his unwieldy vessel with a massive ballast in the shape of elucidation and comment: an elaborate argument unfolding the 'unlikely story' act by act; a 'characterism' of the chief dramatis personae (in the manner of *Every Man out of his Humour*, but far less pithy and brilliant in style); and an address to the Reader, requiring him, with a mixture of menace and entreaty, to read; the whole clinched with a title-page, which proclaims the play to have been 'neuer acted, but most negligently play'd by some, the Kings Seruants. And more squeamishly beheld, and censured by others, the Kings Subiects. . . . Now, at last, set at liberty to the Readers . . . to be iudged.'

The justice of the blow which closed the career of *The New Inn* has never been disputed. Even his 'son' Carew, the most distinguished of his contemporary defenders, tempered his comfortable words with candid though kindly criticism. And posterity, even when most bent upon vindicating Jonson from his traducers, has scarcely qualified the verdict of the first night's audience.

At the same time some reserves must be made. The staple of the play is far from being of uniform texture.

the original more nearly than the 1631 text. The fact that 'sweepings' is pointless without 'Brome' appears decisive of their relative priority.

The worst things in it are as bad as they can be, lifeless as drama, poor as writing, tedious to hear and to see—the mere rotten debris of Jonson's genius. 'The drunkards and the noises of the inn', the crew of inchoate figures whose dreary gibes and 'jests so nominal' support with such unlucky persistence the character of the Light Heart, are mere pathological specimens,—the gropings of an imagination which in this direction was all but exhausted, under the galvanic stimulus of a valiant will. And Jonson's own massive self-confidence flagged towards the end as he handled them, so that he refrained from 'haling' them in to 'vent' in the fifth act those 'vapours in the place of wit' which so seriously damage its predecessors. The 'Humour' vein, whose first sprightly runnings had created the excellent comedy of thirty years before, now dribbles wearily out in poor travesties of the well-known types, or unsuccessful crosses and variations of them. The military braggart, the astute serving-man, are recognizable still in Sir Glorious Tipto and Ferret,—shadowy kinsmen of Bobadill and Brainworm. Pierce and Jordan, inn servants and members of the militia, talk tap-room and barrack-room phrases intermixed without attaining genuine vitality in either capacity; and Fly, a more ambitiously designed amalgam of the scholar, gipsy, and parasite, remains a recipe or specification for a character less human than the worst Elizabethan clown's journeyman-like imitation of humanity.[1]

But the play is far from being all on this level. If the vein of humorous observation was all but exhausted, if the 'judgement', always liable to strange lapses, here failed altogether, the acute and ingenious fancy and the sustained power of style were little impaired. To this extent the 'brain' still held its own. The fund of romantic poetry which the masterpieces of his maturity had obscured still

[1] Some of the 'horsey' dialogue of these personages was, however, thought worth conveying into a revised version of Fletcher's *Love's Pilgrimage* (1635). The origin of the parallel passages in these two plays has been much discussed; but internal evidence appears to us decisive in favour of the view just indicated.

survived, attenuated and impoverished, but capable, at moments, of a fitful and uncertain splendour, and offering, at other moments, alluring glimpses of effects beyond the actual reach of the palsied hand. No reader can mistake the resolute attempt to plot romantically which has determined the main lines of the present play. Here, too, much of the invention is extravagant, even monstrous. But some of it is noble and beautiful; and where it fails, it is by pushing to an outrageous extreme the characteristic motives of romance. Families broken up and finally restored, children separated from parents, brought up under strange disguises and at last transformed and recovered, were the staple of romantic story. But it would be hard to find a parallel in any school of romance to the vicissitudes and disguises of the Frampul family; the head of which, to adopt Gifford's incisive summary, 'abandons his home, turns travelling tinker, showman, and finally innkeeper, because his wife had brought him two daughters'; while the wife herself also runs away, 'leaves her title and estate to her eldest daughter, steals her youngest, and sells her in the disguise of a boy to her own husband, whom she does not recognize, and continues to live with him under the appearance of a drunken Irish nurse with a patch over one eye (as an effectual screen) and a bottle of usquebaugh at her girdle'. Not the least audacious feature of the design is that all the members of this Protean family—father, mother, and two daughters—are found living, unknown to each other, in the same inn. This was indeed to take the kingdom of romance by storm; and Jonson in effect plies the traditional machinery of transformation and disguise with a vigour which comes near to effacing every vestige of the characters it is applied to. The Host may be allowed to retain some traces of the genial country gentleman, and 'Frank' some hint of girlish sparkle and sprightliness; but the 'vertuous Gentlewoman, *Sylly's* daughter of the South' is obliterated in the mean and sordid apparition of the Nurse; and the second 'disguise' of Frank, the supposed boy, in the garments proper to her actual but unsuspected sex, though not unparalleled in the later Elizabethan drama,[1] is a device only too characteristic of the decline of a powerful brain, which still invents, but with a formal and mechanical ingenuity, and retains a less and less hold upon the freshness and the charm of life.

But parts of the play have no inconsiderable measure of that freshness and that charm. Joyous reminiscences of Rabelais and Cockayne linger, faded and subdued, about this hostelry of the Light Heart, this Host who so pleasantly enforces the 'great charter' of his Thelema which will tolerate everything sooner than the sullen guest. Yet it is no dissolute gaiety that he presides over. He confesses to have been 'borne to somewhat aboue' his 'trade', and betrays his good stock by his sterling sense of honour no less than by the 'vein of salte and sharpnesse', the 'strikings vpon learning' which disclose themselves, unexpectedly, 'vnder his cap'. His strictures on the depravity of the modern page fall indeed into the Juvenalian tone to which Jonson's own comic mirth had always inclined, and accord but ill with the fashions of the Light Heart. They resemble the jeremiads of the elder Kno'well. The Host is here in danger of the 'sullen' mood he has just checked. With some abruptness he is recalled to his proper part, and Juvenal is transformed into Horace, a genial spectator at the theatre of life; diverting himself like Jaques, but not cynically, with the shifting scenes of that play the world:

and if I haue got
A seat, to sit at ease here, i' mine Inne,
To see the *Comedy*; and laugh, and chuck
At the variety, and throng of humors,
And dispositions, that come iustling in,
And out still, as they one droue hence another;
Why, will you enuy me my happinesse?[2]

---

[1] Gifford pointed out a similar combination in *The Widow*, where a girl, Martia, disguised as a man, assumes what some of the persons in the play take to be the disguise of a woman, with the result that when she marries Francisco, the laugh goes against the jesters.

[2] I. iii. 134-40.

The part of Lovel, like that of the Host, afforded opportunities for an actor, and both were, as Jonson expressly owns, 'played well'. Something of abstract formalism lurked, no doubt, in this juxtaposition of the 'melancholy' with the 'cheerful' man; but the circumstances and complexion of Lovel's 'melancholy' were of a kind unfamiliar, if not new, to Jonson's art. 'Melancholy' as a fashionable affectation, or an effeminate foible, he had pilloried often enough; but Lovel is no fellow of the Matthews, the Bobadills, nor even of the amorous Duke in *Twelfth Night*. His melancholy is neither an affectation nor a natural quality of temperament, but the outward expression of a passion which he has renounced but cannot extinguish 'A compleat Gentleman, a Souldier, and a Scholer', he appears, and is meant to appear; an ideal, if not heroic character, of a romantic complexion rarely treated sympathetically by Jonson. That he is a supreme success cannot be said, but he is assuredly no failure, though doubtless less a product of dramatic imagination than of elaborating intellect. There is hardly anything comic about him. But the picture of the busy futilities in which his 'melancholy' finds relief might pass for a mocking travesty of Dürer's great print;—'Melancholia' still the 'mother of invention', but of invention which only ploughs the sand and weaves the air:

         Here, your master,
And you ha' beene this fortnight, drawing fleas
Out of my mattes, and pounding 'hem in cages
Cut out of cards, & those rop'd round with pack-thred,
Drawn thorow birdlime! a fine subtilty![1]

But Lovel's capacity for finding an absorbing interest in solemn trivialities stands him later in good stead, and ends in turning what began as triviality into serious and significant action. The 'Sports' which the Lady invites him to share were in substance little more than a well-bred drawing-room counterpart of these gross diversions. The cult of

[1] I. i. 24–8.

'Platonic love' had, since the accession of Charles and the advent of Henrietta Maria, become a courtly fashion. It was one of the symptoms of that reaction against the hearty, gross-living Renascence which fills the later sixteenth and early seventeenth centuries, in western Europe, with euphuisms, pastoralisms, preciosities, and other experiments of an adventurous, but groping, instinct of refinement. All these phenomena had their ideal and beautiful side; but all lent themselves only too readily to perverse and tasteless extravagance; the most fatuous in its occasional developments, as it was the sublimest in origin, was the 'Love' which assumed Plato's name. England had no Hôtel de Rambouillet, but Henrietta Maria had, as princess, felt its attractions; and the 'new love' which Howell spoke of as prevailing, in the early thirties, at the English Court was a parallel, if not a derivative phenomenon; marking a change in the fashionable tone towards women, quite as pronounced as the change in ideals of phrase and style which the *précieuses* made current and their provincial imitators 'ridiculous'. The brutal licence of the Jacobean Court yielded, under Charles, to a refined but artificial gallantry, which found in the ideal language of Plato about love a seemly vesture, or a specious disguise. Jonson has chosen to associate this Platonic speech with the pleadings of a 'Court of Love',—a blend of antique and medieval matter which in a more natural setting than that of this play would appear strangely incongruous, but which matches its artificial context well enough. It was a blend familiar to Jonson's own practice in the Masque, where Oberon, for instance, and his knights are introduced by the coarse antics of Silenus and his Satyrs. These and similar precedents, however, can hardly have been very reassuring to an audience bent upon comedy and encouraged by the vigorous preparations of the first act to expect it. When the plot threatens, at the opening of the third act, to resolve itself into the story of the Sports of Lady Frampul, the older spectators may well have remembered with apprehension the sumptuous pastimes of *Cynthia's Revels*. From any complete dissolution, however, of the nerve and fibre of dramatic plot in the amenities of a drawing-room game *The New Inn* is preserved by the character of Lovel. Reluctantly enough he enters on the imposed task, the praise of true love, which is to win him the single, ceremonial, and passionless kiss. But one must not *badiner avec l'amour*; and Lovel, without swerving an inch from the conditions of the game, plays it with an impassioned earnestness which shatters the woof of elegant make-believe, and startles the merry and fantastical soul of Lady Frances into love. Jonson's handling of this romantic motive does not indeed approach Musset's in charm, pathos, or grace; and the repetition of the 'Court of Love' in the fourth act, with no change of circumstance beyond the new topic—valour—proposed for discourse, was a daring, and perhaps fatal, outrage upon the demand of every audience that a plot shall move otherwise than by beating time. But Lovel's speeches are finely written, and their supposed effect is not incredible. And his lofty conception of the nature of love is set off by the grosser notion of Lord Beaumont, albeit this be

a fable of *Plato's*, in his Banquet,
And vtter'd, there, by *Aristophanes*.

APPENDIX VIII

'THE NEW INN' AND FLETCHER'S 'LOVE'S PILGRIMAGE'

The facts referred to in the note on p. 193, are briefly these : (1) *Love's Pilgrimage* was 'renewed' for the King's men in September, 1635; Herbert's office-book, as reported by Malone, shows that he charged a fee, and that the play had therefore undergone alterations (Fleay, *Biog. Chron.* i. 193); (2) The first scene contains a number of close textual correspondences with two scenes (II. v and III. i) of *The New Inn*. Some of the speeches freely render the same ideas. Internal evidence makes decidedly for the view that *The New Inn* scenes are the original, which the reviser of *Love's Pilgrimage* adapted with varying skill to his purpose. Jonson's Tipto, flaunting his Spanish ceremony upon the homely Host of Barnet, is, with all his extravagance, a Jonsonian type. His burlesque account of his own fastidious etiquette,

> I would not speake vnto a Cooke of quality . . .
> In *Cuerpo*! (II. v. 57-9.)

was apparently, spoken in the first person, too *outré* for the reviser, and he turns it into a description of a certain 'master of ceremonies':

> I will tell thee of him:
> He would not speak with an Ambassadors Cook,
> See a cold bake-meat from a foreign part,
> In cuerpo (I. i.)

The extravagance of the passage is certainly better carried off thus. But the passage itself is, in all the identical parts (about three-fourths of the whole), thoroughly Jonsonian, and its introduction is unmistakably forced. The bits in this passage peculiar to the *Love's Pilgrimage* are also absurdly inferior, like the third line in the above extract. Compare, again, Tipto's vaunt,

> Your *Spanish* Host is neuer seen in *Cuerpo*,
> Without his *Paramento's*, cloake, and sword,
> (II. v. 72, 73.)

with the corresponding lines of Incubo:

> Such [i. e. a master of ceremonies]
> Have I heard him oft say, ought every Host
> Within the Catholique kings dominions
> Be in his own house.

The fact that the scene of the *Love's Pilgrimage* is in Spain, and the unceremonious Host a Spanish host, would sufficiently explain the substitution for Tipto's categorical assertion of this pious wish. The converse is decidedly less natural. A comparison of III. i of our play with the close of the same scene of *Love's Pilgrimage* confirms the view that the former was the source. The stable talk of Pierce, Trundle, Peck, Tipto, and Fly reappears as a dialogue between Diego, the Host, and Lazaro. Poor as the talk is, it belongs to the plan of the play; while Lazaro appears only in this scene and is strictly otiose. The distribution of the dialogue in *The New Inn* is more pointed, but occasionally hard to follow; the corresponding passages of the *Pilgrimage* are often smoother, but suggest an inferior intelligence. Compare the following:

> *Fly.* . . . 'tis an office meritorious,
>   To tith such soundly.
> *Pei.*   And a graziers may.
> *Fer.* O they are pinching puckfists!
> *Tru.*   And suspicious.
> *Pei.* Suffer before the masters face, sometimes.

with   (III. i. 149-52.)

> *Diego.* . . . 'tis a meritorious office
>   To tythe him soundly.
> *Laz.*   And a Grazier may
> (For those are pinching puckfoysts, and suspitious)
>   Suffer a mist before his eyes sometimes too, . . .

Pierce says that a grazier's horse may sometimes be made the victim of a trick before its master's very eyes. Partly owing to the interruptions of Ferret and Trundle, this is not at once obvious. The author of the second passage uses nearly the same words but expresses something quite different, viz. that the master, looking on, is the victim of an hallucination. This passage is certainly easier; but just for that reason it is hardly credible that the obscurer first passage should have been altered from it; the hypothesis that the second was the work of a reviser who stumbled at the harshness of the line, and possibly did not understand it, appears greatly preferable to the view that this simple and straightforward verson of the matter was revised into the more difficult text of *The New Inn*. For the same reason it is impossible to accept the rather surprising surmise at which Mr. Tennant, at the close of his able argument (p. lxxi), arrives, viz. that the variations of *Love's Pilgrimage* are taken from a player's copy of *The New Inn*, which 'rigorously revised', before going to the press in 1631, the text in which we now read it. In this case we should have to suppose that Jonson himself, appealing from the audience who had damned the play to the reader whose approval might still be won, and willing, as the change from 'Cis' to 'Prue' shows, to remove sources of offence even when he saw no reason for it, nevertheless deliberately altered easier expressions into harsh ones. Mr. Tennant hardly credits the possibility of a reviser whose 'mental make-up' would have permitted him to convert *The New Inn* passages into those of the *Pilgrimage*. But he is willing, if we do not misunderstand him, to believe that Jonson himself was capable of writing, in 1629, what an obscure and unknown reviser can hardly be conceived to have written.

INTRODUCTION TO
'THE MAGNETIC LADY'

THE MAGNETIC LADY

The Magnetick Lady, or Humors Reconcil'd was first published in the Folio edition of 1640. It had been licensed to the King's men on October 12, 1632, when the book-keeper of the Blackfriars Theatre paid £2 for the privilege. A contemporary letter, dated September 20th of the year, fixes the composition of the play to the preceding weeks or months, and leaves no doubt that it was performed the same autumn. 'Ben Jonson, (who, I thought, had bene dead) hath written a play against next terme called the Magnetick lady.'[1] Its career on the stage opened inauspiciously, and the unlucky auspices were on the whole fulfilled. The players chose to enrich their parts freely with offensive oaths. On being summoned to answer this offence before the High Commission Court, they attempted to lay the blame upon the author and the Master of the Revels. Jonson, however, justified himself, and in a second petition to the court they confessed that they alone were responsible, whereupon the court 'laid the whole fault' upon them. Jonson's private enemies were busy too. Inigo and Butter attended the first night's performance, and, if we may trust the scurrilous verses of Gill, went into convulsions of scornful laughter at the ridiculous dullness of their old assailant's work. Such applause as it may have received from friends and 'sons' seems to have been given rather to the poet than to the play. James Howell, one of the latter, intimated his opinion of it without disguise, though in delicate and pleasant terms. 'You were mad', he wrote to Jonson, 'when you writ your *Fox*, and madder when you writ your *Alchemist*; ... and when you writ your *Epigrams* and the *Magnetic Lady* you were not so mad. ... The madness I mean is

[1] John Pory to Sir Thomas Puckering, in B. M. Harley MS. 7000, fol. 336. Gill's verses also, reflecting on the play, were evidently written before the close of the year.

that divine fury ... that Ovid speaks of'.[1] This tempered appreciation marks nearly the high-water mark of *The Magnetic Lady's* fame. Langbaine tells us that it was 'generally accounted an excellent play', but this vague statement is less typical of opinion about it than Dryden's well-known inclusion of it among its author's 'dotages'. Among recent critics, only Swinburne, and in some degree the last American editor of the play, Dr. H. W. Peck, have seriously qualified this adverse verdict. For Swinburne, 'the higher genius of Ben Jonson as a comic poet' here showed itself in 'one brilliant flash of parting splendour before the approaching sunset'. And he points especially to the opening scenes as examples of a notable 'revival of the comic power and renewal of the dramatic instinct'.

Swinburne's phrases perhaps over-accentuate the incidental vivacities of which Jonson was never incapable. What is certain is that he here recurred, frankly, even ostentatiously, to the methods and devices by which his earlier comedies had first won fame. 'Stay and see his last *Act*, his *Catastrophe*', counsels the 'Boy' at the close of Act iv, exactly as his counterpart might have done at the same point in *Epicoene* or *The Alchemist*, 'how hee will perplexe that, or spring some fresh cheat, to entertain the *Spectators*, with a convenient delight, till some unexpected, and new encounter breake out to rectifie all, and make good the *Conclusion*.' The stamp of old age is surely set upon the play; but it is the old age of a veteran captivated by the memory of his prime, and seeking, if for the most part ineffectively, to recover its secret.

In a fashion which recalls the dying Gaunt's nice playing with his name, Jonson, old and bed-ridden, sports with the fancy of the 'circle' so nearly run, whose perimeter this last adventure was to complete. The comedy which closed the poet's round of life was itself contrived to suggest a circle in the scheme of its plot; a circle with a 'magnetic

---

[1] Howell's Letter, addressed to 'Father Ben', dated January 27, 1629, but evidently later.

mistress' as its centre, and a crowd of heterogeneous Humours revolving about her, whose disorderly and often 'diametral' antagonisms are kept within bounds and in the end 'reconciled' by the 'magisterial wit' of Master Circumference, or 'Compass'. Apart, however, from the plan of geometrical and magnetic allusion, the device indicated no radical novelty of plan even among Jonson's own plots. Precisely his most artful plot-structures might have been described in similar terms. Volpone and Subtle are each a 'magnetic centre' whose fascination holds a miscellaneous herd of Humours in its sway, their rivalries and jealousies being artfully manipulated and arranged by a shrewd confidant. But Mosca and Face are completely objective creations, like every other figure in these masterpieces of Jonson's prime; whereas Compass recalls the arch-contrivers of *Every Man out of his Humour* and *Cynthia's Revels* and *Poetaster*, in whom it is so easy to recognize Jonson himself pulling the threads of the intrigue and manipulating the issues of the plot to his own glory. Compass need not be identified with Jonson, to whom he expressly refers by name; but the Jonsonian traits in his character as drawn by himself are unmistakable:

> You know I am a Scholler,
> And part a Souldier; I have beene imployed,
> By some the greatest States-men o' the kingdome,
> These many yeares: and in my time convers'd
> With sundry humors. . . .   (I. i. 19 f.)

But the intrigue which is actually built upon this quasi-geometric plan is of a kind virtually new in Jonson's art; and, if wanting in freshness of execution, shows powers of ingenious combination which he had never surpassed. The humours of courtship and match-making, so fertile an ingredient in later fiction and drama, had remained, like the graver passion and pathos of love, virtually unexplored by the first great master of Humours. They belonged, for him, to the background of life, and interested him even less as an artist than as a man. He had satirized in earlier days the foibles of married life—the fatuous complacency of husbands, the intrigues of citizens' wives with courtiers; but the preference of wives to maids which he apparently confessed to Drummond had been characteristic also of his choice of feminine types in drama. In the later group of Comedies, as we have seen, this preference no longer holds good. Pecunia and Lady Frampul are marriageable heiresses, and their relations with those who design, or desire, to marry them occupy a large space in the respective plays. But the 'humours' of courtship and match-making are scarcely hinted in either. Young Penniboy has a rival, of whose existence we are from time to time reminded, and Lovell is no bad embodiment of the melancholy of passionate resignation. But the fantastic tricks which the neighbourhood of a young woman with a fortune will induce in a worldly community, the jealousies of rival suitors, the plots and counterplots of domestic factions, the opinionativeness of guardians, the partisanship of aunts and the craft of nurses—into all this fruitful field of satire, so sedulously explored by the latterday novelist and playwright, Jonson had hitherto merely made a casual incursion. He now, in *The Magnetic Lady*, took complete possession of it. Whatever damaging criticism, in other respects, may be brought to bear upon the sorry heroine and on the sordid suits of which she is the object, her value in the economy of the drama cannot be denied. The hand of the well-portioned niece (be she called Placentia or Pleasance) is the central preoccupation of every member of this motley company. Its disposal, in one way or another, is the business which sets them all in motion, and provokes or 'feeds' the characteristic humour of each. Compared with any of the earlier Humour plays, even with *Every Man in his Humour* itself, the plot is singularly compact and well organized. But its compactness is not obtained without some audacious assumptions. Compass wins his triumphs too easily; his victims play palpably into his hands. Jonson had in other days been accused of abusing lawyers; he rebutted the charge successfully enough in the Epilogue to the *Poetaster*; but those who resented the sarcasms of the law-student Ovid might well have felt the profession to be yet more gravely compromised by the helpless surrender of Practice, 'the only famous Counsell, o' the kingdome', to the wiles of Compass (IV. ii).

For the rest, few of the characters altogether realize the lively expectations aroused by the preliminary description of them in the first act. Some of these analyses are as forcible in thought and phrase as any which Jonson has left. The analytic description of character had now become a literary fashion; and Jonson himself, by his analyses of the dramatis personae of *Every Man out of his Humour* thirty years before, had powerfully contributed to establish it. Hall, Overbury, and Earle had all, in the interim, produced their well-known collections; and some traces of the epigrammatic preciousness which the whole school affected may be discerned in the 'epigrams' delivered by Compass (but 'made' by 'a great clerk As any is of his bulk, Ben Jonson') upon Palate, Practice, Moth, Rut, Silkworm, and Bias. Though not without individual oddities, they are all palpably intended to be professional types; men who have taken the ply of their calling, and whose philosophy ('for all men', as Compass says, 'are philosophers, to their inches') is an astute and methodical pursuit of its ends. Sir Diaphanous is the 'Courtier extraordinary' who

> by diet
> Of meates, and drinkes; his temperate exercise;
> Choise musick; frequent bathes; his horary shifts
> Of Shirts and Wast-coats; meanes to immortalize
> Mortality it selfe. (I. vi. 4–8.)

Sir Interest has reduced his thrift to principles, and will tell you instantly by logarithms (perhaps the first literary allusion to Napier's invention) the utmost profit of a stock employed;[1] Bias is 'the very Agat Of State, & Politie: cut

---

[1] I. vi. 35.

from the Quar Of Macchiavel.'[1] Something, too, of the detail, and possibly of the choice of figures, is due to Chaucer's great gallery of English types. Master Practice, 'My Ladies lawyer! Or man of Law', who is 'so dedicate to his profession, And the preferments goe along with it',[2] that another Armada would hardly rouse him, owes something to the more famous man of law who was the busiest of men, and seemed yet busier than he was. Parson Palate, or Palate Please, who makes all the matches of the parish and knows the wardmote quest better than the Levitic law, unites the persuasive unction of the Frere with the cheery secularity of the Monk. Doctor Rut, however, is drawn in more sombre colours than the doctor of Physic, and might be taken to personate all those notorious qualities of the profession which Sir Thomas Browne, just a year afterwards, was at so much pains to show that one of its members did not share.

Women figure in unusual numbers among the characters and play an even more than correspondingly important part in the action. Jonson had painted women often enough in their relations with men—ambitious citizens' wives, brilliant and brazen courtesans, or English varieties of the *Femme savante*, like the Collegiate Ladies. But with the more specifically feminine side of women's life, the 'women's matters', 'smock-secrets' of the nursery and the boudoir, he had never deigned to occupy himself and his audiences at large. In *The Magnetic Lady* the dramatic capacities of feminine intrigue are explored and exploited with a security rarely exhibited elsewhere than in this play. The 'heroines', Placentia and Pleasance, are indeed little more than lay figures, passive prizes, or tokens of the prize, for which the game is played; and the Magnetic Mistress herself looks on somewhat helplessly at the movements and counter-movements induced by the 'magnetism' which she exercises, but can hardly be said to possess. But the below-stairs women have all touches of vivacity, and the

[1] I. vii. 29–31.   [2] I. vi. 15, 16.

'gossip and she-parasite' and arch-intriguer, Polish, is perhaps the best woman Jonson ever drew. She is of the sisterhood of Juliet's Nurse and of Mrs. Gamp; not to be matched, indeed, with either in finished consistency of conception or in force of execution, but sufficiently attesting Jonson's intimate understanding of this type of womanhood, with its sinister blend of gossiping volubility and callous heart. Abler and more daring than the Nurse, she has nevertheless moments which appear to be reminiscent of the earlier and more famous gossip; as when she is expounding the virtues of the late Master and Mistress Steel, the parents of her charge (who, like Juliet, is fourteen years old):

> Mr. *Steele*, was liberall,
> And a fine man; and she a dainty Dame,
> And a religious, and a bountifull.   (I. iv. 62-4.)

But such resemblances are soon lost sight of when the course of the plot strips off her mask of unctuous fidelity, and exhibits her, first as the bold intriguer, and finally as the brazen proclaimer of her own treachery. Intermittent the dramatic vitality of this comedy confessedly is; but the decisive moment, when the game of concealment is played out and 'truth is breaking forth on every side', and Polish, secure, as she thinks, of the prize, snatches the glory of confession from the helpless lips of Goody Keep, is as effective as anything in Jonson's later comedy; while her final discomfiture by Bias's refusal of her daughter on any terms, recalls the sudden abysmal collapse of Mosca or of Morose at the moment of seeming triumph. In logical rigour, at least, the denouement of our play falls nothing short of these.

Many as were the new shifts which Jonson tried in these later plays, he did not easily resign his old masterful habit of intervening to assist the judgement of the audience. The present intermezzos are only less vivacious in execution and less happy in invention than those of *The Staple of News*. The Boy who presides over this dramatic 'shop' (which recalls the φροντιστήριον of the *Clouds*) is a 'tender juvenal' such as Jonson delighted to draw, less brilliant and exquisite than Shakespeare's Moth, but higher built in learning, one of the redoubtable Children of the comic stage compounded with a budding scholar who had learnt Terence in the third form at Westminster. The Boy, like the Cordatus of earlier days, is charged with the task of rebutting criticisms upon the play, and in general is speaking Jonson's mind about it. But this humorously extravagant refutation is twice as effective as Crites' or Asper's sententious scorn; and Damplay's easy surrenders ('A shrewd Boy! and has mee every where!') give a sportive air to the whole debate. A first act entirely occupied with deploying the persons of the drama on the stage and describing their characters was in itself an audacious jest played upon the audience; and Jonson is only carrying the jest a step farther when he makes the Boy retort to the objection that there is nothing done in it, or concluded: 'A fine peice of Logick! Doe you looke, Master *Damplay*, for conclusions in a *Protasis*? I thought the Law of *Comedy* had reserv'd them to the *Catastrophe*.'

INTRODUCTION TO
'THE SAD SHEPHERD'

THE SAD SHEPHERD

I

The Sad Shepherd was first published in the second volume of the Folio edition of Jonson's works, with the date 1641. Found in its present fragmentary form among Jonson's papers after his death, 'it was nevertheless', we are told on good contemporary evidence, 'judg'd a Piece of too much worth to be laid aside, by the Learned and Honourable Sir Kenelme Digby, who published', i. e. edited, 'that volume'.[1] No further traces of Jonson's work, beyond those here published, have ever been found, nor have the investigations of several generations of scholars enabled us to solve with any certainty the problems to which the extant fragment gives rise.[2] Is *The Sad Shepherd* the surviving remnant of a finished play, or was it left incomplete? And, in either case, when was it written? The first is little more than a curious speculation; the second closely concerns the history of Jonson's mind and art. To both, merely an adumbration of a reply can at present be offered.

The 'fragment' consists of two complete acts and about half the third, out of the five intended. But the prefixed arguments carry the story half an act farther than the text, the argument of the entire third act being prefixed to the extant portion of it; and both the list of persons and the description of the scenery carry us a little farther still. Reuben 'the reconciler', who closes the list of 'Persons', and his 'Cell', mentioned among the items of the 'Landtshape', would doubtless have figured in the fifth act. These facts point, on the whole, to the conclusion that the

[1] H. Moseley, Address to the Reader prefixed to *Last Remains of Sir John Suckling*, 1659.
[2] A continuation, not devoid of skill, was published by Waldron in 1783. It was reprinted by Dr. Greg in his valuable edition of *The Sad Shepherd* (1905).

play was plotted out, but never completely executed. But they are quite consistent with the view that the remaining scenes were actually executed, and subsequently lost. The analogy of the other fragments included in this Folio may be quoted on either side. The editor's note to the fragment of *Mortimer* runs : 'Hee dy'd, and left it unfinished,' or in other copies: 'Left unfinished.' This, as Dr. Greg says, offers a presumption that the incompleteness, in cases where a similar statement is not made, was due to some other, or not known by the editor to be due to the same, cause. But in the elegy on Lady Venetia Digby[1] the editor notes expressly at the close of the ninth piece: 'The Tenth, being her Inscription, or Crowne, is lost'. We might here, equally, presume that the absence of a similar attestation rendered probable some other cause. The simple words 'The End', added at the close of *The Sad Shepherd*, are most naturally taken to indicate that this was all that, so far as any one knew, had ever existed. And Jonson was known to have been engaged upon a work of this kind. The obituary tribute of Lord Falkland in *Jonsonus Virbius* (1638) recalls, as if it were a familiar matter of fact, that

> Not long before his *Death*, our *Woods* he meant
> To *visit*, and descend from *Thames* to *Trent*.[2]

It is difficult to resist the inference that Jonson was actually at work upon the play, or preparing it for performance, within at most a few years of his end. The existence of the finished Prologue clearly indicates that the play was on the way to completion, but in no way precludes the view that the poet's work on it was interrupted by a sudden seizure, or by death itself.

The arguments for holding *The Sad Shepherd* to have been left incomplete naturally also go to support the view that it was the work of his last years. The express testimony of Falkland above quoted, coupled with the opening line of the Prologue, ' He that hath feasted you these forty

---

[1] *Underwoods*, lxxxiv. [2] *Jonsonus Virbius*, p. 8.

yeares', forms a piece of evidence, not conclusive indeed, but certainly far weightier than any that has been hitherto brought forward to the contrary. It is idle to urge that this or the other lines in the Prologue apply better to the second, or to the third, decade of the century, and that the date 'forty' was altered from 'twenty', or from 'thirty', to suit a later revival, when these *ex hypothesi* incongruous passages were allowed to stand.[1] At the same time (so delicately are the rival probabilities balanced), it may be granted that—apart from the 'forty years'—the Prologue is quite as well suited to a date about 1615, and that we could easily believe it to have been originally written for his earlier 'pastoral', *The May Lord*, which he described to Drummond in 1619, and then revived for *The Sad Shepherd*, were there a grain of evidence for the connexion. The play itself, on all grounds of style and form, would, of course, be less amazing as an achievement of Jonson's forties than of his sixties. But on any hypothesis of date it reveals a Jonson whom we could not have completely anticipated from anything else that he has left. It is a splendid anomaly: the tests of internal evidence fail completely; and the only external evidence available must have the decisive weight.

Only two other pieces of supposed external evidence pointing to a different conclusion have so far been produced. (1) Gifford long ago called attention to the resemblance between the opening lines of *The Sad Shepherd* and a passage in Goffe's *Careless Shepherdess*, performed in 1629. As a matter of course he declared that Goffe had 'imitated this passage'—together with 'many others' which he does not specify and which the close scrutiny of subsequent

[1] A clue to the date may, however, some day be found in the lines:
> But here's an Heresie of late let fall;
> That Mirth by no meanes fits a *Pastorall*.

Dr. Greg has plausibly supposed Jonson to refer to criticisms hypothetically passed upon his 'son' Randolph's *Amyntas*. The 'Heresy' can hardly have left no trace of itself in print.

critics has failed to detect. Goffe's play, it is true, includes two lyrics from Shirley's *Triumph of Beauty*. But it is not probable that there is imitation on either side here. Goffe's lines, hardly less beautiful than Jonson's, are by no means very like them; an imitator capable of expanding Jonson's thought with so delicate a touch would have shown his quality in other passages of the play; whereas this one, by general consent, stands alone. The circumstances point rather to a common source; no conclusions can at present be founded upon them.

(2) More recently an attempt has been made by Mr. Fleay to show that *The Sad Shepherd* was described by Jonson to Drummond; that it is, in a word, to be identified with the 'pastoral' which he called *The May Lord*, and is thus anterior in date to January, 1619. The theory has some plausible points, but we agree with Dr. Greg in holding it to be, in the present state of the evidence, untenable. Jonson's words as reported by Drummond run: 'He hath a pastorall intitled the May Lord, his own name is Alkin, Ethra the Countess of Bedfoords, Mogibell Overberry, the old Countesse of Suffolk ane inchanteress; other names are given to Somersets Lady, Pembrook, the Countesse of Rutland, Lady Wroth. In his first storie Alkin commeth in mending his broken pipe. Contrary to all other pastoralls, he bringeth the Clownes making mirth and foolish Sports.'

Three points only in all this afford the slightest foothold for Mr. Fleay's supposition: (1) The name Alkin (Alken) occurs in both; (2) 'Contrary to all other pastoralls' there is 'mirth' in both; (3) Belvoir Castle, near which the scene of *The Sad Shepherd* is laid, was the seat of the Countess of Rutland and her husband. It is enough to reply to (1) that Alken's action does not, in the extant first half of *The Sad Shepherd*, correspond with that ascribed to him. His description of the Witch's dimble and of her ways ('I wonder such a storie could be told of her dire deeds,' comments John), must be held to be his 'first storie', if any there be, but there is no question there of 'mending a broken pipe'. (2) It is clear from the Prologue to *The Sad Shepherd* that the admission of 'mirth' in pastoral was not, with Jonson, a passing caprice, but a deliberate principle; the expression of his intention to set back the confined frontiers to which pastoral had become restricted and restore the freer air and the more varied moods and keys of Theocritus. If *The May Lord* and *The Sad Shepherd*, therefore, were distinct pieces, it would be prima facie probable that both would contain mirthful elements, and the fact that this is attested of both has very little value as an argument for their identity. (3) Lady Rutland played in *The May Lord*, and Mr. Fleay is confident that she and the earl are Marian and Robin in *The Sad Shepherd*. But even if they were, that by no means adds to the likelihood that *The Sad Shepherd* was *The May Lord*; for the countess's name occurs, apparently, in a position of secondary importance, and the earl's does not occur at all. There is nothing to show that *The May Lord* was specially connected, by its supposed scene, with the house of Rutland rather than with that of Bedford or Pembroke. By its supposed scene *The Sad Shepherd* was clearly so connected; but there is not the slightest evidence that the connexion went any farther.

We agree then with Dr. Greg, whose scholarly discussion we have done little more than summarize, in holding that the identity of *The Sad Shepherd* with *The May Lord* is, in the present state of the evidence, untenable. But his further contention, that *The May Lord* was more probably a series of 'pastoral eclogues' than a play, is less easy to accept. As shown above, Aiken's account of the Witch in *The Sad Shepherd* is actually called a 'storie'; it is therefore hazardous to argue that Drummond's reference to 'his first storie' implies that the whole pastoral was in narrative form. Nor is it easy to suppose that the identification of the persons does not point to some kind of performance.

II

Fragment as the piece is, the scope of Jonson's purpose in this his one extant essay in pastoral drama is not difficult to discern. The play is, he declares in effect in the Prologue, right English stuff,—cloth pulled from English flocks, and yet able to match that of Sicily and Greece. It is an attempt to make the beautiful Greek genre of pastoral at home on English soil, to create a truly English pastoral, as rich and various as the Greek, but taking its character and colour more freely from the rural usage and tradition of England than had hitherto been usual.

The problem was not quite simple. English shepherd life, whatever its homely charm for eyes sated with the artifice of courts, was not, like the Greek, a soil in which poetry sprang spontaneously into flower and fruit. The imaginative realism of the age of Wordsworth or of Millet might extort a yet deeper beauty from its often uncouth rusticity, but in natural charm it was obviously far poorer. Theocritus could take up the shepherd world of Sicily, hardly changed in substance, into the gracious poetry of his *Idylls*; the love lays, dirges, and singing matches of his shepherds only render with a finer skill indigenous modes of song; their carved bowls, enwreathed with vine and acanthus, only translate into musical words the artistry of native chisels. The typical English shepherd of Jonson's time, on the other hand, was fairly enough represented by Shakespeare's Corin, 'a true labourer, whose pride is to see his ewes graze and his lambs suck'; his typical humour was reflected in the jests and horse-play of the 'Second Pastoral' in the Towneley plays; his love-making in the unsentimental duel of Robin and Makin; while his habitual preoccupations were better expressed in that primitive 'Shepherd's Calendar' which instructed the shepherd when to wean or to shear, than in the poetic pastoral for which Spenser borrowed that homely title. Competitions in poetry were not the way of the English shepherd; he preferred a dog-match on the slopes of Cotswold. Doubtless in Elizabethan England—'merry', pre-Puritan England—song abounded, and the shepherd sang like the rest; Drayton was not remembering Theocritus or Vergil but describing Warwickshire when he made his 'Melanthus' sing the lark up at dawn with a 'country roundelay', and lead his flock home 'like a king' with the bagpipes at night.[1] But between this casual singing of shepherds and the custom and cult of shepherd song the distance was great, and pastoralism as we know it could never have been generated by English pastoral life alone.

It would have been well for English poetry had pastoralism entered it in the form created or re-created (for Stesichorus had made shepherd songs three centuries before) by Theocritus. The transformation effected in pastoral by the subtle artistry of Vergil opened up many new paths for pastoral poetry. In Vergil the shepherd is already half a symbol, and the landscape setting dreamy and unreal; but the unreality itself becomes a clue to new ideal values which go far to compensate for the loss of the more sinewy substance of the poetry they replace. Yet the same symbolism, which proved so noble an instrument in the hands of Vergil and Dante, served far more readily in meaner or grosser hands to reduce poetry to the lower level of satire or didactic, of political or theological polemics. The Carmelite Baptista, pleasantly surnamed Mantuanus after the master he believed himself to rival, showed the utmost virtuosity in exploiting pastoral symbolism in the service of his political and ecclesiastical creed, and the fluent and elegant Latin verse, which made him a classic in all the schools north of the Alps, spread the vogue of his polemical pastoralism. His contemporary Sannazaro, nearly at the same time, gave the first powerful impulse to the development of the effeminate and sentimental side of pastoralism, thenceforth denoted by the title of his famous romance the *Arcadia*. Satire and sentimentality formed the staple of sixteenth-century

[1] *Muses' Elysium*, Nymphal vi.

pastoralism—a sorry stuff, disastrous for poor wits, yet capable of yielding rare beauties in the hands of genius. In England it did so again and again. Spenser sounded all the notes of pastoral tradition with impartial enthusiasm in the *Calendar*, redeeming even political allegory and conventional love by the bewitching melodic discoveries of his verse. Sidney blew the horn of martial adventure among the sheepcotes of Arcadia. Drayton let in the fresh air of English meads and woodlands upon the scenery of exotic pastoral. And a host of lyric poets found, like Marlowe, in the simple romance of pastoral love-making, food for entrancing song. During the last twenty years of the queen's reign almost all lyric was winged with pastoral inspiration or coloured by pastoral scenery and circumstance. It was, in fact, in lyric almost alone that pastoral poetry, during the sixteenth century, found entirely congenial expression. Pastoral romance, in spite of the immense prestige of Sidney, ended in barren failure; while some of the most imperishable songs of the age have come to us imbedded in the very mortal setting of the romances. For the soul of the earliest pastoral had lain in its lyric elements, in the love-song and the elegy; and these remained its most enduring hold upon English poets. Whereas both romance and drama, demanding a wealth of action and character which the tenuous frame of pastoral eclogue could ill supply, sank into rapid decay. It was in the elegy alone—'some dirge of Lycidas or Astrophel', Thyrsis or Adonais—that noble poetry continued, on occasion, to borrow the pastoral form.

Yet it was natural that, in the years when drama was becoming the supreme form of literary expression in English, the attempt should be made to draw upon the fragile beauty of pastoral for the material of English plays. The founders of pastoral drama, Tasso and Guarini, had shown extraordinary skill in turning the slender material to the utmost dramatic account. But even they had enlarged the sphere of strict pastoral by calling into play the pagan gods.

Diana avenges a broken vow of maidenhood or a breach of fidelity, Venus an unrequited passion. Transported to the stage of Elizabethan England, pastoral drama had even less chance of thriving by the virtue of pastoralism alone. Even at Court, where the first experiments with this exotic kind were made, and where its cultured unreality found a relatively congenial atmosphere, its purveyors discreetly seasoned pastoral with more piquant matter. Sidney introduced a comic pedant among the shepherds of his *Lady of May*; Lyly, following Guarini's example, brought divinities into his *Gallathea*, and these altogether dominate the pastoral scenes of Peele's *Arraignment of Paris*. Even Daniel, so little in sympathy with the crude mixtures which appealed to the popular taste, introduced litigation and quack medicine into *The Queen's Arcadia* (1605). Severer tests awaited pastoral drama written for the popular stage; and the first dramatist who made the attempt, Fletcher, suffered disaster notwithstanding the brilliant lyric qualities, nowhere surpassed in pastoral drama, which distinguish *The Faithful Shepherdess* (1609). Fletcher had in fact scarcely attempted to lift either his personages or his action out of the unreality of pastoral convention; he had merely clothed the actors and the incidents of a universal amorousness in an atmosphere of exquisite music. Shakespeare, a few years before, and again a few years later, showed a better way. Though the poet of *As You Like It* and *The Winter's Tale* merely played brilliantly with pastoral motives, they breathe the finest essence of the pastoral ideal; literary pastoralism itself is introduced only to be gaily derided in Phoebe and Silvius, and set off against the homely reality of Corin and Audrey; while between these stands the glorious creation of Rosalind, 'pastoral' enough to be wooed by verses carved on trees, but reducing both the faded fiction and the dull actuality to insignificance in the radiance of her ideal but living humanity. In *The Winter's Tale* literary pastoralism is no longer glanced at, yet without it we should never have had the exquisite creation of Perdita, no princess playing the

shepherdess in Arcady, but a true shepherd-maid who yet
'nothing does or seems',
> But smacks of something greater than herself,
> Too noble for this place.

Moreover, without probably intending in the least to invigorate pastoral drama, Shakespeare had in *As You Like It* provided his successors with a fruitful suggestion by bringing his pastoral folks from the fields into the woods. Sidney's Arcadia had its woodlands, and Tasso's a woodland nymph courted by his shepherd hero; but these were merely variations of the Arcadian conventions. Shakespeare's Arden, though not without its exotic touches, breathes the enchantment of an English forest, and the intercourse of its shepherds, real and feigned, with its foresters to the manner born or 'brothers in exile', opened up new possibilities for English pastoral, which one fellow-poet at least was, consciously or not, to turn to account.

III

Pastoral drama had, then, when Jonson wrote, already a rich history behind it on the English stage. Imitation of his contemporaries was not in Jonson's way. But to take up motives already used, and show how much more might be made of them by a master both of antique literature and of realist observation, was a procedure quite in conformity with the genius of the author of *Sejanus*. And *The Sad Shepherd* does in fact surpass all its predecessors, if we put Shakespeare *hors de concours*, in bold and free extension of the nation's pastoral field, while Fletcher alone excelled the lyrical beauty of his purely pastoral songs. Where he moves within the pastoral tradition he redeems its conventionality by enchanting grace; where he breaks away from it he abounds in the life and truth that pastoral art so long had lacked.

Jonson is in fact, as no English pastoral poet before him had been, emancipated from those symbolical and satirical applications of pastoralism which had captivated the sixteenth century. Mantuan and Marot, Sidney and Spenser, do not, as pastoralists, exist for him. Even Vergil hardly counts. There is no slavish imitation of any one, but it is plainly the originator of pastoral, Theocritus, who has moulded most effectually Jonson's conception and handling of his pastoral subject, alike by breadth and variety of motives, and the freshness and nearness to life of his art. The shepherds of Theocritus were not yet courtiers or politicians in disguise, speaking the uniformly highflown language which Jonson disliked in Guarini and Sidney, but countrymen whose discourse is the 'speech actually spoken by men', set only to the music of exquisite verse. Their dirges and serenades are lyric moments in lives abounding with other moods and other concerns, and we hear no less distinctly the gay discourse of friends making holiday, or the light bantering talk of comrades over their work. Above all, the scenery is that of no fantastic Arcadia, but of the real Sicily, and it is painted with the crisp, individualizing touch of one who is rendering what he has seen, not what he has vaguely dreamed. The wooded lawns of Aetna, the streams cool from the high snows, the meadows of asphodel and cytisus, the glowing noontide, with the cicada's shrill music everywhere, the yellow bees drinking at the spring, and the lizard sleeping 'like a shadow' on the hot stone wall—all this, and scores of similar traits, the ultimate source of Arcadian landscape but dissolved away in its nebulous outlines, retained their potent appeal to the realist in Jonson, and contributed to the fresh and vivid painting of rustic scenery which distinguishes *The Sad Shepherd* of this ingrained Londoner from all other earlier pastoral save Shakespeare's. The veracity of the Greek has helped Jonson to be veraciously English.

But the Theocritean veracity, being at the same time exquisitely poetic, also helped Jonson here to find, with a sureness of tact far beyond his wont, the poetic side of truth. Now the English shepherd world, as we have seen, could not here match the Sicilian. But there was one region of English rustic life no less rich in poetry, no less steeped in romantic traditions which bore the very *cachet* of the race. The English greenwood, and especially Sherwood Forest, with its legends of Robin Hood, was the best equivalent Jonson's England could provide for the lawns of Aetna and their pastoral tears and mirth. And for drama, the Robin Hood legends offered a far richer and more fruitful source than all the rudimentary stories of Theocritus taken together. To graft the frail exotic growth of pastoral upon the robust stock of English greenwood poetry was a stroke of genius, for which even Shakespeare's pastoral Arden had only partially prepared the way. Far from invoking the national memories of England's greenwood hero, Robin Hood, Shakespeare had deliberately effaced or assuaged all the traces of the Gamelyn tale of Sherwood still retained in Lodge's romance; while in the only extant plays which touch the Robin Hood legends before Jonson, Munday's *Downfall* and *Death of Robert Earl of Huntingdon*, the handling is too perfunctory to require notice.

IV

Jonson's title, *The Sad Shepherd, or A Tale of Robin Hood*, thus marks the union by him of two traditions distinct in origin and character. And their poetic characters remain distinct in his treatment, though not more diverse than the more naturalistic and the more lyric element in the poetry of Theocritus. Aeglamour the Sad Shepherd is purely lyric, as the Sicilian shepherd spontaneously became at the bidding of joy or grief, but was not by habit. Robin Hood and his men correspond rather to the Sicilian shepherd in his daily garb, pursuing his craft and gathering as he goes its chance boons of wit and mirth; while their cheery Germanic humour allies them to the blithe natural gaiety so soon to be lost in the regulation melancholies and despairs of the later pastoral tradition. In the story of

Aeglamour and Earine there is no question of translating the classical shepherd into terms of English life, but rather of emulating his exquisite yet quite un-English music.

The intermingling of poetic styles so sharply contrasted in the same drama has disturbed some excellent critics. Yet Jonson has done much by tact of handling to modulate and harmonize them. The homelier and the more delicate inhabitants of Sherwood are invested in a common atmosphere of poetry analogous, in its lower degree, to the magic which subtly attunes together the princes, clowns, and fairies of the *Midsummer Night's Dream*. Even the rudest of Robin Hood's men speak in verse, and some of them, like Tuck, are of a finer breed than their prototypes in the ballads; while Robin and Marian themselves speak a language admirably fresh and natural in its heartiness and gaiety, yet, none the less, choicely phrased and cadenced; so that this pair mediates as it were between the homelier figures in the company and the frankly poetic 'Sad Shepherd' and his lost love. But Aeglamour and Earine, on their part too, are withdrawn by many delicate touches from the atmosphere of traditional pastoral. They utter their Sicilian plaints among English meads; Earine is thought to be drowned in English Trent, while English local colour and pastoral convention mingle when we are told

> how *Dove*,
> *Deane, Eye,* and *Erwash, Idell, Snite,* and *Soare,*
> Each broke his Vrne, and twenty waters more,
> That swell'd proud *Trent*, shrunke themselves dry.[1]

While in such passages as that in which Aeglamour questions Much about the drowned body of his love—

> Ha' you swept the River say you? and not found her?
> *Much.* For Fowle, and Fish wee have.
> *Aegl.* O not for her?[2]—

the Sicilian poetry of lyric love and the English of woodland adventure are brought together in a single natural and moving situation, not the less effectually that it throws

[1] I. v. 53–6.   [2] I. iii. 31, 32.

their opposite preoccupations—the lost maiden and the fish and fowl—into sharp relief.

Jonson's handling of these contrasted traditions was, in fact, largely determined, as this instance illustrates, by his pronounced predilections as a dramatist. It was not exclusively determined by them, for material so hard to accommodate to his powerful English realism would then probably have been crushed out of existence altogether. He deliberately accepted the pastoral material. But he meant to make a pastoral drama on lines of his own. We know that he strongly disapproved of the pastoral dramas of his predecessors. Sidney and Guarini, he told Drummond, 'make every man speak as well as themselves, forgetting decorum'.[1] And *decorum*, or the correspondence of speech and demeanour with character, Jonson meant to be one of the distinguishing notes of his own pastoral drama. 'Decorum' was compatible with realism, but did not imply it, and Jonson satisfied it completely by finding, for characters which range, like these, from the fanciful to the observed, modes of expression which follow a corresponding gamut from the most ethereal lyric to the homeliest pedestrian speech. The high-wrought lyric phraseology which conventional pastoral assigns equally to all persons and situations is, in our drama, confined to the expression of high-wrought lyrical moods, and hence belongs to characters like Aeglamour, whose moods are solely lyrical. Aeglamour's 'lovely wail' stands out from the plainer eloquence of his associates, but not more than his 'deep-hurt phantsie' and his fevered grief stand out from their joyous, healthy animation. The beautiful extravagances of impassioned imagination, of common pastoral, recover their truth as the language of a mind which passion has thus violently transformed. If flowers spring up in Earine's footsteps (I. i), if 'the whole Earth sicken when she dies', and the little rivers shrink themselves dry, this is felt as the flush of

---

[1] *Convers.* xviii. 611 ; cf. iv. 4–5, with explicit reference to the *Pastor Fido*.

a lover's fevered fancy; as a pathetic individual aberration in a normal world, not as the symptom of a pervading caprice.

For the rest this abnormal mood and character, as abnormal in Jonson's drama as in life, finds in him a wonderfully complete response. The lyric poet who slept in the formidable master of humours never spoke more authentically than in Aeglamour's opening lament, 'Here she was wont to goe! and here! and here!' and in his passionate outburst in reply to Robin's kindly exhortation to mix with us

In all the profer'd solace of the Spring.

Of Earine herself we have hardly any distinct glimpse apart from the glamour in which her lover's passion invests her. There she seems less a woman than a 'lovely apparition', holding in herself all the magic of spring, while wholly exempt from the abstractions of allegory. She is imagined indeed rather in the vein of primitive myth than of allegory; and her adventures are perhaps modelled on those told of Daphnis, the spirit of spring. Like Daphnis she is enclosed in a tree, and her supposed drowning in Trent may reflect the plunge of Daphnis in the cool river wave when the dog-days came on.

The other shepherds and maidens are of a less exalted lyricism; they express more ordinary moods in language less high-flown, if hardly less choice. Their speech matches in refined beauty at least the more pedestrian passages of the *Aminta*; it has flashes worthy of Tasso at his best. But the conception of character shows little subservience to the school of literary pastoral. Love is delightfully fresh and natural, remote alike from the prudish asceticism and from the impudent wantonness which were part of its dramatic stock-in-trade, and had been freely exploited by Fletcher. But with the natural love of Robin and Marian, we quit the pastoral world altogether. Passion speaks no more in Aeglamour's lyric eloquence, but in quip and crank and gay repartee. Love-making has a different *ethos*; the lover is a cheery craftsman, not a leisured sentimentalist. Pastoral orthodoxy held that 'the truest Lovers are least fortunate', and recited the 'Lovers Scriptures' to prove it; 'jolly Robin' defies such augury, for he

                       the story is
Of all beatitude in Love.

In his mouth is fitly put the glowing description of the happy age, which still might be,

              when on the Plaines
The Wood-men met the Damsells, . . .
And all did either love, or were belov'd.[1]

And as the blitheness of Robin and Marian is opposed to the 'melodious despair' of conventional pastoral, so are their energy and resource to the pastoral indolence. When Robin, in common with the whole company of shepherd guests, is dumbfounded by the amazing transformation of the supposed Marian, he alone refuses to succumb to the spell. 'The best is silence,' says Lionel; 'And to await the issue,' adds Alken the wise. 'The dead, or lazie wait for't,' cries Robin; 'I will find it.'[2]

And it is especially Robin and his train who justify (so far as our fragment goes) the prospect of 'mirth' defiantly held out in the Prologue to the 'heretics' who opined

      That Mirth by no means fits a Pastorall.

V

Effective drama, however, in Jonson's sense, demanded more sinister elements than this blithe woodland society readily provided. His predecessors in pastoral drama, as we have seen, had met this need in their characteristic way, by calling in malign figures from the classical pastoral world, just as some of them provided their sanctions and retributions by the aid of the divinities of Olympus. The Satyr was a yet more obvious resort for the modern dramatist.

[1] I. iv. 42–7.   [2] I. vii. 37, 38.

These shaggy kobolds of the Greek woodlands with their uncanny blend of insatiable animal appetites and superhuman power, had been dreaded and shunned by the Greek shepherd; and in the idealized shepherd life of the literary pastoral they never ceased to be at least a remote and possible peril. But it was pastoral drama and pastoral romance which made the fortune of the Satyr. In general he threatens or attempts outrage upon one or more of the shepherdesses—often, as in the *Aminta*, the heroine; her lover, accepted or disdained, intervenes in time, and her 'cruelty' in the latter case yields after a sufficient interval to gratitude and reward. More rarely, the wantonness of the Satyr is subordinate to his malignity; so in the *Pastor Fido*, he betrays the human lovers to the agents of the goddess whose law they have broken. Rarely, the Satyr is a benign and friendly character. In some of the followers of Tasso and Guarini a Centaur, or a Triton, takes the Satyr's place.

The English Pastoralists before Jonson had taken over the Satyr, for the most part, with an altered character and function. Italian cynicism dwelt on his goatish aspect, and made him an embodiment of unbridled lust; the Elizabethan saw in his uncouth figure only rude and untaught nature, capable of warm impressions and childlike devotion. The wild wood people are discovered listening rapt to the teaching of Una, and one who is half a Satyr by birth becomes her rescuer and escort.[1] Hence perhaps, though with added touches of Ariel, the charming conception of the Satyr in Fletcher's *Faithful Shepherdess*, where there are other reminiscences of Spenser. And so it is not astonishing that in the 'Elysian' pastoral world of Drayton,[2] where the evil things of antique myth grow innocuous, the Satyr loses his wanton nature (though the maids still shudder at his dangerous repute), and becomes a harmless, even pathetic creature, mourning over the lost woodlands once his haunt. In the Satyr's place, as contriver of harms in his Shepherd

[1] *Faerie Queene*, I. vi.   [2] *Muses' Elysium*, Nymphal x.

drama, Fletcher had put a Shepherd; a change which, however suggested, was certainly in keeping with the confirmed humanism of the drama of 1608. His 'sullen Shepherd' nevertheless falls nothing short, in the monotony of his malice and salacity, of any satyr, devil, or god in literature. Jonson, we know, thought highly of *The Faithful Shepherdess*, and his Lorel has recognizable affinities with the Sullen Shepherd. But his group of malign powers was at once more complex and more English than Fletcher's. Maudlin the Witch, with her son, her daughter, and her attendant fiend—all summoned up for the frustration of the happiness of the shepherds and hunters—illustrate the unfailing lavishness, and the prevalent realism, of Jonson's invention. Not Fletcher, far less Spenser, but rather his old friend ('esteemed' or not) Michael Drayton, was his nearest English precursor in this latter repect. But Drayton's method was different. Olympus and Parnassus seem to have poured forth their people, if we listen to their names only, upon the pages of his Elysium. But whatever they may be called, the most unmistakable English men and maids, hale and buxom, blithe and frolic, discover themselves in the faces and forms that bear these classic labels and attributes. Venus and Cupid, trespassing furtively in the Elysium from which they have been sternly excluded, become a merry English wife and her 'little lad'; they take ferry, and she chats gaily with the ferryman, who marvels at the 'little dapper elf', 'half bird half boy', and finds it passing strange 'to have a child have wings to fly, and yet want eyes to see'. Drayton, in some sense the 'brave heroic mind' *par excellence* among all the Elizabethans, dared these incongruities with impunity, such is the charm of the English freshness and homeliness which his magic throws upon the most exotic figures. Here and there, in the Masques, Jonson had approached this arch and jocund mode of acclimatizing antique myth. But in *The Sad Shepherd*, boldly varied like the courses of the banquet he provides, he avoids at least this kind and degree of incongruity. He gives his shepherds a Greek, as well as Romance and English names; no classic deities or monsters invade the scene, as thoroughly English as Drayton's, in which they meet and revel. Save for a passing allusion by the love-sick Aeglamour to the days (long gone by moreover)

when *Cupid* smil'd,
And *Venus* led the *Graces* out to dance,[1]

or by Maudlin to Hecate,[2] who was already associated with northern witchcraft, all explicit intrusion of the classic myth-world is avoided; and even a bare reference to antiquity is rare. Classical myth has nevertheless left a very definite impress upon the poetry and upon the plot of *The Sad Shepherd*. Sometimes a Greek mythical trait is simply transferred to the English scene, as in the mourning of Nature for Earine. With more vigour of inventions he finds an effectual native equivalent for the *Satyr*. As Robin Hood and his huntsmen offered the nearest English equivalent of the poetic shepherds of Sicily, so the salacious and malignant Satyr-folk found a parallel in the Witch's son. Lorel, the rude swineherd, attempts the seduction of the captured Earine, as Tasso's Satyr that of Sylvia; and his mother's magic arts supplement the deficiencies of his own untutored wit. It may be supposed that Aeglamour would finally have rescued his lost mistress, like Aminta, from her captivity. Lorel's actual 'love-craft', as well as his form and feature, are, however, modelled upon those of a wooer blunter but more honest than this Satyr—the Cyclops Polypheme of Theocritus. Like Polypheme, he has to plead that a 'camus'd' nose and a hairy face ought not to count too heavily against a lover who can offer his mistress such stores of milk and cheese, and can pipe like never another of his fellows.[3] Other traits are rendered, with delicate tact, in terms of English life and scenery. Polypheme inhabits a cave shaded by laurels and cypresses, and overgrown with ivy and vine, and a torrent

---

[1] I. v. 48, 49.   [2] II. iii. 42.   [3] Theocritus, xi. 32–4, 38.

descending from the snows of Aetna provides a draught divinely cold through the livelong heats of the Sicilian summer. Lorel dwells in a hut ; oak, beech, chestnut, and poplar grow before his door, and 'twa trilland brooks' fresh from their springs ' make a river, to refresh my feet '. Polypheme woos with gifts of young bears, Lorel with badger-cubs. And each has a mother who, though she has been the occasion of her son's passion, refuses to have any part in furthering it. ' 'Tis all my mother's fault,' complains Polypheme; 'she never once put in a kind word for me with thee.'[1] This may well be the germ of the scene where Maud and Douce step aside and listen while Lorel unfolds his rustic love-craft, and then roundly rail at his boorish mode of wooing a gracious nymph.

Lorel is indeed, so far as the extant story shows, little more than his mother's tool: the one formidable malign power is the Witch herself. In the spells and enchantments of witchcraft Jonson found an equivalent, which could not fail to thrill an English audience, for those arbitrary interpositions of Diana or Venus which even in Italian spectators could generate but a faint academic interest. But the colouring, as with Lorel, is partly derived from a kindred Theocritean scene; here, like the deserted wife Simaetha, she plies her spells to the whirling of a brazen magic wheel.[2] Simaetha propitiates Hecate—'dread Hecate, whom the young dogs tremble at', as she paces among the tombs, and prays Queen Moon to shine full ; Maudlin turns her wheel on a moonlight night ' when our dame Hecate

> Made it her gaing-night, over the Kirk-yard,
> With all the bark and parish tykes set at her.[3]

And her magic wheel is a spindle the threads of which are wrought, with the spells she utters, into the magic robe she is to wear: a picture which might have carried us far from the homely associations of Sherwood into the neighbourhood of Shakespeare's homeless witches who seem not like the inhabitants of earth and yet are on it, were it not that

---

[1] Theocritus, xi. 67-8.   [2] Ibid. ii. 30.   [3] II. iii. 43, 44.

the robe is wrought by a Gipsy, and that the witch and the 'sewster' are sitting 'under the towne turne-pike'. But modern witch-lore was the source of Maudlin's actual devices in the plot, which appear to have consisted mainly of deceptive personation. Douce's personation of Earine probably has its origin in Fletcher's Amarillis-Amoret, perhaps in Spenser's Duessa-Una. More original than Maudlin herself is the picture of the gloomy dimble where she dwells—a sinister counterpart of the elvish woodlands of the *Midsummer Night's Dream*. The Witches' cavern in Macbeth is like themselves without locality; the horrible ingredients of their cauldron are gathered from far and near, from sea and land, with nothing in common but their monstrosity. Jonson's Maudlin is a more commonplace creation than these; unequivocally human and feminine, without a hint of the cosmic sublimity which gives the 'weird sisters', 'posters of the sea and land', an illusive resemblance to the Fates. She is a palpable inhabitant of the earth, and the spot of earth she inhabits is rank with a teeming luxuriance of the malign plant and animal life that ministers to her arts:

> the venom'd Plants
> Wherewith she kill's,

the sad mandrake, whose groans are deathful, nightshade and hemlock, adder's tongue, and martagan. Horror and melancholy hang about the place, and the Romanticism of the unborn Shelley is prefigured in lurid lines which tell how it lies

Close by the ruines of a shaken Abbey,
Torne, with an Earth-quake, down unto the ground,
'Mongst graves, and grotts, neare an old Charnell house.[1]

Of Puck-hairy, Maudlin's attendant goblin, little can be said. He enters the play only with the fragmentary third act, and in spite of his claim to be to Maudlin what Mephistopheles had been to Faustus, appears to be as unequivocally human and natural as Jonson's supernatural beings habitu-

[1] II. viii. 17-19.

ally are. No kinsman of the impish Puck, hardly even of Jonson's own hapless outwitted Pug, he has the air of a sagacious and wary steward to a flighty and enterprising mistress, whom he alternately deludes and protects, while she on her part 'thinks she does all', and he, on his, complains of the hardships of his service. There can be no doubt that, in the finished play, Puck-hairy's protection would have proved futile, that Maudlin would have been caught, and Earine released; and Puck-hairy, if not anxious about the issue, yet feels, like Satan, in *The Devil is an Ass*, that the game of baffling the schemes of men is arduous and troublesome. What his fate was to be it is in vain to guess. But the last we hear of Maudlin indicates that Jonson imagined her final scene in delightful keeping with the pervading wood-craft spirit of the piece; when her spells and charms are wrought, the jolly huntsmen led by Alken will track her again to the dimble where she sits like a hare in her form—('for a witch is a kind of hare'—and 'marks the weather as the hare does')—and

   make this hunting of the Witch, as famous,
As any other blast of Venerie.[1]

[1] II. viii. 70, 71.

THE ADDITIONS TO
'THE SPANISH TRAGEDY'

APPENDIX IX

THE ADDITIONS TO 'THE SPANISH TRAGEDY'

The Elizabethan practice of adapting old plays to the tastes of the day has greatly multiplied the critical problems incident in any case to a dramatic literature largely of unknown or disputed authorship. In the *cause célèbre* of *Hamlet*, owing to the loss of the old play, a final judgement will probably never be pronounced. In the case of the Second or Third Parts of *Henry VI* both the original and the adapted versions are extant, and the problem is only one of authorship. In a third group the old play was merely provided with 'additions'. Marlowe's *Faustus* in its final form is a famous example of this type; and to it belongs also *The Spanish Tragedy* of Kyd, for 'adicyons' to which Henslowe, according to his own entries in his Diary, twice 'lent' considerable sums, in 1601-2, to 'Benjamin Jonson'. Here the prima facie evidence of authorship is clear, and the problem arises solely from the extreme disparity between Jonson's known work and that here ascribed to him. It is true that this known work of his abounds in warnings against a too rigid determination of what he could and could not do; the 'robustness' of his comic satire might seem incompatible with the delicate poetry of his Masques; and the loss of all his early work, with the probability that *Every Man out of His Humour* marks a deliberate and pronounced revolution in his dramatic technique, makes it impossible to exclude the possibility of a 'romantic' vein in him, normally suppressed but occasionally, for special purposes, indulged. This view was entertained and ably urged by one of the acutest interpreters of the Elizabethan drama, John Addington Symonds.[1] To a great extent this view of Jonson is our own. Whether it suffices to justify Jonson's claim to the Additions to *The Spanish Tragedy*, it is the purpose of the present note to decide.

[1] *Ben Jonson*, pp. 15, 16.

238   *The Additions to*

The entries in question are as follows :

Lent unto m^r alleyn, the 25 of septmb₃ 1601 to lend vnto Bengemen Johnson vpon his writtinge of his adicians in geronymo the some of—————————————— } xxxx[a]

vnto bengemy Johnsone
Lent ₔ at the a poyntment of E Alleyn and w^m birde the 22 of June 1602 in earneste of a Boocke called Richard crockbacke, & for new adicyons for Jeronymo the some of——————— } x[li]

Diary, folios 94, 106 verso (ed. Greg, pp. 149, 168). According to these entries, Jonson was twice commissioned by Henslowe to write 'additions' to this popular play, Alleyn, and in the second case also Birde, presumably guaranteeing their due execution. Further, some 'additions', described as new, were in the same year incorporated in Kyd's play ; a new edition of it being issued at the close of 1602 with the following title-page :

' The | Spanish Tragedie : | Containing the lamen | table end of Don Horatio, and Bel-Imperia : | with the pittifull death of olde | Hieronimo. | Newly corrected, amended, and enlarged with | new additions of the Painters part, and | others, as it hath of late been | diuers times acted. | Imprinted at London . . . 1602.'

It is natural to identify the additions here advertised with those which Jonson a few months before had been paid to compose. But the known reluctance of theatre companies to allow their plays to be published while still earning money on the stage, introduces the suspicion that Jonson's additions of June, 1602, were too recent to be published in the same year, and therefore that the additions that were so published, and the authorship of which is in dispute, were not by him.

In this 'amended' form the famous old play renewed its youth, and a second quarto, substantially identical with this, appeared early in the following year, 1603 ; others appearing in 1611, 1615, 1618, 1623, and 1633. There can be no doubt that this success was due to the 'additions' so alluringly emphasized in the title-page. They did not indeed avail to silence all cavils at the expense of a play that had become by 1600 a favourite butt for the wits. Jonson, after as before, stood in the forefront of these cavillers. In 1598 he had made the play the favourite reading of Bobadill and the Town Gull. In 1600 he introduced another 'whom it hath pleas'd nature to furnish with more beard, then braine', swearing ' *That the old Hieronimo*, (as it was first acted) *was the onely best, and iudiciously pend play of Europe*'.[1] And even in 1614 he pronounced authoritatively in the Induction to *Bartholomew Fair*, that 'Hee that will sweare, *Ieronimo*, or *Andronicus* are the best playes, yet, shall passe vnexcepted at, heere, as a man whose Iudgment shewes it is constant, and hath stood still, these fiue and twentie or thirtie yeeres'. In this, Jonson's only explicit reference, as distinguished from the numerous allusions and quotations, to the play after the date of the 'Additions', it will be seen that he entirely ignores them. The only passage in which he might be understood to distinguish a revised from the original form of the play—that in *Cynthia's Revels*—was written, and printed, before the date of these additions. No inference affecting the present question can therefore be drawn from the words 'as it was first acted', pointed as they seem. And there is nothing else to suggest, as Dr. Boas thinks, 'a personal motive for belittling the play' derived from his own authorship of the 'Additions'.[2] If any inference could be drawn from the *Bartholomew Fair* passage, it would be that the scenes to which the play was so largely indebted for its persistent popularity were due to some fellow-dramatist—such as Shakespeare—whose writing was uncongenial to him and wholly unlike his own, and of whose technical methods he strongly disapproved. No such inference, of course, can be justly drawn from so slender a basis of fact. But it would be far truer to the view which modern criticism almost unanimously has taken of these scenes than that which accepts as decisive Henslowe's ascription of them to Jonson.

They consist of five passages (ed. Boas, II. v. 46-98; III. ii. 65-74; III. xi. 2-50; III. 12 A; IV. iv. 168-217), the fourth being an entire scene; together some 320 lines. They are all devoted to the elaboration of a single motive,—the harrowing grief of Hieronymo for his son. Since Kyd wrote, the Elizabethans had discovered resources of imaginative expression far beyond his, and these scenes are, as imaginative renderings of passion,

---

[1] *Cynthia's Revels*, Induction.   [2] *Kyd's Works*, p. lxxxvii.

worthy of comparison with the best that, in 1601, they had done. As Dr. Boas has pointed out, however, in his acute discussion, their dramaturgical value is by no means equal to their literary quality. The finest of them, in particular, the famous 'Painter' scene so prominently announced on the title-pages, is in its root-motive—the visit to the bereaved Hieronymo of another father of a lost son—a replica of the original scene which immediately follows; and the Painter's visit—at midnight, to the garden-bower where Horatio had perished—achieves its superb imaginative effect at the cost of gross unlikelihood; a kind of expense which it was not characteristic of Kyd—and still less, we may add, of Jonson—to incur. His dangerous frankness to Lorenzo in the Second Addition (III. ii. 65 f.):

> In troth my Lord it is a thing of nothing,
> The murder of a Sonne, or so:

is psychologically defensible in a man whose reason is mastered by grief, but, like the First (II. v. 46 f.), the Third (III. xi. 2 f.), and the Fourth (III. xii. A), disturbs the coherence of the total effect by the abruptness with which we are carried to and fro from the raving Hieronymo to the sane one, and from impetuously disordered eloquence to Kyd's stately but somewhat mechanical decasyllabics. The sharpness of these transitions was itself a technical fault in a literary fabric not designed to resemble mosaic. Even where, as in the Third Addition, both the 'inlaid' piece and its immediate context are highly imaginative, the change of manner and *tempo* (at l. 50) is strikingly abrupt; the more so as these fifty lines have no dramatic link with the context either at the opening or the close, Hieronymo's first line after the insertion (l. 51),

> Good leaue haue you: nay, I pray you goe,

responding to its immediate predecessor in the original (l. 1),

> By your leaue sir,

not to what intervenes. The author of the 'Additions', we must conclude, was a poet of rare poetic and tragic power, but either a rather indifferent or a rather unscrupulous workman.

How far does Jonson fulfil this character? We may consider, in the first place, his treatment of similar topics and situations elsewhere. We know that in 1598 Meres (in common doubtless with cultivated Elizabethan playgoers in general) reckoned him among the notable contemporary writers of tragedy. But of his early tragedies nothing unfortunately has survived. From the five years intervening between Mere's reference and *Sejanus* we have a few titles. Jonson himself, we cannot doubt, deliberately excluded all his earlier tragic writing from his Collected Works. He may have condemned it as inferior in quality, or as composed on principles of tragic art other than those which his ripe taste approved. It is natural to conclude, as most critics have done, that these earlier tragedies were more 'Elizabethan', more 'romantic', than *Sejanus* and *Cataline*. But this carries us little way, and leaves wholly unanswered the one vital question, whether this earlier tragedy of Jonson was allied—as the 'Additions' surely are—not only in untutored freedom of workmanship, but in imaginative genius, to the tragedy of Shakespeare and Webster. In default of tragedy, however, we have fortunately at least a tragi-comedy, which falls short of tragedy only in its happy end, which is still untouched by Jonson's later 'classical' technique, and which further offers a proximate parallel to the very situation so powerfully elaborated in the 'Additions'.

The Case is Altered, as we have seen, was produced in 1599. Some two years earlier Jonson had acquired peculiar familiarity both with *The Spanish Tragedy* and with the role and situation of Hieronymo by playing that part himself on Henslowe's stage. It is likely enough that he elaborated the Plautine story of Hegio and his 'captive' son with a reminiscence of this famous and familiar role; for Count Ferneze describes his loss with a passion which makes him more like Hieronymo than Hegio. That Jonson's own not very emotional nature was yet keenly sensitive to the pathos of this form of bereavement we may gather from the verses called forth four years later by the death of his boy—'Ben Jonson his best piece of poetry'.[1] The situation of Count Ferneze was, then, one likely to elicit whatever capacity for rendering the pathos of a son's loss Jonson possessed. It is as immaterial for this comparison that Camillo is, unlike Horatio, ultimately restored, as that at the time of the supposed action he has been lost for nineteen years instead of for a few hours. Jonson makes

[1] *Epigram* xlv.

Ferneze still agitated with the passion of his loss. He chances to use the words 'my only son', and 'that word *only*' strikes his heart cold and gives it a deep wound. The memory of 'that black and fearful night' when he lost Camillo is still as fresh as if it had been yesterday, and he breaks off the narrative,—

> my heart is great.
> Sorrow is faint; and passion makes me sweat.
> (I. ix.)

When Camillo actually appears (v. ix), his father, supposing him to be Chamont, is about to consign him to the gallows; but his hand is stayed by an apparition of the phantom form of his son standing 'betwixt him and me'. He bursts into tears and turns aside:

> What a child am I
> To haue a child? Ay me, my son, my son.

This hallucination is Ferneze's (and Jonson's) nearest approach to the unreason of grief.

A comparison of these passages with the 'Additions' discloses differences more radical than can be explained by the greater vehemence of Hieronymo's grief, or by its more definitely unhinging effect upon his brain. Both the psychology and the poetry are of a wholly different order. Jonson's description of Ferneze's symptoms is competent and well expressed, but without one rare touch, one penetrating or memorable trait; on the whole, his emotion is described from without, not from within. His reception, for instance, of the news of Camillo's capture is not very convincing:

> Ill newes of my sonne,
> My deere and onely sonne, Ile lay my soule.
> Ay me accurs'd, thought of his death doth wound me,
> And the report of it will kill me quite.
> (III. iv.)

Nor his outburst under hallucination:

> What miracle is this? tis my own fancy
> Carues this impression in me, my soft nature,
> That euer hath retaind such foolish pitty. . . .
> (v. ix.)

This is the language of analysis rather than of possession.

The verse throughout is Jonson's uniform, regular, measured blank, without either the subtle modulations or the bold departures from the norm which add so much to the moving power of Hieronymo's outbursts.

If Jonson wrote the 'Additions' he had to represent a father doubtless more overwhelmed by grief than Ferneze, and it may well have been precisely his madness that drew the public and of which the management desired a more plentiful and piquant supply. We know what tumults of incoherence the typical Elizabethan accepted, and produced, as 'madness' under such conditions; and it is hard to believe that Jonson, the most 'rational' of them all, could here have found and walked securely on the path known otherwise almost alone to the poet of Ophelia and of Lear. Hieronymo's 'lunacy' is, no more than theirs, incoherent; its wildest fancies are held together by the one torturing thought which they transfigure and transform when he bids his men

> Light me your torches at the mid of noone
> When as the Sun-God rides in all his glorie;

the thread of reason in his unreason leads him from the Sun to 'yonder pale faced Hee-cat there, the Moone', who did not shine that night his son was murdered. The transition that follows is a wonderful stroke, equally daring and true:

> Had the Moone shone, in my boyes face (there was a kind of grace
> That I know) nay, I doe know, had the murderer seene him,
> His weapon would haue fall'n and cut the earth,
> Had he been framed of naught but blood and death.

So the Tree becomes a living and malicious thing in his hands:

> I set it of a kiernnell:
> And when our hot Spaine coulde not let it grow,
> But that the infant and the humaine sap
> Began to wither, duly twice a morning
> Would I be sprinkling it with fountaine water.
> At last it grewe, and grewe, and bore, and bore,
> Till at the length it grew a gallowes, and did beare our sonne.
> It bore thy fruit and mine: O wicked, wicked plant.

The ensuing colloquy with the Painter recalls yet unwritten work of Shakespeare at more than one point. When he retorts to the Painter, who also had lost a son, and 'no man did holde a sonne so deare',

> What not as thine? that's a lie,
> As massie as the earth, I had a sonne,
> Whose least vnuallued haire did waigh
> A thousand of thy sonnes,

we think of Hamlet's frenzy in the grave of Ophelia—

> What is he whose grief
> Bears such an emphasis?

And the temper of his proposal to his comrade in grief to

> range this hidious orchard vp and downe,
> Like to two Lyons reaued of their yong,

may even, more faintly, recall Lear's desire to 'talk a word with this same learned Theban', whose 'daughters have brought him to this pass'.

To prove that Jonson cannot have written these scenes is of course impossible. But to admit that he may have written them is to strain almost to breaking-point the theory which would credit even his rugged nature with incalculable reserves of power, only on this one occasion disclosed. Such reserves, it may be said, are revealed in the rare loveliness of *The Sad Shepherd*, the astonishing creation of his late maturity, perhaps of his last years. But the lyric beauty which distinguishes this fragment does not differ in kind from that scattered profusely through his Masques. It in no way resembles the tragic work of Shakespeare, to which the 'Additions', as many critics from Coleridge onwards have suggested, show points of kinship. It might be argued that the 'Additions' are not more different from *The Sad Shepherd* than *King Lear* from the *Midsummer Night's Dream*. But that would be to consider only the utterly disparate substance and temper, and to ignore the subtle affinities of style and verse which permeate even chronologically and poetically remote portions of Shakespeare's work. No such links can be discovered between the 'Additions' and any part of Jonson's authentic writing. And we can come to yet closer grips with the problem. For if Jonson wrote the 'Additions', he was moving with full mastery, in 1601, at a level of poetic and tragic expression to which, two years before, when his dramatic fortunes still hung in the balance, and again two years later, when he was deliberately seeking to procure a reversal, in tragedy, of the popular condemnation of his comedies, he showed equally little power and inclination to rise. That the

The Spanish Tragedy 245

Jonson who at twenty-six wrote *The Case is Altered* should at twenty-eight have been capable of writing the 'Additions' may not be beyond belief. But is it credible that one who was capable of the 'Additions' should for the rest of his life betray no hint of the same quality and kind of power?

There remains, of course, the stubborn fact of Henslowe's entries. But the knowledge and accuracy of this illiterate manager are not such as to justify unconditional trust. Both entries indicate transactions not simply between Henslowe and Jonson, but through the mediation of third persons. The sums in both cases were 'lent' upon work undertaken, but not yet, apparently, handed in. Such a statement cannot guarantee, if there is strong internal evidence to the contrary, that the work undertaken by Jonson was not carried out by some one else. This, unless judgement be held in complete suspense, appears to us to be the least vulnerable conclusion.

INTRODUCTION TO MASQUES AND ENTERTAINMENTS

Inigo Jones's design for a Nymph in 'Chloridia'

MASQUES AND ENTERTAINMENTS

'LIGHTLY built', said Schiller, 'is the car of Thespis; like Charon's barque it carries only shades and phantoms; and if rude life presses aboard, the frail craft threatens to capsize, being fit only for flitting ghosts to tread. Semblance must never match reality; if Nature triumphs, Art is overcome.'[2] The age which has seen the drama vitalized by the realism of Ibsen and his successors may well demur to the unqualified emphasis of this assertion. 'Rude life', thrusting in among the unsubstantial phantoms of an overconventional or academic art, is more apt to ballast the frail craft than to capsize it. If the drama does not exist solely in virtue of holding up a glass to reality, this condition has rarely damaged it, and is indeed one of its surest paths to excellence. But there are some species of literary art in which a certain remoteness from reality, a phantomlike detachment not merely from matter-of-fact experience but from the very possibility of actual existence, is one of the conditions of the medium in which the artist operates and of the effect at which he aims. Like music and sculpture, the Fable, for instance, and the Pastoral are founded upon a certain negation of realism; a Fable in which the animals grunt or neigh instead of talking, a Pastoral in which the shepherds' 'simplicity' does not shadow forth some noble matter, affect us

[1] Every writer on the Masque is under heavy obligations to two remarkable monographs: R. Brotanek, *Die englischen Maskenspiele* (1902), and P. Reyher, *Les Masques anglais* (1909). The section on the Pre-Jonsonian Masque in the present introduction is much indebted, in particular, to Brotanek's able sifting and discussion of the material. Reference may also be made, for this section, to Dr. E. K. Chambers's valuable survey in *The Mediaeval Stage*, ch. xvii, and Dr. W. W. Greg's *A List of Masques, Pageants, &c.* Dr. Chambers's chapters on the Masque in his *Elizabethan Stage* appeared only when the present Introduction was complete.
[2] Schiller, *An Goethe, als er den* Mahomet *von Voltaire auf die Bühne brachte* (1800).

like the music which imitates sounds, or the painted statue.

What is true of Pastoral and of Fable appears to mark the character, not less, of a literary *genre* more fugitive, local, and temporary than either—the Court Masque, as shaped and practised by a few men of genius for a single generation during the first half of the seventeenth century. An 'unsubstantial pageant' indeed, based on the capricious taste and the insecure poetic enthusiasms of a Court. Threatened on the one side by the regular drama, then just reaching its supreme heights of humanity and passion, and in danger, on the other, of being engulfed in the abysses of a soulless magnificence, the Masque sustained a precarious existence, and came in fact to an early and final dissolution. The Civil Wars, which suspended the vitality of the drama, extinguished, save for a casual flicker or two in the early Commonwealth, that of the Masque; and this was one, and not the least worthy or beautiful, of the traditions which the Court of the Restoration could not, and did not attempt to, restore. Neither Jonson himself, nor those two or three others whom he allowed to be capable, 'next himself, of making a Masque', succeeded in rooting it in English soil. The noble poetry of *Comus* only accentuates the perishable quality of the Masque-form which it transgresses or ignores. But Jonson, refining this form, yet working within it, triumphs, not once or twice only, over its infirmity; and these little pieces, on which he lavished his rare double gift of comic invention and lyric grace, reflect better than any other part of his work, equally narrow in compass, the fertility and varied capacity of his genius.

When, towards the close of 1604, Jonson was called upon to produce his first Masque, the Court entertainment that went by that name had a long and complicated history behind it. The name itself had been somewhat less than a century in use. But it is tolerably clear that what began about 1512, it has often been said under Italian influence, to be called a 'Masque' differed in no intrinsic quality from

Masques and Entertainments

the 'disguisings' and 'mummings' which had for a century and more [1] preceded them in England, and of which we first have a distinct description in the later fourteenth century.[2] The band of one hundred and thirty Londoners who, in 1377, rode 'disguizedly aparailed' as esquires, knights, cardinals, emperor, pope, and devils, to Prince Richard at Kennington, entered the hall, and, after playing at dice with him, danced with the company, exhibit with perfect clearness three features which the later Masque consistently retained. (1) The *dance*, executed by the 'disguised' persons or masquers, remained to the last the culminating and indispensable event towards which the whole preceding action, however superior in dramatic interest, was designed to lead up. That the dance and the 'disguise', to our feeling so little connected, had an historic nexus is indicated by the frequent emergence of the dance-motive in the dramatically developed Masque, in situations where it is irrelevant or discordant. The dance, as a social festival, was originally mimetic, and the mask its principal instrument of mimicry. (2) The abrupt *entrance* of the disguised persons—a company of ostensible strangers—into the festive hall was a piquant moment, which, again, the later Masque persistently retained. And while the dance became little more than a rudimentary survival in the matured Masque, the entrance or disclosure of the masquers was turned to brilliant poetic and dramatic account in a score of ways, on the

[1] Hall describes how 'on the day of the Epiphany at night, the king with a xi other were disguised, after the maner of Italie, called a maske, a thyng not sene afore in Englande'. Hall had himself described disguisings closely similar as recently as 1510. The Revels account describing the provision, on the later occasion, of 'long gowns and hoods with hats after the manner of maskelyng in Etaly' is consistent with the view that 'the thyng not sene afore in Englande' was merely the Italian mode of 'disguise'. But Reyher, *u. s.* p. 20, gives reasons for holding that whereas the 'mummers' and 'disguisers' performed in strict silence, the 'masquers' talked with their ladies. This innovation in technique was in any case one of the causes of the rapid popularity of the Masque as a Court entertainment.

[2] The use of 'masks' (*larvae, viseres*) for various sportive purposes is of course much older; Chambers's *Mediaeval Stage*, i, p. 391, regards it as 'the most direct legacy to Christmas' of the Roman Kalends celebrations.

successive development and fluctuating vogue of which the history of the later Masque largely depends. (3) And to the last, the masquers, like the disguised citizens of 1377, *took part with the courtly spectators* in the dance.

But in every point of art beyond the dance and the disguise the early mummings were quite rudimentary. The mummers neither spoke nor sang; they supported imaginary parts, but without the stimulus of an imaginary action or scenic accompaniments. From the standpoint of the developed Masque they were a company of players elaborately dressed for performance, but without a stage, scenery, music, plot, dialogue, or voice. All these things were added by degrees, lifting the Masque ultimately to a level of artistic and poetic achievement in which the original masqued dance itself had a very slender share. While the dance elsewhere, especially among the country-folk, often grew into a rude dramatic sport, in the Masque it remained, on the whole, a mere nucleus, gracious and dignified, but unfruitful, about which the dramatic elements gradually gathered. And both the persistence of the dance, and its resistance to dramatic development, were powerfully promoted by the change in the personnel of the Masque which was involved when, at some time before the end of the fifteenth century, the masqued dance was carried out, not by disguised and privileged outsiders, but by members of the Court circle itself. By the opening of the sixteenth century the Masque (still called a 'disguising') had made striking advances in elaboration. All the resources of courtly art were called in to the celebration of the marriage of Prince Arthur to Catharine of Aragon in 1501. The dance was now introduced and preceded by 'pageants proper and subtile'. In some of them the dancers were already visible from the first, looking out from the windows of the castle, whence they presently descend. In others they were hidden, for instance, in the bosom of a 'mountain', which at a given moment suddenly opened, when they sallied forth and danced as before. But this was by no means the limit

Masques and Entertainments 253

of what had been achieved at this date. Some of the pageants referred to exhibit both speech and song and the germs of dramatic action. Eight ladies appear in a castle ; a ship approaches manned by Hope and Desire, who seek the promise of their favour in the name of eight knights. The envoys receive a negative reply, which they communicate to the suitors. The knights thereupon proceed to attack the castle, which presently yields, and then the nascent and tentative drama dissolves, and besiegers and besieged engage in the inevitable dance.[1]

For another century, however, these beginnings of dramatic dialogue made little advance within the narrow province of the Masque, notwithstanding the rapid progress of play-making and stagecraft during the same period and to a great extent in the same courtly *milieu*. This was due to no nicety of critical discrimination between what was proper to the two spheres,—the exuberance of Elizabethan art swept over these distinctions, or huddled several species together as in Polonius's playbill,—but simply to the different nature of the personnel. The noble amateurs who took part in these diversions completely answered the purpose of stately spectacle as they sat, magnificently caparisoned, at the windows of their castles and arbours, descended thence in dignified procession, and finally mingled in the courtly coranto or galliot. But they rarely either were, or aspired to be, qualified for the lively yet exacting dramatic 'interludes', performed by hired professional players, which beguiled the impatient expectation of the courtly audience 'till the disguising came in'.[2]

To a less dramatic form of speech, on the other hand, the conditions of the disguising were directly favourable, viz. the explanatory monologue. In proportion as the device embodied in the disguising grew in subtlety, arose the need for an interpreter or 'presenter' who should at once introduce the persons and describe their situation. The

[1] Collier, *Hist. Dram. Poetry*, i. 58 ; Brotanek, *u. s.* p. 26.
[2] Starkey's *Booke of certaine Triumphs*, quoted by Brotanek, p. 7.

'presenter' was not necessarily one of them. He might be, and often was, an accomplished professional writer or speaker, paid for his services; the prototype, in fact, both of the acting 'presenter' of the later Masque, and of the Masque-writer himself. This usage is already fully developed in the recently discovered disguisings of Lydgate (1427–30).[1] In the Tudor disguisings it is frequent, though by no means invariable. In 1517, when the pageant of the 'Gardyn de Esperans' was brought into the palace hall, 'Master Cornish', in a scarlet gown 'like a stranger', explained its purport, after which the six knights and ladies who were seen walking in the garden 'descended and danced'.[2] A famous later example is the speech composed by Gascoigne for the 'Venetian' Masquerade at Lord Mountacute's in 1575.

Up to the last decade of the queen's reign, then, the Elizabethan Masque showed, on the whole, little power of coherent development. Fettered by its aristocratic exclusiveness, it was unable freely to assimilate the dramatic and poetic invention of which the age was so prolific. How to bring that infertile aristocratic nucleus into productive union with those richer and stronger elements of art was itself a problem for the inventor of poetic forms, not soon, nor easily, solved. In the meantime, however, several allied forms of festive entertainment were being vigorously cultivated under less rigid conditions. Some of these were drawn into loose inorganic connexion with the Masque of the sixteenth century. They acquired a greater importance by being taken up into the liberated and mature Masque of the Jacobean age.

Of all such allied species it will suffice for the purpose of the Jonsonian Masque to mention two: the dramatic 'tourney', or 'barriers', and the dramatic monologue.

---

[1] Cf. Hammond, *Anglia*, xxii, 364; Brotanek, *u.s.* p. 306; Chambers, *u.s.* p. 396.
[2] *Letters and Papers . . . of Henry VIII*, ii, 1509; quoted by Brotanek, p. 77.

Masques and Entertainments 255

From the time of Edward III the institution of the tournament, always hovering on the verge between battle and sport, had passed readily into a dramatic game between fictitious characters in an imaginary cause. Thus in 1331 Edward III and his Court rode to the lists in Cheap arrayed as Tartars; in 1343 'the pope' and 'twelve cardinals' encountered all comers in Smithfield.[1] The still more spectacular and more artificial chivalry of the sixteenth century found expression in a long series of these military disguisings, where the combat proper was approached, like the dance in the regular Masque, through an avenue of magnificent preliminaries, or even became little more than the critical final scene of a fantastic plot. The most famous example is the 'Triumph' of 1581 in which Sidney and Fulke Greville, with two others, personating 'the four Foster Children of Desire' appear before the 'Castle of Perfect Beauty', where the queen is seated, offer to defend her rights against all comers, bombard the castle with flowers and perfumed water, and then, finally, engage in the tourney.[2] In other cases the tourney, or the besieged castle, was brought into the framework of the Masque, as introductory to the dance. Thus in the show, already noticed, at Prince Arthur's wedding, the knights besiege the ladies in the Castle of Love; in that at the marriage of Princess Mary in 1518, knights, distinct from the 'disguisers' proper, emerged from a cave 'and faught a fair tourney', and when they were departed, the disguisers descended from their rock and 'danced a great space'.[3]

1. The Dramatic Tourney.

If the mimetic tourney promoted the advance of the Masque towards dramatic action, the character monologue and dialogue promoted its advance towards dramatic speech. The masked courtly dancers who personated negroes, or Russians, or sailors, did not usually carry personation beyond the use of disguising dress. But on the frequent

2. Character Monologues and Dialogues.

---

[1] Chambers, *Mediaeval Stage*, i. 392.
[2] Nichols, *Progresses of Elizabeth*, ii. 310 f.; cf. Brotanek, p. 28.
[3] Hall, *Henry VIII*, fol. 66; cf. Brotanek, p. 20.

progresses of Elizabeth, where a nobleman or a city provided the indispensable entertainment, and where courtly persons were sometimes less available than lively wits, the custom grew up of offering more vivacious personations, with characteristic speech, gesture, and action. A 'porter' at Kenilworth blusters at the throng who seek admission (1575); a 'hermit' at Theobalds complains to the queen that Burghley has driven him from his quiet seclusion (1591).[1] Or the ancient fashion of the 'dispute' or *tenson* is borrowed, as in the contemporary Italian *contrasti* and in some of Heywood's *Interludes*. A gardener and a mole-hunter, for instance, dispute for the possession of a casket which the former had dug up: they solve the difficulty by presenting it to Elizabeth. And these two elements, the explanatory speech and the debate, compose the substance of the graceful entertainment which, with one possible exception, may be placed at the head of all the English Masques of the sixteenth century—Sidney's *The Lady of May* (1578). Often the character speeches served to introduce the tourney, as in Bacon's debate of the Hermit, Statesman, and Soldier (1595), who encounter Essex as he enters the lists, and seek in turn to convert him to their own way of life; while his squire repels all alike with the plea that he is vowed to the service of his mistress, the Queen.[2] A debate upon the rival merits of 'Riches' and 'Love' had similarly introduced a tourney at the betrothal of the Princess Mary.[3] In this way important advances were made towards the articulate dramatic expression achieved in the later Masque. Moreover, the conflicts of ideals easily assumed an ethical colouring; sympathy was sought for the one, satire and ridicule heaped on the other. And independently of all satire, the taste for the grotesque, so vigorously developed at the Courts of the Tudors, tempered the elegances of the Masque and all kindred forms

---

[1] Brotanek, *u.s.* pp. 40-1, summarily describes the numerous class-types represented.
[2] Nichols, *Progresses of Elizabeth*, iii. 372; Brotanek, p. 42.
[3] Brotanek, p. 86.

of courtly entertainment with oddities and antics not perhaps very unlike those which had amused the Court of Edward III. A 'Mask of Cats' was performed before Edward VI; masques of apes and dragons before Elizabeth.[1] These performances of 'Antics' reached their apotheosis in the Jonsonian 'Antimasque'.

The character-speeches and dialogues did valuable service in raising the intellectual quality of the entertainments provided for the queen; and Elizabeth's own well-understood tastes encouraged every advance in this direction. But the absence of scenery and spectacle, for which they often provided a willingly accepted excuse, involved some impoverishment even in strictly dramatic effect. In particular, the sudden apparitions or transformations which, as we have seen, were found, in a rudimentary form, in the earliest extant disguises, had little or no counterpart in entertainments where the decisive effect was sought in an effective epigram or a crushing argument. Even so graceful and witty a Masque as *The Lady of May* is inferior, as a piece of dramatic action, to many of the shows performed under Henry VII or Henry VIII. The merit of bringing these two fruitful sources of dramatic effect for the first time together appears to belong to a class in whom the taste for wit and the taste for spectacle were a corporate tradition—the students of the Inns of Court. The *Gesta Grayorum* describes the performance, in 1595, of two Masques, the bearing of which upon the subsequent growth of the species was first recognized by Brotanek.[2] In both the Masque of the Knights of the Helmet (6 January 1595) and Davison's more famous Masque of Proteus (Shrovetide, 1595) dramatic dialogue is freely introduced. But in both it also serves to convey a simple but effective dramatic plot, leading to a climax which resolves itself into the stately closing dances proper to the regular Masque. The

---

[1] Loseley MSS., quoted by Brotanek, p. 49.
[2] Nichols, *Progresses of Elizabeth*, iii. 262 f., 297 f.; Brotanek, p. 133 f.; cf. Reyher, p. 146 f.

Knights of the Helmet have captured three monsters, enemies of the Prince of Purpoole. The monsters prove to be Envy, Malcontent, and Folly, and are dismissed from the Prince's presence, while the knights, after conveying them forth, return, splendidly habited, to take part in the dance. The 'masquers' are here, therefore, present and visible from the first. But their change of garb foreshadows one variety, not the least effective, of the later transition to the Masque proper—that, namely, in which, as in *Lovers Made Men*, the 'masquers' appear in the Antimasque suffering some misfortune or disability, from which at the opening of the Masque proper they are suddenly relieved. The Masque of *Proteus and the Rock Adamantine*, on the other hand, is an example of the other type of transition, where the masquers suddenly emerge, and thereby initiate the statelier closing scene. Prince Henry and his knights are here at the outset unseen in the recesses of the Magnet Rock. There they remain while Proteus and the Prince's Squire hold a conversation which explains the situation to the audience; a device showing a great advance in dramatic technique upon the single explanatory speech, while the dialogue itself is in wit and humour not unworthy of its date. The Squire demonstrates to Proteus that the Prince has solved the problem laid down by the sea-god as the condition of his deliverance; whereupon Proteus, at the end of his subterfuges, opens the Rock, the Prince and his knights emerge, and the dance ensues.

More than two years of James's reign had passed when Jonson was called on for his first Masque. But he had already shown his quality in slighter festive shows of the same kind. The triumphal progress of the new king from Edinburgh to London in the summer of 1603, and the Coronation procession through the City in the following March, were occasions hardly paralleled within living memory, and they were celebrated with unprecedented lavishness and elaboration. The resources of every kind at the disposal of the noble or civic entertainer were immeasurably greater than those which had served to welcome Elizabeth forty-five years before. In wealth of poetic and dramatic talent, above all, there could be no comparison. The later occasion, no doubt, lacked those deeper notes of joyous relief, of ecstatic deliverance, which made the simple devices of Elizabeth's Coronation pageant so impressive and moving. Set beside even the somewhat tarnished and faded majesty of her last years, the King of Scots was not an imposing figure; nor was the impending invasion of north-countrymen an event likely to stimulate his new subjects to livelier coruscations of enthusiastic fancy. The one aspect under which the accession of James was of national importance, the union of the two countries under one crown, counted for little more than did the fact that he was a Protestant. How slight a share the reforming fervour so pointedly shown at Elizabeth's accession had in the welcome prepared for her successor may be gathered from the significant fact that Jonson, now a Roman Catholic, was repeatedly called to assist, and that he complied without the slightest difficulty. No descending figure presented a Bible to the new Defender of the Faith. That he was not only a Protestant but a doughty theological dogmatist was well known; yet the Protestant note is hardly ever struck in these festivities. No sturdier champion of the Reformation, as he understood it, then sat upon any throne; but what counted with his English hosts was his pretension, at least as loudly emphasized, to be a man of the Renascence. The pupil of Buchanan had some title to his master's praise, as he assuredly merited his grave warnings; in any case his repute as a scholar who loved to exhibit and to exercise his erudition, gave the cue to all his entertainers. Classical antiquity was everywhere called in to supply the machinery of the festive devices, and men of letters who received commissions to provide the speeches and the songs were, with rare exceptions, men of known accomplishment in classical study. The pre-eminence of Jonson in this respect had already been made evident two years before by *Poetaster*; and though he had since then withdrawn into sullen retirement, 'scorning the world', it was no secret to his noble friends that he was at work upon the Tacitean tragedy of *Sejanus*, produced a few months later. It is thus not surprising that it fell to Jonson to provide the first extant Entertainment designed to welcome the royal party on their journey southwards. It was given to the queen and prince by Sir Robert Spencer, their host at Althorp, the king having gone forward. A *Particular Entertainment of the Queen and Prince at Althrope*,[1] as Jonson's title ran, does not, as a piece of artistic invention, stand above the best of the Court entertainments of the previous reign, and follows them closely in general type. The Fairy Queen and a bevy of fairies had welcomed Elizabeth with song and speech at Elvetham,[2] as they now welcomed James's consort at Althorp; 'wild men', fauns, Sylvanus, had on other occasions testified, like Jonson's Satyr, by their homage, to her power over the savage breast; and the bantering dialogue between the Satyr and the Fairies is matched in dramatic vivacity by Sidney's *Lady of May*, and the chaffing colloquy of Pan and the two Shepherdesses which amused Elizabeth at Bisham.[3] The contrast between a ruder and a more refined element among those who brought their homage was at least as old as the days when the Morris dance had, at a certain point of the ceremonial, regularly interrupted the stately measures. But these familiar features were rendered by Jonson with a command of gracious poetic speech not surpassed certainly, and very rarely approached, in any Elizabethan entertainment. With a delicacy seemingly unlike him, but always at his call, he has marked the distinction between the wilder and the choicer creatures of the woods, by the colouring and movement of the verse. The Satyr is a charming creation; and Jonson, who used his classicism with the freedom of a poet, not with the rigour of a pedant,

Althorp Entertainment, June, 1603.

---

[1] This pronunciation is still locally current.
[2] Nichols, *Progresses of Elizabeth*, iii. 101.   [3] Ibid. iii. 133.

Masques and Entertainments 261

has enriched the character with some traits of the native Puck, without impairing the *naïveté* of the shaggy wood-god. In this freakish, elemental creature, contrasted with the courtly and decorous fairies, there is already a hint of the Antimasque.

The reception of the king nine months later in the City involved problems of a different kind. Jonson devised the first and last of a series of shows given at different points between the City and Whitehall; Dekker, his recent antagonist in the 'Stage Quarrel', providing the rest. The weighty critical remarks appended to the First Part of the Entertainment at Fen Church show how seriously Jonson had reflected on the theory of these devices. Posterity may regret the lavish expenditure of his learning and ingenuity upon 'toys' so perishable. The Entertainments add little to his fame, however they may have advanced his fortunes. But he clearly thought the task of expressing the welcome of a capital city to its sovereign one worthy of the artist as well as of the citizen; and he carried it out in a fashion which only fell short of doing justice to the dignity of the City by doing more than justice to the dignity of James. The slightness of these shows was no reason, with Jonson, for perfunctory treatment; he carved the clay as assiduously and with as much cunning of hand and of thought as though it were marble. He lays down the theory of 'these devices' in the terms which Aristotle applies to the drama.[1] More exclusively than ever he addressed himself to the elect; the throng of groundlings, who were able to enforce their judgement in the Globe or the Revels, might here be ignored; and the possibility of using a recondite, symbolic speech, eloquent to 'the sharpe and learned', was assuredly one of the bonds which

Entertainment at the Coronation, March 15 1604.

[1] '... the very site, fabricke, strength, policie, dignitie, and affections of the Citie were all laid downe to life: The nature and propertie of these Deuices being, to present alwaies some one entire bodie, or figure, consisting of distinct members, and each of those expressing it selfe, in the own actiue spheare, yet all, with that generall harmonie so connexed, and disposed, as no one little part can be missing to the illustration of the whole' (Folio, 1616, p. 848).

attached Jonson to the Masque. 'And for the multitude, no doubt but their grounded iudgements did gaze, said it was fine, and were satisfied.'[1] But even the 'sharpe and learned' must have been put on their mettle by inventions so recondite as that of the Strand show, where Electra, the last of the seven sister Pleiades, who, according to the poets, had fled from the constellation as a comet *dissolutis crinibus* in grief at the fall of Troy, returns weeping with joy at the advent of the new sovereign. With this legend Jonson, adroitly enough, interwove Pliny's account of the comet which appeared at Rome shortly after the death of Caesar, and was heralded as a good omen by the future Augustus:

> Long maist thou liue, and see me thus appeare,
> As omenous a comet ...[2]

says Electra. The Fates, who had plunged Italy in civil war after those earlier auspices, accepted the omen in the disastrous sense which English usage favoured, and Jonson's masterful Latinity chose to ignore. But it is easy to detect under Electra's exalted prophecy the note of grave counsel. In these weighty lines, as still more strikingly in the *Panegyre*, composed for James when he opened Parliament a few days later,[3] the poet addressed the king with a dignified because wholly unaffected assumption of their complete equality, yet without a phrase which need have recalled to the son of Queen Mary the hectoring of Knox or even the plain-speaking of his own tutor Buchanan. *Solus Rex, et Poeta non quotannis nascitur*, wrote Jonson at the close of his 'panegyre'; and the epigram admirably sums up the spirit which marked his dealings with the Court from first to last. Divine right he accepted without reserve, but he instinctively emphasized the side of the doctrine least favourable to royal arrogance. Kings

---

[1] Folio, 1616, p. 849.   [2] Ibid. p. 862.
[3] Published with the two preceding Entertainments, March 19, 1603-4. Dekker issued a detailed account of his own share of the performance. Stephen Harrison, the architect, issued a full text with engravings of the 'devices'.

... by Heauen, are plac'd vpon his throne,
To rule like Heauen; and haue no more, their owne,
As they are men, then men.[1]

Private hospitalities on a splendid scale followed the national welcome. On 1st May the king and queen were entertained by Sir William Cornwallis in his house at Highgate, and Jonson was again called in to provide the Entertainment. This he did in two very charming scenes. No native English figures, like the fairies of the Althorp piece, are permitted to share with the antique divinities the honour of welcoming the learned king; but Jonson has contrived, with a skill only possible to one in whom scholarship and poetry fertilized each other, to make his classical symbolism serviceable for an English holiday festival. It is May morning, and the master of the Ocean and his beauteous Oriana themselves go a-maying like the rest. At the house gates they are welcomed by the household gods; but this hospitable rite is only the preliminary grace to the banquet prepared for them, and the Penates guide them through the house into the luxuriant garden beyond,[2] where Mercury, cavalierly dismissing their escort, leads them to the bower where 'for her moneth, the yeerely delicate *May* keepes state'.[3] The song of her attendant spirits, Aurora, Zephyrus, and Flora, and the hardly less lyric speech of Maia herself are the crown and climax of the whole: the song, of homelier texture, pleasantly alive with the wing and note of English birds; the speech, more curiously wrought, and laden with the perfumes and savours of the South, and the joyous riot of the Greek woodlands. The charm of both pieces lies, however, rather in the *entrain* of the verse-music than in any noticeable magic of phrase. The afternoon show has a different kind of merit. It is a kind of prelude to the Jonsonian Antimasque, a prelude still tentative and cautious. But the taste for a gross-

Entertainment at Highgate, May 1, 1604.

[1] Folio, 1616, pp. 866–7.
[2] Gifford's title for this Entertainment, 'The Penates', was therefore not well chosen.
[3] Folio, 1616, p. 881.

flavoured dish as an item in an otherwise exquisitely refined banquet was deeply engrained in polite England. And the courtly audience would doubtless have relished Pan's rough humour and rollicking rhythms, after the sweets of Maia, even had his 'salt' not been 'tempered' by the presence of Mercury.[1]

On two later occasions Jonson was called on for entertainments of this slighter and less formal kind, and these may be briefly noticed in this place. The scene of both was the Earl of Salisbury's house at Theobalds; and in each of them, in addition to the king, a distinguished foreign guest was present, whose ignorance of English involved certain peculiar features in the composition. The first, *The Entertainment of the two Kings of Great Britain and Denmark*, on 24 July 1606, is in reality merely a device with an explanatory speech, the latter being rendered in Latin elegiacs for the benefit of King Christian. The second, of more interest, was written for a less ordinary occasion: the transfer of Theobalds by Salisbury to James, who gave Hatfield in exchange on 22 May 1607. With great skill Jonson contrives out of the occasion a dramatic scene flattering to both subject and sovereign. The Genius of the house, plunged in grief at the approaching departure of the master, receives, at first with incredulous amazement, then with joyful acclamation, the news of the splendid destiny which the Fates have in store for him. It was a simple but effective motive; and the execution shows the freedom and boldness in this kind of work which were to be expected from one who had now become the most redoubtable of the makers of the courtly Masque.

The versatile brilliance, erudition, and resource shown by Jonson in the festivities of March and May appear to have told in high quarters. The Masque of the previous Christmas (1603), *The Vision of the Twelve Goddesses*, had been

[1] It is hardly necessary to notice the scandal which rumour has attached to the name of Dorothy Cornwallis, who probably acted Maia. If the rumour was true, would Jonson have ventured to represent her as the mother of a son?

provided by Samuel Daniel. Daniel stood high in favour with courtly circles, and Jonson had been ignominiously expelled, with his friend John Roe, from Hampton Court. But the impression made by the Entertainments of the following spring was strong enough to outweigh both these disadvantages, and it was Jonson who was called on for the Christmas-season Masque for 1604–5. With the ensuing Twelfth Night begins accordingly the long series of Jonsonian Masques.

The first of Jonson's Masques was indeed due to the direct incentive of 'the most magnificent of Queenes'. The epithet was given to her in the printed title-page of the Quarto text,[1] and aptly figured the expanded ambitions of the new phase of Masque which was to replace the relatively frugal entertainments of Elizabeth.[2] Anne herself, with a bevy of noble ladies, designed to figure in the masqued dance, to which everything else in the Masque was in theory subordinate. She even gave an explicit indication of the kind of spectacle she desired. 'It was her Maiesties will', reports Jonson, 'to haue them' (the masquers) '*Black-mores* at first';[3] from which we may gather that she contemplated some transformation scene in which their blackness was removed.[4] The idea was anything but novel, disguising as negresses having been a favourite fashion with the ladies of Elizabeth. But the fable is wholly of Jonson's devising, and at once lifts the Masque to the higher level of ingenious and graceful invention from which in his hands it never fell.[5]

Masque of Blackness, January 6, 1605.

[1] *The Character of Two royall Masques. The one of Blacknesse, The other of Beautie. Personated by the most magnificent of Queenes Anne Queene of Great Britaine, &c. With her honorable Ladyes, 1605. and 1608. at white-hall.*
[2] M. Feuillerat's admirable study, *Le Bureau des Menus Plaisirs*, shows how much luxury of dress and equipment these 'relatively frugal' entertainments nevertheless admitted.
[3] Folio, p. 893.
[4] It is piquant to recall that, ten days before the performance of the *Masque of Blackness*, the queen had witnessed the first Court performance of *Othello* (Dec. 26, 1604). But it would be idle to suspect any connexion.
[5] Miss E. Welsford, in 'Italian Influence on the English Court Masques' (*Modern Language Review*, Oct. 1923), believes that both

It is a fantastic but graceful variation of the Phoebus and Phaeton legend, delicately touched to modern, national, and courtly issues. Already, in this earliest of the long series of his Masques, Jonson showed himself an adept in the art of blowing these glittering bubbles of invention—airy woof with just enough of substance to catch the light and radiate colour, and detain the delicate foot of the spirit of poetry and song. The queen's crude demand for 'blackmoors' yielded in his hands, with the powerful support of the scenic artist, to whose 'design and act', he tells us, 'the bodily part' of the entertainment was due, a fantasia on the theme, despicable to neither poet nor painter, of Blackness. The scene is imagined in the spirit of Bacon's just remark that a bright pattern upon a dark ground is more pleasing than the reverse arrangement. The 'ground' is 'an obscure and cloudy night-piece', with 'a vast sea' stretching to the horizon. Upon these dark waters and against this cloudy sky was seen the brilliant apparition of a concave shell, like mother-of-pearl, in which the masquers were seated, their blackness set off by azure and silver and profusion of pearl.[1] The darkness-and-light contrast is taken up and pursued through fresh developments in the subtler medium of verse. The vision of 'a face, all circumfus'd with light' in the waters of the lake where the tropical maidens sit cooling their soft limbs, foreshadows the mild and healing lustre of the northern land,

>   Whose termination (of the *Greeke*)
>   Sounds TANIA,

to which the vision enigmatically directs them. Black Mauritania, swarth Lusitania, rich Aquitania, yield nothing to their quest; but when Oceanus points to

---

Jonson and Jones 'drew their inspiration' from a tournament held in 1579 in the Pitti Palace, Florence. But she gives no evidence beyond general resemblances, and she allows that 'they certainly did not initiate their models with any exactness'. Both men, it may be added, were at that date six years old.

[1] Coloured drawings of the dresses for the masquers and their light-bearers are preserved at Chatsworth, among the Inigo Jones sketches (Walpole Society's Catalogue, nos. 1, 4).

Masques and Entertainments

This *Land,* that lifts into the temperate ayre
His snowy cliffe,

as '*Albion* the faire', and the silver splendour of the moon breaks out upon that cloudy night-piece, the recurring *Leitmotiv* announces their arrival at their goal even before the mention of 'Britania' has justified the too scholastic oracle. And in Aethiopia's parting prescription to her bright nymphs there is a kindred gleam of moonlight and sea foam and the birth of Aphrodite; abruptly closed however by a touch of the matter-of-fact, even uncouth, prosaist who was never very far from Jonson the lyric poet: 'Your faces dry, and all is done.' But the closing songs have great beauty; the wistful call ' whose cadences were iterated by a double *eccho*, from seuerall parts of the land '—

Daughters of the subtle floud,
Doe not let earth longer intertayne you—

has a hint of the pathos of Arnold's merman; as the whole Masque, with its tale of primeval wanderings, and its incessant sound of the sea, its elaborate artifice, its sumptuous Jacobean candlelight, has, notwithstanding, something not wholly alien to the *Odyssey*.

Structurally, however, the *Masque of Blackness* is still relatively immature; it does not exhibit some features which Jonson subsequently adopted and thenceforth retained. In particular, the masquers, in whose descent and dance the whole is to culminate, were from the first present and visible.

The intended sequel to the *Masque of Blackness* was *Hymenaei*, originally designed for the Twelfth Night of the following January 5, year, 1606. But that winter, and again in the winter of 1606. 1606-7, great Court weddings intervened, for which specifically wedding Masques were desired, and it was only in 1607-8 that Jonson was at length called upon to complete his invention. The *Masque of Beauty* is thus divided by three years from the *Masque of Blackness,* and it shows an advance in maturity of structure hardly to be understood without reference to the intervening examples. One of these, performed on Twelfth Night, 1606, was the work of Jonson himself. The *Hymenaei*, though not the finest of his wedding Masques, is more pregnant with thought and learning, and altogether richer in Jonsonian characteristics than its predecessor; not the least noticeable among them being the provision of this monument of abstruse and erudite allusion for the marriage of two children—'two noble *Maides* Of different sexe'—whose sinister precocity could not be foreseen. But rare indeed are the fresh and natural touches in the earlier Jacobean Masques. Realism was an affection of its declining years, almost a symptom of its decadence; its characteristic and typical beauty is a beauty of artifice, or, at least, a beauty like that of a fortunate symbol or allegory, due as much to the charm of the figure as to its truth. The *Hymenaei* is distinguished from the *Masque of Blackness* at once by its bold use of allegory, and by its archaeological severity. The *Blackness* was a whimsical fantasia coloured with classical materials. The *Hymenaei* draws much more largely upon those 'most high, and heartie *inuentions*, . . . grounded vpon *antiquitie*, and solide *learnings*', and 'though sounding to present occasions, . . . yet alwayes laying hold on more remou'd *mysteries*',[1] which Jonson now desiderates for the Masque. Here also he acknowledged that 'the *Designe & Act*' of the whole were due to 'Maister Ynygo Iones'.[2] The framework of an antique wedding ceremonial is, with singular skill, welded into an allegory of marriage; which, if medieval in scheme, is Greek, even Platonic, in conception: the riot or Affections and Humours subdued by Reason and her ally Hymen. The standing war between the wayward impulses and appetencies of men and the canons of moderation and good sense was a congenial theme with Jonson, and had a few years earlier been a principal source of his comedy. It supplied in this Masque an early example of the conflict of abstractions which later on became the habitual structural

---

[1] Folio, 1616, p. 911.
[2] In the Quarto text; Jonson later suppressed the acknowledgement.

motive of Jonson's Masques. The Affections and Humours,—
> The foure vntemp'red *Humors* are broke out,
> And with their wild *Affections*, goe about
> To rauish all Religion—[1]

enter to the accompaniment of 'a kind of contentious Musique'; and there is a moment of alarm, when they suddenly draw their swords, encompass the altar of Hymen, and disturb the ceremonies, while the virgins and youths fly to keep their hallowed lights untouched. A few years later Jonson would probably have introduced these as an Antimasque, and treated then with the deliberate and genial *grotesquerie* which he indulged, for example, in the portrayal of Comus and his rout. But the Antimasque is here still latent; the Affections and Humours are personated by gentlemen, 'gloriously attired'; they take part in the Main Masque with the ladies who figure the faculties of marriage; and their disturbance is little more than a lively sword-dance at the close of their stately preliminary measure, in designed accordance with the mock show of violence in the Roman marriage-rite. As the final song of the Masque Jonson had, in the same spirit, naturally thought of the Epithalamion, in which the ancient celebration culminated; but to this last piece of antiquarianism his courtly audience appears to have imperfectly responded. Only one stave of his fine sinewy adaptation of Catullus was sung; but he took his revenge by printing it entire in the published version, with a preface announcing his hearty forgiveness of 'their ignorance whom it chanceth not to please'.

The Introduction to this Masque, issued with the first edition of it in the course of 1606, contains some of Jonson's weightiest utterances, in part already quoted, on the theory of the Masque at large; a branch of art still, like no other, in a quite fluid and indeterminate state, wholly untouched by authoritative traditions or example. Drawn, by courtly command rather than by any 'study' of his, into the work of masque-writing, he could not get far

[1] Folio, 1616, p. 914.

without setting the stamp of his intellectual idealism upon a genre which so readily degenerated into a splendid but momentary feast of the senses. For him, at least, 'magnificence in the outward celebration', however becoming and seemly, was only of value as the vehicle, or 'body' of these 'high, and heartie *inuentions*, to furnish the inward parts'; without which 'the glorie of all these *solemnities* had perish'd like a blaze, and gone out, in the *beholders* eyes'. This vigorous critical manifesto—couched in his most nervous and animated prose—was clearly intended for the address of some contemporary theorist, who had derided his lavish prodigality of thought and learning upon 'these transitorie deuices'; and there can be little doubt, as Brotanek has shown,[1] that the culprit was the poet Daniel, whose Court Masque for the first Twelfth Night of the new reign had been so signally outshone by that produced by Jonson for the second. It was in the Preface to his *Vision of the Twelve Goddesses* (1604) that Daniel delivered his somewhat illiberal strictures upon those who strive 'to shewe most wit about these Puntillos of Dreames and showes', insinuating that such zealots 'are sure sicke of a disease they cannot hide, & would faine haue the world to thinke them very deeply learned in all misteries whatsoeuer'.[2] Daniel had obviously been nettled by the 'captious censures' passed upon his Masque. The truth is that the *Vision* was by no means qualified to satisfy the standards applied, in January 1604, to a Court Masque. In invention it falls far behind the best Elizabethan examples,—a mere procession of goddesses, introduced (since they are seen in a 'Vision') by Night and Sleep. Even the verse and phrasing are stiff and hard, throwing into vivid relief the supple strength of Jonson's 'well-torned lines'; and 'well-languaged' Daniel permits himself such a monstrosity for the sake of rhyme as 'addrests' for 'addresses',[3] and such frigid intricacies as the third stanza of the song of the

---

[1] *Die englischen Maskenspiele*, p. 184.
[2] *The Vision of the 12. Goddesses*, sig. B.
[3] Ibid., sig. B 4.

Graces. A Shelley or a Goethe might successfully have criticized Jonson's too self-conscious art in the name of a more ethereal and in the full sense visionary poetry; but Daniel's *Vision* is ethereal only in its unsubstantial thinness, and properly provoked Jonson's sarcastic reference to the 'ayrie tasts' which left his full table to batten on their 'cleane emptie trenchers'; 'where perhaps a few *Italian* herbs, pick'd vp, and made into a *sallade*, may find sweeter acceptance, than all, the most nourishing, and sound meates of the world'.[1]

In the *Barriers*, performed on the night following the marriage, Jonson was contented to fall in more closely with Tudor precedent. A debate between two disguised persons or abstractions had, as we have seen, been a common prelude to a tilt. In essential structure the present piece is far more elementary than Bacon's Introduction to the Essex tourney noticed above, and it is closely anticipated by a *Barriers* described by Hall,[2] when 'two persones plaied a dialog theffect whereof was whether riches were better then loue'. Failing to agree, they call in six knights to decide the issue by battle. The tourney ensues. Finally, 'an olde man with a siluer berd' intervenes to resolve the strife by the courtly conclusion that 'love & riches, both be necessarie for princes'. Jonson's debate between Truth and Opinion is similarly first committed to the arbitrament of arms, and then resolved by the apparition of the Angel. But on this simple theme Jonson has lavished all the splendour of his rhetoric, and the impressive swing of his verse. The rash attempt to capture the exquisite Catullian poetry of maidenhood was indeed unlucky; translation at all times tended to impose the meticulous scholar upon the poet, and neither maidenhood nor marriage lay within the domain of Jonson's more acute poetic perceptions. But

---

[1] Folio, p. 911. In the last sentence we may suspect an allusion to a more recent illustration of Daniel's theory of the Masque,—a pastoral imitated from Guarini's *Pastor Fido*, and performed at Oxford in August, 1605 (Nichols, *Progresses of James*, i, p. 553; Reyher, *u.s.* p. 164).
[2] 'The xix yere of Kyng Henry the VIII,' fol., 1576.

'Truth' was a theme which engaged all the strenuous idealism of his nature, and Gifford's epithet 'magnificent' is not more than is due to the picture of her descent:

> She weares a robe ench'as'd with eagles eyes,
> To signifie her sight in *mysteries*;
> Vpon each shoulder sits a milke-white doue,
> And at her feet doe witty serpents moue:
> Her spacious armes doe reach from *East* to *West*,
> And you may see her heart shine through her brest.[1]

Masque of Beauty, January 10, 1608.

This was the only Court Masque of the Christmas season 1605–6. In the following season, too, the Christmas Masque was replaced by a wedding Masque, Campion's *Masque for Lord Hayes*, performed on Twelfth Night, 1607.

Two successive Twelfth Nights had thus been given up to the celebration of Court marriages. For 1608 yet another was in prospect; but the wedding of Viscount Haddington finally took place at Shrovetide, and the magnificent Masque which Jonson was commissioned to prepare for it did not stand in the way of the ordinary Christmas festivities. The queen accordingly bethought her of the old *Masque of Blackness*, and called upon Jonson to 'thinke on some fit presentment, which should answere the former, still keeping them the same persons, the daughters of NIGER, but their beauties varied, according to promise, and their time of absence excus'd, with foure more added to their number'. These somewhat matter-of-fact demands were a challenge to Jonson's invention, and he answered them like a poet. The poetry of the *Masque of Beauty* is certainly not inferior to that of its predecessor, and its 'fable' is much better. The voyage of the Ethiopian maidens to Albion for the improvement of their complexion had, as story, little intrinsic advantage over any modern journey to a fashionable watering-place with a similar object. The appearance of the lurid figure of Night, in the background, mad with resentment at the slight to her colour, and interposing like the Odyssean Poseidon to

[1] Folio, 1616, p. 932.

detain them in interminable wanderings in the ocean, adds an element of dramatic conflict, of epic peril and suspense, of which the story, as story, was much in need. Not much, it is true, is made of Night's hostility; it does not enter into or affect the structure of the Masque at all, even by a 'contentious music', far less by an armed assault like that of the angered Humours and Affections in *Hymenaei*. To this extent the *Masque of Beauty* marks a less advance towards the mature Masque-structure than does its predecessor. The malign spells of Night have been already shattered when the scene opens, and her activity is merely reported, not seen. But the 'report', conveyed in the dialogue of Januarius and Boreas, is full of implicit drama, from Boreas's first entrance—'blustering forth' upon the stage, and inquiring in his 'rude voice' for Albion, Neptune's son,—to his account of how the storm-tost Ethiopian maidens prayed him 'for the loue of my Orythyia',
  Whose verie name did heat my frostie brest,
  And made me shake my snow-fill'd wings and crest,
to bear home their sad news. One could wish that these dramatic germs had been permitted to expand. All the ingenuity and splendour of scenic invention are concentrated upon the floating island of Beauty, an apparition which Jonson makes a show of justifying by references to Pliny and Cardan,[1] but which, with its elaborate Palladian technique, clearly bears the mark of Inigo's hand— Renascence classicism imposed upon medieval allegory.

But if the imperious claims of spectacle may be suspected to have checked the development of drama, the spectacular elements have not been altogether barren for poetry. The dance, to which the whole action was bound to lead up, might seem likely to incur grudging treatment at the hands of a poet so jealous of the claims of his own art. Jonson found nevertheless, it is clear, an artistic delight in these graceful intricacies of interwoven movement, describing them with unwonted enthusiasm,—'a most curious *Daunce*, full of

[1] Folio, 1616, p. 903.

excellent deuice, and change', a 'second dance, more subtle, and full of change, then the former', 'a third most elegant, and curious dance, and not to be describ'd againe, by any art, but that of their owne footing',[1] and the like. And despite this last deprecatory phrase, Jonson himself found language worthy of the loftiest claims that dancing can advance, in the stately staves of song which follow and precede the closing dances of the Beauty Masque; winning for these inarticulate callisthenic parentheses the significance of being the last and truest embodiment of beauty itself,— that motion which, at the beginning of things, divine Love taught and Beauty fulfilled. If Jonson hardly, like Milton, gave the Masque an ethical soul, he everywhere quickened and replenished its brain; and with all their differences, there is no other Masque-writer whom Milton so often recalls, or from whom he learnt so much. Both these austere scholars in their way spiritualized the favourite amusement of a light-living society. Where Milton informed the courtly convention of virtue with the Puritan passion for righteousness, Jonson clothed the gallantry of the cavalier in the sublime formulas and paradoxes of antique speculation.

> When *Loue*, at first, did mooue
> From out of *Chaos*, brightned
> So was the world, and lightned,
> As now!
>   .   .   .   .   .   .
> It was for *Beauty*, that the World was made,
> And where she raignes, *Loues* lights admit no shade.[2]

The *Masque of Beauty* evidently pleased its audience and excited some curiosity among those who had not witnessed it.[3] It was, indeed, without doubt, in a literary

---

[1] Folio, 1616, pp. 909-10.   [2] Folio, p. 908.
[3] On the 29th January Rowland Whyte wrote to the Earl of Shrewsbury saying that he would have liked to send him a manuscript copy, but had been unable to procure one from Jonson, who pleaded that he was busy with the Haddington Masque, due for performance and actually performed ten days later (Nichols, *Progresses of James*, ii. 175). It was published, shortly after, with the *Masque of Blackness*. The music set by his friend Ferrabosco to some of the songs in both,

sense, the finest Masque yet produced. It stood out from its predecessors not only in strength and delicacy of poetic invention, but also in the choice, even austere, taste, the lofty sense of the dignity of poetic art, by which the invention was controlled. Yet Jonson's critical disdain was not without its sterile side. In Masque as in drama he at first peremptorily rejected many rude devices and motives of popular stagecraft which an artist of more imaginative sympathy would have assimilated and transformed. The jesting clown and fool whom Shakespeare put to so wonderful and varied a use Jonson sternly excluded from his comedy. Had the Masque been equally under his control, it is likely that he would have dealt similar measure to some of the extravagances of the Antimasque. But the Masque-writer was subject to a control more arbitrary and more absolute than any exercised by the play-house manager or by his public. The queen, in particular, repeatedly furnished indications of her wishes with which the most ruggedly independent of poets could but comply. But if Jonson perforce surrendered some things he would have preferred to keep, and admitted some that he would have chosen to exclude, he showed singular adroitness in accommodating his concessions to his art. When the Antimasque was first introduced cannot be precisely determined, many masques of the early seventeenth century having perished; the first known use of the term is Jonson's in the preface to *The Masque of Queens* in the following year. But it is plain from this preface that the vogue of the Antimasque, as a rude or grotesque foil to the refinement of the Main Masque, had already set in, and that 'others' had given examples of it. One of these was certainly Campion, who in his Masque at Lord Hayes's wedding, 1607, had introduced the palpably burlesque, or as the phrase was, 'antic', effect of a dance of trees; the ostensible trees being later 'transformed' into the men which had doubtless contributed to the effect, was published by the latter in his *Ayres* in the following year.

who danced the Main Masque. Jonson, called upon to contribute to the celebration of another Scottish wedding with another masque, followed this precedent so far as to introduce what he clearly intended to pass for an Anti-masque.[1] But the gulf is wide between that burlesque dance of trees, and this jocund company of boys, representing 'the sports, and prettie lightnesses that accompanie *Loue*'. The boys were 'antickly' attired, they 'fell into a subtle *capriccious Daunce*, to as odde a *Musique*', 'nodding with their antique faces, with other varietie of ridiculous gesture'.[2] But these 'antics' are not themselves 'capricious'; they do not form an irrelevant parenthesis or 'interlude' of gaiety, thrust, like the old mummers' masquerade, into the middle of a solemn show, for the relief of the spectators. The gaiety arises quite naturally out of the situation which Jonson has devised—itself a happy example of his skill in embroidering antique legend. The story of 'runaway Cupid', pursued by Mother Venus and her Graces, and finally 'apprehended', lends itself quite as readily to the lighter as to the loftier mood of Love-poetry. The dainty idyll of Moschus, in which it was told, had been imitated again and again, in Italy and especially in France. Spenser had enshrined it in the *Calendar* for March; Barnaby Barnes had at least adapted the French adaptations.[3] Jonson, ignoring all other predecessors but Moschus himself, has told it in a dialogue full of those sprightly touches which the masculine vigour and weight of the Jonsonian manner make the more apparent. From this middle tone of quest and discovery, where one part is anxiety and three parts the zest of sport, the passage is easy and natural to the undisguised oddities and subtleties

*Masque at Lord Haddington's wedding (*Hue and Cry After Cupid*), February 9, 1608.*

---

[1] '... since the last yeere,' in the Masque at Lord Haddington's wedding, 'I had an *anti-masque* of boyes' (Preface to *Masque of Queens*, Folio, p. 945). Daniel in the following year introduced what he called an 'Antemasque' into his *The Queen's Wake*. But this was strictly, as the name implies, a show preliminary to, not in contrast with, the Main Masque. See the lucid discussion by Reyher, *u. s.* 170 f.
[2] Folio, 1616, p. 938.   [3] Cf. Lee, *Elizabethan Sonnets*, I. lxxviii.

of Cupid and his boys, on the one side, and, on the other, to the lofty if ill-sustained hymn of the Graces to Love: a hymn which starts with the 'crying' of the lost runaway, the wanton boy, among the Beauties, and culminates in a superb paean over Love, the immortal Lord of Heaven and earth, and master of gods and men, conveyed in one of the loftiest stanzas Jonson ever wrote:

> At his sight, the *sunne* hath turned,
> NEPTVNE in the waters, burned;
> *Hell* hath felt a greater heat:
> IOVE himselfe forsooke his seate:
> From the *center*, to the *skie*,
> Are his *trophœes* reared hie.[1]

The Main Masque, like the Antimasque, is introduced with great ingenuity; Jonson was obviously bent upon eliminating the crude unmotived sequences of so many royal entertainments. The inevitable burst of splendour, out of which the masquers, a yet more splendid 'light in light', emerged for their stately dance, is provided by a marvellous globe, forged by Vulcan as a wedding gift; the necessary explanation of its abstruse symbolism was managed, not by a set describer or 'showman', provided for the purpose, but in the most natural way by the divine workman himself; while the final opening of the sphere, the culminating moment, in the common apprehension, of the whole, is also brought about by the shattering hammer-stroke of the southern Thor:

Cleaue solid Rock, and bring the wonder forth.[2]

Thus the idle magnificence of the Main Masque is tempered and dignified by being brought into contact with the spirit of labour and of craftsmanship; as the boisterous unreason of the Antic-dance is touched with the laughter of love and the blitheness of the chase.

The year 1608, which had seen two fine Masques from Jonson's hand, was crowned by the composition of a third, in a literary sense the most splendid of the whole series.

The Masque of Queens, February 2, 1609.

[1] Folio, 1616, p. 936.   [2] Folio, 1616, p. 940.

The Masque of Queens Celebrated From the House of Fame was originally designed for the usual New Year festivities at Whitehall; but, as a letter of Chamberlain's informs us, its performance was postponed to Candlemas. This was the third occasion on which the queen had honoured herself by 'vsing' Jonson's 'seruices', as he puts it, to her 'personall presentations', and he exerted himself to produce a Masque of surpassing quality. Once more, too, the queen, who had twice 'instructed' the poet with such gratifying success, provided him with express directions; and once more the royal word, lightly cast forth upon the waters, brought in a harvest of poetic sheaves wholly disproportioned to its own worth.[1] Her suggestion, however, shows how alive she was to the new opportunities of entertainment which the Masque in Jonson's hands was rapidly evolving. 'Her *Maiestie*', reports Jonson, and the passage (already referred to) is a *locus classicus* for the whole history of the Masque '(best knowing, that a principall part of life, in these *spectacles,* lay in their varietie), had commanded me to thinke on some *dance,* or shew, that might precede hers, and haue the place of a foile or false *Masque*'.[2] It is clear from this that the queen had pronounced in favour of the Antimasque, understood in this sense as a 'foil' or contrast to the 'Grand' or 'Main' Masque; henceforth the Antimasque's place in the Court entertainments was assured; it was not merely of Court standing, *hoffähig,* but indispensable there. But everything indicates that the queen's notion of the Antimasque hardly went beyond 'variety' and contrast—something that would throw into effective relief the dignity and refinement of the Main Masque and the noble masquers; in other words, something conspicuously undignified and unrefined. Jonson, however, was far from content with this; he demanded in the whole entertainment the unity

---

[1] Miss Welsford (*u. s.*) points out resemblances to *Il Giudizio di Paridi*, a pastoral comedy performed at Florence in October, 1608, but admits that there was 'no direct borrowing'.
[2] Folio, 1616, p. 945.

of a work of art; and this was at least endangered by a radical bisection into Masque and 'foil'. Even his own experiment with the 'antics' and oddities of Cupid's boys had purchased 'variety' at too great a cost to dignity to be repeated here. Whatever concession Jonson in the sequel made, reluctantly to the spirit of burlesque, more willingly, if against his first intentions, to the genius of Comedy, in *The Masque of Queens* he meant to produce a dramatic poem, everywhere in consonance with the dignity and tone of poetry, and sustaining in all its parts the 'current and fall' of a single device. He put aside burlesque therefore altogether, and fell, with admirable instinct, upon a region of existence far more profoundly opposed than the most outrageous burlesque to the gracious charm and courtly elegance of the Main Masque, and yet pregnant with the poetry which charm and elegance admit, but which only an Aristophanes or a Pope can extort from burlesque. Some two years before Jonson wrote, Shakespeare had wrought out of the foul and horrible witch-world the sublimity and awe of supreme tragedy. The witchery of *Macbeth* had assuredly impressed the author of *The Masque of Queens*; but his own witch-poetry can endure that dangerous comparison. It reaches, at its highest, less amazing heights; but it is more equally sustained on a level of noble if not consummate verse, and it is without those descents which in *Macbeth* tempt us to admit interpolation. The ease with which the master of comic humours guides his 'less presumptuous car' through the thick and murky air of the witches' inferno, where Shakespeare and Milton rode supreme, may well strike us. But it ought to surprise no reader who remembers what feasts of poetry Jonson had, four years before, extorted from the foulness of Volpone, and was about to elicit from the corruption of Mammon. It is true that Jonson, here as always, had the whole ancient and modern literature of his subject to draw upon, and that his witches' incantations are to those of *Macbeth*, in respect of abstruse and minute learning, somewhat as *Sejanus* to

Julius Caesar; true also, that Jonson may quite probably, in this case as in that, have had a mind to show how a really learned poet managed these matters. Yet it was something more than learned industry which achieved the weird horror of many of Jonson's strokes; the uncanny effect of scenery and atmosphere, the 'spurging of a dead man's eyes' under the evening star, the dismal groan of the uprooted mandrake crossed by the dawn-song of the cock. The exhortation of Ate belongs to another, perhaps less exacting, kind of poetry. The embodied 'opposites of Fame and Glory' occupy this Jonsonian hell, as the torments of life gather at the gate of Vergil's Avernus, of which Claudian doubtless thought in the passage which Jonson himself quotes.[1] Even finer is her 'Invocation' to the fiends and furies—

> You, that haue seene me ride, when HECATE
> Durst not take chariot; when the boistrous sea,
> Without a breath of wind, hath knock'd the skie;
> And that hath thundred, IOVE not knowing why. . . .

To this high ceremonial speech succeed, one after another, the 'murmuring charms'; the stately iambics pass over into agitated anapaests and clanging spondees; for long the hideous rites remain without effect; suspense grows keener, the music more hurried and impatient; confused noises fill the air. Ate, though her 'rage beginnes to swell' at the stubborn delay of the awful powers she invokes—'Darkness, Deuils, Night, and Hell',—yet preserves a relative composure, marked by a graver and more temperate rhythm, and by her complete mastery of the tumultuous throng. There can have been few more impressive moments in the Jacobean Masque than the instant silence imposed upon the 'barking, howling, hissing, and confusion of noyse' by her 'Stay!' like the sudden stillness of a general rest interrupting the climax of a modern orchestra. In all this, and much more, Jonson

---

[1] Folio, 1616, p. 948. The passage is *In Rufinum*, i. 27–34.

Masques and Entertainments 281

unfolded a curious artistry in rhythm rare with him, and not common in his contemporaries.[1]

A 'foil' so magnificent imposed a serious task upon the poet of the Main Masque. But the argument of the whole, which the Main Masque had chiefly to convey, was of the blended heroic and ethical temper to which the poet in Jonson always responded; and the scene in which Perseus, 'expressing heroique, and masculine Vertue', discloses the bright bevy of queens who sit enthroned in the House of Fame, has the dignity of a massively simple monument reposing on a gnarled and curiously wrought base. If Jonson drew upon Chaucer for the outward semblance of Fame's 'glorious house'—

Built of all sounding brasse, whose columnes bee
Men-making *Poets,*

he breathed into it the spirit not of Chaucer but of Milton. Not the gay insouciance of the author of *The Hous of Fame,* but the strenuous note of *Lycidas* sounds, recognizably, in the cadences of this ruder but not less masculine verse. The device of the eleven famous queens, led by his own, was itself obviously borrowed from *The Legend of Good Women*; and the treatment of Anne of Denmark's companions in Fame is as cursory as that of Anne of Bohemia's precursors in 'Goodness' is perfunctory. To the readers of the Masque, however, Jonson made some compensation in the pithy chronicles of those wasted wights which he subjoined in printing it. In this Masque indeed the prose commentary becomes comparable in importance with the verse text; not merely, like the marginal prose of *The Ancient Mariner,* summarizing the poetry in another and hardly less beautiful speech, but stepping in to interpret the inarticulate magnificence of the scenic show. The prose of Jonson, here as elsewhere, is not 'another harmony' but a variety of the same; and it intervenes between the speeches or the songs like the plainer, but not

[1] Cf. Campion's comment on the 'modern writers'' use of enchantment, prefixed to *The Description of a Maske,* 1614.

less well wrought, passages in a variegated surface of the same metal. Least of all to be spared is the description of the central moment, when, in the heat of the magical dance, 'full of præposterous change, and gesticulation', 'on the sodaine, was heard a sound of lowd musique, as if many instruments had made one blast; with which not onely the *Hags* themselves, but the *hell*, into which they ran, quite vanished, and the whole face of the *Scene* altred, scarce suffring the memory of such a thing; But in the place of it, appeared a glorious, and magnificent building, figuring the *house of fame*, in the top of which, were discouered the *12. masquers*, sitting vpon a throne triumphall, erected in forme of a *pyramide*, and circled with all store of light'.[1] This adds emphasis even to the scornful comment of Heroic Virtue's opening speech:

> So should, at FAMES lowd sound, and VERTVES sight,
> All darke, and enuious witchcraft flie the light.

The 'opposites of Fame', to be completely vanquished, had not only to disappear, but to be forgotten. Their oblivion set the seal on the triumph of Virtue.

Prince Henry's Barriers, January 6, 1610.
The Quarto text of *The Masque of Queens* Jonson dedicated, not to the queen on whom he had there conferred so splendid a celebration, but to her eldest son. Prince Henry, still a boy of fifteen, had already given signs of future distinction both in letters and in arms, and under the courtly deference of Jonson's fine dedication it is easy to read not merely genuine admiration but an almost fatherly tenderness and pride; his own dead son ('Ben Jonson his best piece of poetry'[2]), whom he had lost at seven, some six years before, would have been within two years of the same age. Henry had shown a keen interest in the great Masque, and had requested Jonson to provide a clue to the abstruse learning with which it was packed,

---

[1] Folio, 1616, p. 956. Inigo Jones's sketch for the House of Fame has been preserved, and is one of the earliest drawings we possess of a masque-scene. It is reproduced in the Walpole Society's *Catalogue* of Inigo Jones's designs for masques, Plate IV.
[2] *Epigram* xlv, 10.

by 'retriuing the particular *Authorities*'. The task was a severe ordeal even to the most learned of Jacobean poets, who had 'writ out of fulnesse, and memory of my former readings', and not from materials expressly collected and arranged. He had concluded by expressing to his 'most excellent *Prince* and *onely Delicacy* of *Man-kind*' the hope that, should he survive to the 'Age of your Actions', 'I may write, at nights, the deedes of your dayes'. The occasion came sooner than either thought. The prince, while still in his sixteenth year, obtained the consent of James to his solemn investiture with the title of Prince of Wales, and the occasion was fixed for January, 1610. The form of the celebration was in keeping with Henry's tastes. With a passion for tourneys and all other chivalrous exercises far beyond the wont of the other princes of his time, coupled with a no less genuine love of letters, the semi-dramatic festivity of 'Barriers' was as it were made for his mind. He threw himself into the device with great gusto. At Christmas, 1609, a challenge was delivered in the name of Meliadus, Lord of the Isles (an ancient title of the Scottish heir apparent), to all knights of Great Britain to the Barriers on June 4 following. The name was the prince's choice, and apparently became his customary style in the martial sports and masquerades. Drummond sang his elegy under this name, and turned it into an anagram (*Miles a deo*), misspelling it for the purpose (Mœliades).[1] When Jonson accordingly was called upon to provide the 'Speeches' or scenic framework to the Tilting, his cue was already in a great degree defined. The Lord of the Isles involved Arthur; the romantic scenery and personnel were given. But Jonson's invention played freely with his theme, and it is instructive to contrast the little drama which serves as setting to these 'Barriers' of Prince Henry with the simple debate which had sufficed to introduce the Essex wedding-tourney. Not only is the 'plot' much more significant and beautiful in the later piece, but it has a far

[1] *Teares, on the death of Mœliades*, 1613.

greater relative importance. In the Essex Barriers the fight is the decisive event, to whose arbitrament the two debaters appeal when argument proves unavailing. In Prince Henry's it is merely a practical illustration of the recovery of Chivalry from her long sleep, which is already consummated before a sword is drawn. And whatever we may think of the kind of chivalry which the age of James I awakened and the age of Elizabeth had lulled, which lay inert when Ralegh was daring the might of Spain, and started into life when for Spain's gratification he languished in the Tower, the restoration of chivalry was for the soldier poet who had sung of 'True Soldiers'[1] no conventional theme, as one fears that Truth's praise of marriage had been to the husband then enjoying a five years' separation from his 'honest shrew'. Such poetry as these speeches exhibit gathers chiefly about this legend of Chivalry: her House ruined, her arms cobwebbed and rusty; and then her dramatic waking at the charm of Meliadus's name pronounced by Merlin:

> Were it from death that name would wake mee. Say Which is the Knight?[2]

The purely Arthurian parts, on the other hand, are imperfectly vitalized; Merlin's long summary of English history has more solidity than grace, and can have done little to conciliate the attention of spectators impatient for the Tilt.

Oberon, the Faery Prince, January 1, 1611. The new Prince of Wales whose career was thus so happily inaugurated at once began to take his part in the Court entertainments. For the Christmas festivities of 1610–11 no less than three Masques were commissioned, one by the prince and two by the queen; two of the three from Jonson. *Oberon, the Faery Prince*, the prince's Masque, is not poetically among the finest of the series, but it is a good example of his skill in weaving new story and situation out of the mythic materials of different times and

---

[1] *Epigram* cviii.   [2] Folio, 1616, p. 974.

Inigo Jones's design for 'the first

cene' in the Masque of 'Oberon'

peoples; while in structural unity it marks, like its companion, *Love Freed from Ignorance and Folly*, a notable advance upon the otherwise far greater *Masque of Queens*. It was a felicitous thought to seek the contrasted effects of the Main Masque and the Antimasque in the Fairy and the Satyr; kindred births, originally of the naïve folk-genius of the Teuton and the Greek, but touched or moulded later by the more conscious artistry of poets. The homely elf of the German forests, gathering courtly grace in the faerie of French romance, had finally arrayed himself in all the glory of chivalry as the elfin knight of Spenser. The Satyr, on the contrary, through all the phases of the far more brilliant, profound, and many-sided culture of Greece, was never drawn within its charmed circle, except as an embodiment, in marble or in verse, of frank animality and rude nature. In 1610 the Fairy tradition was still plastic to the poet's hand, and the brilliant developments it had received during the previous twenty years from Spenser, Shakespeare, and Drayton, had invested that tradition in an atmosphere of literary associations which he could at will invoke. The Satyr tradition, though less plastic, was clearly defined, and of perennial piquancy and charm. Jonson handles both with vivacity, in verse more frequently melodious than is his wont. His masquers are knights,

preseru'd
In *Faery* land, for good they haue descru'd ;
they wait upon Oberon in company with courtly 'Faies' who look disdainfully upon

the course, and countrey *Faery*,
That doth haunt the harth, or dairy ;[1]

and with heavy Sylvans, who sleep at their watch; so that the household of Oberon already embraces representatives of all the myth-peoples who compose the Masque ; a circumstance which makes greatly for its unity of effect. The most important contribution to this is, however, the figure of

[1] Folio, 1616, pp. 981, 983.

Silenus, who, in a fashion of which we have no previous example, intervenes both in Masque and Antimasque, mediating artistically between them. In the Antimasque Silenus, 'prefect' of the Satyrs (somewhat after the fashion of the Sixth *Eclogue* of Vergil), asserts a precarious control over his 'wags', and mildly rebukes their wanton antics as they leap among the rocks in the eerie light of the new-risen moon, or fling a mocking hymn at that pale-faced luminary, sick for Endymion's love. And when Oberon's palace opens, and Oberon and the knights are seen enthroned, it is Silenus who is charged with the delivery of the noble praise to 'the state' which ushers in the 'solemn rites' of the Main Masque.

Love Freed from Ignorance and Folly, February 3, 1611.

Still finer than the prince's Masque was the queen's. The *Love Freed from Ignorance and Folly* was apparently produced a few days before the *Oberon*. It was expected to cost her, together with a second Masque of which nothing is known, 'but £600';[1] a low estimate which it is hard to believe was not exceeded when we learn that, besides the usual splendour of dresses and scenery, no less than sixty-six musicians were employed, playing a multitude of different instruments. The wandering or pilgrim motive of the *Masque of Beauty* is here resumed with far more delicate and resourceful art. The bevy of bright ladies who have sailed out of the East under Love's conduct to Ultima Thule, seeking Phoebus where he nightly feasts with Ocean, encounter livelier perils than their swarthy predecessors. The envy of Night, which has held the Ethiopians captive, is only known by report, and is no longer dangerous when they appear. But here the scene opens on the very crisis of the pilgrims' fate. Love, their escort, is a captive, and the genius of malign ignorance comes forth dancing to 'a strange Musique of wilde Instruments', 'leading LOVE bound'. The Sphinx is a somewhat unexpected symbol for Ignorance, even for Ignorance 'the enemy' (as it always was for Jonson) 'of Love, and Beauty'. But he thought of

[1] John More to Sir R. Winwood, December 15, 1610.

Inigo Jones's design for

the Masque of 'Oberon'

it, as his by no means superfluous commentary explains, as the kind of pretentious fatuity which, like witchcraft and alchemy, 'still couets, to enwrap it selfe in darke, and obscure tearmes, and betray that way, whereas true loue affects to expresse it selfe, with all clearenesse, and simplicitie';[1] words which sound like an echo of the scorn which the author of *The Alchemist* had a few months before poured upon the practitioners of that pseudo-science. The imbroglio, in any case, aptly fits the characters of this Jonsonian sphinx. 'Tyranne Loue' is posed with a riddle which he must solve as the price of freedom. To convey the subjection of Love to Ignorance by his inability to guess the riddle which the symbol of Ignorance propounds is not, it must be allowed, very lucid allegory. But the working out of the situation, where decisive moments of the Masque are directly brought about by Love's successive guesses, marks the greatest advance yet made by Jonson in the problem of dramatically vitalizing the Masque within the limits of the Masque form. Love, instead of 'finding out the way', blunders into a wrong solution, brilliantly building up a fabric of plausible guesses, only to see it shattered by the disclosure of an incurable flaw; whereupon the Sphinx, with the scornful smile of Apollo pronouncing sentence upon Marsyas, summons her brood of Follies to carry him off; and when they swarm upon the stage and engage in their wild dance about their victim, the drama reaches its crisis, and the Antimasque its climax, at once. The ultimate triumph of the masquers, equally *de rigueur*, is brought about by a similarly dramatic procedure. No sudden overpowering splendour blots out from dazzled senses 'the very memory' of triumphant Ignorance and Folly; simply, Love, taught by the Muses' priests where the true solution is to be sought, immediately discovers it, and his rapturous *Heureka* ('''Tis done, 'tis done. I haue found it out') breaks the spell of the Sphinx's power and banishes her with her baneful brood; while on the other

[1] Folio, 1616, p. 985, note a.

side enter the Graces, and as they crown victorious liberated Love, lead on the measured dances of the Main Masque with one of the happiest of Jonson's lyrics:

> A crowne, a crowne for LOVES bright head,
>   Without whose happie wit
> All forme, and beautie had beene dead,
>   And we had di'd with it.

It is a pity that the solution, thus fortunately discovered, rests upon a basis so precarious as the majesty of James the First. But we have to face the fundamental flaw of the whole Masque-genre,—the radical insincerity which a man of genius writing for the entertainment of his sovereign can only in the rarest cases escape. And if Jonson was neither a Vergil nor a Goethe, James had still fewer pretensions to be either an Augustus or a Karl August.

Love Restored, January 6, 1612.

Love Freed from Ignorance and Folly, though one of the less costly of the Jacobean Masques, was apparently not produced without some inconvenience to the embarrassed Treasury, and it is possible, as Brotanek suggests, that the second Masque contemplated when More wrote to Winwood in the middle of December may have been omitted on economical grounds, or indeed never have existed at all. *Love Restored* is in any case not this second Masque, as Nichols thought. The apparent affinity of title in the two Masques covers no real resemblance,—a sufficient proof that they were not produced at the same season. *Love Restored* would have been a blundering title had the Masque been a companion piece to *Love Freed*; the personation of Love standing in no such relation as the title suggests to his capture. Several allusions moreover exclude an earlier date than the beginning of 1612.[1]

---

[1] E. g. 'so Catholique a cockscombe as CORYAT', and 'the *Christmas* cutpurse'. Coryat's *Crudities* was published in the summer of 1611. Brotanek first pointed out the account, in a letter of John Chamberlain, 31 December 1611, of the detection of a pickpocket at Court, to which Jonson alludes. Mainly on this ground he assigns the Masque to Twelfth Night, 1612. Mr. Simpson (*Every Man in his Humour*, p. xxxiv) argued that the Masque was one of those performed at Somerset's wedding in Dec.–Jan. 1613–14. But the series of masques and shows

Love Freed from Ignorance and Folly had itself contained no hint of the financial straits which had so direct and ominous a bearing upon the very existence of this expensive form of art. But in its successor, *Love Restored*, Jonson with felicitous humour took the financial situation, and the controversies which had grown out of it or found fresh food in it, as the groundwork of the plot. The angry criticisms passed, with growing assurance and menace, upon the Court Masques proceeded from two distinct though overlapping classes, and rested on two distinct grounds. To the Puritan the Masque was a branch of the abhorred drama, and the fact that it was designed to amuse, at an extravagant cost, an aristocratic audience and a royal champion of divine right did very little to qualify his disesteem. And many grave citizens who were not Puritans took exception to the enormous sums spent upon the soon forgotten pastime of an hour. Jonson, who had done, and to the end did, his best to 'grace the Masque with elegancy', would doubtless have sympathized with a qualified and discriminating criticism of the attempt to 'daub it with cost'. But he catered for sumptuous tastes, and in the company of prodigal artists like Inigo Jones; and his 'elegancy', if it did not actually occasion fresh expenditure, simply turned the stream of gold which he could not check into a more artistic channel. In any case he frankly took up the gauntlet of the critics, Puritan and economist alike, and branded both in the figure of Plutus, who, disguised as Love, gains entrance to the Court to denounce, in hoarse tones and with the Puritan accent, its favourite pastime: 'I tell thee, I will haue no more masquing; I will not buy a false, and fleeting delight so deare: The merry madnesse of one hower shall not cost me the repentance of an age.'[1] Plutus, wearing the mask of Love, was now the reigning god, 'making friendships, contracts, mariages, and almost

known to have been performed at these festivities appears to exclude this possibility. Cf. Chambers, *Elizabethan Stage*, iii. 387 f. Mr. Simpson now concurs in this view.
[1] Folio, 1616, p. 990.

religion; begetting, breeding, and holding the neerest respects of mankind; and vsurping all those offices in this Age of gold, which LOVE himselfe perform'd in the golden age'.[1] To this despot of frugal pastimes, gloomy countenance, and utilitarian economics, Jonson with his usual felicity opposes the very genius of old English country mirth and festive jest, Robin Goodfellow; and it is significant that as Plutus, the enemy, won admission by disguising himself, so Robin, the friend, after vainly 'translating' himself into a succession of other shapes, gets in by simply sticking to his own and giving out that he was a part of the Device. Not much, it is true, of the *naïveté* of 'the honest plaine countrey spirit and harmelesse', who 'sweepes the harth, and the house cleane',[2] has survived his conversion into a mouthpiece of Jonsonian polemics. At moments a reminiscence of the Shakespearian Puck may be suspected, as in ''Tis you, mortalls, that are fooles'.[3] But on the whole his value as a character is sacrificed to his value as a discoverer and denouncer of the sham character of another. Even his pleasant malice, when most arch, as in his personation of the Puritan feather-dealer—'We are all *masquers* sometimes'—suggests the irony of the man of the world, not the exuberant fun of the boy-sprite. For the rest, this prose prelude altogether overshadows the Main Masque which follows. It is not regular Antimasque; the comic actions and dialogue which originally served to introduce the grotesque dance having here altogether extruded it. This exclusion remained exceptional; but the distinction in other respects between the Antimasque and a scene from prose comedy of real life became in Jonson's hands a vanishing quantity, and the grotesque dance, though retained, proportionately anomalous. *Love Restored* opens this later phase of Jonsonian Antimasque. One cannot but contrast with the immense vivacity of the portrayal of Plutus the impostor, the pale and perfunctory enumeration of the ten companions of true Love, the noble virtues which

[1] Folio, 1616, p. 993.   [2] Ibid. p. 990.   [3] Ibid. p. 993.

adorn a Court.¹ But Jonson's scorn, though not more genuine, was always more fruitful than his admiration.

During the autumn of 1612 and the first half of 1613 Jonson was absent in France. This is the reason why the most extraordinary festive occasion of the reign of James—the wedding of Princess Elizabeth, was graced by no contribution from the most distinguished of its writers of Masques. *A Challenge at Tilt*, December, January, 1613–14. His absence was, however, the opportunity of rivals or friends only less distinguished than he; not only of Chapman and Fletcher, whose merits in Masque-making he placed next to his own; but Beaumont and Campion, whom posterity considers at least as well entitled to this honour.² Towards the close of the year a more sinister marriage called for a further provision of wedding Masques. The principal Masque was again written by Campion—the so-called *Squires' Masque*. But Jonson, far from refusing to take part in the celebration of this adulterous second marriage, as Gifford suggests, contributed two pieces: one *The Irish Masque* on December 29; and the *Challenge at Tilt*, with its sequel the Tilt proper, produced on the following day and on January 1. Neither piece is of the first importance, but the second contains some of his most brilliant and beautiful prose, and the homely humour of the first found such favour with the courtly audience that it was repeated five days later, on 3 January 1614.³

In the *Challenge at Tilt*, and its sequel, Jonson reverted to the simpler structure of the Barriers which he had composed for the first marriage of the bride. Here too, a simple debate between two opponents, instead of the ambitious dramatic apparatus of Prince Henry's Barriers,

---

¹ '... one *harmonie* Of *honor*, and of *courtesie*, True *valure*, and *vrbanitie*, Of *confidence*, *alacritie*, Of *promptnesse*, and of *industrie*, *Habilitie*, *Realitie*' (Folio, p. 994).

² T. Campion, *The Lords' Masque*, 14 Feb. 1613; G. Chapman, *Masque of the Middle Temple and Lincoln's Inn*, 15 Feb. 1613; F. Beaumont, *Masque of the Inner Temple and Grays Inn*, 20 Feb. 1613.

³ Brotanek, p. 350, shows that this, not 10 January, is the date of the repetition.

U 2

provided the ostensible occasion of the fight. But in dramatic vivacity both the earlier Barriers fall short of this charming quarrel of Eros and Anteros, and (after the mock battle) their reconciliation, as subtle and profound as it is gracious, by Hymen. Truth and Opinion exchange plea and counterplea with a dignity not devoid of stiffness and formality, and in stately and sententious verse which does little to mitigate this effect. But the two Cupids, of man's love ('the nobler creature') and woman's ('the purer'), 'strive' with one another like boys—boys of genius, and their emulous tirades flow from their lips with a winged eloquence rare in Jonson's prose.

> Was it not I that yester-night wayted on the *Bride*, into the nuptiall chamber, and against the *Bride-groome* came, made her the throne of loue? Had I not lighted my torches in her eyes? Planted my mothers roses in her cheekes? were not her eye browes bent to the fashion of my bow? and her lookes ready to be loos'd thence, like my shafts? Had I not ripned kisses on her lips, fit for a MERCVRY to gather? and made her language sweeter then his vpon her tongue? was not the girdle about her, he was to vntie, my mothers? wherein all the ioyes and delights of loue, were woven.[1]

The solution, again, of the earlier Barriers is not without awkwardness; the champions of opinion being 'reconciled' with those of Truth, while Opinion herself—'adulterate Truth'—is ignominiously dismissed. The Hymen of the later piece provides a better ground for the reconciliation of the champions: 'This is a strife, wherein you both winne, and begets a concord worthy all married mindes emulation, when the louer transformes himselfe into the person of his belou'd, as you two doe now.'[2]

The Irish Masque, December 29, 1613, and January 3, 1614.

In *The Irish Masque* Jonson essayed a new genre. Ostensible imitation of the dress and habits of other nationalities had been a common device of the sixteenth-century entertainments. Jonson's own first Masque had turned to account at least the 'Blackness' of the

---

[1] Folio, 1616, p. 996.   [2] Ibid. p. 1000.

Ethiopians. The Irish too had figured in several shows.[1] But it is doubtful whether realism in these performances went much beyond the use of the characteristic Irish 'mantle'. Jonson brought to the management of the 'national' Masque the thoroughness of a scholar and the virtuosity of a keen observer of the highways and byways of speech. He had early shown remarkable command of rustic dialect in the *Tale of a Tub*. Shakespeare had dallied at moments with this somewhat cheap form of comedy, and even used occasionally its opportunities for equivoque. But the 'English' of Jonson's Dennis and Dermont and Howell and Rhees is far more elaborate and drastic than that of Captain Macmorris and Parson Evans; unfortunately it is also, in almost the same degree, less funny. The device itself provides a simple but ingenious machinery for the sequence of Antimasque and Masque. The 'imbasheters' sent by the Irish as a sign of their devotion to James, to the wedding, have lost their festive dresses on the voyage. The four footmen come forward to explain the mishap to the royal presence, and after getting out the story with digressions and interruptions worthy of Dogberry and Verges, dance their rude Antimasque. Then the gentlemen ambassadors appear, in Irish mantles instead of their Court dresses, and dance 'to a solemnne musique of harpes'; finally, the presence of the king effects a transformation in keeping with all masquing etiquette, and the masquers 'let fall their slough' and come forth arrayed in their orthodox masquing apparel. It adds to the amusement, and marks a further step in the intrusion of comic realism upon the rigour of Masque convention, that after the appearance and first dance of the masquers, the familiar 'footmen' of the Antimasque again intervene, with a 'How like tow tish

---

[1] An inventory of the Masque-dresses from the beginning of Henry VIII's reign includes 'mantles according to the Irish fashion' (Collier, *Hist. Dram. Poetry*, i. 80). At Christmas, 1551, an Irish man and woman figured in a Masque; a masque of 1557 consisted of 'Almaynes, Pilgrymes, and Irishemen, with their insidents and accomplishes accordingly' (ibid. i. 163). See Brotanek, pp. 37-8.

YAMISH?'[1] to be cut short and finally dismissed by the Civil Gentlemen of their nation, and the Bard who presently sums up with a loyalist moral this equivocal 'compliment' (as Gifford calls it) to the unhappy country which had so recently experienced the policy of the 'peace-making' king.

Mercury Vindicated from the Alchemists at Court, January 6 and 8, 1615.[2]

Three years, probably, had now elapsed since Jonson last produced the regular Twelfth Night Masque at Court. Like the great comedy *Bartholomew Fair*, which had been his principal work during 1614, and more signally than any earlier Masque, *Mercury Vindicated* is saturated with the flavour of Jonson's mind. In the play the very fabric of comedy had been forced to expand and relax to accommodate the prodigious turmoil of the plot. In the Masque he compelled the courtly conventions of its form to convey a peculiarly lively expresssion of his special vein of humour and of his most intimate aims in art. Hitherto, the ideas or content of the Masque, where they were not, as in the *Masque of Blackness,* a mere fantastic thread for song and dance, had usually been drawn from commonplaces of Renascence sentiment, as the opposition of Fame and Envy, or of the higher and the lower Love. Both Love and Fame had been sung in Jonson's time in loftier and more memorable strains than his: he found passable music for these standing themes, but we rarely think of him when we remember their poets. But of alchemy Jonson was the poet *par excellence*; and none the less that to the more obviously poetic aspects of alchemy he remained scornfully inaccessible. While Marlowe and Shakespeare drew tragic horror or magic enchantment from the magician's cell, Jonson fastened with annihilating power upon the mass of sham ritual and pseudo-erudition which they called their science and their art, and made grim sport for posterity over the illusions of their dupes. In the

---
[1] Folio, 1616, p. 1003.
[2] The chronological order of this Masque and *The Golden Age* is doubted by Mr. Chambers (*Elizabethan Stage,* iii. 389). But the authority of the Folio, passed through the press by Jonson himself, is here decisive

Masque the focus of ridicule is transferred from the dupes to the 'artists' themselves and the 'imperfect creatures' of their craft. The satire of *The Alchemist* had turned upon their pretension to make gold. Here, availing himself of the famous legend of the artificial man who emerged from the crucible of Paracelsus, he devised a gruesome company of inchoate or mutilated beings—men badly made by these rude and self-constituted 'journeymen of nature'. It was an excellent satiric device to identify these unlucky abortions of the laboratory with the types of eccentric or extravagant humanity in which Jonson as a comic dramatist had from the first found his good. The profusion of various material thus provided perhaps induced Jonson to borrow here for the first time the device of the double Antimasque-dance which had for some years been in vogue. The innovation was probably not attractive to him, and he did not permanently adopt it. But it offered a ready means of adding to the vivacity and impressiveness of the comic introduction to the Main Masque; enabling him to introduce in separate grotesque dances the 'troupe of threedbare Alchymists' and their 'imperfect creatures, with helmes of lymbecks on their heads'.[1] In the transition to the Main Masque, on the other hand, Jonson falls back from the dramatic sequences so skilfully obtained in his recent Masques to the sudden Transformation scenes of the *Hymenaei* or *The Masque of Queens*. The clue to the symbolism, briefly touched in the preluding speech of Mercury, had been fully given in the fine opening song of 'Cyclope' as he tends the fire in the Alchemists' laboratory. Nature is old and lamed, and the Sun, her friend and ally, disarmed by the spell of winter. Now is the time for 'soft, subtile fire', the 'soule of art', to do its part in creation against the usurped monopoly of Nature and the Sun. And things looked bad enough for Nature, as Jonson well knew, in the London and Whitehall of 1615.

---

[1] Folio, 1616, p. 1008.

> Looke, but how few confesse her now,
>   In cheeke or browe!
> From euery head, almost, how she is frighted.
>   The very age abhorres her so,
>   That it learnes to speake and goe
> As if by art alone it could be righted.[1]

But none knew better, too, than Jonson that 'Nature' was not exhausted nor exhaustible; and the apparition of the 'glorious bowre' whence Nature with wise Prometheus descends leading the masquers forth 'to shew they are the creatures of the Sunne' echoes, or anticipates, not inaptly the fine paragraph of the *Discoveries* headed '*Natura non effœta*', in which Jonson so completely made his own a thought of the younger Pliny: 'I cannot thinke *Nature* is so spent, and decay'd, that she can bring forth nothing worth her former yeares. She is alwayes the same, like her selfe: And when she collects her strength, is abler still. Men are decay'd, and *studies*: Shee is not.'[2] But in 'vindicating' Nature from the 'imperfect creatures' of the laboratory, Jonson was implicitly carrying on his own Humanist crusade against the literature which offered 'monsters' instead of 'men'. What he had said, in weighty sententious couplets, in the Prologue to *Every Man in His Humour*, he conveyed with admirable deftness in the symbolic and mythological language of the Masque when he made Mercury, escaped from the crucibles of alchemy, fling his parting defiance to the 'old *Smug* here of *Lemnos*, and his smoaky familie', and proclaim his allegiance to 'the Maiesty of this light, whose *Mercury* henceforth I professe to be, and neuer againe the *Philosophers*'. It must be owned that there is more poetry in the conception than in the verse. Nature's songs open with a charming stanza ('How yong and fresh am I to night'), but pass into triviality. And Prometheus is permitted some approaches to buffoonery, and Nature has one exasperating rhyme.[3] But the whole is worthily

---

[1] Folio, 1616, p. 1004.
[2] Folio, 1640, p. 89. Cf. Pliny, *Epist.* vi. 21.
[3] 'Laughters' and 'daughters' (Folio, 1616, p. 1009).

summed up and concluded in the single harsh but pregnant line:
> They are not worth his light, goe backward from the Sun.

Jonson's next Twelfth Night Masque, a year later, marks a sharp divergence, in some important points, from his recent practice. The loose and unstable combination of lyrical and dramatic, of ideal and comic elements, and of verse and prose, which the Masque never ceased to be, had shown a steady bias, during the last five years, on the side of comic and dramatic prose. In *Love Restored, The Irish Masque*, and *Mercury Vindicated*, the vivacity and elaboration of the comic scene which introduced the Antimasque made this the focus of the whole entertainment, and foreshadowed an ultimate reduction of the stately Main Masque to the function of a formal Epilogue,—a consummation at least approached in *The Metamorphosed Gipsies*. But in *The Golden Age Restored* this process was suddenly reversed. The action is of a classic simplicity becoming the theme; and the verse in which it is uniformly conveyed is always, even in dialogue, lyric in character, richly and continuously rhymed, and, for Jonson, unusually melodious and beautiful. What there is of drama is moreover unfolded almost wholly in the Main Masque, an unusually variegated woof of intermingled dialogue, dance, and song; while the Antimasque in its turn sinks to the proportions of a rudiment,[1] and, like that of *The Masque of Queens*, has no comic intention or effect. As if to emphasize the insignificance of the Antimasque, Pallas descends at the outset to announce that the Iron Age with his embattled Evils is about to cease, 'frustrated' instantly by the glance of her shield. The brief tumult and clash of arms which follows, and the Iron Age's stirring summons to his brood, are thus fraught with even less of dramatic suspense than the usual

The Golden Age Restored, January 1 and 6, 1616.

---

[1] Compare the simple enumeration of the Evils here with the similar enumeration of the Virtues in the Main Masque of *Love Restored*, and the elaborate portraits of the 'imperfect creatures' in *Mercury Vindicated*.

ostentatious hostilities of the Antimasque, always destined to collapse before the triumph of Virtue, or Nature, or Fame. Yet there are touches in the Antimasque which, curt and reticent as they are, suggest more definite and personal allusions than are commonly to be detected in the satirist's conventional catalogue of evils. The Countess of Somerset and her husband had been brought to trial, a few months before, for the hideous crime of which they were shortly to be convicted; and Jonson, who had joined in celebrating both her first and her second wedding, now keenly regretted his participation, and did his best to conceal it from posterity by cutting out all reference to it in the text of these Masques, published shortly after in the collected edition of his works. Yet it would be strange if no veiled allusion had escaped him in a description of the insurgent evils of the age composed at such a moment. And every courtly ear that heard Pallas recount how

> IOVE can endure no longer,
> Your great ones should your lesse inuade,

and the Iron Age number among the brood of Avarice 'thy babe last borne, smooth Trecherie', must have instantly thought of the insidious murder wrought by the all-powerful favourite and his wife upon the helpless prisoner in the Tower.

For the rest, the transformation of the Evils into statues by Pallas's shield is an apt example of a kind of impressive effect open to the Masque but denied to the drama. The most original feature of the ensuing scene is the introduction of the four old English poets, Chaucer, Gower, Lydgate and Spenser, as protagonists of the restored Golden Age. None of the four enjoyed, elsewhere, any peculiar marks of Jonson's esteem. The recovery of the 'buried art' of John Lydgate can hardly have seemed a prospect for which it was worth while to obliterate the living art of Shakespeare and Donne; and Spenser, whose matter and manner he equally disliked, doubtless owes his inclusion among the poets of Elysium to the flavour of an older day conveyed by his antique phrase, rather than to his poetry. But that the

restored Golden Age should be led on by English poets—
'farre-fam'd spirits of this happie Ile'—instead of by the
inmates of the classic Elysium, marks another step in
the gradual assimilation of the Masque to English circumstance and scenery. Beyond these names and phrases,
however, there is little that is English in this Golden Age.
The old English poets appear isolated and somewhat
incongruous figures in an earthly Elysium imagined in the
spirit of Hesiod and the fourth *Eclogue* and mainly furnished
from their resources. But in the final stanzas Jonson
beautifully amends the most palpable flaw in the traditional
conception of the Golden Age—its blank incapacity of
growth—by making the Age and the poets co-operate
through their song in its endurance and their own immortality:

>   Like lights about ASTRAEA's throne,
>   You here must shine, and all be one,
>   In feruor and in flame.
>   That by your vnion she may grow,
>   And, you sustaining her, may know
>   The age still by her name.
>
>   Who vowes, against or heat or cold,
>   To spin you garments of her gold,
>   That want may touch you neuer,
>   And making garlands every hower,
>   To write your names in some new flower,
>   That you may liue for euer.

A greater poet than Jonson might have reached out from
this graceful fancy to Goethe's sublime vision of the
'Erdgeist', who weaves on the roaring loom of Time
the living garment of God. But the Masque, child of
luxury and pastime, not of speculative imagination or
probing thought, throve in the atmosphere of lofty commonplace; and among the grounds of Jonson's supremacy as a
Masque poet was his consistent use of lofty commonplaces
as the motives to which he brought his real originality of
invention and of technique. The great man, Jowett is

reported to have said, is he who does original things in a conventional way.

Christmas his Masque, Christmas, 1616. The busy year which had seen the appearance of a comedy (*The Devil is an Ass*), a Masque, and the laboriously revised edition of his collected works, closed with a *jeu d'esprit*. The humour, such as it is, of *Christmas his Masque* begins with the title: the name of these stately shows being borrowed with Saturnalian freedom for a boisterous travesty. The 'Masque' is (substantially) indeed of 'merry Christmas's' own making, and is nothing more nor less than a Christmas mummery or procession of grotesque types: Misrule, Gambol, Carol, Minc'd-Pie, Baby-Cake, and the rest. Satiric piquancy is, however, characteristically given to the device by the fiction that Christmas had originally made his 'Masque' for the gross apprehensions of a City audience. 'It was intended I confesse for Curryers Hall, but because the weather has beene open, and the Livory were not at leisure to see it till a good frost came that they cannot worke, I thought it convenient, with some little alterations, and the Groome of the *Revells* hand to 't, to fit it for a higher place, which I have done; and though I say it, another manner of devise then your Newyeares night.'[1] Events intervene to trouble the execution of the 'device'. Jonson had already in *Love Restored* made sport with the adventures of enterprising citizens and others in the attempt to get admission to the scene of the Masque, and Robin Goodfellow's graphic report is varied with much pleasantry in the escapades of Venus ('Good Lady Venus of Pudding-lane') and her hopeful son Cupid ('Prentise in Love-lane with a Bugle-maker, that makes of your Bobs, and Bird-bolts for Ladies'). Cupid's imperfect discharge of his part, and his fond mother's vain encouragements ('Tis a good child, speake out, hold up your head Love') issuing only in Christmas's scornful comment: 'Nay, he is out enough, you may take him away, and begin your Dance; this it is

[1] Folio, 1640 (Masques), p. 1. From this point the text of the Masques is quoted from the 1640 Folio.

to have speeches'), make excellent burlesque. The 'interruptions' contributed by Jonson as a supplement to the show 'intended for Curriers' Hall' illustrate the immense advance made by the Masque, even in its lightest and loosest mood, since the days of the sixteenth-century mumming, old-fashioned Christmas fare which Jonson now serves up with this pleasant Jacobean garnish of comic by-play.

In the Christmas Masque Jonson had fallen back upon the homeliest native traditions of festive revelry. Its successor, produced some six weeks later, was designed for an occasion which demanded a complete subordination of the national elements of the Court Masque. Written for performance before the Ambassador Extraordinary of the French King, at the house of the late Ambassador of James to France, *Lovers Made Men* moves wholly among the familiar figures of classical myth, then the common possession of well-bred Europe. In consideration of the foreign ambassador, the whole Masque was, further, sung in recitative, as Jonson tells us, 'after the Italian manner'. It is, in effect, the earliest operatic piece in the language, and the history of opera would have been different indeed had its composers been provided with such a libretto as that for which Master Nicholas Lanier 'made both the Scene, and the Musicke'. Jonson has composed no daintier and more gracious verse than these speeches and songs, with their intricately interwoven rhymes and quick interchanging rhythms. The plot is a Lucianic variation upon the theme of Charon and the river Lethe, deftly arranged to yield the normal movement and counter-movement of the Antimasque and Main Masque in the most simple and natural way. The Masque being performed, it would seem, exclusively by noble persons, as often happened in the country-house entertainments, it was probably convenient that the Antimasque should be played by them also, instead of by professional players. This would of itself suggest to a poet of Jonson's resource that the Antimasquers, instead

Lovers made Men, February 22, 1617.

of being, as usual, flung into obscurity or annihilation by the triumphant apparition of the Main Masque, might reappear in it as their healed or 'transformed' former selves. The device had already been practised, ten years before, by Campion in his wedding Masque for Lord Hayes.[1] The myth of Lethe furnished an obvious means of effecting this. But the application to Lovers,

> tost upon those frantique seas,
> Whence VENVS sprung,

and *made men* once more by the oblivious draught which releases them from Love's frenzied illusions, belongs to Jonson alone, and reflects his unromantic view of passion. The erotic verse of his own and most other ages abundantly exemplified the hyperbolic phrases upon which his satiric raillery fastens. But it was a happy exercise of the Masque-maker's cunning to convert these victims of Love's consuming flames and whelming waters, ecstatically persuaded that they had 'died for Love', into material for an Antimasque, as examples of the 'imperfect creatures' who there exhibited their 'antic faces' and 'ridiculous gestures'. The Lovers, brought to the brink of Lethe's stream, 'stoope to the water, and dance forth their Antimasque in severall gestures, as they liv'd in love',—presently to emerge restored to the disillusioned common sense, the temperate wit, the 'humanity', waited on by 'cheerfulness' and 'readiness', which for Jonson made so large a part of the sterling substance of Man. The contrasts and gradations in this Masque are of singular delicacy and refinement; and the harmony of total effect, in which it so much surpasses many Masques of greater magnificence, is greatly promoted by the continuous relations of Mercury and Cupid, whose Attic figures intermingle in changing attitudes round the whole circuit of the little piece. They are champions of opposite causes, but neither is completely suppressed; each contributes something to the final issue. The 'Lovers'

---

[1] *The Discription of a Maske, Presented before the Kinges Maiestie at White Hall . . . in honour of the Lord Hayes, and his Bride*, 1607.

have followed Cupid's lure and been deaf to Mercury's; but in the Court-world for whose pastime the Masque was written, Lord Love was far too potent to be slighted, and the 'Men', transformed by Lethe, forget only the foolish violence of passion, and joyously continue to love, but *love with wit*.

In the Christmas Masque of 1617, as in its predecessor, *Vision of Delight*, Jonson turned to account the traditional Saturnalian licence of the season. But he now brought to bear upon this homely motive all his resources of invention and art. *Christmas his Masque* was a boisterous substitute for the Masque, a Saturnalia of popular revelry thrust in upon the courtly scene in its place. The *Vision of Delight* is a true Masque, but one complying with the spirit of the time; allowing free scope to an emancipated fancy, and in its own composition admitting an occasional relaxation of the rigour of the game. In the opening verses Delight announces the program of a chartered Epicureanism. Earth and air and the ingenious brain of man are to furnish forth a joyous variety show, suitable to the exacting appetites and the brief patience of a Court:

<blockquote>
Let your shewes be new, as strange,
let them oft and sweetly varie;
Let them haste so to their change,
as the Seers may not tarrie.[1]
</blockquote>

The first Antimasque, 'A she Monster delivered of sixe *Burratines*, that dance with six *Pantalones*', immediately enters, with no other prelude or explanation than these verses, which it appears to illustrate. Jonson here was obviously infringing, for a special purpose, the refined technique which he had been steadily elaborating for the dramatic and natural introduction of the Antimasque.[2] Then Night rises, and calls upon 'Phant'sie', in an eloquent song, to create the fantastic distorted population of dreams and darkness:

---
[1] Folio, p. 16.
[2] This point is well made by Brotanek, *u.s.* p. 146.

>   Breake *Phant'sie* from thy cave of cloud
>   and spread thy purple wings;
>   Now all thy figures are allow'd,
>   and various shapes of things.[1]

Phantasy's speech, which follows, is a genuine Antimasque (in the extended sense), wholly in keeping, in its rollicking incoherence, with the Phantasms ('the second Antimasque') whose dance it introduces. But Fancy does not reign solely here; she is not, like the witches in *The Masque of Queens*, or Comus in the *Pleasure Reconciled*, a purely antagonistic power, belonging wholly to the Antimasque. After playing the leading part there she banishes the incoherent Phantasms, and remains to preside sympathetically over the Masque proper, in which the stories of Nature are not distorted but only seen in vision before their time. The Vision of the Spring ecstatically described by Wonder ('Wonder must speake, or breake') approaches the sensuous opulence and exaltation of Keats as nearly as Jonson's classical sobriety of phrase permits. But the modern reader's pleasure in these rare woodland notes of old Ben is abruptly cut short when Phantasy, turning to 'the State', proffers the explanation of the wondrous vision, foreshadowed indeed by the apparition of 'Peace':

>   Behold a King
>   Whose presence maketh this perpetuall *Spring*.[2]

The word recalls us from Fancy's brief emancipation to the bondage of tasteless flattery which even the doughtiest of Jacobean poets complacently endured. Beautiful as it is, the *Vision of Delight* bears the marks of decadence, and it is not surprising that among the post-Jonsonian Masque-writers it found special favour. In both Shirley's *Triumph of Peace* (1634) and Jordan's *Fancy's Festivals* (1657) 'Fancy' is adopted as the presenter, or as the teeming mother, of the marvels of the show.[3]

Pleasure Reconciled to Virtue, January 6, 1618. If not wholly exempt from the same flaw, the very interesting Masque of the ensuing Twelfth Night exhibits it in a far less injurious form. *Pleasure Reconciled to Virtue*,

---

[1] Folio, p. 17.   [2] Ibid. p. 20.   [3] Brotanek, p. 222.

notwithstanding the angry reception it experienced, may on the whole be counted among the Masques in which Jonson has most dexterously united high courtesy with sage and salutary counsel.

Comus, for Jonson, is the god of the gross pleasures that 'extinguish man' and destroy themselves. He haunts a grove of Bacchic ivy about the base of Atlas, the 'hill of knowledge', and his attendant rout hail him in a Falstaffian hymn of rollicking verse and greasy prose, fit prelude to the dance of bottle- and tun-shaped men which follows. Then Hercules, fresh from the slaying of the earth-giant Antaeus, appears, and indignantly annihilates the grove with this second tribe of earth-born monsters. Comus is the hero of the first Antimasque, and vanishes with it. But Pleasure does not share his fall, and is seen sitting aloft with Virtue, while the chorus invite the 'great friend and servant of the good' to rest after his toil. Yet another variety of earth's monstrous brood, the Pigmies, think to surprise their enemy asleep, and their futilities make a 'second Antimasque' which perhaps gave a hint to the author of Lilliput. Then at length Mercury descending communicates the tidings of the twelve princes who, having

> beene bred
> In this rough mountaine, and neere *Atlas* head,
> The hill of knowledge,[1]

are now to profit by the reconciliation of Virtue with Pleasure, and be admitted into the garden of the Hesperides. Then the mountain opens in the approved way, and the twelve masquers descend in triumph for the dances and songs of the Main Masque. These leave no doubt how Jonson intended the 'reconciliation' to be understood. His garden of the Hesperides was clearly no garden of Adonis or Armida, and if it had been, there is no fear they should grow soft or effeminate, since Pleasure is now 'the servant'

---

[1] Folio, p. 26.

of Virtue, and acts only at her bidding. 'Royal education' is to be a laborious and exacting discipline. It is also to be a discipline in skill and technique, in arts and science. Hence they are led on by Daedalus the wise, who is able to 'give them lawes to all their motions', and lead them through 'any laborinth, though it be of love'. In three songs of unusual subtlety the wise Daedalus unfolds his wisdom. Jonson, as an artist, knows that if pleasure and virtue are anywhere 'reconciled', it is in the joyous exercise of trained skill in art; and he weaves the intricate figures of the masquers' dance ingeniously into the substance of the poetry when he makes Daedalus invite them so to

> enterweave the curious knot
> As ev'n th' observer scarce may know
> Which lines are Pleasures, and which not.[1]

Love was less intimately known to Jonson than art, and we must not look for such poetry from him as the 'reconciliation of Virtue and Pleasure' in this 'subt'lest maze of all' would have evoked from many a lesser poet. But there is at least singular adroitness in the turn by which Daedalus, preluding the dance with the ladies, calls the masquers to their last exercise of delightful virtue in the 'laborinth of beautie':

> Go choose among—But with a minde
> as gentle as the stroaking winde
> runs ore the gentler flowers.
> And so let all your actions smile
> As if they meant not to beguile
> the Ladies, but the houres.[2]

But this pleasant occupation does not signify their final release from the ardours of toil. Shakespeare had laughed at his academic repudiators of love: Jonson summons his lovers back from the 'sports' which Virtue permits to the life of strenuous labour she enjoins:

[1] Folio, p. 27. [2] Ibid. p. 28.

> These, these are houres by Vertue spar'd
> Her selfe, she being her owne reward:
>   But she will have you know,
>   That though
> Her sports be soft, her life is hard:
>   You must returne unto the Hill
>   and there advance
>   With labour, and inhabit still
>   that height and Crowne,
> From whence you ever may looke downe
>   upon triumphed chance.[1]

This is not remote from the spirit of Milton's *Comus*, and the culminating words of the song,—

> In Heaven . . . is Vertues seate,
>   Strive to keepe her your own,
> Tis onely she can make you great,
>   Though place here make you knowne—

have only been touched to a finer issue in the closing verses of his epilogue. For Milton had clearly studied *Pleasure Reconciled*, and the earlier *Comus* may well be held to excel the later as much in suppleness and fertility of scenic invention, relatively to its scale, as it falls short of it in splendour of poetry. And Jonson's invention is applied wholly within the lines of the accepted Masque form. With secure and experienced skill he rearranges the legend of Hercules so as to lead naturally up to the contrasted effects of Main Masque and Antimasque; while Milton, loftily and somewhat stiffly taking his own way, achieves his end in the main by the aid of his own consummate resources, making but slight and perfunctory concessions to the traditional technique. To the grotesque, rustic, and buffoon effects which had now established themselves firmly in the rollicking measures or colloquial prose of the Antimasque, Milton refuses to concede a single syllable of his Attic (or Doric) verse. Comus's rout of 'oughly-headed monsters' enter (in the stage direction) 'making a riotous and unruly noise', but

[1] Ibid. p. 29.

their riot and unruliness find countenance only in the purport of their leader's speech, a tissue of the most delicate literary embroidery veiling the foulest things in the woof of indirect imagery and allusion. The dance of rustics at the close is so gratuitous and unrelated to the plot that its existence is scarcely noticed and can hardly be explained except as a reluctant concession to the demand for the now almost universal second Antimasque;[1] a purpose, however, to which its place in the Masque is entirely unsuited. The sudden and decisive change of scene and temper which regularly comes with the apparition of the masquers has only a formal parallel in the change of scene from the gloomy wood to the splendour of Comus's 'stately palace set out with all manner of deliciousness'. For this change normally announces that the dramatic conflict between higher and lower powers has now issued in the decisive triumph of the good, which has only to be celebrated in song and dance. But Milton, while offering something superficially like the splendid apparitions to which his audience were accustomed, has altogether detached these elements from their original purpose. The burst of light and colour does not mark the final triumph of good, and the consequent resolution of dramatic stress, but the threatening predominance of evil, and it ushers in the most enthralling dramatic crisis in the whole poem. Drama has thus encroached notably upon the proper domains of song and dance. The persons it has almost completely annexed. The young Egertons assuredly did not quarrel with the poet who released them from roles of dignified passivity habitually assigned to the noble masquers, and gave them the exacting parts commonly handed over to professional actors. But it was an innovation which made havoc of the traditional Masque scheme. Instead of emerging together at a given solemn moment, they play their parts in the whole Masque, have their exits and their entrances in all respects like the persons of a drama. If, in short, we allow

[1] *Comus*, 952-60.

Comus to be rightly called, as Milton called it, a Masque, we must add that it is one in which the spirit of drama has broken free from the Masque in everything that concerns scheme and composition, while retaining a few unimportant traces of a nominal allegiance. In conception, on the other hand, it is a genuine and unmistakable Masque. The conflict of good and evil powers, the unconditional triumph of good, the pervading flavour of debate, were all gratifying and congenial to the militant Puritan poet. These motives too he carried out with a force and intensity not approached by Jonson even when he is most inspired. But Jonson's example was probably the strongest influence which led him to Masque at all. And none of Jonson's Masques was more in his mind than the earlier and, with all its inferiority, splendid and ingenious *Comus* produced by the elder scholar-poet sixteen years before.

'The Masque is poor', wrote Sir Edward Sherburne categorically to Carleton of the *Pleasure Reconciled*; 'and Inigo Jones has lost reputation, for something extraordinary was expected, as it was the first in which the prince ever played.'[1] Jonson was called upon for an improved version, with, presumably, a more emphatic recognition of this *début* of the Prince of Wales. He was not accustomed to have his work returned, and in the version prepared for print concealed the fact by the audacious statement that 'this pleas'd the KING so well, as he would see it againe, when it was presented with these additions,' the 'additions' being in fact the new version of the offending Antimasque. '*For the Honour of Wales*' means, of course, for the honour of the Prince of Wales. The high destiny of Atlas is now transferred to Snowdon. Like *The Irish Masque*, this Welsh Antimasque is full of lively touches of national character and speech; the flavour of the humour is not very rich or subtle, but it is unmistakably Welsh. And the grotesque dialogue and songs give place at the close to a

For the Honour of Wales, February 17, 1618.

---
[1] *Calendar of State Papers, Domestic Series*, 1623-5, p. 552. Cf. Brotanek's discussion, pp. 203, 353.

passage of dignified praise for a nation 'unconquer'd, and most loving liberty, yet . . . never mutinous (and please your Majestie;) but stout, valiant, courteous, hospitable, temperate, ingenious, capable of all good Arts, most lovingly constant, charitable, great Antiquaries'.[1] Griffith's 'apology' for his nation, so oddly prefixed to the invasion of Comus and his crew, was assuredly in Milton's mind when he opened his own *Comus* with a brief but noble tribute to the 'old and haughty nation, proud in arms', over which Lord Bridgewater was called to preside. The new and the old piece, performed together at the ensuing Shrovetide, were now highly successful, and a contemporary letter gives us a valuable indication of the kind and direction of the influence which Court taste exercised upon the development of the Masque. 'The tuesday night [Shrovetide] the Prince his Maske was very excellent well performed of the Prince. . . . It was much better liked than twelveth night; by reason of the newe Conceites and antemaskes, and pleasant merry speeches . . . by suche as counterfeited Welse men.'[2]

Entertainment at Blackfriars (? May 20, 1620). News from the New World Discovered in the Moon, January 6, 1621.

An unusually long interval of silence, so far at least as the Court was concerned, followed the double Masque of 1617–18. During the following winter season Jonson was absent from Court, having set out in the autumn upon his walk to Edinburgh, and spending the festive days and nights in memorable (and happily remembered) talk with the young Laird of Hawthornden. Another hand had accordingly provided the Twelfth Night Masque of 1618–19; but only to establish more firmly the supremacy of Jonson. 'I have heard from Court', Drummond wrote to him, shortly after they parted, 'that the late Mask was not so approved of the King as in former times, and that your absence was regretted. Such applause hath true worth, even of those who otherwise are not for it.'[3] Jonson seems,

---
[1] Folio, pp. 37–8.
[2] Chamberlain to Carleton, February 22, 1618. *State Papers, Domestic, James I*, xcvi. 27.
[3] Appendix II, xii.

notwithstanding, to have taken no part in the festivities of the following Christmas also. 'Marry', says the printer, in *News from the New World*, 'he [Jonson] has beene restive, they say, ever since [his return from Scotland], for we have had nothing from him; he has set out nothing, I am sure.'[1] Contemporary letters leave little doubt that this Masque was produced for the Twelfth Night of 1621; nor would there have been much point in the complaint of his 'restiveness' had not the interval since his return been longer than the year which normally intervened between Masque and Masque.

Jonson had indeed probably produced during this interval an Entertainment not intended for the press, but performed in the house of the Earl of Newcastle in Blackfriars. Internal evidence shows that it celebrated a christening, doubtless that of Charles Cavendish on May 20, 1620. It is preserved in Harley MS. 4955, ff. 48–52, and was printed by Gifford. It exploits pleasantly enough, on general Masque lines, the gay and grave aspects of the occasion, Rabelaisian humours of Dugge and her colleagues of the Nursery preluding as a kind of Antimasque the grave and dignified speech of the 'Mathematician' who forecasts the thread of that life, to be spun by the fates 'out of the whitest wool'. The occasion derived added importance from the presence of Prince Charles ('he with the blue riband'), and probably also of the king, as godfather.

The *News from the New World* betrays a decided loosening of Jonson's sense for the capricious and fantastical genius of the Masque. Beyond any of its predecessors, it is marked by the approximation to comedy which was one of the paths to decay and ruin for the Masque as such. The characteristic features of the Masque appear as colourless and perfunctory rudiments. The apparition of the masquers, and the device which explains it, are slight and poorly invented; never had the exacting conventions of Court-compliment extorted from Jonson a fable at once

[1] Folio, p. 42.

so monstrous and so tame as that of the royal race who 'rapt above the Moone far in speculation of your vertues, have remain'd there intranc'd certaine houres, with wonder of the pietie, wisdome, Majesty reflected by you, on them, from the Divine light, to which onely you are lesse'.[1] The covey of 'Volatees' who enter for the Antimasque, 'a race of Creatures like men, but are indeed a sort of Fowle, in part covered with feathers, . . . that hop from Island to Island', have little of the virtue of Antimasque figures; their puerile oddness is neither significantly grotesque nor humorously expressive. The whole vitality of the Masque lies in the admirable comic scene which has shot up, as it were, within this slight framework of prescribed Masque form. Jonson had, it is true, shown a decided inclination to attenuate the division between these two dramatic modes. But he had never opened the barriers, and let in the rich flood of comic realism to fertilize the delicate but arid soil of the Masque, with so little reserve as here. In *Love Restored* and *Mercury Vindicated* the scene was undisguised London and the talk packed with topical allusion and phrase, but the persons still included figures drawn from the mythic or allegorical spheres which had always been the principal sources of the Masque population. Only pieces composed altogether, like the *Irish*, *Welsh*, and *Christmas* 'Masques', in a perceptibly ruder and homelier key, anticipate the manner which prevails in *News from the New World*, and from which henceforth Jonson rarely turned aside. The two Heralds, the Printer, Factor, and Chronicler, whose talk is a key to the philosophy of the production, distribution, and consumption of News as understood and practised in 1621, might, as personages, have stepped out of any of Jonson's London comedies, and several of them did, in effect, step over, shortly after, into *The Staple of News*. The fantastic order of things, which in general controls the events of a Masque, survives only as a topic of talk, not as a factor in the action. Throughout

[1] Folio, pp. 44-5.

Masques and Entertainments 313

this scene the Moon-world and its discovery remain merely a piece of 'wonderful strange News' which we class with the reports 'from Libtzig', in the Comedy,[1] as burlesque exposure of the ways of the contemporary news-market. But towards the close a change comes over the spirit of the scene,—a change quite other than the transition from Antimasque to Main Masque. By a process not completely justified to the reader's feelings, we are, as it were, hitched out of the world of comic realism, where romance exists only as ludicrous make-believe, into the world of the Masque, where it is the order of the day. While we are still laughing at the yarns of the Second Herald, they suddenly come true; and before we have ceased enjoying the Munchausenisms with which they bamboozle the enterprising Factor and Chronicler, we find ourselves in their place, compelled to accept them as imaginative fact. For the rest, the Moon-world proves as fertile in the hands of Jonson the comic satirist, as it proves tame in the hands of Jonson the poet. Some fresh subjects, too, had recently emerged, which invited the sledge-hammer of the author of *The Alchemist*. The yet more insidious and pretentious jugglery of the 'Rosy Cross', in particular, had won a dangerous vogue, and Jonson returned to the attack again, later on, in *The Fortunate Isles*.

In the following summer, after a long interval, Jonson was again called upon to contribute to the entertainment of James at a country-seat. Villiers, Marquis of Buckingham, who gave the commission, was now at the acme of a career which owed its outward splendour to the prodigality and reckless favouritism of the king; and he prepared a commensurate welcome for his master when, early in August, the latter became his guest at Burley-on-the-Hill. On the king's entrance to the house a porter conveyed in dignified couplets the gratitude of the prodigal's favourite. The Masque which presently followed seems to have pleased James's not very fastidious taste beyond

The Gipsies Metamorphosed, August 3 and 5, and September, 1621.

[1] *Staple of News*, III. ii. 97.

any other Masque of the day; so that it was repeated, two days later, at Belvoir, the home of the marchioness, and again, during the following month, at Windsor; in each case with variations and additions. In this, as in most of the other extant private Masques, especially when performed in the country, noble and courtly persons took a more active part than at Whitehall, where professional actors were more readily available; a circumstance which had an important bearing, here as in the *Lovers made Men*, upon the structure of the Masque. The most obvious way of giving artistic unity to the radically heterogeneous Antimasque and Main Masque was to make them represent phases in the career of the same persons; to let the 'imperfect creatures' of the former, instead of being exterminated or dispersed by the powers of good, merely shuffle off the coil of their disabilities, and reappear 'metamorphosed' as noble masquers to celebrate their triumph in stately dance and song. This procedure, however, laid upon the noble personages the burden of acting, instead of merely sufficing for the dance and song; and the burden would doubtless have been more often assumed had shoulders capable of it been more common. It testifies to the energy with which Buckingham and his family threw themselves into the unique welcome which they now offered to James, that both he and his brother, John, Viscount Purbeck, played leading parts in the vivacious Antimasque which here, as in the *News from the New World* and most of its successors, provides the savour as well as the substance of the feast. It is true that the properly dramatic elements of Antimasque are here reduced to the barest minimum. There is no plot whatever; compared with the simple yet felicitously invented stories of all the recent Masques, the device of the famous *Gipsy* Masque must be called extremely meagre, especially when we consider its portentous length. Jonson felt this, and in the epilogue which closed the Windsor performance anticipated criticism by twitting pleasantly 'good Ben' with having omitted to explain how the Gipsies came to be 'metamorphosed'. Dramatic reason, in truth, there is none; but they were wanted for the Main Masque, and the actual situation emerged through the thin woof of fiction. Plot interest, however, is here obviously less Jonson's concern than character and manners. As a study of national types, speech, and usage, the *Gipsy* Masque goes beyond either the *Irish* or the *Welsh* Masques which preceded it in this kind. The studious care which Jonson, unlike all his dramatic contemporaries, lavished on the things which flourish in our literary studios as 'local colour', 'flavour of the soil', 'dialect', is one of the sources of the 'modern' air his work so commonly has for us. If there is no attempt to capture the romance of gipsy life, if the hinted possibility of such a tale as the famous *Preciosa* which Cervantes had published just ten years before remains a barren germ,[1] the things which the Gipsies actually do are expressively natural and characteristic, the homely everyday signs and symptoms of the gipsy race. Singing and dancing, telling fortunes to gentle and simple, with shrewd attention to the susceptibilities of the one and the pockets of the other; merry tales of the feats, escapades, and gallantries of famous rogues;—such things are the staple of the *Gipsy* Masque, as they are, *mutatis mutandis*, of *The Jolly Beggars* itself. If Jonson does not rival the enormous *entrain*, the lyrical gusto, of Burns, we must still recognize how felicitously he has caught the gipsy tone, how boldly and skilfully he has used the privileges of a realist up to the verge of the limits imposed by courtly convention, and how wide, on the whole how healthily wide, those limits were. It is true the realism is not uniform; it fluctuates, advances, and recedes. The Captain's first 'aim' at the 'lucky bird' in the throne of state is a clever adaptation of the tentative processes of the gipsy fortune-teller; but his speech of eulogy after 'discovering' the king, and most of the 'fortunes' told to the Buckingham circle which follow, are

[1] Cf. the horse laden with stolen children, led in by the Jackman.

lyrics as choice and elegant as Jonson's art could fashion. The Second Gipsy's forecast to the Prince of Wales, in particular, challenges comparison with Jonson's finest epithalamia, and is as charming in phrase as unlucky in its auspices.[1] There is imaginative splendour (not destroyed by its intrinsic unreason) in the conception of the Morning and Evening Star lighting to her bridal chamber the daughter of the world-empire of Spain. The fortunes of the group of lords (from the Lord Chamberlain to the Earl of Buccleugh) which were substituted for the ladies' fortunes at the Windsor performance are of ruder texture, and no doubt hastily written. The last-named does not appear in Jonson's manuscript at all. The extraordinary success of the Masque was clearly due in the main to the zest of the personal allusions. Jonson had, in fact, discovered a literary substitute, fresh and unexplored, for the antiquated institution of the Court fool.

Masque of Augurs, January 6, May 6, 1622.
The singular success of the *Gipsy* Masque was not without influence upon Jonson's subsequent Masque-making. He was far, even now, from having reached a satisfying solution of the problems in structure and composition imposed by this *genre*. His earlier efforts had been concentrated upon developing the Antimasque proper, and giving dignity and refinement to this 'foil' of the Main Masque by the poetic significance of the contrast it symbolized. Since his return from Scotland he had shown little interest in this solution, but had laid hold with great vivacity of another method, already in vogue, of achieving the required contrast of tone and *ethos*. The comic Induction appears already in an advanced stage of development in *News from the New World*, while the Antimasque proper dwindles to a meagre formality. But the union of the Induction with the Main Masque there, as we have seen, is not yet free from awkwardness. None of the personages appears to have, at the outset, any connexion with a Masque; suddenly, with scarcely a word of warning, the

[1] Folio, p. 57.

Herald's cock-and-bull stories are enacted before our eyes. The *Gipsy* Masque, on the other hand, together with the *Irish* and the *Welsh*, owed much of their comic zest to the lively representation of the efforts of rustics or vagabonds to entertain their king. But here the Main Masque, in its turn, lost much of its old distinction and supremacy; and became merely a final scene, in a graver tone and more sententious verse, by persons more sumptuously arrayed, addressing (as in the *Irish* Masque) or identical with (as in the *Gipsies*) the persons of the Induction. In the *Masque of Augurs* Jonson tried to secure all the humour and dramatic vitality of these comic interludes, but at the same time to retain or restore the lofty if abstract magnificence of the mythic Main Masque. This meant, or seemed to mean, a complete severance between Main Masque and Induction, and a consequent surrender of the various subtle devices for their harmonious connexion which had for so long been his study. In the *Neptune's Triumph* he was to discover a happy way of evading this dilemma; for the present he accepted it and threw himself with amazing energy into the task of materializing its defects, and turning its very real advantages to the utmost account. The comic Induction, in the first place, is a true induction, a dramatic *Prolog im Theater*, not a first scene of the piece. The amusing group of characters from the docks who smuggle themselves in at the Buttery entrance of Whitehall, having heard that 'the Christmas invention was drawne drie at Court; and that neither the KINGS Poet, nor his Architect had wherewithall left to entertaine so much as a Baboone of quality',[1] and so aspire, out of their 'allegiance to wit', 'to fill up the *vacuum* with some pretty presentation' of their own, provide a delightful piece of irony; and we gather readily enough what the king's poet thought about fashionable Antimasques little more rational than the dance of John Urson's 'sweet and learned' bears.[2] The figure of Vangoose, the projector of Masques—'a

[1] Folio, pp. 82-3.   [2] Ibid. p. 83.

Brittaine born, but hath learn'd to misuse his owne tongue in travell, and now speaks all languages in ill English',[1] heightens this satire with the peculiar sarcasm which, for Jonson and his readers, the title of 'projector' conveys. Vangoose thrives by battening his public on spectacular marvels barren of intellectual appeal: anything prodigious and heterogeneous will serve his turn; the Turks and their thirty thousand janissaries fighting in the air, or 'all de whole brave Pilgrim o' de World, ... here, dere, every where', wandering towards their respective shrines. His idea of an Antimasque is exactly modelled upon the demand he profitably supplies; and when the groom, curious to see his show, but aware that the Court had a very different entertainment on hand, innocently asks: 'But what has all this to doe with our Maske?' he gets an answer which sums up the grosser philosophy of the matter in a nutshell: 'O sir, all de better vor an Antick-maske, de more absurd it be, and vrom de purpose, it be ever all de better. If it goe from de nature of de ting, it is de more Art.'[2] Here, however, comes in one of those abrupt 'faults' in the literary stratification which the transition of Antimasque from Main Masque so easily occasioned. It is not that the scenery changes, but that a different bias is infused into the atmosphere. Exactly as in the *News from the New World*, the fundamental presumption of the scene passes over from satire to symbolism; the rags that were derided are woven into the vesture of poetry; the absurd and meaningless pilgrims of Vangoose acquire significance as types of all the devious and erring pursuits and enterprises of men, the 'fine labyrinths' and 'brave error' in the world, which fear, or fail to find, the light. When Apollo, accordingly, breaks forth 'with the opening of the light', upon this 'perplex'd Dance of straying and deform'd Pilgrims', so

[1] The king's architect, it may be added, was as far from being gravelled for lack of matter as the king's poet. He actually staged the present Masque, and a sketch for the College of Augurs by him is preserved at Chatsworth (Walpole Society's *Catalogue*, no. 63).
[2] Ibid. p. 86.

Masques and Entertainments 319

that they are 'all frighted away', Vangoose's rubbish is no doubt ignominiously abolished; but only after it has been implicitly accepted, revalued, and built into the fabric of Jonson's work.

The Main Masque, which follows, is a monument of Jonson's extraordinary erudition. Unfortunately it is also a crucial example of the actually inhibitory or paralysing effect which the jealous ἀκριβεία of the scholar exercised upon the nerve and spirit of the poet. The conception of Apollo in his glory scattering the wandering deformities of earth, like creeping things suddenly exposed to the blaze of day, is indeed magnificent; but alas for the Muses whom this club-footed and iron-throated divinity led on in dance and song! He recites his manifold functions in classic mythology with exhaustive accuracy; and the recital is a catalogue. He calls up his legendary sons, each attested and authenticated by a sheaf of quotations, and the call is a bald list of names. Grace of phrase or epithet in these very quotations is reduced to the lowest terms. Yet the poverty of this little domestic scene, if hardly designed, is not injudicious. Approached through a more imposing avenue of poetry, the Apolline address to James, the prince of peace whom at Jove's command he visits, must have appeared a grievous anticlimax. The parade of persons, mythological and allegorical, is, however, unusually ample and elaborate; and the Olympian praise of the peace-loving king, who, 'whilst the World about him is at ods' (it being the fifth year of the War),

> Sits Crowned Lord here of himselfe, and smiles
> To see the erring mazes of mankinde,[1]

is doubtless sincere, and aptly resumes the key-note of the Main Masque.

In the Masque of the following Twelfth Night, Jonson carried the hazardous infusion of the methods of his comic muse into the fragile body of the Masque, yet a step farther. The note of personal satire, so frequent and so

Time Vindicated to Himself and to his Honours, January 6, 1623.

[1] Folio, p. 87.

formidable 'when Jonson's sock was on', had already been sounded with growing frequency in his entertainments at Whitehall. But *Time Vindicated* is a missile directed with all the power of his art, at the king's cost and in the king's presence, at a single man. George Wither, 'the gentleman-like Satyre', was a decidedly more questionable mark than the enterprising newsmongers of whom he had made game the previous year. He was a true poet, author of pastoral verse yet choicer than Jonson's own, and of songs which Jonson never approached. He was also a satirist who, if he made many enemies at Court, had contrived, apparently through the mediation of the Princess Elizabeth, to secure a large measure of the king's impulsive clemency, and was about to be compromised by a peculiarly unscrupulous exercise of his favour.[1] His works were moreover widely read, and to judge by the number of editions, keenly relished. In 1621 his *Wither's Motto* had led to fresh troubles both with the administration and with the Stationers' Company, ending again in his liberation and the enhanced sale of the book. It does not appear that Jonson's ridicule of Wither provoked any active resentment; but the courtly audience evidently thought he was flying at dangerous game. 'Ben Jonson', wrote Chamberlain on January 25, 'is like to hear of it on both sides of the head, for personating George Withers, a poet, or poetaster he terms him, as hunting after some, by being a *chronomastix*, or whipper of the time; which is become so tender an argument, that it must not be admitted in jest or earnest'.[2]

The attack upon Wither is effected in a plot of unusual

[1] His *Satyr to the King* had perhaps helped to obtain his release in 1614. At the date of the *Time Vindicated* he had been for some years occupied in versifying the hymns interspersed through the Bible. By a royal patent dated February 17, 1622-3, a virtual monopoly in this was granted to Wither, while a further proclamation, a few months later, prohibited 'the binding of any psalm-book in metre, without a copy of the said work annexed' (Rymer's *Foedera*, xvii. 454, cited by F. Sidgwick, *Poetry of Wither*, I. xxxii).

[2] *State Papers, Domestic, James I*, 1623, cxxxvii. 27.

intricacy. Under the guidance of Inigo Jones the use of movable painted scenery in the Masque was making rapid advances, and inevitably reacted upon its literary structure and composition. The scene was here three times changed.[1] At the outset was discovered 'a prospective of Whitehall' itself. The second scene—'the Masquers in a cloud'—introduced the Main Masque in the customary way. And yet again 'the whole Scene changd to a Wood', with new characters, and a fresh turn of the plot. This was a recent innovation of Inigo's, introduced by him in Campion's *Lords' Masque*, 1613. Thus the dramatically rudimentary Main Masque of the early years, a stately succession of songs and dances, becomes a little drama in two scenes, with move and countermove, and lively altercations. The Antimasque, also, is in a manner divided against itself, the Tumblers and Jugglers driving the Curious away. The process which evolved the dramatic conflict of Antimasque and Main Masque out of a ceremonial masquerade has repeated itself on a smaller scale in each. There are thus two, if not three, conflicts, and two sets of combatants, a situation not favourable to clearness of issue. The Masque touches, at different points, *The Masque of Queens* and the *Pleasure Reconciled to Virtue*; resuming and interweaving motives derived from both those well-springs of poetic ethics—true fame and noble breeding. Time (identified in accordance with a late Greek etymology with Saturn, $Κρόνος$ for $Χρόνος$) is that proximate Golden Age which the advent of James had inaugurated. Fame, his servant, goes forth to summon 'all sorts of persons worthy' to a great spectacle, the Saturnalia of the new Saturnian realm. The Antimasque-scene is a vivacious picture of the noisy caterers for reputation who, like Chaucer's Rumour, are the enemies of Fame, and feed, like flies, upon the corrupted parts of Time. They chaff Fame, not without wit, as a 'time-server', and overwhelm her with a torrent of lively sallies and sarcasms

[1] Herbert's Office-book copied by Malone, *Variorum Shakespeare*, iii. 147.

against which she makes little head. For them the Saturnian reign is a Roman Saturnalia of universal licence where men might do and talk all that they list. Chronomastix, their leader, would gladly ingratiate himself with Fame, the dear mistress for whose sake alone, he is made to insinuate, he had lashed the Time—

> not for hope I have the *Time*
> Will grow the better by it. To serve *Fame*
> Is all my end, and get my selfe a name;[1]

and offers to drop his lash and 'love the Time', only to meet a scathing repulse. Jonson felt a peculiar scorn for the kind of reputation which the author of *Wither's Motto* just then enjoyed, as the idol of prentices and pudding wives. He hardly foresaw that when this noisy Bacchanalia had died down, and his own critical counterblast itself survived only for scholars, there would still 'ascend' the pure and 'bell-like' fame of George Wither.

Not inferior to Chronomastix are the brilliant etchings of his special confederates—the ragged rascals who print his prohibited works by glow-worm light in hollow trees;[1] the schoolmaster who translates him into pure Satyric Latin and hangs his school with his sharp sentences; the soldier who recites him at all tables, and drives respect for him into incredulous pates at the dagger point.[2] Even these do not exhaust the variety of the Antimasque-scene. The second dance of Tumblers and Jugglers who chase away the Curious is a kind of ironical Antimasque, introduced by Fame for their behoof. They 'only hunt for novelty, not truth',[3] and now they have it.

The two scenes of the Main Masque are written with much archness and charm. In the days of *The Masque of*

---

[1] Folio, p. 94.
[2] The printer is George Wood, whose presses were destroyed in 1621 and 1622, just before this Masque, and again in 1624, just after it. He printed Wither's *Scholar's Purgatory*. The schoolmaster is Alexander Gill, High Master of St. Paul's School. The soldier we have not identified.
[3] Folio, p. 97.

Masques and Entertainments

Queens a pageant of illustrious names would have sufficed to 'vindicate' Time, and with their apparition all antagonism would vanish. But it is just at this point that the second *leitmotiv* of the Masque, the competition of Venus and Diana, or Love and Sport, first seriously emerges, and instead of being swiftly assuaged is carried, with gathering emphasis, to an unforeseen climax. Diana-Hecate, ' Queene of shades ', appears at the outset, like Night in the *Masque of Beauty*, to have detained the young 'glories of the Time ', whose release has now been brought about in her despite by the intervention of Love. The pleasant railleries of Cupid, and 'a jocund Sport', sent into the Court

> To breed delight, and a desire
> Of being delighted, in the nobler sort,[1]

play daintily upon the theme, as they summon the masquers, in different tones, to the dance, the Sport of Love. Finally the scene changes to the woods, and Diana, attended by her champion Hippolytus, indignant at the calumnies of Venus, claims for her noble exercises the better part in the rearing of the 'glories' which vindicate Time. So Daedalus in the *Pleasure Reconciled* had led the chosen youths back, after brief respite, to the Hill. Once more, the strenuous craftsman of art ends on a note of energy and labour and temperance in love, which assuredly he did not catch from his audience, but might have caught from his victim; for Chronomastix was the author of that great protest against sentimentality,

> Shall I wasting in despair
> Die because a woman's fair?

The closing verses, strong in the gentleness of a rugged spirit, sound a note of humanity as rare as it was grievously needed in the seventeenth century.'

The Masque was in general a winter entertainment. *Pan's Anniversary*, 1620-4.

[1] Ibid. p. 100.

Most of the recorded summer Masques were either incidental to the royal progresses through the country, or marked some extraordinary or exceptional occasion at Court. *Pan's Anniversary* was first printed after Jonson's death, and no contemporary notice gives any clue to its occasion or date. But internal evidence points to its having been produced in summer, and in special honour of James; most probably for his birthday, June 19. The Folio date (1625) is in this case certainly wrong, since James died in the spring of that year (March 27). All technical criteria place it among the Masques which followed Jonson's return from Scotland; but the year cannot be decisively fixed. Brotanek[1] assigns it to 1620, on the ground of a contemporary account for disguises corresponding to those of the Antimasque figures.[2] This would make it the first Masque written since his return. But the allusions to this event in the *News from the New World* (January, 1621) indicate, as has already been noticed, that at that date since his return he had put out nothing, and that his silence had been long enough to excite remark. In point of technique, the affinities of *Pan's Anniversary* are decidedly with the Masques of 1623–4 rather than with those of 1620–1. The two presenters, the old Shepherd and the Fencer, whose antagonism finds expression in Main Masque and Antimasque, have their nearest analogue in the duel of Cook and Poet in the *Neptune's Triumph*. And the second Antimasque thrust into the midst of the dignified composure of the Main Masque is again most nearly paralleled in the Cook's provocative dish (of pickled sailors) which interrupts the last course of the Poet's lyric banquet. The motley crew of 'Boeotians', the tooth-drawer, juggler, mousetrap-maker, tinderbox-man, and 'my learned Theban, the tinker',[3] are

---

[1] *u. s.*, p. 357.
[2] A bill 'ffor the Princes Maske' printed in *Notes and Queries*, December 22, 1855.
[3] It is difficult not to suppose, with Steevens, that Jonson here remembered *King Lear*. Gifford, of course, falls upon him savagely for the suggestion.

fully comparable in wit and vivacity with the confederates of Chronomastix. The Fencer and Shepherd are faintly drawn compared to the Cook and Poet; and the entrance of the second Antimasque is less artfully explained. We may probably see in the choice of a Fencer as leader of the Antimasque-crew a subtle compliment to the king's well-known horror of drawn swords; just as their 'Boeotian' understandings convey a compliment to his wit, and the Arcadian celebration of 'the best of Singers, *Pan*', one even less deserved to his verses. In another kind, the opening song and speeches of the Nymphs and Shepherd, diffuse and over-quaint as they are ('bright Dayes-eyes, and the lips of Cowes'), have some of the breath and aroma of a June meadow. The old Shepherd's speech is little more than a catalogue of flowers. But it has somewhat of Milton's curious skill, and was assuredly not unknown to the author of *Lycidas*.

If the Masque form readily lent itself to personal satire, it was still better fitted to celebrate a great national event. The definite breaking-off of the proposed Spanish marriage was indeed an event of national significance, and the nation realized it to the full. Neither regard for the aged king, whose deep-laid policy was foiled, nor fear of his resentment, could restrain the exultation with which England welcomed Prince Charles, when he landed, an unplighted man, in October, 1623. The hatred of Spain, which animated the popular triumph, found free expression some months later in Middleton's *A Game of Chess*. Jonson, writing for a Court still sensitive under recent defeat, necessarily touched this side of the matter with the greatest delicacy. But it is easy to read between the lines the true ground of the rejoicing over the 'safe' return of our 'happy pledge', and the kind of 'safety' meant. Three months had elapsed since the prince landed, and Jonson adroitly elicits a compliment from the apparent delay. It was necessary, explains the poet, to withhold 'this music' until the din of the vulgar had died away, *Neptune's Triumph for the Return of Albion*. Designed for performance on January 6, 1624.

> And every Songster had sung out his fit;
till
>   all the Countrey, and the Citie-wit,
> Of bells, and bonfires, and good cheere was spent,
> And *Neptunes Guard* had drunke all that they meant.
> . . . .
> The *Muses* then might venter, undeterr'd,
> For they love, then, to sing when they are heard.[1]

Jonson was doubtless of the same mind; but the Poet is not to be identified with Jonson, and stands for only one element in the complex and full-blooded Jonsonian Masque. Jonson himself, far from jealously secluding the Poet's courtly music from the 'vulgar's chime' and the 'good cheere', was interweaving the Poet's elegant academic strain with the most genially Epicurean of all his Antimasque-roles—the humours of his 'brother poet', the Cook. The Poet, entering abstractedly with his device for the celebration, is roughly called to account by this rival, who, if anywhere, may claim to be in his 'room and region' in the Banqueting House at Whitehall. The comparison of Cook and Poet was a traditional jest of later Greece, and Jonson elaborates it in his most Aristophanic vein. Structurally, the part of the Cook is important. The plan of treating Antimasque and Main Masque as rival shows presented by two antagonists of corresponding character was perhaps the most effective of all devices for connecting them; it was, however, one of the last to be discovered. Jonson had perhaps already used it in *Pan's Anniversary*; but the Fencer and Shepherd are faintly conceived and slightly modelled in comparison with this Cervantean couple; the man of prose congenially enthroned at last in the world of meat and drink, and the idealist become the most unprofitable of the king's servants, a holiday spectacle, resorted to once a year for a jest. The Antimasque being the Cook's contribution to the entertainment in the Poet's despite, he is naturally a stout defender of the Antimasque at large; which the Poet disdains.

[1] Folio, pp. 108-9.

Cooke. But where's your *Antimasque* now, all this while?
I hearken after them.
Poet.   Faith, we have none.
Cooke. None?
Poet. None, I assure you, neither doe I thinke them
A worthy part of presentation,
Being things so *heterogene*, to all devise,
Mere *By-workes*, and at best *Out-landish* nothings.[1]

This was not, of course, Jonson's own opinion of the Antimasque as such. But it fairly conveys his opinion of the Antimasque as it tended to become, or actually became, in less worthy hands. One recent innovation of his own Antimasque technique is again, as in the *Pan's Anniversary* and less fully in *Time Vindicated*, exhibited here: the introduction of a number of diverse figures,—the human ingredients of the 'learned child's' gallimaufry. A more eccentric peculiarity, also found in the first-named piece, and marking a further relaxation in the rigour of Masque-structure, is the introduction of the second Antimasque in the middle of the Main Masque. This grotesque interruption to the prophetic solemnities of the Poet, when the time for grotesquerie should, by all Masque usage, be over, is adroitly brought into line with the character of the presenter by the presenter himself. These 'fine salt Seaboyes shall relish like *Anchoves*, or *Caveare*, to drawe downe a cup of *Nectar*, in the skirts of a night'.[2] The Cook, in short, would not be true to his office if he did not enter the Hall again towards the close of the feast with a piquant relish to help down the last glass. In comparison with this the second entry of the discontented Thebans in *Pan's Anniversary* is decidedly inartificial. A word must be added on the graceful lyrics of the Main Masque. Jonson was not very often again to write verse of so much charm as Proteus's song, 'Why do you weare the Silkewormes toyles?'; nor, in the sea-poetry of the Masques, curiously wrought with fantastic imagery and mythic

---

[1] Ibid. pp. 109-10.   [2] Ibid. p. 116.

allusion, as it habitually and properly is, is this scene easily surpassed.

The Fortunate Isles and their Union, January 9, 1625.

The *Neptune's Triumph* was never performed under that name. A dispute for precedence between the French and Spanish ambassadors invited for the original performance led to its first being postponed and finally abandoned.[1] The serious portions, however, Jonson introduced with slight changes into the Twelfth Night Masque of the following year, supported by an entirely new Antimasque induction. Circumstances had in the meantime completely changed. The prince's return, no longer quite recent on the original occasion, had become ancient history; and the abortive Spanish match was entirely superseded in the general interest by the betrothal in November, 1624, and impending marriage of the prince to Henrietta Maria of France. The Rose and 'the bright Lily' were to be joined, but their union was still 'a prophecy', not an accomplished fact. Jonson sought to retain as much of the original Masque as could be accommodated to the new circumstances, and also to keep the original musical score. The lyric dialogue of the songs thus follows precisely the old measures. The old scenery and the old fable reappear, as on the humbler stages of the City, with new label and commentary. The moving Island which joins itself to the shore of Britain is no longer the prince's returning ship, but one of the Fortunate Isles, attracted by the fame of that rival Isle of the Blessed in which James was king. Instead of the prince and Buckingham and their companions, 'the old musicians', Stesichorus and Arion, Linus and Orpheus, outdo each other amid eternal feast and song. Both the story and the verse have suffered in the process of 'translation'. Much more important is the new Antimasque scene. This Jonsonian burlesque of Faustus and Mephistopheles is good enough to reconcile us to the loss even of his Cook and Poet. The Masque moreover per-

---

[1] Letter from Chamberlain, 17 Jan. 1624: Nichols, *Progresses of James I*, iv. 802.

mitted what Comedy, for Jonson, forbade, the introduction of one of those 'airy Spirits' themselves whom his conjurer professed to have at beck and call. A new and ingenious turn is thus given to his familiar satire upon the pretenders to abstruse knowledge or superhuman powers.

The Brethren of the Rosy Cross, who had become notorious about 1618, and had been already glanced at in the *News from the New World*, are not actually brought upon the stage, like the Alchemists of *Mercury Vindicated* or of the Comedy. They are indirectly derided in the person of their disappointed votary, Merefool, who, after nine days of labour and prayer, is still 'gaping for the flie they promis'd him', and of the 'aëry jocular spirit' who finds his opportunity in this situation. Johphiel (doubtless so called from the planet he personates) is a creature of both the worlds in which Jonson is a master; a Subtle armed with the magic of Puck, and a Puck who can put on the solemn plausibilities of Subtle. He can bamboozle Merefool and introduce the emigrant Isle of the Blessed in grave and dignified verse. He plays the part of Cook and Poet at once, as presenter; but the second Antimasque, which was a specifically culinary jest, falls away. The first half of the scene might have passed in the London Laboratory; all the shifts by which the impostor bolstered up his precarious reputation are ridiculed in the person of this spirit who mixes in the game for his sport. The humour of the second half is more ambiguous. Satire and Lucianic fancy appear to contend in Jonson's mind, leaving it uncertain whether we are meant to conceive the show of ancient worthies and modern vagabonds whom Merefool does not wish to see but puts up with, as a mocking vision conjured up by the airy spirit, or as merely (what they of course actually were) the company of players in disguise. The realist in Jonson was always liable to encroach upon the fancy of which the Masque was the proper sphere. These vigorous sketches of rogues, in the metre and manner of Skelton, are notable early examples of the historical dramatic lyric. 'The worshipfull *Poet Laureat* to King *Harry*' and his pungent verse were clearly to the mind of the militant 'poet-laureate' to King James.

Masque of Owls, August 19, 1624.

To the interval between *Neptune's Triumph* and its revival as *The Fortunate Isles* belongs a little entertainment of which it was convenient to reserve a notice to this place. The *Masque of Owls at Kenelworth*, wrongly dated by the Folio in 1626, was performed, according to contemporary correspondence, on August 19, 1624.[1] In the sense which the term had acquired in the mature technique of the day, this so-called Masque has no right to the title. But in keeping with the old Warwickshire worthy, Captain Cox, whose ghost he invoked, Jonson fell back on an elementary and archaic form of Masque,—a simple series of grotesque characters. Their successive speeches are written in a genial doggerel, like that given to Skelton shortly afterwards in *The Fortunate Isles*. The impossible Folio date (when the 'prince' referred to in the second line had become king) cannot of course be ascribed to Jonson.

Love's Trivmph through Callipolis, January 9, 1631.

In the Christmas season festivities of the first five years of the new reign, Jonson took no part. At length, in 1630–1, he was again commissioned, with Jones, to provide the Twelfth Night Masque. He had during this interval returned to the drama, with qualified success; the momentary triumph of *The Staple of News* having been followed, in 1629, by the contemptuous rejection of *The New Inn*. It is impossible to ignore that, in the two companion Masques produced for the mutual entertainment of the king and queen in the early months of 1631, we have but a faint reflection of the genius of the great Masque-maker who had celebrated their betrothal. The skeleton of a complete Masque is there; its articulations are even exceptionally intricate and minute; but the poet has thrown the task of making them live for the senses and imagination mainly upon his coadjutor Inigo, furnishing himself little

---

[1] *Cal. of State Papers, Domestic James I*, 21 Aug., 1624, Chamberlain to Carleton: '... presented ... two dayes since.'

more than bald inventories and lists of names. When Jonson, shortly after, published the *Love's Triumph* with their two names as the 'Inventors', but his own first, the architect violently resented his 'usurpation'. Whoever compares the poet's bare list of the 'depraved lovers',—'a glorious boasting Lover, a whining ballading Lover, an adventurous romance Lover', and so on,—with the architect's brilliant sketches of these figures, now at Chatsworth,[1] or with Ben's own not less brilliant word-etchings in the *Time Vindicated* or the *Pan's Anniversary*, will find Inigo's claims not wholly unjust and his anger not wholly inexcusable. The fable itself was, it would seem, their joint production 'after some debate of cogitation with our selves'. To Inigo, in any case, must be due whatever effect was derived from the device of representing the association of the various 'depravities' of love with the dress and character of the 'four principal European nations', which Jonson does not so much as name. A certain sociological interest belongs to the theme, the 'Inventors' having played upon the fashonable caprice or cult of (so-called) 'Platonic love'. The radical insincerity of this movement made it an unhappily stimulating soil for the worst failing of the Masque-genre. A few years earlier Jonson might have touched with power the ideal of which the popular 'Platonism' offered a futile travesty. But these frigid songs and hymns of Euphemus and Euclia, this shadowy Triumph through a yet more shadowy Callipolis, when set beside the gracious and sparkling love poetry of the Epithalamia or *Love Freed from Ignorance and Folly*, intimate more forcibly the decay than the purification of love.

The companion masque, in which the queen and fourteen of her ladies played the ceremonial parts, is built upon a theme more purely fantastic, but of more intrinsic charm. Chloris, the goddess of flowers, who is to become a star on earth, since

Chloridia, February 22, 1631.

---

[1] Walpole Society's *Catalogue*, Nos. 68–78.

> *Jove* will have Earth to have her starres
> And lights, no lesse then Heaven,

opens up vistas of Shelleyan imagery of stars and flowers. The suggestion is not impaired by the delicately imagined lyric dialogues of Zephyr and the Fountains speeding or welcoming the gentle Spring. But Spring has her foes— winds, lightnings, rains, and evil spirits—who impede the divine decree and—dance the Antimasque. The Antimasque is here, formally, as in the *Love's Triumph*, unusually elaborate, no less than eight separate 'Entries' of different groups succeeding in unbroken sequence. These are, however, merely described, in phrases almost as brief as the label-epithets of the decadent lovers. The dwarf's inductory tale of the 'revolt' of Cupid recalls the vivacious prose of earlier days.

The King's Entertainment at Welbeck, May, 1633.

The rupture with Inigo, made final by the publication of *Love's Triumph*, brought to a close Jonson's long connexion with the Masques at Court, where the influence of the imperious and masterful architect was now at its height. Jonson's mantle descended in part upon men not altogether worthy of it; upon a Carew and a Shirley, as well as upon an Aurelian Townshend; and the year 1634, which witnessed Shirley's *The Triumph of Peace* and Carew's *Coelum Britannicum* as well as *Comus*, must be counted among the most distinguished in the brief annals of the English Masque. The report of these alien splendours doubtless reached the palsied poet in his sick-chamber. But he still had staunch friends among the noble houses; and in particular the Earl (afterwards Duke) of Newcastle and his wife twice honoured themselves by calling upon him to provide entertainment for Charles at their great Nottinghamshire homes. In May, 1633, the king in his progress north passed the night at Worksop, and dined with the earl at Welbeck. 'This entertainment cost my lord between four and five thousand pounds,' writes the duchess; and Clarendon describes it as of unprecedented magnificence; 'and would be still thought very prodigious if the same noble person had not, within a year or two afterwards, made the King and Queen a more stupendous entertainment, which God be thanked, . . . no man ever after imitated;' namely the feast at Bolsover in the following year. The Welbeck welcome, though unpretending, shows the variety of resource which the old poet still retained. On the analogy of the *Barriers*, in which Jonson had repeatedly distinguished himself, he was asked to provide a literary setting. There is a characteristic mixture of the grammarian and the combatant in the quaint device presented by Master Accidence, schoolmaster of Mansfield, and Father Fitzale, herald of Darby, the learned antiquary of the north, where Stub of Stub-hall, the rustic bridegroom, contends with six bold bachelors of two wide counties at the Quintain, in honour of his rustic bride. The painting of rustics recalls the *Tale of a Tub*. On the other hand it is hard to believe that the mind which laboured, on the whole with so little effect, upon this Sherwood scene was nearly at the same time, or had at all recently been, weaving the exquisite harmonies of *The Sad Shepherd*. The closing address to the king, which in the manner of a Main Masque breaks in upon the 'rudeness', is dignified, and at times majestic, in thought and expression.

Charles was pleased with the entertainment, and the queen, who had not been present, had no difficulty in persuading him the next year to make another progress to the north and invite the sumptuous hospitality of Nottinghamshire once again. The king accordingly desired the Earl of Newcastle to prepare a repetition of the same agreeable experience. The earl, doubtless welcoming this evidence of the royal satisfaction with his former costly effort, prepared to outdo it. Instead of merely entertaining the king to dinner, he lodged the Court in his Welbeck house, and once more employed the tried hand of the old master, 'sparing nothing', as the duchess relates, 'that might add splendour to that feast, which both their Majesties were pleased to honour with their presence'. 'It cost him in all', she adds,

Love's Welcome at Bolsover, July 30, 1634.

'between fourteen and fifteen thousand pounds.' It can hardly be said that the second entertainment was of proportionate merit. In spite of the title, however, it is wholly unlike the first. Even in these last runnings of Jonson's fancy, there is no abatement of the fertile invention which from the first had been among his conspicuous merits. He is so free from the vices of system and the grooves of habit that his technique is hard to grasp. Decay appears only in the less perfect co-ordination and dramatic vitalization of the motives lavishly flung forth. The entertainment here is varied enough, but it is in truth a potpourri. The opening ' welcome' song, of tenors and a bass alternately, to king and queen is charmingly written. A dance of Mechanics follows, as a sort of Antimasque. It opens with a remarkable passage. Jonson could not resist the opportunity of ridiculing before the king and queen the man who had ousted him from their favour. It was a dangerous game; but the king and queen must have been made of sterner stuff than they were, if they did not enjoy this portrait of the important and opinionated architect :—' A busie man! And yet I must seeme busier then I am, (as the Poet sings, but which of them, I will not now trouble my selfe to tell you) '.[1] The ensuing contest of Eros and Anteros had been used by Jonson in much the same way in *A Challenge at Tilt* to represent the rival or antagonistic loves of husband and wife. Philalethes, who cuts short the strife of their 'little wits', concludes the whole with an ageing poet's benediction upon the married pair.

The Masque genre had some deep-seated vices which Ben—and even Milton—could not eradicate. But the spectacle remains impressive of the Titan playing with bubbles and butterflies and rainbows, and struggling, not with complete success, yet never with utter failure, to weave enduring art out of these unsubstantial materials.

[1] Folio, p. 282.

Inigo Jones's design

scene in 'Chloridia'

INTRODUCTION TO
THE POEMS

THE POEMS

THE Poems of Jonson—including in the term all his non-dramatic verse—were never completely collected by himself, and have not hitherto been, as a whole, critically edited. They have come down to us under conditions of very unequal authenticity. We may distinguish the following groups:

I. Poems edited by Jonson himself in the Folio of 1616. These comprise the *Epigrams* and *The Forest*.

II. Poems published in the Second Volume of the Folio in 1640: the *Underwoods*. Some of these were no doubt collected by Jonson; but many must have been added by his editor Digby, who was doubtless also responsible for the arrangement—or confusion—of the whole, as well as for the revision of the printed text.

III. Poems not included in either of the foregoing collections; chiefly eulogistic and commemorative verses prefixed to the works of other authors. Most of them were incorporated by Cunningham in the *Underwoods*. Others we now publish for the first time. The whole are here collected under the rubric *Ungathered Verse*.

Jonson's main preoccupation in poetry was the drama. Here predominantly the work was done by which he will endure, and by which his final significance is to be measured. It was not done with fluent ease. But whatever the process, the immense energy and volume of his intellect and personality were completely bodied forth in drama alone. Even the Masque was in comparison only a beautiful *parergon*.

Jonson wrote, however, a large amount of non-dramatic verse; and while the great dramatic harvest was all but completely gathered in before his forty-fifth year, this slenderer reaping continued through the whole of his literary life, and the latest sheaves were not altogether the lightest or the worst.

Practically, the whole of these scattered pieces of verse are what are called 'occasional'. They arose directly out of particular events in Jonson's experience, or out of actual relations with friends or foes. His 'Epistles', for instance, are never imaginary, like those which Ovid and his own friend Drayton devised for heroic personages of the past. They reflect, moreover, this experience and these relations simply and directly, with a minimum of literary elaboration or adornment, and with an eye to immediate practical effect. The death of Edward King may be said to have occasioned *Lycidas*; but only in the sense that that event let loose a train of impassioned meditation of vastly greater scope and deeper interest. The death of Vincent Corbet or the marriage of Weston are, for Jonson, not merely occasions for his poetical utterance, but the proper theme, upon which he permits himself only the simplest variations. This personal poetry has in extraordinary measure the special virtue of its kind; it is charged with personality, alive with individual expression and temperament. But these 'occasional' utterances of one who had no equal in his time as an inventor of dramatic character and plot owe almost nothing, either in motif, structure, or atmosphere, to invention. Observation and thought, in active alliance, engross the field, and the shaping imagination which was the birthright of the author of *Volpone* and *The Alchemist* appears all but completely suspended.

It is certainly remarkable that a poet who could put a story so powerfully into action in drama should have left such slight indications of his power of telling one. The foremost English champion of the Renascence could hardly be wholly without that 'Epic ambition' which the Renascence everywhere engendered. Nor was he, as the record of his poems projected or destroyed makes clear. 'Epic ambition', it is pretty clear, helped to beguile, if it did not induce, that nine years' abstention from drama which is at first sight so hard to explain. At Hawthornden he is full of epic schemes and notions; above all he designs 'an Epick Poeme intitled *Heroologia*, of the Worthies of his country, rowsed by Fame,'[1]—a conception of Epic, it may be noted, very far from suggesting servile adherence either to Homer, Vergil, or Aristotle. After his return he 'sang' his journey into Scotland, 'with all th' adventures',[2] and shortly afterwards the story of Proserpine; both were lost in the fire. The *Heroologia* would have been a Jonsonian supplement in heroic couplets to his friend Drayton's *Polyolbion*, which he thought would have been excellent 'if he had performed what he promised to writte, the deeds of all the Worthies';[3] even as it was, he declared to Drayton himself that he was 'ravished with every song'.[4] All these 'heroic' devices, however, came to naught, and a tragic irony has permitted to survive as the sole example of Jonson's epic quality the hideous and unsavoury burlesque known as the 'Famous Voyage'.[5]

If epic ambition occupied or controlled a season or two of Jonson's maturity, the ambition of the lyric poet was early cherished, steadily maintained, and never definitely put by. If not a born singer, he had, on the lowest estimate, an extraordinary talent for simulating song. A juster criticism will allow that this great and laborious artist occasionally achieves, in song, magic of that rare kind which, though it cannot be captured by art and labour, presupposes them. In most of the native forms of lyric he showed little interest, and he expressed a characteristic disdain for the stanza. But he did more than any one else to point the way for English poetry to certain kinds of lyric in which antiquity had done immortal things.[6] For the 'Epigram', which his

---

[1] *Conversations*, i.   [2] *Underwoods*, xliii. 95.
[3] *Conversations*, iii. 25–7.   [4] *Ungathered Verse*, xxx. 53, 54.
[5] *Epigram* cxxxiii.
[6] His notion of the *possible* kinds of verse composition is fairly indicated in *Epigram* cxii, where he complains that the 'weak gamester in Poetry' pursues him through drama, epic, ode, elegy, satire, and epigram.

English predecessors had narrowed down to an exercise of wit and fancy, he vindicated the larger scope of Martial, in some points even that of the Greek Anthology. He revived the lyric 'Epitaph', and produced a few which even in that last-named treasure-house of beauty would not have been out of place. And he was the first Englishman to attempt, with adequate knowledge, to acclimatize the most sumptuous of antique lyric forms, the Pindaric Ode. No doubt the tunes were often plain and pedestrian enough for which he invoked the lyre of Pindar or Simonides. Occasionally, in the effort to reach their high-pitched strains, he strikes a false note and collapses into bathos. On the other hand, when moving on the lower level of relatively prosaic kinds, like the Epistle and the Satire, he sometimes rises without effort, by the sheer on-thrust of mind, to accesses of eloquence which are not far from the fervour of song.

Jonson had, in his rich but somewhat oddly assorted mental endowment, some qualities of the lyric poet in extraordinary measure; of others, and those perhaps the most essential, he had less than many minor singers of his time. His speech had the personal accent which communicates individual quality and colour to whatever matter it conveys. He had the vehement and passionate temperament without which song is apt to be only a gracious exercise. But he had no native well-spring of verse music; and such music as he wins by his extraordinarily cunning artistry is rarely ineffable. His passion, again, was not on the whole the high-wrought enthusiasm which cannot utter itself sufficiently save through rhythm and figure. Anger and scorn were keener and more potent with him than love; and anger, though it may 'make dull men witty', is apt to infuse into the very utterances which it impels something which impedes and disintegrates the lyric quality; to steal away the magic from melody; at best to reduce its airy fabric to commoner and grosser terms, as the music of Shelley himself becomes a ruder and earthier thing when it wings his indignation against Gifford or Castlereagh. Jonson's faults did not lie in the direction of unreality of mind, and he cannot be accused of putting his lyrical instruments to merely factitious use. He used them for his own needs, at the prompting of actual occasions, and these for the most part such as lent themselves best to the lower levels of poetic expression. He appears as the implacable satirist, the self-constituted *censor morum*, the savage and often foul-mouthed reviler of personal antagonists of either sex. Or again, he is the staunch friend, the shrewd counsellor, the genial guest, the comrade of scholars, the 'father' of the tribe of Ben. But at times even occasions like these provoke him to utterance which is lyric in intention or in form. And in other cases the situation itself brought with it lyric suggestions which he did not decline. A 'Celia' and a 'Charis' could inspire love-songs of rare beauty, if not love; the death of children, of old friends, of noble women, of Shakespeare, could draw from him strains of lofty and felicitous commemoration. And a few of the finest poems had no definable personal occasion at all.

These three groups correspond to three recognized literary types, which may be used to describe them: 'Satire', 'Epistle', 'Lyric'. In the following survey we shall follow the lines of these groups. This involves no doubt the partial redistribution of some of the classes recognized by Jonson himself, and in particular of the class which he distinguished by a special rubric and set at the head of the whole collection,—the Epigram. But however admirable may have been Jonson's conception of the scope and possibilities of this genre, the Jonsonian book of *Epigrams* is in fact a quite unmanageable wilderness of verse-kinds ranging from the ugly brutality of 'Gut' to the delicate grace of 'Salathiel Pavy' or the dignified force of the 'Savile'.[1] We need not consider the 'Famous Voyage'; a bad joke which by way of a further joke, equally bad, he chose to include. He was too scholarly to use terms loosely, and he

[1] *Epigrams* cxviii, cxx, xcv.

had classical authority for all the innovations he seriously claimed. But he used his authority freely, and pegged out ampler domains than he had lyric genius adequately to fill. As the Epigrams range from gross prose to daintiest poetry, so the Elegies include kinds so diverse as the satire and the dirge. The Epistles are fairly homogeneous, but a large number of the Epigrams are Epistles under another name, and cannot without risk of confusion be treated apart. They all belong to that pleasant division of his verse which was addressed to friends. For offending foes, whether gods or men, he had a formidable counterpart to the Epistle, which he called an 'Expostulation' or an 'Execration'. In the third group will be noticed all the verse of definitely lyric intention as expressed in the choice of form; from the songs and brief snatches of verse in which Jonson's fugitive lyrical charm is most often caught, to the Odes, often pedestrian in effect, but never in aim.

I.

By far the greater part of the 'satirical' verse of Jonson is included in that comprehensive division of his poems which he called *Epigrams*. This antique species has to-day forgone most of its old prestige, maintaining for the most part a precarious footing on the very verge of poetry, or frankly accepting a place beyond it as mere versified jest. The Epigram of ingenious wit derived from Martial, and from Martial in his coarsest and least poetic vein; its vogue always denoted the dominance of Latin over Greek, and of silver Latin over Augustan, authority. In such periods, the nobler and less restricted model of epigrams offered by the Greek anthology was ignored. But every return to closer intimacy with the Hellenic world has induced the attempt to recover it. The chiselled epigrams of Landor, cameos of concentrated intellectual beauty, probably come nearer to the finest things in the Anthology than anything else in modern literature. Shelley translated some of Plato's 'epigrams' with exquisite skill. Goethe's *Venetian Epi-*

grams and *Vier Jahreszeiten* and Schiller's *Tabulae votivae* reflected the Hellenizing humanism of Weimar. Jonson, the chief of Jacobean humanists, strove similarly to recover for the Epigram some of its antique liberty and range. In knowledge of what the Greeks had achieved in Epigram he far surpassed Goethe and Schiller and probably Landor; but the ripest Greek scholar of Jacobean England was also one of its least Greek minds, and his ripe scholarship only at rare moments bore comparable fruit.

It is clear that Jonson set an unusual, and to his contemporaries doubtless astonishing, value upon Epigram, as upon his own performances in it. When he collected and arranged his poems in 1612-14, it was the epigrams that he set in the forefront of the lyric pieces, ushering them in with a special preface and dedication to Pembroke as 'the ripest of my studies'. All the other pieces,—epistles, songs, odes,—thus implicitly disparaged, were thrust promiscuously together under the colourless rubric *The Forest,* as 'Miscellaneous poems' not requiring classification. Even so, *The Forest* numbers only fifteen pieces, the *Epigrams* one hundred and thirty-three. The later epigrams, it is true, Jonson, or more probably his posthumous editor, deprived of their pride of place, and they jostle on equal terms with odes, elegies, sonnets, and epistles, in the huge tangled labyrinth of the *Underwoods*. But he never ceased to claim for Epigram the status of poetry. 'Even one alone verse sometimes makes a perfect *Poeme*', he writes (perhaps after Scaliger) in the *Discoveries*, quoting two single-line epigrams of Martial's as examples.[1] Few epigrammatists have nevertheless subjected the definition of 'a poem' to a severer strain than Jonson in some parts of this collection, as few have given it, now and then, more splendid illustration.

Jonson's vigorous culture of the Epigram was not an isolated phenomenon, and the vogue it was rapidly acquiring in his generation resulted from a concurrence of many

[1] *Discoveries*, 1640, p. 125, 'What meane you by a Poeme?'

cognate tendencies in early seventeenth-century temper and wit. In the sixteenth century, despite the clumsy experiments of a Wyat, and the copious industry which secured his sobriquet for 'Heywood the Epigrammatist', the Epigram remained on the whole exceptional, even anomalous. Early Elizabethan writing was habitually expansive and diffuse, simple and direct. Euphuism was one of the first symptoms of a growing taste for pointed statement, witty allusion, quick and amusing turns of thought; all of which it at the same time powerfully furthered.[1] The same taste was fostered by those collections of pictorial enigmas known as the Emblem-books. Here and there they colour a Shakespearian image, and they provided the key to much of the recondite and fantastic wit of the school of Donne. In Donne himself recondite figure was but one of the modes in which a genius as fiery as it was subtle forged for itself articulate expression; but the force of his example made 'metaphysical wit' a current resource with poets whose elementary emotions could have been adequately rendered without its aid. The rapid triumph of recondite wit of various kinds in early seventeenth-century writing over the melodious and transparent diffuseness of Spenser marks in some sort the triumph of epigram over allegory. The set of literary style in this direction from about 1600 is as evident in prose as in verse, in talk as in writing, and was powerfully fostered by other specific influences, in particular by two classical examples of epigrammatic prose,—the *Characters* of Theophrastus (edited by Casaubon in 1597), and the earliest (and most epigrammatic) *Essays* of Bacon, published in the same year. Both books were naturally familiar to Jonson.

A further influence of a different kind contributed to extend the vogue of the Epigram in the early seventeenth century, but at the same time to narrow its scope. The first decade of the century was in a special sense the day of

[1] We may recall the marked preference of the Elizabethans for the epigrammatic close in the Sonnet.

Satire, as the previous decade had been, in non-dramatic verse, the day of the Sonnet. Lodge and Hall had laid hold of the authoritative weapon of Juvenal and Horace, neglected, strangely enough, until then. Jonson himself had put comedy to the service of satire with a thoroughness and resource unparalleled since Aristophanes. Men who did not dispose of ordnance of this calibre availed themselves willingly of the light but stinging missile so dexterously handled by Martial, and the effective use of which by the 'two mute satyrs' Pasquil and Marforio was one of the sensations of contemporary Rome.[1] At the same time, the non-satirical categories of the Epigram, though somewhat obscured, were not altogether lost sight of. For Puttenham 'a merry conceit' may be an epigram as well as a 'bitter taunt'; and the epigram of compliment, if imperfectly recognized in theory, suffered no perdition in use.

The Collections of Epigrams put forward in England from 1596 onward were of very different origin and calibre, and disclose various notions of the nature and purpose of the species. But they reflect on the whole the general view that the Epigram was a brief and pointed mode of satire.[2]

---

[1] *The Arte of English Poesie*, 1589, i, ch. 27.

[2] i. Sir John Davies. Printed at the end of Marlowe's *Ovid's Elegies*, ostensibly at Middelburg, before 1598.
 ii. Thomas Bastard, *Chrestoleros. Seuen bookes of Epigrames*, 1598.
 iii. Edward Guilpin, *Skialetheia. Or a shadowe of Truth in certaine Epigrams and Satyres*, 1598.
 iv. John Weever, *Epigrammes in the oldest cut and newest fashion*, 1599.
 v. John Owen, *Epigrammata*, 1607 and later. Jonson described him as 'a pure Pedantique Schoolmaster, . . . and hath no thinge good in him, his Epigrames being bare narrations' (*Conversations*, xii). Lessing delivers an equally sharp judgement upon Owen's 'pedantry' and abstractness (*Zerstreute Anmerkungen über das Epigramm*, section 2). But see the more sympathetic judgement of a more recent Latinist, Professor Bensly, in *Camb. Lit. Hist.* vol. iv.
 vi. John Heath. *Two Centuries of Epigrams*, 1610, contemptuously referred to by Jonson in *Discoveries*, 1640, p. 97.
 vii. John Davies of Hereford, *The Scourge of Folly. Consisting of satyricall Epigramms, and others in honour of many noble and worthy Persons of our Land*, c. 1612. Cf. Corser, *Collectanea*, v.
 viii. Sir John Harington, *Epigrammes*, 1613. Jonson told Harington, on being asked for his opinion, that his epigrams were 'Narrations, and not Epigrames' (*Conversations*, iii. 39, 40).

The forty-eight epigrams of Sir John Davies (before 1598) probably did much to set the tone. He was hailed by an admiring follower, Guilpin, as 'our English Martial', and ten or a dozen years later Davies and Weever still supplied the standard by which, as Jonson complains, his own epigrams were tried and condemned.[1] The Sonnet had always been an epigram *in posse*, and Davies's epigrams are in effect sonnets, or easy variations upon the sonnet form, a series of one to four quatrains usually clinched by a stinging final couplet. With one possible exception (*Epigram* xxxvi, 'Of Tobacco') they are all 'sharp and tooth'd', and some are very gross. But Davies was not altogether unjustified in speaking of his 'merry rhymes'; he carves and flays his antagonist without mercy, but with the air rather of one exercising a new and effective rapier of which he has just mastered the tricks, than of a deadly hater of either social abuses or his fellow-men.

Such a conception was rudely traversed by a considerable number of the epigrams of which Jonson put forth the 'First Book' in 1616. A collection of *Epigrams* which contained pieces of pure pathos, such as the epitaphs on his children, enthusiastic odes like the lines to the Countess of Bedford, and weighty epistles, like those to Sir Henry Savile,[2] inevitably provoked critical comment among the 'mere English censurers' whose notions of epigram were drawn from the current modern instances. Jonson was, however, far from throwing over the conventional variety of the species, and he chastises some of his critics, by anticipation, with epigrams which in brevity and abusiveness, if not in point, can have left them little ground for complaint:

> PLAY-WRIGHT me reades, and still my verses damnes,
> He sayes, I want the tongue of *Epigrammes*;
> I haue no salt.[3]
> Surly, 'for greatnesse sake', may 'heare my *Epigrammes*,

---

[1] *Epigram* xviii, 'To my meere English Censurer'.
[2] *Epigrams* xxii, xlv, lxxvi, xciv, xcv. [3] *Epigr.* xlix.

but like of none '.[1] The 'mere English censurer' thinks his way in epigrams 'new', for he has seen

> DAVIS, and WEEVER, and the best haue beene,
> And mine come nothing like;

he is roughly informed that the 'new' way is 'the old way, and the true', and bidden cultivate faith in default of knowledge.[2] And in the epigram 'To my Booke' (ii) Jonson sarcastically hits off the popular notion of the genre:

> It will be look'd for, booke, when some but see
> Thy title, *Epigrammes*, and nam'd of mee,
> Thou shouldst be bold, licentious, full of gall,
> Wormewood, and sulphure, sharpe, and tooth'd withall;
> Become a petulant thing, hurle inke, and wit,
> As mad-men stones: not caring whom they hit.

If the reader really did 'look for' this, Jonson himself had given him some excuse; for he had early won a certain reputation as an 'epigrammatist' precisely in the sharp and biting kind.

> How you translating-scholler? you can make
> A stabbing *Satir*, or an *Epigram*,
> And think you carry iust *Rhamnusia*'s whippe
> To lash the patient.

So Mavortius addresses Chrisoganus (Jonson) in Marston's revised *Histriomastix*.[3] No doubt Jonson, as his habit was, overdid the role, so congenial to him, of *unus contra mundum*, and ignored the presence, beside the vulgar prejudice he so defiantly exposes, of more enlightened conceptions and a less rigidly limited practice.[4] But on the whole his recriminations hit the mark.

---

[1] *Epigr.* xxviii.   [2] *Epigr.* xviii.
[3] *Histriomastix*, 1610, sig. B 4 verso, Act ii. The date of revision is August, 1599. Jonson had at that date at least produced the epigram upon the 'two damned villains' who sought to entrap him in prison ('On Spies', *Epigr.* lix; Drummond, *Convers.*, xiii), and probably others. Marston, his admiring friend at this time, had doubtless heard him recite it.
[4] As examples of the complimentary epigram we may recall the two addressed by Bastard in his *Chrestoleros* (1598) to Sir Henry Wotton, and those written by Sir Edward Herbert in 1604 (*Convers.*, v), and Dunbar in 1616, to Jonson himself.

It was another question whether Jonson was right in claiming, as he so emphatically did, to have restored 'the old way, and the true' of epigram, which the modern world had deserted. What did he mean by the old way? There is no doubt that he had in view, primarily, the Roman master of Epigram. Martial was a notable favourite with Jonson. He singled out his works, with those of three other satirists, Horace, Juvenal, and Persius, from the whole of Latin literature as to be read 'for delight',[1] and recommended him in the weightier company of Quintilian and Tacitus for Drummond's special study.[2] Jonson was not the man to prostrate himself before any predecessor, ancient or modern, whatever his authority; but there are plenty of evidences in his epigrams of the value he set on Martial's.[3] The copy used by Jonson in later life is still extant, with occasional characteristic marginal comments,[4] and English editors like Farnaby were glad to draw upon his library for rare editions and otherwise inaccessible emendations.[5] Martial's situation, again, had points of resemblance to Jonson's. Both enjoyed peculiar favour with their sovereign; but James was no Domitian, and it was literary foppery rather than courtly adulation that led Jonson to emulate the monstrous compliments by which Martial purchased his precarious immunity.[6] Martial, too, had run counter in various points to current notions of the Epigram, and had retorted upon his critics by putting them in his book. There were sticklers for brevity, for instance, who resented his vivacious tirades of a dozen or twenty lines, and whom he disposed of with the retort:

---

[1] *Convers.*, ix. [2] *Convers.*, ii.
[3] Two epigrams (Martial, viii. 77 and x. 47) were translated by Jonson. We hear of his reading 'some Epigrams of Martial' with his younger fellow-playwright Field (*Convers.*, xi).
[4] Cf. Appendix IV in vol. i, pp. 253-4.
[5] Cf. Farnaby's grateful reference to Jonson's service in providing him with Scriver's edition, 'quem nulla mea aut amicorum cura parare potuit'; and Jonson's letter (printed in vol. ii Appendix II, xxii) presenting a copy of 'Farnabii mei Martialis' to his friend Brigges in 1623.
[6] *Epigr.* xxxvi.

'Non sunt longa quibus nihil est quod demere possis;'[1] There were sticklers too, for gall and vinegar, who revolted against his occasional tender touches and were advised to take 'Vaticana' if they wanted a bitter.[2] There were others who regretted the old Roman severity and decorum—Cato's and Cornelius's of the Domitian age—to whom he bluntly retorted that prurience was indispensable to the epigram, and that riotous wantonness was better than prudery.[3] On these and other matters Martial had explained his standpoint in a combative preface—itself an excellent example of epigrammatic prose. Like Jonson[4] he claimed to have used the epigram with a humanity, a regard for persons, quite contrary to precedent. No one's honour had been touched, whatever their social or personal insignificance; and he pointedly protested against the 'malicious interpreter' who construed harmless general assertions as personal abuse. Then, changing his ground, he had declared, with insolent assurance, that lascivious freedom of speech is the 'tongue of Epigrams', appealing to Catullus and other ancients in its support, and warning Cato not to bring his sour face into this theatre of licensed vice; 'or else, if he will enter, let him mind the play'.

It is certain that Jonson was extremely conscious of these precedents; that he was, in fact, very willing to be regarded as the Martial of his time and country. In a number of points he courted comparison with the Roman master, and even where he dissented from Martial's procedure he commonly expressed his dissent in terms borrowed from Martial. One may even suspect that Martial's preface to the 'First Book' of his Epigrams is the ultimate ground of Jonson's preface, and of the title 'Book I' which ushers in a collec-

---

[1] Martial, ii. 27.
[2] Martial, x. 45. Jonson borrowed this quotation in the prefatory remarks to *Hymenaei*.
[3] Martial, i. 35.
[4] Jonson actually borrowed some of Martial's phrases in defending himself to Lord Salisbury in the matter of *Eastward Ho*. See Appendix II, vol. i, p. 196.

tion approximately equal in number to Martial's first Book, but which, unlike his, remained without a sequel.

The point on which, to judge from his preface, Jonson most decisively detached himself from Martial was in regard to the right, or rather duty, of foul speech. Jonson significantly makes 'Playwright' quarrel with his examples for being without 'salt' (i. e. wantonness), the 'tongue of epigrams'—the very phrase (*veram Epigrammaton linguam*) used by Martial in his own person in his own defence. And he closes his preface with an equally pointed reference to Martial's 'theatre' and the inhospitable reception accorded there to 'Cato'. It is not Cato but the men of impudent and wanton riot whom Jonson warns that they will 'publish their faces, at their perill, in my *Theater*, where CATO, if he liu'd, might enter without scandall'. Jonson, again, points out that many of his epigrams are devoted to the commemoration of 'good, and great names', of which Martial says nothing.

But when we turn from the two prefaces to the collections which they introduce, the divergences appear less striking. Neither poet quite lived up, or down, to his program. Martial might warn off the decorous Cato, but he permitted himself to write and even to publish very many epigrams to which the decorous Cato would have warmly responded, while Jonson, who warned off the wanton and the impudent, admitted quite as many which only this class of auditor could thoroughly relish. And if Martial dwells only upon his satirical epigrams, he like Jonson had many pleasant epistles and touching epitaphs. Jonson's claim to have gone his own way was nevertheless not altogether baseless. We have only to open the *Epigrams* of Sir John Davies to recognize that even Jonson's gross and scurrilous specimens may represent a certain advance in, or towards, decency; and Jonson at his grossest is in fact as much less gross than Martial as, at his wittiest, he is less witty. The friendly and genial epigrams in Jonson are certainly more numerous, if also, again, more dull. Yet Jonson's friendship, as it appears in these epigrams, if less vivaciously expressed, is made of more sterling stuff. And it is only in the tenderer vein of Epitaph that Martial really anticipates Jonson. The stately Epitaph, of the type which culminates in Browne's 'Underneath this sable hearse', is his own.

Upon the technique of Epigram, as upon its proper topics, Jonson expressed very decided opinions. We gather from the *Conversations*, as quoted in the note on p. 345, that he condemned two kinds of current epigram on technical grounds:

1. 'Bare narrations' like those of Harington and Owen;
2. Those which, like some of Sir J. Davies's, 'expressed in the end what should have been understood by what was said'.

These criticisms reflect on the whole the standpoint of Martial. The one clearly demands that the Epigram, in so far as it relates an incident, shall cap the narration with some kind of reflection; the other, that the reflection shall not be quite obvious or otiose. Though we have no further hints of Jonson's theory of Epigram, he had certainly read the *Poetice* of Scaliger. Epigram is there defined to be of two kinds: containing either a mere indication of a person, or thing, or action; or deducing something from premisses.[1] The first comes nearer to the original sense of an 'inscription', and to the epigram of the Greeks with its cameo-like directness and simplicity. The second expresses at least one important variety of the 'pointed' epigram which Martial founded and made classical.[2] A more psychological and less scholastic formula, which is also much truer to the rich variety of the Martialian *point*, was given by Lessing, when, keeping close to the origin of the Epigram, he compared the two 'parts' to the monument and the inscription, the one exciting curiosity which the other satisfies. His

---

[1] *Poetice*, iii. 126.
[2] As Lessing points out in his beautiful essay on the epigram referred to above, Scaliger's two kinds are in reality closely connected; the 'inscription' in the former corresponding to the conclusion in the other.

strong logical bias perhaps led him to give too decided preference to the type of epigram which concludes with a brilliant summing-up of the matter, or with a telling general principle of which, as in the epigram to Decianus,[1] it is an unsuspected case. Lessing thus gave but a grudging recognition to the element of surprise in epigram. Yet surprise was undoubtedly a favourite device with Martial as with all his followers. The facts are first artfully recited so as to make a certain explanation appear obvious; the true solution is then suddenly sprung upon us in the last line or the last word;—as when 'Santra', through twenty lines an omnivorous glutton, is transformed by the single word *vendit* into a wretched collector of scraps for sale.[2] Jonson's practice on the whole conforms to his own canons, but it shows only a partial conformity either to Martial or to any other authority. A large proportion of his epigrams are, however, unmistakably modelled on one or other of various Martialian types. The modelling is not very skilful, but the intention is clear. The two parts—description and comment or point—can be distinguished; and though the point seldom or never vies with Martial's in brilliance, it is also seldom of the otiose or obvious kind which Jonson reprehends. An example of the more logical type is the epigram on Brainhardy (xvi); where the conclusion—an ironic consolation to a brawler who was always picking quarrels but evaded settling them ('He that dares damne himselfe, dares more then fight')—may be compared with Martial's question to the kindred spirit who committed suicide for fear of being killed: ' Hic, rogo, non furor est, ne moriare mori?' The epigram on 'Giles and Joan' (xlii), the married pair who always agree—in their opinion of each other—is another good example of the logical but not otiose summing up.[3] Or the conclusion, while still logical, may aim at surprise, as in *Epigram* xxxvii, 'On Chev'rill the Lawyer', one of Jonson's neatest examples. Cheveril, who

---

[1] Martial, i. 8.   [2] Martial, vii. 20.
[3] It is probably an expansion of Martial, viii. 35.

will never lose a client, takes fees from both sides and pleases both ;

> For while he melts his greace
> For this: that winnes, for whom he holds his peace.

But the heavy lunge of Jonson's wit was not well suited for this light rapier-play; and his most energetic strokes sometimes fall flat. In many of the epigrams Martialian effects are obviously aimed at and as obviously missed. The laboriously accumulated traits of Don Surly's ambition to be 'great' (xxviii) deserve a better conclusion than that in which they culminate, or collapse:

> SVRLY, vse other arts, these only can
> Stile thee a most great foole, but no great man.[1]

In other cases he provides some more or less plausible substitute for the point proper. A 'narration', for instance, is capped with an unexpected catastrophe instead of with a biting comment; the dramatist, as it were, intervening in aid of the epigrammatist. Such is the final revulsion of fortune in the adventures of 'Lieutenant Shift' (xii). A hint of a similar turning of the tables as in prospect concludes the survey of the career of 'Poet-ape' (lvi). Sometimes the epigram ends with a sudden and violent change of key, as where the fine address 'To True Soldiers' (cviii) culminates in an unexpected lunge at any of the other breed who may be in the audience:

> He that not trusts me, hauing vow'd thus much,
> But 's angry for the Captayne, still: is such.[2]

But a large number of epigrams betray a different attitude towards the precedent and authority of Martial.

---

[1] The type, not uncommon in Martial, is that in which an epithet, reiterated again and again in an ostensibly favourable sense, is finally turned to sarcastic account; as in ii. 7:

> Declamas belle, causas agis, Attice, belle,
> Historias bellas, carmina bella facis, . . .
> Nil bene cum facias, facias tamen omnia belle,
> Vis dicam quid sis? magnus es ardalio.

[2] The nearest approach perhaps to this revulsion of tone in Martial is the transition in the last line of the 'Erotion' (v. 37) from the sympathetic tribute to the dead child to a jibe at Paetus. Cf. Lessing, *u. s.* § 3.

The mechanism of the pointed conclusion is neglected, the point displaced, or multiplied, or forgone altogether. With all his imperious scholarship and his despotic art, the natural man in Jonson was stronger still; and, in Epigram, his natural man demanded the vigorous utterance of vigorous thoughts as they arose, and rebelled against the calculated reticences and reserves of the literary strategist. The cool finesse which keeps expression steadily in the rear of thought until the moment comes for a final decisive stroke was, like other kinds of ironical self-effacement, not very congenial to him. Sometimes he delivers his most telling shot with impatient vehemence at the outset; a strong phrase breaks from him in the opening couplet, and the rest is comment and illustration, or surly gnawing of the bone. Thus, the whole pith of the 'English Monsieur' (lxxxviii) is concentrated in the first lines:

> Would you beleeue, when you this MOVNSIEVR see,
> That his whole body should speake *french*, not he?

Or the point is discounted before it arrives, as in the excellently conceived epigram on 'Mime' (cxxix). The foolish mimic whom the town crowds to see, without whose company no supper or excursion is complete, and who supposes that he is admired because his buffoonery is popular, is a capital butt for irony; but Jonson's insuppressible scorn breaks out in the question: 'Thinks't thou, MIME, this is great?'

This piece illustrates also a frequent structural feature of the Martialian epigram much more congenial to Jonson than the point—the sequence of parallel statements preliminary to it. In Martial the sequence is usually graduated, advancing by successive nuances, each assertion a shade more hyperbolic than the last, as in the well-known epigram, where the minute 'estate' dwindles in the course of twenty lines from a window garden to a nutshell.[1] Jonson effects his sequences with a fiercer vehemence and a less discriminating control; you

[1] Martial, xi. 18.

think he will drop the rapier of the modern 'Martial', and take to his fists like the Englishman he is. This conflict of methods is recognizable in most of the satirical character-sketches; with more of contriving artistry in the 'Weak Gamester' (cxii) and in 'Poet-ape' (lvi), with more disorder and impatience in 'Surly' (xxviii) and the 'Town's Honest Man' (cxv).

But Jonson's debt to Martial is easily overstated. What he directly borrowed in situation, topic, point, is but a small proportion of the whole. As a satirist he was no man's disciple; the springs of satiric observation and satiric expression were native in him. It was his own world of London, not reminiscences of Martial, that furnished the provocation and the cue. He is at his best in those incisive character-portraits to which the persons of the comedies owe so much of their vividness. This portrait gallery of sordid and shady types, the refuse of the City and the Court, has obvious analogies among the motley population of the comedies. 'Shift' has a kinsman of the same name in *Every Man out of His Humour*; 'Voluptuous Beast' (xxv) is a variation—or a first sketch—of Volpone. But, on the whole, these epigrams lay bare a lower and fouler stratum of Jacobean humanity, and they render what they expose with a harder, a crueler, less humorous, and less plastic touch. It is rare that humour and irony hold the balance with so much success against indignation and invective as in the sketch of the too knowing politicians, 'ripe at six and twenty', in the 'New Cry' (xcii) who

> Keepe a *starre*-chamber sentence close, twelue dayes:
> And whisper what a Proclamation sayes.

The brief couplets and quatrains interspersed among these portraits and sketches are almost without exception inferior; rude without being incisive, brutal without compensating power, and sometimes gross without mitigating humour. Jonson's somewhat saturnine strength needed more room and verge than these minute areas where 'nec serpens habitare tota possit'. His great galleon of a mind wanted space for its evolutions. All his command of brief and weighty phrase does not prevent most of them from being flat and dull. Their brevity creates an expectation of wit which is imperfectly gratified. Whereas in the longer pieces, where the effect depends on a succession of strokes, immense powers of cumulated and iterated assault have full play, and gather swing and momentum in the process.

But the *Epigrams*, like the plays of the first volume of the Folio, do not adequately exhibit the range of Jonson's capacity. Half his then existing plays were not printed there, and at least one epigram, for intelligible reasons, he withheld.[1] In sheer brutality the epigram on Mistress Bulstrode, 'The Court Pucell' (*Und.* xlix), falls little short of Martial's verses to Galla; and more cannot be said. Donne's elegies upon her indicate—after making allowances for the *de mortuis nil nisi bonum* convention of the Elegy— a very different view of her character. Jonson himself could find eulogistic terms for her in the epitaph included in the *Ungathered Verse* (ix).

After the date of the Folio, the satirical epigram fell into disuse with Jonson. Only two or three examples remain; but these indicate undiminished interest in the genre and its characteristic forms. One, on the failure of the Royal Household to supply the poet's sack (*Und.* lxviii), is a sonnet. And the couplets and quatrains—probably always less congenial to him—disappear altogether. The 'Epigram of Inigo Jones',[2] earlier and far better than the more familiar 'Expostulation'—adapted from Martial, xii. 61— is hardly surpassed in Jonson's writings for dry withering ferocity. It has concentration and irony; it plants its sting the deeper by scornfully refusing to sting at all:

Thy Forehead is too narrow for my Brand.

In the epigram 'to the Household', 1630, probably the last

---

[1] Jonson alludes to it in the *Conversations*, v. 103-4.
[2] *Ungathered Verse*, xxxvi.

of all the satirical group, he for once exchanges the bludgeon, his too habitual weapon, for a light single-stick, and brings his quarrel home to the negligent powers of the Buttery which refused him his laureate allowance of wine, incisively enough but without bluster and noise.

Jonson's disuse of the satiric epigram is, in part, explained by the less frequent provocations to satire which marked the relatively prosperous and fortunate years of his later prime, and by the strong motives for suppressing it with which poverty and sickness and the loss of Court favour provided his old age. The epigrams of these years are mainly brief epistles to friends or occasional verses to the Court. But there were moments when pent-up anger broke through all the barriers imposed by prudence, and then the conventional restraints of Epigram, loosely as Jonson had interpreted them, did not always suffice. The 'Expostulation' to Inigo Jones gains little by the free rein which Jonson has given to his rancour. Even as a piece of invective it fatally lacks sinew, while its force as argument is impaired by the blind and futile cavils which mingle with the just charges, involving the architect of genius in the same anathema as the too ambitious stage-manager who took 'painting and carpentry' to be 'the soul of Masque'. The man thus thrown off his balance by human ill will could bear the stings and arrows of misfortune with admirable temper. A decade earlier, a disaster more serious than any inflicted by Inigo had been met by him with a stoical good humour from which these angry whinings are a sad descent. The 'Execration upon Vulcan', which so pleasantly simulates satiric invective, hardly has its match in the verse of serio-comic bravery.

Finally, in a little group of pieces concerned mainly with Women, Jonson lays bare the savage cynicism of which in his dealings with them he was at no time incapable, and which was even his normal disposition towards all but certain exceptional members of the sex. When he undertook in this mood to analyse the constitution of woman, his crucible was apt to yield few ingredients but vanity and lust. His most forcible expression of this temper is the so-called Elegy: 'Let me be what I am' (*Und.* xlii). It is a brief, pregnant 'philosophy of clothes'—in the sense of Swift rather than of Carlyle—clothes which create a factitious atmosphere in which men are dazzled, captivated, and deceived. 'Fooles ... love a Goat in Velvet', silk allures a rhyming songster, 'the Cittie Cap's a charme'. Jonson himself is inured to these beguilements; he lives, and has lived twenty years—

> Where I may handle Silke, as free, and neere,
> As any Mercer; or the whale-bone man
> That quilts those bodies, I have leave to span:
> Have eaten with the Beauties, and the Wits,
> And Braveries of Court, and felt their fits
> Of love, and hate: and came so nigh to know
> Whether their faces were their owne, or no.

But the sex has its use: it provides the poets with a theme, and even those who cannot love must affect love if they wish to be read. Consequently Jonson himself, with his fifty odd years, 'as Horace fat' and 'as Anacreon old', laims the right to rhyme of beauty with the rest.

'Elegy' was a strangely chosen name for such a piece; yet Jonson did not classify his poems arbitrarily. Perhaps of all contemporary poets he was, alike as man and as artist, the least obviously qualified for the most feminine and delicate of poetic genres as practised by his Roman masters. To be *mollis*, even *flebilis*, was the recognized function of 'Elegia', and Jonson is the standing type of 'robustness'; while his pathos, though genuine and moving, was of a simple kind, hardly stirred save by the death of children. Equally outside, rather than beyond, the scope of his verse, save at those fortunate moments which in his case we have always to reckon with, were the fine staple and fastidious polish traditional in Elegy.[1] Both in

---

[1] 'Dicite quo pariter carmen *tenuastis* in antro? ...
　　Exactus tenui pumice versus eat
　　Quo me Fama levat terra sublimis. ...'

Greece and Rome the Elegy, though not rigidly confined in range of mood or topic, became habitually the expression either of mourning or of erotic passion. In the hands of Propertius and Catullus it developed a singular splendour and intensity, in those of Tibullus and Ovid an unsurpassed elegance and grace. Quintilian recognized its value in the training of an orator.[1] Yet, originating as it did, the Roman Elegy could not but develop other notes than that of erotic passion pure and simple. The lover addressed a mistress who was bound to him at most by such mutual vows as Propertius and Cynthia had once exchanged; hence infidelities, suspicions, jealousies, expostulations, pleadings, objurgations, were far commoner provocations of elegy than simple love. Thus there enters into the complex texture of the Roman elegiac something that only differs from satirical invective by the underlying passion which in fact gives it its intensity. Propertius, when Cynthia is unfaithful, can send her reflections upon the women of Rome in contrast to the devoted wives of India and the martial maids of Sparta (iii. 13, 14), such as, *mutatis mutandis*, Musset, disillusioned, might have sent to Georges Sand. And towards husbands or other guardians the 'elegiac' lover naturally falls into a tone still further removed from tender sentiment. 'Sing of flower-crowned lovers at another man's door by night, and the trophies of their drunken flight, so that he who would deceive strict husbands may learn by thy lays how to serenade the girls out of their locked chambers', was the counsel of Calliope to her poet.[2]

It is, then, doubtless this secondary vein of Elegy that Jonson had in mind when he called his cynical piece of invective by that name. Passion is indeed wholly absent; no foiled or deserted lover is here venting his bitterness on the sex at large. But the sardonic observer, making his

says Propertius (iii. 1. 5 f.), addressing the Manes of the Greek masters of Elegy, Callimachus and Philetas.

[1] *Inst. Orat.* x. 1. 93.   [2] Propertius, iii. 3. 47–50.

stern catalogue of foibles and frailties, approaches the disillusioned lover often in phrase if not in temper. And towards the husbands Jonson uses a cavalier tone still nearer to that of Propertius, and perhaps overheard from him:

> Fathers, and Husbands, I doe claime a right
> In all that is call'd lovely.[1]

It was thus only an occasional strident note of the Propertian elegy, torn out of its passionate context, which finds echo in this dry and hard piece of cynicism, probably the least elegiac composition, in the usual sense, which ever in England claimed that name. Jonson, in fact, went his own way with Elegy; like his friend Drayton, whose elegies, published a few years earlier (1619–20), are mostly familiar epistles to friends, as remote as this from the elegiac temper.

To that temper one English poet alone—his other friend, Donne—had, before Jonson, given powerful expression.[2] And Jonson himself came far nearer elsewhere to the elegy of passion and of mourning. But, though huddled up together in the tangled chaos of the *Underwoods*, these belong in fact to a different province of his mind and art; to the rarer but not less real Ben who honoured and was honoured by a host of friends, 'on this side of idolatry, as much as any'; who could at least command the language of passion for women, and probably excited passion in them, and in whom there ran a vein, not very strong or substantial, but delicate and beautiful, of tenderness and pity.

II

To Jonson in this more amiable aspect the poems of the first collected edition do, quantitatively, perhaps somewhat more than justice. In *The Forest* we see it all but exclusively; in the chequered field of the *Epigrams* it has an

---

[1] *Und.* xlii. 11, 12.
[2] Donne's earliest extant elegy appears to date from 1596, when he was twenty-three.

The Poems

even share. Jonson was clearly concerned, as we have seen, that these 'ripest of my studies' should not be confounded with the purely savage and licentious epigrams of convention, and laid emphasis, in the dedication to Pembroke, upon the poems of lofty praise freely dispersed among the examples of severe, but honest, reprehension. Against the perils incident to the latter he looked for the earl's protection: 'In thankes whereof, I returne you the honor of leading forth so many good, and great names (as my verses mention on the better part) to their remembrance with posteritie.' Of good and great names there is no lack, and in an age accustomed to extravagant flattery Jonson may claim on the whole to have praised with judgement, independence, and sincerity. If he ever seems to throw all three to the winds, it is generally where Martial had been guilty of a like perversity before him. Martial had prostrated himself before Domitian, and similar self-prostration was henceforth good epigrammatic form. This partly explains some epigrams addressed to the king and queen in which Jonson might seem to have resolved to compound by extravagant hyperbole for brutal frankness elsewhere. Martial's monstrous flattery of the 'divine' Domitian he reproves indeed, but only to insinuate that it would be plain truth applied to James, who 'cannot flatter'd bee' (xxxvi). And in one at least of the epigrams of his last years to Charles and his queen, he adopts the Martialesque tradition in this respect without reserve.[1] Others, however, of this last group are conceived in a natural strain, devoid neither of humour nor of pathos; and the epigram to Charles 'for a hundred pounds he sent me in my sicknesse' in 1629 [2] is honourable to both.

In the long series of the 'epigrams' to his friends and

---

[1] *Und.* lxvi, 'An Epigram To the Queene, then lying in. 1630.' We must not make Jonson responsible for a future which he could not foresee; but the comparison of 'Mary, the Mother of our Prince' to 'Mary, the Mother of our Lord' gains little in felicity for us from the reflection that the infant was destined to become Charles II.

[2] *Und.* lxii.

comrades this natural and unstudied address is a chief, sometimes the only, merit. With all their variety of thought and phrase, they are singularly uniform in tone. They are in the main short familiar epistles, loosely constructed and with little care for point or climax. And they convey good counsel and good sense in compact and weighty phrase, grave but rarely passionate, unconstrained but never gay. They do not strike us, like Milton's sonnets to his intimates, as the stately relaxations of one who did not easily unbend; but they are almost as devoid of the lighter moods and tones of good fellowship and literary camaraderie. His massive and sustained emotion, whether of love or hate, carries him forward with a momentum too blunt for badinage or irony, too even for the coruscations of playful or incisive wit. The 'great overplus' of this latter gift, which at the Mermaid or the Triple Tun outdid the meat and wine, is very successfully controlled in his epigrams. Nor do they often leave us in doubt, as Martial's sometimes do, whether to take them for agreeable banter or for cutting retorts disguised in the phrases of pleasantry. If a seeming slight was put upon him by a friend or host, he never, so far as we know, took playful vengeance for it in a gay and lively sally, like the 'Donasti, Lupe, rus sub urbe nobis';[1] he more probably 'looked black' and spoke his mind in a blunt retort delivered, like the famous 'My Lord, you promised I should dine with you, but I do not', from his place at the bottom of Lord Salisbury's table[2]; or in a resentful allusion, like the 'I ask'd a lord a buck, and he denyed me', which prefaces his acknowledgement of the contrasted generosity of Lucy Bedford (lxxxiv). Despite his arrogance, however, and the air of 'surly virtue' as native to him as to his namesake, these epistolary epigrams convey a sense of strong and weighty character, which in Martial's, with all his brilliant versatility and inexhaustible play of wit, we miss.

The personal accent of Jonson, more doggedly self-assertive and unmistakable than that of any other man

[1] Martial, xi. 18.   [2] *Conversations*, xiii. 318–19.

of letters of his time, persists like a deep-sustained burden through these brief, and often pedestrian, utterances. Jonson's egoism is always there, but it is spontaneous and involuntary,—the mere volume as it were of the man's nature discharging itself along the channels of expression.

With hardly a change of phrase, this account of the epistolary epigrams may be applied to the pieces which he chose to distinguish from them as 'Epistles'. If he put his 'Epigrams' in a Book by themselves, and his 'Epistles' in the miscellaneous collection of *The Forest*, it was chiefly because the *Epigrams* of Martial were in reality so clearly distinguishable from the *Epistles* of Horace. The epigram, in Jonson's hands, when he was addressing a familiar friend, strove as it were towards the miscellaneous discursiveness, and the easy limits, of the 'epistle'. In the second volume of the Folio the distinction, though formally maintained, is no longer pressed; and the two kinds meet and mingle promiscuously, doubtless with Jonson's intention, in the *Underwoods*. And at frequent intervals throughout his career he was throwing off little pieces which share their common qualities with these 'epigrams' and 'epistles', —verses addressed, for the most part, to fellow authors and published in the forefront of their books. They were hence, as a rule, not incorporated during Jonson's lifetime in his collected works.

The last class, in spite of the temptations it offered to conventional eulogy, rises far above the level of ordinary complimentary verse, and conveys much salutary criticism or counsel, thinly if at all disguised. But Jonson's quality is still better seen when he is not dealing with literary merit, but with manhood and character. 'Iephson, thou man of men' (*Epigr.* cxvi), 'Vvedale, thou piece of the first times' (cxxv)—such opening words sound like the call of antique heroism in the emasculate age of James I; and Milton may have remembered them when, a generation later, he addressed a greater than Jephson as 'our chief of men'. Jonson's delight in this primeval strength and grit sometimes gives an eloquence to his verse, to which it does not naturally incline, as in the second 'epigram' to Benjamin Rudyerd (cxxii). But most often his speech is rugged, hardy, unadorned, like the pristine humanity it so willingly describes; and the few and simple images usually accentuate rugged strength like this in the man. Burghley is the captain

> That in all tempests, never quit the helme,
> But stood unshaken in his Deeds, and Name.[1]

Sir John Radcliffe, the solitary remnant of his house, stands

> like a columne, ... left alone,
> For the great marke of vertue, ...
> ... to shew the times what you all were.[2]

And in Sir Henry Savile he saw the incorruptible soul of Tacitus, the type, for him, of the historian who 'dares not write things false, nor hide things true'.[3] Of lawyers, as of soldiers, no one said sharper or more savage things. But to the exceptional man of either profession, Jonson, like Meredith, would make superb amends. Such an atonement is the fine character of Benn, the Recorder of London.[4]

The Augustans too had looked back to the hardy simplicity of their ancestors, and Jonson consciously echoed the glowing prophecy of the Fourth *Eclogue* when he hailed in a Rudyerd, or an Egerton, men who renewed 'the aged SATVRNE's age',[5]—'the worlds pure gold, and wise simplicitie';—or in whom 'the *Virgin*, long-since fled, ... return'd'. But the convention, if it was one, was strongly rooted in character; and the accent both of his praise and of his friendship is distinctive and his own. The joy in hardihood and heroism ran deeper in him, one suspects, than in Horace, if it found expression in less splendid and memorable phrase. In Jonson's relations with his noble friends too, we find a haughty and critical sensitiveness which hardly marked the relations of Horace with Maecenas or Agrippa, and which gives distinction and

---

[1] *Und.* xxx. [2] *Epigr.* xciii. [3] *Epigr.* xcv. [4] *Und.* xxxiii.
[5] *Epigr.* cxxii, lxxiv.

quality to the thinner and harder vein of poetry in which it is conveyed. When he congratulates Salisbury upon his accession to the treasurership,[1] he proudly insists on the disinterestedness of his joy. He is 'glad', not like those that have new hopes, or suits, nor like old dependants, nor for fashion, nor flattery, nor wit,—

> But I am glad to see that time suruiue,
> Where merit is not sepulcher'd aliue.

He had sometimes praised too generously, and 'preferr'd men past their termes', but even this was, he declared, 'with purpose to have made them such';[2] and later he came to scrutinize jealously merit and persons,

> and vexe it many dayes
> Before men get a verse: much lesse a Praise.

And if the man he had praised proved unworthy, his mortification was poignant; once or twice it stung him to a lyric intensity of which he was normally incapable. It was at such a moment that he turned upon his treacherous Muse, in the sixty-fifth *Epigram*, with the fierceness of a deceived lover—

> Away, and leaue me, thou thing most abhord,
> That hast betray'd me to a worthlesse lord;
> Made me commit most fierce idolatrie
> To a great image through thy luxurie.
> . . . .
> With me thou leau'st an happier *Muse* then thee,
> And which thou brought'st me, welcome pouertie.
> Shee shall instruct my after-thoughts to write
> Things manly, and not smelling parasite.
> But I repent me: Stay. Who e're is rais'd,
> For worth he has not, He is tax'd, not prais'd.

The epigrams to the men of his more intimate circle are of great interest, if only for the varied glimpses they offer of Jonson's kindlier moods, but their value as literature lies less in any commanding merit of form or phrase than in the force with which the hearty friendship of a proud and self-centred man expresses itself in every line. The

[1] *Epigr.* lxiv. [2] *Und.* xiv, 'An Epistle to Master Iohn Selden'.

numerous pieces addressed to Sir John and William Roe almost all have this charm in a high degree.[1] How quaintly affectionate are the very openings, 'Glad-mention'd ROE', 'ROE (and my ioy to name)'. And without invoking comparisons utterly beyond Ben's compass, like Dante's confession to Virgil, it would be hard to find a tribute of scholar to master comparable either for moving eloquence or for the calibre of both with the famous lines to Camden—

>   most reuerend head, to whom I owe
> All that I am in arts, all that I know.
> (How nothing 's that?) [2]

But Jonson, with all his generous warmth, lacked the finer graces of familiarity; while his native power of criticism, which made him exceptionally aware of the literary infirmities of his best friends, could not well be allowed free play even in 'epigrams' addressed to them. Even lines so terse and pregnant as those to Donne,—'the delight of PHŒBVS, and each *Muse*',[3]—are less shrewdly expressive than the tantalizing dictum reported by Drummond: he esteemed Donne 'the first poet in the world in some things'.[4] The trumpet-note of scorn for the mob of all ranks ('The wise, and many-herded *Bench*, that sits Vpon the Life, and Death of *Playes*, and *Wits*') rings as loudly as that of indignant friendship through the fine lines sent to John Fletcher after the failure of *The Faithful Shepherdess*.[5] The lines to Beaumont[6] are among the most engaging of his tributes to his younger friends, but cannot be matched in vigour or in verve with the epistle to the unknown applicant for inclusion among his 'sons',[7] or even with Beaumont's own delightful epistle to Jonson himself. The epigram to Overbury (cxiii)—as glaringly at fault in its assured forecast of the future as Jonson's prophecies usually were—contains some fine lines:

---

[1] *Epigr.* xxvii, xxxii–iii, lxx, cxxviii.   [2] *Epigr.* xiv.
[3] *Epigr.* xxiii; cf. xcvi.   [4] *Conversations*, vii. 117.
[5] *Ungathered Verse*, viii.   [6] *Epigr.* lv.   [7] *Und.* xlvii.

So, where thou liu'st thou mak'st life vnderstood!
Where, what makes other great, doth keepe thee good!

Of the later epigrams of this class, it will suffice to mention the 'Epigram to a Friend, and Sonne' (perhaps Lucius Cary),[1] a document of friendship even more than of sonship, and touched with a peculiar sense of the preciousness of 'rare friends'.

In the verse addressed to his women friends, Jonson, like the majority of men, is on the whole more brilliant and less sincere. The recipients were all above him in station, Bedfords, Wroths, Rutlands, Aubignys, Covels, Carys,—most of them at one time or another his hostesses; and he observes certain ceremonial formalities with them which he does not observe with their husbands or with men of similar rank.[2]

The famous lines to the Countess of Bedford,[3] 'Lucy the bright',—the finest of all Jonson's epigrams,—clearly indicates the extent, and the limits, of his capacity for friendships with women. The enthusiasm which glows in these quatrains, and wings on its way verses which for once have charm, wells from a source by no means so deep in Jonson's brain as the close-knit fervour of the lines to Camden or to Selden. Not merely was chivalry alien to his nature, but even the most admirable qualities of individual women had to conquer their way to his recognition through a medium of cynical distrust and disparagement of the sex at large. In this very collection, only a couple of pages from the beautiful morning hymn to the Countess of Bedford, the reader comes upon an epigram which suggests in the plainest terms that all women are harlots.

[1] *Und.* lxix.
[2] Thus he addresses these ladies uniformly with 'you', the men, even the king, almost invariably with 'thou'. This is of course in some cases the 'thou' of poetry, not of intimate friendship; but the fact remains that he did not avail himself even of the poetic usage in addressing Lady Bedford or Lady Aubigny. The only exception, we think, is Lady Venetia Digby, the 'Muse' of his last years.
[3] *Epigr.* lxxvi.

And of that morning hymn itself it may be said that it honours the countess either for masculine virtues or for virtues in which men and women have equal share. She is credited with scarcely a single definitely feminine attribute, and the finest lines are those which convey a compliment to her strength of mind in terms suggestive of a man's superiority to feminine avocations:

> Onely a learned, and a manly soule
> I purpos'd her; that should, with euen powers,
> The rock, the spindle, and the sheeres controule
> Of destinie, and spin her owne free houres.

The equally famous epigram to the Countess of Rutland (lxxix), offers to the daughter of Sidney a similar lofty eulogy at the cost of her sex. With other women, or with the same on other occasions, he indulges a vein of playful fancy rarely seen in his verses to men, and not very natural to him. The epigram to Mistress Cary (cxxvi), for instance, is a trifle, not without gaiety or elegance; but it is the sort of thing that a score of contemporary poets would have done better than Jonson.

III

It was under the stimulus of these courtly friendships, and of the agreeable hospitalities in which they found expression, that Jonson began to write the more expanded and flexible epigrams which he called 'Epistles'. The town-bred English Horace had no farm among the Surrey hills, and, had he had one, would hardly have fled there with Horatian rapture from the civic 'dust and wheels'.[1] But he was not without his sober pleasure in the amenities

---

[1] There is indeed a tradition, which we cannot trace back farther than Manning and Bray's *History of Surrey*, 1804 (vol. ii, p. 180), that Jonson used to retire to Swain's Farm at Leigh near Reigate, and that a room in this house was called his 'study'. An elaborate account of the house is printed, evidently without verification, in the fourth edition of Murray's *Handbook of Surrey*, 1888 (p. 52). The old timbered front has been stuccoed over; the ingle-nook of the old kitchen has been turned into a modern fire-place with two side-cupboards; and no old panelling or old furniture has been in the house for at least eighty years.

of country life, and when Maecenas summoned him to be his guest at Penshurst or Durance, relished the choice but free and unostentatious life there, and rewarded host and hostess, on his return, with such epistles as those which open *The Forest*. For subtle touches of description we look indeed in vain; Jonson's eye and ear were not of the quality which captures new rareties of sensation; of colours and of perfume they are almost bare; both Wither and Browne surpassed Jonson in the rendering of the idyllic charm which he nevertheless clearly felt. Fresh and individual notes now and then occur, such as the fine touch in the epistle to Wroth:[1]

> if thou list the night in watch to breake,
> A-bed canst heare the loud stag speake.

But these flashes of vivid experience are rare, and sometimes give place to decorative embellishments in the style of pseudo-classic Pastoral;—Pan and Bacchus feasting under the Kentish beeches of Penshurst, or the fish and fowl eager for the honour of furnishing the table of the Sidneys:

> The painted partrich lyes in every field,
> And, for thy messe, is willing to be kill'd.

Jonson was a more arrogant man than Horace, and his praise of the even-handed hospitality of Penshurst is delivered with shrewd side-glances of disdain for hosts who had shown less regard for his privileges as a guest. He may have had in mind how Horace set off his patron's delicately considerate benefactions by an amusing picture of the aggressive hospitality of the Calabrian boor.[2] But the difference in temper and geniality is palpable and not to Jonson's advantage either as artist or as man.

With the vein of half-ironic philosophizing which flavours so happily the rural enthusiasms of Horace, Jonson had still less affinity. No school of secular thought occupied in the culture of Jacobean England precisely the position which Stoicism and Epicureanism held in Augustan Rome,

---

[1] *Forest*, iii.   [2] Horace, *Ep.* i. 7. 15 f.

as the recognized creeds of the intellectual aristocracy, toyed with or jested at by the world of fashion. The nearest approach to such a philosophic faith might be found in certain impressive commonplaces of the Renascence, for a century and more the common possession of cultivated Europe;—the power of poetry to immortalize, the triumph of man over death by Fame. They were the coinage of poets rather than of thinkers, and persisted as a literary faith without striking deep root in conviction or greatly affecting conduct. But underneath these exalted speculative affirmations of the poets there lay in Jonson's mind ethical ideas of immense potency and grip, though never by him brought into philosophic shape; ideas most nearly akin to Stoicism, had the Stoic's capacity to 'endure and renounce' been quickened with heroic energy and daring.

Such was the stuff of the Jonsonian counsel dispensed in Epigram and Epistle to his friends. In the epistle to Elizabeth Countess of Rutland,[1] for instance, the Renascence commonplace of beauty immortalized by poetry appears reinvigorated by his own energetic self-consciousness. To the daughter of 'godlike Sidney' he confided the literary ambitions more loftily proclaimed in the Preface to *Volpone*, and in which she herself was to have a share. The epistle which follows,[2] to Lady Aubigny, the young wife of his five years' host, is a remarkable example of Jonson's critical and discriminating praise. But the pace quickens, and a more individual colour comes into the diction, when he turns from direct eulogy to chastise those who praise her for the wrong things,—for the fortune which is irrelevant, or the beauty which any fool can see; and the 'other great wiues' whom her purity and fidelity put to the blush.

IV

The Epistles scattered through the *Underwoods* were probably all written after the Folio of 1616 was prepared for press, though in some cases before its actual publication.

---

[1] *Forest*, xii. [2] *Forest*, xiii.

The Poems

In this kind of writing Jonson's strength suffered no material decline; two or three of these later epistles rank amongst his strongest and most memorable work. Even the 'begging letter' which he sent to the lord treasurer in 1631[1] when his Muse lay

> Fix'd to the bed, and boords, unlike to win
> Health, or scarce breath, as she had never bin,

owes its pathos to no suggestion of mental decay. At the head stand the two kindred epistles to Sir Edward Sackville (xiii) and Master Colby (xv). The half-idyllic temper of the 'Penshurst' and 'Durance' here gives place to a rougher and sterner mood more familiar to Jonson. Great part of both is occupied with scathing pictures of the shady side of Jacobean London, etched with a concentrated vigour which he had never surpassed. But in the anger is heard, yet more unmistakably than usual, the accent of a noble spirit, grieving over the cankers that festered in the blood of England. Very likely the memory of personal slights rankled also; but personal irritation, if present, finds no distinct expression. Jonson had suffered much from tactless givers, who chose the wrong time or place, or were only anxious to get rid of a troublesome suppliant. But he exposed in a much graver tone the corrupt givers who lavished their wealth on roisterers and swaggerers:

> him that last was made,
> Or stands to be'n Commission o' the blade.

The ideal giver and the ideal warrior were for Jonson, if not kindred characters, yet natural allies; and he delineated both to Sackville in sterling and memorable phrases:

> They are the Noblest benefits, and sinke
> Deepest in Man, of which when he doth thinke,
> The memorie delights him more, from whom,
> Then what he hath receiv'd.

The military swashbucklers he disposed of, like Spenser before him, by distinguishing from their mere 'lust obscene,

---

[1] *Und.* lxxi.

or appetite of offending', the valour which discerns good or ill. The weight and pregnancy of Jonson's writing never stood him in better stead than when, towards the close of this epistle, he set forth his sober ethics of patient self-amendment,—the creed not of a sluggish spirit, but of a realist in morals as in art, who knew that growth must be by degrees, and achievement have its roots in daily practice.

> I have the lyst of mine owne faults to know,
> Looke to and cure; Hee's not a man hath none,
> But like to be, that every day mends one,
> And feeles it.

The temper of the epistle is near akin to that of Wordsworth's *Happy Warrior*, one verse of which these lines directly recall. Wordsworth's contemporary, Horne Tooke, knew them by heart.

The 'Colby' epistle (xv) similarly recalls Wordsworth's War Sonnets. No threatened invasion, indeed, was now in question, and Jonson's appeal to his friend has no other motive than to rouse him from the lethargy of vicious ease. His indictment of his country is tempered by none of the tenderness of 'the lover' or 'the child', which mingles in Wordsworth's. The country was in deadly peril indeed, but only from itself; and Jonson holds up the mirror with a fierce passion of abhorrence which saw no resource but in a manly advance into a field where the body may bleed but the conscience remains intact.[1]

Not less fine is the 'Epistle to Selden' (xiv), the chief of contemporary English scholars; a worthy counterpart, by a fellow-scholar, of the disciple's 'epigram' he had once offered to Camden; and inviting comparison even with the memorial poem on 'Master William Shakespeare and what he hath left us' itself. He had latterly, he confesses, become more wary and circumspect in praise. But here these cautions were of no avail.

---

[1] This epistle may be compared in theme and contrasted in manner with Donne's spirited epistolary expostulation with Sir Henry Goodyere (*Poems*, ed. Grierson, i, p. 183).

> I yeeld, I yeeld, the matter of your praise
> Flowes in upon me, and I cannot raise
> A banke against it.

In Selden Jonson hailed a 'Monarch in Letters', as he was presently to hail in Shakespeare the 'Soule of the Age'; and the former 'Title of Honour', though it has not worn so well as the latter, was perhaps conferred with more sincere conviction. Selden was for him the ideal scholar-historian, who had retrieved the image of the past from the confusions and errors of tradition, and presented it to the world in a style full of 'excellent seasoning' and 'masculine elocution'. Theirs was an age given to huge agglomerations of erudition; Jonson, too ready himself to embarrass the conduct of business with a prodigal excess of detail, honours in his friend the shaping and organizing mind:

> I wonder'd at the richnesse, but am lost,
> To see the workmanship so' exceed the cost![1]

Selden had dedicated his book to no noble patron, but to his 'most beloved friend, and Chamber-fellow' Edward Heyward; a procedure which Jonson, without practising it himself, could heartily appreciate and praise, adding moreover a felicitous tribute to the 'chamber-fellow', as one who had wrought

> In the same Mines of knowledge; and thence brought
> Humanitie enough to be a friend,
> And strength to be a Champion, and defend
> Thy gift 'gainst envie.

Less equal and sustained, but even more vivid and individual in its finest passages, is the 'Epistle answering to one that asked to be Sealed of the Tribe of BEN' (xlvii). It is, in effect, less an 'answer' to a request than an outburst of impassioned thought about friendship, not very apposite to the particular application that prompted it. The applicant had encountered Ben in an hour when his

[1] One may compare the spirit of Jonson's rule for the Apollo banquets: 'Epulae delectu potius, quam sumptu, parantor.'

genius for fellowship had been mortified, and his proud self-sufficiency put upon its mettle by recent rebuffs. He was not thinking of his 'sons' and their devotion, but of his own superiority to the world's censure, and he faces the ardour of the would-be disciple with impressive but irrelevant assurances of his power to stand alone. And he follows up this yet more formidably with a picture of the false friend, etched as incisively as Hamlet's, and under its general profile disclosing the unmistakable features of the fellow-artist who for the time had superseded him at Court. Years of amicable copartnership had only filmed, not healed, the sore, and we find him, as if those years were cancelled, repeating the fierce old phrases of the epigram on 'The Town's Honest Man' (cxv);—the newsmonger and tale-bearer, who will jest on all souls that are absent, even the dead, and who lives in 'the wild Anarchie of Drinke'.[1] Yet the old scorn is still vital, and is uttered with a richness of fancy and allusion which lifts it into poetry without detracting a whit from its bitter animus. He had venomously played, in the epigram, upon Inigo's professional accomplishments: he was his 'owne fames architect' and an 'inginer in slanders, of all fashions'. He now turns the very Court Masques themselves, in which Inigo had, as he thought, usurped his place, into material for ridicule of the friendship which like those 'Glorious Scenes' was 'built with canvasse, paper, and false lights', with fevery heats and colds, 'Oylie Expansions' and 'shrunke durtie folds'. While the personal application cannot be mistaken, the expression is lifted, with occasional lapses, above personality. Jonson is no longer, as in the Epigram, concentrating his power on abuse. But the virus of the Inigo affair now only gives an acid relish to the temper of lofty and disdainful self-sufficiency which was the noblest answer within his compass to the tyranny of man and fate.

[1] The phrase thus twice used by Jonson was applied by Drummond, in the interval between them, to himself: 'drink . . . is one of the elements in which he liveth' (*Conversations*, xix. 683–4).

The sense that now his enemies were likely to be more than his match, and that the 'fraile Pitcher' of his art, his 'animated Porc'lane of the Court', would suffer in the encounter with the 'coarser earthen Jarres' there, does not cow his courage for a moment. But it abates his truculence, chastens the stentor shout too common with him, and permits to emerge the note of a Stoic in truer accord with poetry— the deepest strain of his nature:

> Live to that point I will, for which I am man,
> And dwell as in my Center, as I can,
> Still looking to, and ever loving heaven;

and if heaven sent any friendships 'square, well-tagg'd, and permanent', ready to embrace them.

Friends of this sort, of his own rank, Jonson still had, outside as well as within the world of letters. To one of these, an official in the Exchequer, Arthur Squib, he addressed two epistles[1] which may be compared with the epigrams of earlier days to the Roes for affectionate intimacy, while the first expounds his ideal of friendship with all his wonted close-knitted strength.

The true Epistle is not addressed, even indirectly, to the world. Jonson's many copies of verse addressed to his literary comrades, but intended to introduce and recommend their works, have more epistolary quality than such verses in general, simply because Jonson was apt, whatever the audience, to speak to the man he was addressing, and to say the thing he meant. Many of the shorter of them, as has been seen, are virtually 'epigrams', though classed by Jonson apart, or at least not included in his 'Book'. One, far beyond the epigram in scale and scope, has the peculiar intimacy of the epistle in an almost unmatched degree; but, again, breaks away from the epistle, as practised by Jonson, in range and audacity of flight. The 'Vision', as he chooses to call it, 'on the Muses of his friend Michael Drayton' (1627)[2] thus forms a transition from the more pedestrian to the more lyrical group of Jonson's verse. He

[1] *Und.* xlv, liv.   [2] *Ungathered Verse,* xxx.

addresses his old comrade with the rough frankness common between men of tough nature, whose friendship, grounded upon real fraternity of genius and temperament and common passion for the greatest things, can endure quarrels, silence, and loudly expressed 'disesteem' on both sides without serious hurt.[1] A cynical world, however, seizes upon the signs of dissension between its great men. Jonson was evidently concerned to make clear to all and sundry what at bottom he thought of 'Michael':

> It hath beene question'd, MICHAEL, if I bee
> A Friend at all; or, if at all, to thee:
> Because, who make the question, haue not seene
> Those ambling visits, passe in verse, betweene
> Thy *Muse*, and mine, as they expect. 'Tis true:
> You haue not writ to me, nor I to you;
> And, though I now begin, 'tis not to rub
> Hanch against Hanch, or raise a rhiming *Club*
> About the towne: this reck'ning I will pay,
> Without conferring symboles.

Lines like these convey the impression of a type of friendship sufficiently remote from those enshrined in Plato, in Shakespeare's *Sonnets*, and in the Fifth Book of *The Faerie Queene*. Like most of the other things which grew in the strong soil of Jonson's nature, his friendship flowered with no tropical luxuriance or aroma; but its roots struck deep. The declaration would be more effective if it were not so like a challenge to any who might think otherwise. There was something of bravery in the passion of both poets; and the tardy pioneer who had asserted his right to originality so boldly ('I will, yea, and I may') was not likely to resent a too vociferous championship of his claims. But solid conviction and solid truth underlay the bravery; and Drayton's abounding and unequal poetry received in his time no heartier, more heartfelt, or, on the whole, more judicious praise.

With Shakespeare as with Drayton, Jonson's relations had been chequered. No fraternity of genius or community of

---

[1] *Convers.* xi. 153: 'Drayton feared him, and he esteemed not of him.'

aim furnished a permanent ground of fellowship, and Jonson was not the man to overlook the literary heresies of his best friends. On the other hand, Shakespeare was probably hard to quarrel with, while the imperious and arrogant temper which Drayton shared with Jonson only facilitated those 'fears' and 'disesteems' on either side for which Jonson was to make so hearty an amends. And the personal differences with Shakespeare lay far back in the Elizabethan days of the Stage Quarrel; he had himself, moreover, been dead for seven years. The phrases which have grown hackneyed in the modern cult of Shakespeare,— 'Sweet Swan of *Avon*', 'gentle Shakespeare',—if not of his coinage, owe their currency largely to his use. The lines entirely bear out his private confession that he 'loved the man' and 'honoured his memory, on this side idolatry, as much as any'. But they also bear out the indications furnished by the context of that passage that Jonson did not profoundly understand the genius of Shakespeare. Misplaced praise in the public tribute and unreasonable cavils in the private memoranda tell the same tale. It does not much matter whether Jonson is pronouncing roundly that Shakespeare 'wanted art', or praising him for his verses hammered and re-hammered upon the Muses' anvil; neither criticism is at all near the mark. To say, again, that in every verse he
> seemes to shake a Lance,
> As brandish't at the eyes of Ignorance

is to ascribe to him what Jonson himself, and not what Shakespeare, understood by humanity. Against these occasional indications of imperfect perception, or imperfect sincerity, must be set the great phrases which posterity has found it impossible to better and therefore continually repeats:
> Soule of the Age!

and then the still loftier, complementary truth—
> He was not of an age, but for all time!

Jonson never wrote more eloquently than in the central

passages. And how fine is the scornful development of Basse's quaint conceit about making room for Shakespeare in the 'threefold fourfold tomb' of Chaucer, Spenser, and Beaumont:

> I will not lodge thee by
> *Chaucer*, or *Spenser*, or bid *Beaumont* lye
> A little further, to make thee a roome:
> Thou art a Moniment, without a tombe . . .

This is poetry and criticism at once. Of the specific quality of Shakespeare's genius Jonson perhaps understood less than many of his brother poets and dramatists; but the true magnitude of the 'Starre of Poets' in the firmament of universal literature he was the first clearly to proclaim.

V

In temper and afflatus, if not in form, the memorial poem on Shakespeare knocks hard at the gates of lyric. It is rather a song of triumph than an elegy. Written when his loss was no longer recent, and when Englishmen were about to be put for the first time in complete possession of what he had left them, it breathes rather exultation than regret. But it may serve to effect our transition to the poems which death, one of the permanent sources of poetry, has actually touched with its mysterious or pathetic inspiration. They include some of Jonson's finest work; and though all are not of the same quality, there is a perceptible quickening and kindling of the poetic air as we enter these little votive temples. If the verse does not yet sing, it is already of the kindred of song. Jonson is not one of the great poets of death. The same inferiority, both of imagination and of heart, which gave the intellect and senses so dominant a share in the fabrication of his lyrics of love, put beyond his reach either the lyric which thrills us with the intolerable pathos of loss, or that which haunts us with visionary glimpses beyond the grave. The mystery of the passing of souls never touches us in him. Some of the notes of a great and moving requiem were, however, within his compass.

To resume what has already been said, he had in a high degree the Renascence exaltation in the presence of human achievement, and he could commemorate the passing of great men or of beautiful women with a kind of serene magnanimity, as of one assured of the triumph of genius and beauty over death and time. And he had a tenderness for young children, rarely disclosed indeed save at their death, the simple pathos of which he could convey in delicate and moving strains. Of both qualities Jonson gave clearest evidence in the *Epigrams*, where the brevity of the form held in some check the discursive and critical habits of his mind, here peculiarly disastrous. But this very restraint rendered more welcome the ampler vehicle provided by the Elegy, especially as, with the approach of old age, his command of brief and pregnant phrase relaxed. The 'epitaphs' in fact, with one exception, were written before 1621, the threnodic elegies after 1630.

In the commonly pedestrian and too often malodorous wilderness of the Jonsonian 'epigram', the few epitaphs make rare but delectable oases. Of the two themes which touched Jonson's elegiac feeling, the pathos of the death of children is here the more conspicuous. The beautiful epitaph on the boy actor Salathiel Pavy[1] at once caught the public ear, and has always been amongst Jonson's most famous pieces. It does not affect violent or profound grief; but a sorrow which can play with fancies and please itself with dainty caprices of invention is traced as it were in low relief along the child's sarcophagus; Death in tears at his own work, Heaven and Nature disputing for its possession, and the awful Fates themselves convicted of a blunder and striving to make it good. Martial, who excelled in this gracious play of fancy between smiles and tears, probably gave the hint of the conceit in his epitaph on Scorpus;[2] but Jonson has here greatly surpassed his master. The charming pieces on the six-year-old Erotion were naturally

---

[1] *Epigr.* cxx. Pavy died in 1601 or 1602.   [2] Martial, x. 53.

in his mind when he commemorated, probably some years before, his own little daughter [1] and, a year or two after, his first-born son.[2] The former has a simplicity both of feeling and of thought rare in Jonson. To the graceful fancy of the Martialesque epitaph it makes no approach whatever. Nay, one may suspect, in a scholar of Jonson's quality, that a touch of this kind—very charming to our feeling—in the Erotion epitaph is deliberately declined.

> Mollia non rigidus caespes tegat ossa: nec illi,
> terra, gravis fueris: *non fuit illa tibi,*[3]

Martial had written. Jonson prefers the unadorned plainness of
> This graue partakes the fleshly birth.
> Which couer lightly, gentle earth.

The epitaph on his son, though written in his Catholic time, is quite without the theological tinge of the former. It is altogether a riper and more masculine production; that of one who does not merely suffer a loss with resignation, but lays his mind to his grief and gives it expressive form and body. The famous

> here doth lye
> BEN. IONSON his best piece of *poetrie,*

may be called, if we will, a conceit, the conceit of a scholar playing with etymology. But it is one of those conceits which (like the 'puns' of the dying Gaunt) spring from deeper regions of a man's heart and brain than his sober prose.

The 'Epitaph on Elizabeth, L. H.' (cxxiv)—more mysterious in its origin—is again distinct in character. The opening and close are pitched in a quiet and tender key: an unassuming life is over; peace to her memory, do not ask her name. But among these subdued tones of resignation there intervenes, though still in undertone, a more exalted note,—the Renascence faith in the eternity of beauty and virtue:

---

[1] *Epigr.* xxii (*c.* 1595).   [2] *Epigr.* xlv (1603).   [3] Martial, v. 34.

> Vnder-neath this stone doth lye
> As much beautie, as could dye:
> Which in life did harbour giue
> To more vertue, then doth liue.

Less monumental, but of a subtle rhythmical beauty which Jonson rarely bettered, is the epitaph on 'Margaret Ratcliffe' (xl). The artificial acrostic form does not prepare us for poetry so choice, but is hardly detrimental to it, the name thus sounding gradually through the poem and subtly co-operating with it, like a recurring but ever varied rhyme.

After the publication of the Folio, Jonson less often used this stately mode of epigram for commemorative purposes. The lines on the Countess of Pembroke, long ascribed to him, are probably Browne's; and those dedicated, ten years later, to the memory of Drayton are not certainly his. The affectionate familiarity of such earlier epitaphs as that on 'glad-mention'd Roe'[1] reappears in the charming epitaph on Vincent Corbet.[2] But as his own life drew to a close he began to adopt forms which allowed fuller scope than 'epitaph' in its widest interpretation could do, to both feeling and description. The most elaborate and intricate lyric mould at his disposal, the Pindaric Ode, was not too magnificent nor too hard for the commemoration, in 1629, of Sir Henry Morison.[3] Later still, the deaths of two ladies elicited from him two laboured and unequal but deeply felt elegies, the second a veritable cycle of commemorative song, challenging comparison in scale, though not in force, with the 'Charis' of ten or twelve years before.

The elegy on Lady Jane Pawlet (1631)[4] opens in a train of mysterious beauty as unexpected in Jonson as the reminiscence of it in the 'Elegy to the Memory of an unfortunate Lady' is in Pope. But Jonson, at his best Pope's inferior in skill and tact, could not sustain the music on this unfamiliar note; and the unusual opening strain breaks down with a run into the desperate prose of

---

[1] *Epigr.* xxxiii.   [2] *Und.* xii.   [3] *Und.* lxx.   [4] *Und.* lxxxiii.

Shee was the Lady *Jane*, and *Marchionisse*
Of *Winchester*; the Heralds can tell this;

to recover itself, however, in a measure, when, a score of lines farther, Jonson tells movingly of her sufferings and fortitude:

how did her soule assure
Her suffrings, as the body had beene away!
And to her Torturers (her Doctors) say,
Stick on your Cupping-glasses, feare not, put
Your hottest Caustics to, burne, lance, or cut:
'Tis but a body which you can torment,
And I, into the world, all Soule, was sent!

With Venetia Digby Jonson's relations had undoubtedly been closer. He called her his Muse, and had written, some few years earlier, a charming 'epigram' to her upon her husband, Sir Kenelm.[1] The story of the woman whose 'Faire Fame left to Posteritie' he sought to vindicate in these last imperfect strains of his ebbing song has never been adequately told. The character of Venetia Digby, as variously reported to us by her husband, her friends, and the gossip and scandal of the day, is clearly problematic, and might have engaged the interpretative imagination of Browning. The more generous view of her which has latterly won ground assuredly finds some support in the peculiar intensity and delicacy of the praise which Jonson, who could tell women their faults with such brutal candour, when he chose, devoted to the memory of his slandered friend. It is a laboured tribute, moving by the very inadequacy of the lyric powers which struggle for expression, only occasionally striking out a fine phrase. The sustained ease and brightness of 'Charis' are altogether gone. The first and second 'pieces' are of little more than pathological interest. The *terza rima* of the latter, used before Jonson by Wyat and Surrey, Sidney and Daniel, has rarely been so completely denuded of charm and grace. 'The Picture of the Body' (No. 3) hardly emerges into distinctness. But

---

[1] *Und.* lxxviii.

the 'Picture of the Mind' of his 'Muse' was a more provocative theme to the ageing poet, and there are flashes of the old fire and a swing in the rugged verse when he commemorates

> The Voyce so sweet, the words so faire,
> As some soft chime had stroak'd the ayre;
> And, though the sound were parted thence,
> Still left an Eccho in the sense.

The closing 'Elegy on my Muse' is, in spite of inequalities of style and anomalies of metre, not unworthy to be, what it probably was, Jonson's last considerable piece of verse. Rarely had he touched so simply the note of desolate loss as in the opening verses:

> 'Twere time that I dy'd too, now shee is dead,
> Who was my *Muse*, and life of all I sey'd.

But the old poet would not rest on that note; his thoughts, against his wont, passed beyond the grave which he felt himself fast approaching, and the elegy on the dead 'Muse' became an 'apotheosis' of the 'saint'. His conceptions of the celestial life do not differ from those of the simplest devotee; but he utters them with wistful intensity, and his picture of the heavenly society—

> There, all the happy soules, that ever were,
> Shall meet with gladnesse in one *Theatre,*—

was remembered by Milton when he imagined the close of *Lycidas*.

VI

This halting but tender commemoration involuntarily recalls the more eloquent verses which Jonson had made for living ladies in his prime. In the poetry of love he reached his highest note as a singer. The exact measure of his range and faculty in this field depends unfortunately upon the solution of a difficult problem of authenticity. The four Propertian 'elegies' in the *Underwoods*[1] differ totally in spirit as in quality of poetic fibre from the

---

[1] *Und.* xxxviii–xli.

undoubtedly Jonsonian 'elegy' which immediately follows, —a piece of savage satire already noticed. One of them (xxxix) appeared also among the elegies of Donne in 1633, and as all four are unmistakably by the same hand, and strangely recall Donne's strikingly individual manner, while they have no parallel in Jonson, his claim to them, published as they were in the loose, ill-edited collection of the *Underwoods*, and after his death, cannot be asserted with any confidence, and must in our view be abandoned. Woman is, in both groups, the preoccupation of the writer. But to the author of the four 'elegies' woman is a daemonic power, exercising a mysterious spell which, with all his efforts at gaiety of heart, he never evades:

> O, that you could but by dissection see
> How much you are the better part of me;
> How all my Fibres by your Spirit doe move,
> And that there is no life in me, but love. . . .
> Your forme shines here, here fixed in my heart;
> I may dilate my selfe, but not depart.
> Other by common Stars their courses run,
> When I see you, then I doe see my Sun,
> Till then 'tis all but darknesse, that I have,
> Rather then want your light, I wish a grave.[1]

Here surely we have a glimpse of the mystic passion, shot with splendour and with gloom, which womanhood provoked in the genius of Donne. Jonson, whose highest mood towards women was an intellectual admiration, was impervious to this temper.

We turn therefore, with regret, from these powerful 'elegies' to consider Jonson's undoubtedly authentic examples of the lyric of love. The touch and movement of true lyric visit him most readily in metres of quite simple structure and cadence, and his lyric moods are as simple (whatever the literary artifice of their expression) as his metres. Among the crowd of facile and often exquisite love-lyrists, facile in singing love as they were facile in making it, masters of

[1] *Underwoods*, xxxviii. 109–22.

madrigal and the 'lascivious pleasing of a lute', he stands apart, as a nature not prompt either to passion or to pity, and from which song was not lightly won. It is doubtful whether any of his love-songs were in any strict sense inspired by love; certainly there is no sign anywhere of the lyric abandon which in a Burns or a Goethe reaches artistic perfection without a trace of controlling art. At rare moments he catches with extraordinary felicity the glowing phrase and impetuous onrush of triumphant love. But his natural habit as an artist is rather the stately and measured speech of the 'classic' ideal. In most hands this measured speech serves only to express the temperate commonplaces of emotion. But Jonson shares with greater artists, in his best moments, the gift of eliciting a magical expressiveness from the simplest and most unobtrusive turns of phrase and rhythm. Even the little poem set at the head of *The Forest*, to explain 'Why I write not of Love', is something other, and something more, than the ingenious anacreontic which its scheme suggests. He once tried, he says, to capture Love and bind him in his verse, but Love had scorned the bondage of the poets; enough that they had once entangled Mars and his mother in their net, he had wings and wore them not in vain:

> With which he fled me: and againe,
> Into my ri'mes could ne're be got
> By any arte. Then wonder not,
> That since, my numbers are so cold,
> When *Loue* is fled, and I grow old.

The half-playful temper of the imagery insensibly changes, and in the last verses we seem to hear, not an elderly and disenchanted Anacreon, but Landor's Charon, old indeed, yet capable, in the presence of Dirce, of 'forgetting' that he is old, 'and she a shade'. Nor was the poet in fact so old—he was little over forty—but that a 'Charis' still a few years later could touch his sluggish vein, as a 'Celia' had touched him a few years before. It was to 'Celia' that he addressed the one supreme success among his songs. The famous 'Drinke to me, onely, with thine eyes'[1] is, no doubt, little more than a paraphrase of scattered passages in the same work, which Jonson chose and recombined. But it at the very least compels us to qualify the damaging verdict upon Jonson's powers as a translator which almost all his other performances in this kind would authorize. The demon of literalism commonly ousts the poet in Jonson, and distorts his nervous and idiomatic speech into uncouth and even monstrous forms. Here, on the contrary, he has found a setting for the exotic thoughts far stronger, simpler, and nobler than that from which he drew them. Hardly a phrase is substantially changed; but by sheer force of style and of music the whole situation is lifted into a rarer and intenser atmosphere, where the audacities of rhetoric change their complexion and become the spontaneous hyperbole of impassioned speech. No doubt Philostratus must have the credit of having strewed much implicit poetry through his prose. But the skill shown in concentrating and eliciting these scattered potential values is remarkable. 'Put the cup to thy lips, fill it with kisses, and give it me so', is a trivial, even grotesque, elaboration of an idea which could bear only the momentary touch of Jonson's

> Or leaue a kisse but in the cup,
> And Ile not looke for wine.

When on the other hand, as in 'To Celia' (*Forest*, v), Jonson tried the capacity of his English upon a great poet like Catullus, he rarely achieves more than mediocrity. The simple intensity of the

> Soles occidere et redire possunt:
> Nobis, cum semel occidit brevis lux,
> Nox est perpetua una dormienda

offered no vantage-ground for the salient qualities of Jonson's style, and became, 'literally' rendered, merely smooth and insignificant in his

[1] *Forest*, ix.

>   Sunnes, that set, may rise againe:
>   But if once we loose this light,
>   'Tis, with vs, perpetuall night.

Campion came far nearer with the superb Elizabethan Romanticism of his

>   Heau'ns great lampes do diue
>   Into their west, and strait againe reuiue,
>   But soone as once is set our little light,
>   Then must we sleepe one euer-during night.[1]

The poem to Celia in the *Underwoods*[2], which apparently belongs approximately to the same date, must have been deliberately excluded from *The Forest* by Jonson himself. Though called an ode, it has little of the formal tone and metrical intricacy which Jonson habitually sought in that species. The motif is simply a compliment, conveyed with Jonsonian amplitude and elaboration, but which he was neither poet enough nor lover enough to redeem from its traditional banality. Yet the little piece is well made; the octosyllabic couplet, in which it is written, has indeed a way of eliciting unexpected grace of melody from his somewhat harsh and crabbed instrument.

With the completion of the first Folio Jonson's career as a poet of Love might seem to be closed. Yet few of his lyric verses had danced more eloquently from his pen than those which he devoted, a dozen years later, to the celebration of 'Charis'.[3] The poet who had at forty in *The Forest* excused himself for no longer writing of love, 'since *Loue* is fled, and I grow old', now at fifty excuses himself for loving still:

>   Poëts, though divine, are men;
>   Some have lov'd as old agen.

Two of the ten pieces, in form and manner, stand apart from the rest. Of one of these, *Her Triumph* (iv), two stanzas are at least as early as *The Devil is an Ass* (1616), where they appear. It is a sumptuous and glowing romantic hymn heavy with perfume and of a lingering sonorous

---

[1] *A Booke of Ayres*, 1601, i. [2] *Und.* xxvii. [3] *Und.* ii.

music ; interposed amid a succession of blithe anacreontics, as nearly Greek in their buoyant temper and their crisp and vivacious movement as Jonson ever achieved. Wither handled this delicate trochaic measure with a subtler charm, and informed it with a rarer music ; but Jonson's cadences have a classic grace, the effect of which is heightened by the sense of rugged strength in reserve. The seventh lyric diverges both in rhythm and manner from this main group, and from the fourth, alike. It belongs, like the latter, to the time before 1619. It is a pretty piece of dramatic cajolery, and stood high in its author's favour, being, Drummond tells us, among the commonplaces of his repetition at Hawthornden. Charis's 'reply', in ix, is a gay and piquant dramatic lyric, unpleasingly capped, in x, with a drastic example of the cynicism which Jonson could rarely suppress when he undertook to exhibit the inmost nature of women. Within the main group, also, there are perceptible shades of difference. The earlier numbers are more largely built upon motives from classic myth ; Cupid, a *dramatis persona* in ii, iii, and v, becomes merely a decorative arabesque in viii and ix. 'Charis' and *The Forest* give the measure of Jonson's powers in the poetry of love. Could we indeed claim for him the four remarkable 'elegies' already discussed, we should have to speak of his powers in very different terms. The elegy of this Propertian variety, in which Donne was so great, Jonson did not indeed altogether fail to attempt. The two 'elegies' of the *Underwoods*, 'Can Beautie that did prompt me first to write' (xviii) or 'By those bright Eyes, at whose immortall fires' (xix), contain powerful strokes ; but this ingenious play with the mythology of Love and Fortune, this elegant enumeration of bright eyes and flying curls, merely touch the surface of the passion whose dark recesses Donne probed with so strange a power. The elegy in the *In Memoriam* stanza (xxii) has much of Donne's close intellectual texture, but without his sudden splendours and his pervading glow.

The 'Celia' poems and the 'Charis', then, include almost all the best of Jonson's love-lyrics. But most of the other pieces in *The Forest* and the *Underwoods* which approach the character of a song have to do with the relations of men and women, touching these for the most part in a lighter or less personal way, often with an inclination, imperfectly resisted, towards epigram or satire. The playful 'Song'[1] adapted from the Latin, which he by way of penance sent to Lady Pembroke for maintaining that 'Women are but Mens shaddowes', is a pleasant trifle, aerated with a sprightlier and more flippant wit than his own, but reflecting faithfully enough the cynical view of women at large which no admiration for a few ever dislodged from his mind. The cynicism is bitterer in the 'Gentlewoman's Farewell to the World',[2]—another of Jonson's few Dramatic Lyrics;—where the venal world which the 'vertuous and noble' gentlewoman renounces is itself significantly conceived as a woman,—a withered harlot who 'struts and paints' but is inwardly 'shrunk up and old'.

The main division of the *Underwoods* opens with a group of quasi love-lyrics, all probably of the years between the completion of the Folio volume of his *Works* and the Scottish journey. The 'Pastoral Dialogue' (iii), another of the pieces which its author loved to recite, has more of the school than of the fields; and the verses of the shepherd and the shepherdess, though strong and well turned, as well as ingenious, do little to persuade us of the Orphean magic which the singers ascribe to their own or each other's songs. The song 'Oh doe not wanton with those eyes' (iv), which Gifford thought the finest in the language, shows a remarkable command of the resources of impassioned lyrical expression. The restless intellectual energy which so often masters the lyric mood in Jonson, and threatens to turn song into a metrical debate, is here completely harmonized with it; the temper of dialectic is there, but it is the dialectic of passion, not of polemics. How seriously

[1] *The Forest*, vii. See the *Conversations*, xiv. 364–7.   [2] *The Forest*, iv.

elsewhere that temper of dialectic, neither harmonized nor subdued, could impair the execution of a charming lyric motive, is well seen in the stanzas called 'A Nymph's Passion' (vii). Throughout two stanzas her 'passion' must be taken for granted on her, or Jonson's, word; she is wholly occupied with the interesting dilemma, whether she shall tell it and risk the rivalry of the other nymphs, or keep it to herself and miss the satisfaction of their envy. Coleridge, who adapted this piece, with a few alterations, under the title of 'Mutual Passion, altered and modernised from an old poet', struck out the disturbing second stanza.

The pieces which follow in the *Underwoods* all belong to the time of the Scottish journey. The verses on 'The Hourglass' (viii), sent to Drummond after his visit, may be reckoned among the happier of his very unequal translations. The lines on 'My Picture left in Scotland' (ix), sent with these, in order 'that love when it is at full may admit heaping', are little more than a *jeu d'esprit*, but assist with a touch of unequalled vividness our effort to imagine the formidable poet of the 'mountaine belly' and the 'rockie face', as he sat and talked to his host of Hawthornden. In the brief snatch of verse 'Against Jealousy' (x) Jonson's scorn comes as near as his nature permitted to the Poet's 'scorn of scorn':

> Wretched and foolish Jealousie,
> How cam'st thou thus to enter me?
> I ne're was of thy kind: . . .
> I wish the Sun should shine
> On all mens Fruit, and Flowers, as well as mine.

'The Dream' (xi) touches a yet rarer chord. For a poet of his calibre he had few natural affinities with the dream world, and with the poetry that is evolved from, or nurtured upon, dreams. His touch is too incisive and too hard to convey the subtler complexities of soul-life, even had they not commonly escaped his energetic rather than delicate analysis. But he has here seized with a force that recalls Mrs. Meynell's 'Renunciation' Sonnet the mingled rapture and dread of one who has encountered love in the dream state which at once emancipates and enslaves.

VII

Jonson's lyrics of love clearly owe more to the artist than to the lover. In the few 'divine' songs, on the other hand, art is wholly subordinate to religious passion. Jonson's religion rarely appears in his writing, and its inner history is a sealed book to us; but it is plain that he had, together with a permanent and deep-seated interest, half devotional and half scholarly, in theology, moods of rapt absorption in divine things, or of shuddering self-abasement. Sometimes these thoughts fell upon him in company, and then the jesters of the Mermaid would rally him on his 'melancholy'.[1] The noble verses in which he hints this are hardly matched in Jonson, and not often matched in his century, for the grave intensity of accent and impressiveness which belongs to the humility of a great but proud spirit. Lines so poignant and yet so individual as these:

> I know my state, both full of shame, and scorne,
> Conceiu'd in sinne, and vnto labour borne,
> Standing with feare, and must with horror fall,
> And destin'd vnto iudgement, after all,—

or,—

> Yet dare I not complaine, or wish for death
> With holy PAVL, lest it be thought the breath
> Of discontent; or that these prayers bee
> For wearinesse of life, not loue of thee,

might justify us in expecting from Jonson some approach to the religious lyric of George Herbert. For the finest example of such lyric before Herbert, the Jesuit Southwell's 'The Burning Babe', Jonson, it will be recalled, expressed

---

[1] Good, and great GOD, can I not thinke of thee,
But it must, straight, my melancholy bee?
The Forest, xv, 'To Heaven'.
The point of the question was first indicated by Mr. Swinburne (*Study of Ben Jonson*, p. 103).

an almost unexampled fervour of admiration.[1] But the few actual 'Hymns' of Jonson show that such expectations must always have been vain. 'The Sinner's Sacrifice' (i) is almost wholly devoid of the searching individual accent of the lines 'To Heaven'; he reproduces the current theology in the current phrases, or phrases which only depart from current usage to become pedantic. The Hymn 'On the Nativity of my Saviour' can be as little compared with 'The Burning Babe' as with the Ode which the boy Milton had already written some years before Jonson's saw the light.

Most of Jonson's enduring work in lyric was done, as has been said, in forms of simple and unobtrusive metrical structure, such as the octosyllabic couplet and quatrain. For the intricate complexes of rhyme and rhythm in which the lyric invention of his younger contemporaries disported itself he shows, in his independent verse, no marked liking. The lyrics of the Masques, however, which so often force us to reconsider our conception of Jonson's art, make clear that he was not disinclined to metrical intricacy and elaboration, as also that he had no slight skill in their use. And when he was writing without the restrictions imposed by song and dance, he availed himself on occasion of two of the most artificial of all lyrical forms,—the Sonnet and the Ode.

VIII

His dealings with the Sonnet were indeed casual and rare. There is no doubt that he cordially disapproved of this as of every other variety of the stanza form; he 'cursed Petrarch', says Drummond,[2] 'for redacting verses to sonnets', which he compared to the bed of Procrustes. But, as the example shows, it was the rigidity, not the intricacy, of the sonnet form which offended him. The

---

[1] 'So he had written that piece . . . he would have been content to destroy many of his' (*Convers.* xii. 180–2).
[2] *Convers.* iv. 60.

Sonnet had moreover, during its brief but enormous vogue in England, afforded a privileged asylum to the extravagances and inflations of style which Jonson most abhorred. Even Shakespeare and Sidney, its greatest English masters, had jested, on occasion, at the sonnet and the sonneteer.[1] At the date of the *Conversations* its vogue had long declined; a few Scotsmen in the rear of fashion, like Drummond, and an inheritor of the Sidneyan tradition, like Lady Mary Wroth, were its most conspicuous cultivators. But Drummond was his host, and Lady Mary Wroth had been his friend and associate. The sonnets of both were known to Jonson, and possibly his condemnation of the species was the more incisive on that account. It was at least an irony of fate which made it his lot to 'exscribe' the not inelegant sonnets of Lady Wroth's *Urania*, and to cap them with one of his own, telling her how he had become, in that occupation, 'a better lover, and much better Poët'.[2] The sonnet is fluent and skilful enough, but obviously no more than a playful exercise. Four other authentic sonnets are known; one (*Underwoods*, lxviii) has been noticed above. Two occur in dedications; one signed 'Ben Iohnson' in the dedication to Breton's *Melancholike Humours* (1600), the other, signed 'B. I.', is prefixed to *The Passions of the Mind in General*, by T. Wright, a Catholic divine, in the authorized edition of 1604. It does not appear in the pirated edition of 1601.[3]

It was otherwise with the Ode. Jonson wrote odes at all times of his life, and with evident predilection. He was here, moreover, (and the fact is by no means irrelevant) relatively a pioneer. Instead of mingling with the stragglers in the rear of an exhausted fashion, he was opening up, if not a new way in English poetry, yet a new and noble manner, with potencies which he himself could as yet but very imperfectly exhibit or explore.

---

[1] It is significant that in his tributes to both Shakespeare and Drayton he ignores their sonnets.
[2] *Und.* xxviii.
[3] Cf. the note to *Conversations*, iv. 61.

IX

As a recognized poetic genre, the 'Ode' under that name had existed in western European literature for about half a century when Jonson began to write. Its first emergence had everywhere been the symptom of a vigorous, combative, and exacting classicism. The very term, pure Greek, and strange previously to all the western vernaculars, announced hostility to the loose-strung lilting measures of native prosody. Du Bellay in 1549 had called upon the poets of France to turn from 'virelays, rondeaux, and similar *epiceries*' to the writing of 'Elegies','Eclogues', 'Sonnets',and 'Odes'. The last, 'unknown hitherto to the French Muse', were to be kept severely aloof in character from all she had known. They were to be 'sung to a lute well tuned to the Greek and Roman lyre', and not a verse was to be without 'some impress of rare and antique erudition'. In the same year Du Bellay published his own *Odes*, which satisfied the latter canon so well that it was thought desirable to provide them with a commentary. To emulate the difficult and splendid distinction of Pindar was reserved for Du Bellay's friend and chief, Ronsard; the first of French poets to 'Pindarize', as he too frequently and emphatically reminds his readers.[1]

The first four books of Ronsard's *Odes* were published in 1550. They included many which emulate more successfully his other master Horace; and the Pindaric aspirations of the rest are seen, not in any novelty of rhythm or of verse-grouping, for the metres of Pindar were still generally unknown or misunderstood, but only in the abstruse and allusive style, and in the mechanical adoption of the divisions of the choric song—strophe, antistrophe, epode. It attests the keenness of the Humanist sentiment at the French Court that his austere and despotic Hellenism, deliberately denuded of the amiable airs and the easy graces of old France, should

---

[1] On the story of Du Bellay's indebtedness to Ronsard for the form and substance of his odes, see Sainte-Beuve, *Tableau*, p. 333 f.

have at once struck home. A familiar anecdote tells how, when Mellin de Saint-Gelais, the accredited master of the older way, ventured a burlesque reading, in the king's presence, of Ronsard's newly published *Odes*, the Princess Marguérite snatched the volume from his hand and captivated a not perhaps very difficult audience by reading them as they were meant to be read. So began the forty years' sway of the 'prince of poets' and his school; a sway which, as recent investigations have shown, by no means reached its territorial limit at the English Channel.

But neither Pindar nor Horace was destined to have the chief share in determining the character of the Ode in France. Four years after Ronsard's emergence, Henri Estienne published the first edition of 'Anacreon'. In these delicate lyric cameos the prestige of the antique was associated with qualities of charm and gaiety far more congenial to the Gallic temper than the high-wrought sublimity of Pindar. 'L'esprit français se trouvait assez naturellement prédisposé a cette grace insouciante et légère; l'Anacréon, chez nous, était comme préexistant,' says Sainte-Beuve.[1] He acted therefore as a reconciling and harmonizing force, mediating between the new classicism to which in origin he belonged, and the Gallic temper to which he was spiritually akin. Neither Ronsard nor his followers resisted a spell so subtly addressed at once to their Hellenic faith and to their French instinct; and the 'verve férocement Pindarique' of the master became, in the ensuing years, appreciably tempered and assuaged.[2]

If the earliest English sonnets were framed upon Italian example, France, whose influence was so potent upon the later sonnet literature, may claim to have started the English Ode. Its first beginnings were indeed sorry enough. The masculine rudeness of Wyat already promised a noble

---

[1] 'Anacréon au XVIme siècle' (*Tableau*, p. 427 f.).
[2] Ronsard's acquaintance with Anacreon must have begun earlier than the appearance of Estienne's edition. Apart from several decidedly Anacreontic Odes in the second and following books, the 11th ode of that book is a free but graceful rendering of the well-known 'Eros wet'.

art; but in Soothern's crude and blundering adaptations of Ronsard,[1] and the feeble and grotesque 'Odes and Odelets' of Barnabe Barnes,[2] it is hard to recognize any germs of vitality. Of the strength and beauty of the French Ode little indeed was here reproduced. Its quasi-Pindaresque audacities only encouraged the incredible extravagance of third-rate Elizabethan fancy; while the charm and grace of the French Anacreon awaited, in our more stubborn tongue, executants of another calibre than Soothern or Barnes. The former received a condign castigation from the author of the *Art of English Poesie* in 1589.[3] Yet Drayton, the greatest of English ode writers, in the strict sense, before Milton, did not disdain to pay the poor plagiary a compliment, which is indeed his best title to remembrance, as the pioneer in this kind:

> Southerne ...
> Who me pleased'st greatly,
>   As first, therefore more rare,
> Handling thy Harpe neatly.[4]

Neither in this ode, nor in the introductory poem to Goodere, nor in the prose address to the Reader, does Drayton mention Jonson; yet several years before 1605-6, when Drayton wrote, Jonson had already adventured in this kind, in the 'Ode to Desmond', first published it is true long after the poet's death, in the *Underwoods* (xxv). It is plain that Jonson, here as elsewhere, had disdained all modern and contemporary examples. In England there was as yet no one from whom in this matter he could learn, and the French classicists, at the time of his first odes, he could not read. He had clearly gone, as usual, direct to the Greek and Roman masters, subject, as always, to the more authoritative ruling of his own genius. Akin as he was in taste and temperament to Drayton, his chosen path in the

---

[1] *Pandora*, 1584.
[2] *Parthenophil and Parthenophe; Sonnets, Madrigals, Elegies, and Odes* (1593).
[3] Book III, ch. xxii, pp. 259, 260, ed. Arber.
[4] 'To Himself and the Harp.'

Ode diverged sharply at the outset from that which Drayton was to choose, and at no point approached it at all closely. Drayton held a sufficiently lofty estimate of his own powers, but he made no serious attempt to emulate the eagle flights of Pindar, which indeed, he thought, lay altogether beyond the compass of modern song:

> Though wee be All to seeke
> Of PINDAR that Great *Greeke*.

He dallied once or twice with the light themes of Anacreon (*To Cupid*; *An Amouret Anacreontic*) and in light measures not unlike his; he sang, too, with something like Horatian versatility, of love and battle, friendship and good cheer. But through all his reading and reminiscence of the classical Ode, there thrilled, as Professor Elton has well noticed, the short sharp 'twangle' of the British harp. The verse tosses and heaves, clashes and jostles, to beat out of stubborn English vocables hints of melodic effects more proper to the strings; hints fitfully lost and recovered along several lines of tentative rhythm, until they break into the strong and original music of the great harp-song of Agincourt.

No such haunting tune can be detected in the Odes of Jonson. His verse, more powerfully built and cunningly elaborated than Drayton's, was lifted far more rarely by the swing of song, as it was more rarely lighted by those 'brave translunary things' which Drayton had in him as truly as Marlowe. But Jonson's militancy does not break out in heroic hymns like the Agincourt song; it masses itself in weighty exhortation or invective, like the epistle to Colby or the 'Speech according to Horace'.[1] It was rather his distinction, at a time when the vices of fantastic and inflated expression were exercising a growing fascination on writers of every calibre, from Donne to the Water-poet and Davies of Hereford, to have set an example of noble plainness and strength. In his Horatian conciseness and sobriety, and in

[1] *Und.* xv, xliv.

his Horatian power of pregnant and impressive ethical statement, lay indeed his principal asset as a maker of odes; and such virtue as his own possess is chiefly of this kind. He himself knew where his affinity lay, if he hardly recognized his limitations. He might borrow the Alcaic lute, and 'warm himself by Pindar's fire', but Horace was his own.[1] It is in his quality of scholar rather than of poet that Jonson has set his mark most decisively on the history of the English ode. He was the first to attempt the choral ode on the elaborate Pindaric scheme; and a century and a quarter was to elapse before any one else attempted it with an even approximately equal understanding of its nature. The metres of Pindar were first explained to the generality of scholars by Boeckh little more than a century ago.[2] The early 'Pindarizers' formed astonishingly different conceptions of their idol. Some, like Ronsard, imitating the apparently uniform lines of the manuscripts, Pindarized in verses of unvaried length and structure. Others, like Cowley, were captivated by his wealth of intricate rhythms, and reproduced them, as they thought, in stanzas of chaotic irregularity. It is clear that Jonson had penetrated far into the mystery which remained obscure to others so long after his death. The Morison Ode[3] is, in metrical structure, fully as Pindaric as *The Progress of Poesy*. The Desmond Ode is less symmetrical in structure, but bears evident signs of an attempt to assume the Pindaric manner. Little more than historic importance belongs to this class of odes. Jonson himself hardly felt at ease in these magnificent singing robes. And in most of the pieces which he called odes, he falls back upon the simpler and plainer types in which he was more truly master. The empyrean flights of Pindar and the light brush of lyric wings were equally beyond his compass.

Of this last group of odes only two were certainly published, or intended for publication by Jonson himself,—

[1] Second 'Ode to Himself' (1629).
[2] Aug. Boeckh, *Dissertatio de metris Pindari*, 1810.   [3] *Und.* lxx.

the Epode of 1601 and the Birthday Ode to Sir William Sidney, both included in the first volume of the Folio (*Forest*, xi, xiv). Several others, however, had been long extant when *The Forest* was compiled, and must therefore have been deliberately excluded by him. Of these, some appeared after Jonson's death in the second volume of the Folio— the 'Ode to Himself' (*Und.* xxiii); to Desmond (xxv); 'High spirited friend' (xxvi); and Celia (xxvii). Two later odes were included in the same miscellaneous collection: the 'Pindaric Ode' (lxx), and the 'Ode gratulatory' (lxxiv); but not the 'Allegorical Ode', prefixed to Holland's *Pancharis* in 1603. The earliest of the extant odes (before 1600) is beyond question the ode addressed to the Earl of Desmond. It is also one of the earliest examples of his lyric work at large, and may well be as early as anything extant that he has written.[1] In any case it belongs to the experimental, the 'prentice, stage of his craftsmanship in lyric. It is one of the few of his extant pieces which give us a glimpse into the processes of his still immature and tentative art. Rarely indeed do we find Jonson doing explicit homage to another artist in the invocation:

> . . . Arise Invention,
> Wake, and put on the wings of *Pindars* Muse,
>   To towre with my intention
> High, as his mind, that doth advance
> Her upright head, above the reach of Chance,
>   Or the times envie.

Thus confidently, and with a critical *naïveté* not characteristic of him, did the least lyric of the greater poets of his generation seek to hitch his wagon to the Pindaric star. There was more of rivalry than of discipleship in this invocation, and we are not surprised to find the wagon, within a stage or two, quietly unloosed and going as its driver chooses. Not that there is any abrupt revolt; but the unruly impulses of his powerful temperament overcome

---

[1] Desmond was imprisoned in the Tower from 1584 to 1600. His estates were declared forfeit in 1586, and he died in 1601.

the control of a hand still immature. The vein of close-knit ethical reflection into which he falls, for example, in the second and fourth stanzas, though perhaps his line of nearest approach to Pindar, is distinguishable enough from Pindar's oracular and prophetic wisdom:

> No Armour to the mind! he is shot-free
>   From injurie,
> That is not hurt; not he, that is not hit;
>   So fooles, we see,
> Oft scape an Imputation, more through luck, then wit.

But the Pindaric illusion is completely shattered when the satirist breaks in, at the close of the third stanza, with his ugly medical allusions to 'the Anatomie in Surgeons hall, . . . a Statists theame, to read Phlebotomie'. This academic pedantry had little resemblance to the aristocratic hauteur of his original, which Jonson had in mind when he aspired 'to sing my thoughts, in some unvulgar straine'.

If the Desmond ode is still experimental, unequal, and only here and there recognizably authentic and individual, the spirit of Jonson is unmistakably impressed in every line of the two odes 'To Himself'. No one in his generation was to find loftier expression for friendship than he; but the emotions of friendship, when not made acute by tragic pity or terror, are a less potent provocative of impassioned lyric utterance than the anger of a strong man at bay. In every point of structure and style the first 'Ode to Himself' (*Underwoods*, xxiii) usually connected with the Stage Quarrel, but probably not earlier than 1612, stands apart from the Desmond Ode. Instead of the complicated strophe and the laboured execution, the brief ringing lines succeed one another, like hammer strokes, at even intervals, till they are clinched by the single rolling alexandrine. Instead of timorously trying his instrument, he wields it with conscious mastery. Instead of invoking 'Genius' and 'Invention' and the 'wings of Pindar's Muse', he will simply be Himself; 'take in hand his lyre', and 'strike in his proper strain'. And if the music is harsh, the serried rhymes at least crash as his hand sweeps the strings:

> And since our daintie age
> Cannot indure reproofe,
> Make not thyself a Page
> To that strumpet the Stage,
> But sing high and aloofe,
> Safe from the wolves black jaw, and the dull asses hoof.

The note of wounded arrogance is as audible here as that of ideal scorn. Yet this is no 'vulgar strain'.

Nor was it an altogether ignoble anger which inspired the yet fiercer invective of the second 'Ode to Himself' (1629), his retort upon the players and playgoers who refused to tolerate *The New Inn*. Both odes clearly originated in a reverse on the stage. But *The New Inn* reverse was more humiliating in itself and more pitiable, nay tragic, in its circumstances than any that had gone before. It befell one no longer in his vigorous early prime, but bed-ridden and at the verge of old age. But it is 'better playing with a lion's whelp than with an old one, dying'; and the unparalleled fiasco of *The New Inn* evoked an outburst not only more violent, but more powerful and significant in every respect. Even the resolve to try another way in poetry, instead of the 'loathed stage', is declared in strains full as lofty and spirited as the old, and the temper which entertains such a resolve—'though thy nerues be shrunke, and blood be cold'—we may feel to be futile, but it is the pathetic futility of heroism, 'still nursing the unconquerable hope'. The second ode only was published in Jonson's lifetime, in the octavo edition of *The New Inn* (1631).

The single ode, with one exception, which he himself included in his *Works* shows little trace of the personal love or hate which with him habitually bore such an emphasis. Though apparently composed for an occasion, it appears to well up from the depths of his mind, untouched by its more transient or vehement surface-currents. His connexion with Robert Chester, the author of *The Phoenix and the Turtle*, can hardly have been that of intimate friendship. The 'Praeludium' is a kind of introductory *scherzo* on the trite theme, 'What shall I sing, and with what god's help?'(*Forest*, x). The jest is unduly prolonged, with much burly classical jocosity at the cost of the several divinities whose pretensions are dismissed. Ben was not the man to ascribe his inspirations in earnest to any external sources, and the transition from the sportive preliminary to the grave 'Epode' for 'deepe eares' is aptly heralded by a haughty assertion, in the last stanzas, of his own poetic αὐτάρκεια:

> Nor all the ladies of the *Thespian lake*,
> (Though they were crusht into one forme) could make
> A beautie of that merit, that should take
> My *Muse* vp by *commission*: No, I bring
> My owne true fire. Now my thought takes wing.

And, in truth, the strain of the 'Epode'[1] which follows was one which the Elizabethans did not often hear. To the reader of *The Phoenix and the Turtle* the effect must have been startling. The dainty web of fancies and conversations, ingeniously elaborated by the Italian poet and his English translator and commentator, was suddenly rent by this rugged song with its impassioned and merciless veracity. Even Shakespeare—if he indeed was the author of the graceful verses ascribed to him—does little more than twine a few fresh ingenuities of conceit about the quaint emblematic figures of the theme; the wedded fidelity he commemorates loses nothing, in his hands, of the half-fabulous air with which the symbols invest it; like the phoenix, it exists only in a single example, and now that that has perished, love and constancy are dead too. Jonson could play with symbols and allegories as deftly as

---

[1] By 1600, the last line being quoted as Jonson's in *England's Parnassus* of that year (Bang, *Shakespeare-Jahrbuch*, xliv. 157).

any man when he chose, but here he was of another mood, —recalling, not the Shakespeare (or pseudo-Shakespeare) of *The Phoenix and the Turtle* verses at all, but rather the profoundly real Shakespeare of the 129th Sonnet. Jonson was not, any more than Shakespeare, one who 'knew not vice at all': but he entertained no illusions; he read his own breast as he read other men's, and neither cynically denied the existence of virtue nor confounded it with the easy innocence of prudent self-regard. And when he speaks of 'true love', the verse and imagery catch an afflatus, and sometimes a penetrating power, easily distinguished from the conventional glamour of academic eulogy, and possible only to the man who has searched some of the deeper places of human nature:

> That is an essence, farre more gentle, fine,
>   Pure, perfect, nay diuine;
> It is a golden chaine let downe from heauen,
>   Whose linkes are bright, and euen,
> That falls like sleepe on louers, ...
>
> O, who is he, that (in this peace) enioyes
>   Th' *Elixir* of all ioyes?
> A forme more fresh, then are the *Eden* bowers,
>   And lasting, as her flowers:
> Richer then *Time*, and as *Time's* vertue, rare.
>   Sober, as saddest care:
> A fixed thought, an eye vn-taught to glance;
>   Who (blest with such high chance)
> Would, at suggestion of a steepe desire,
>   Cast himselfe from the spire
> Of all his happinesse?

The '*Ode ἀλληγορική*' prefixed to *Pancharis*[1] (1603) is (like the '*Ode ἐνθουσιαστική*' which he contributed to *Love's Martyr* in 1601) in a kind not altogether consonant to his genius. But the 'allegory' is managed with an easy dexterity not very characteristic of him in kinds more congenial;

---

[1] *Pancharis*, by Hugh Holland, a friend of Jonson. Cf. Pearsall Smith, *Life and Letters of Sir H. Wotton*, i. 408. Printed in *Ungathered Verse*, vi.

and it betrays, here and there, Jonson's weighty and massive touch; as in the stanza on Montjoy, who

> more hath wonne
> Then Time hath donne,
> Whose strength is aboue strength;
> And conquers all things, yea it selfe, at length.

The ode to Sir William Sidney (written in 1612)[1] is, with the 'Epode', the only example of the ode included by Jonson among his *Works*, and has a certain interest on that account. It is exempt from the crude unevenness of the Desmond ode, it is made of the same metal throughout, and wrought with finished technical craft. But the metal, though good, is not choice, and it is possible to regret the Desmond patchwork, with its flashes of gold amid the iron. The thought was a commonplace;—a commonplace, however, which had the full weight of Jonson's character and conviction behind it, and which he could therefore drive home with a force and in a phrase which make them his own.

Jonson's earlier odes had thus been in the main tributes of friendship. Whatever else decayed in Jonson, his capacity for making and keeping friends remained fresh; and a little aftermath of odes commemorates these friendships of his latest years. The veteran of sixty furbished up the disused instrument to do honour to his 'sons' and other younger contemporaries. Between 1630 and 1633 he wrote a marriage ode for Jerome Weston, a congratulatory ode to the same friend, and an ode in memory of Sir H. Morison.[2] An 'Epithalamium' was perhaps the kind of ode in which Jonson was least qualified to reach high excellence. To the intoxicating beauty which irradiates the marriage hymns of Spenser, to the lurid splendours of thought and passion which shoot through the nakedness of Donne's, he could offer no approach. The pregnant and close-packed meditation of which he was master was not stirred by a

---

[1] *Forest*, xiv. Sir W. Sidney died on December 3, 1612.
[2] *Underwoods*, lxxv, lxxiv, lxx.

theme for which at bottom he cared less perhaps than any other poet of the day. The gracious fancy which had fashioned the finest wedding Masques in our literature may still have been at his bidding. But it did little to save the Weston wedding ode from some of the worst faults of the genre,—minute particularity divested of the bloom and breath of poetry. It does not even escape the awkward or unlucky touches incident to an elderly man who is seeking to recover, or depict, the passion he has ceased to feel, if indeed he ever felt it. The last vestige of romance is stripped from the solemnities of marriage. Bald and unimpressive narrative can hardly be carried farther than in such a stanza as that which describes the ceremony:

> See, now the Chapell opens; where the King
> And Bishop stay, to consummate the Rites:
> The holy Prelate prayes, then takes the Ring,
> Askes first, Who gives her (I *Charles*) then he plights
>   One in the others hand,
>   Whilst they both stand
> Hearing their charge, and then
> The solemne Quire cries, Joy; and they returne, Amen.

In general the style is dignified, even stately; but without charm. Or, if any there be, it attaches not to the immediate occasion and incidents of the marriage, but to the far-off vision of wedded old age, such as might have fallen to his own lot:

> That when you both are old,
> You find no cold
> There; but, renewed, say,
> (After the last child borne;) This is our wedding day.

A thought for which Rossetti found the language of poetry in his 'last of love',—

> In every kiss sealed fast
> To feel the first kiss and forebode the last.

The less ambitious 'Ode gratulatory' with which Jonson welcomed Lord Weston from his embassy in 1632 is more agreeable to read. If the thought is a commonplace and the expression hardly anywhere informed with the true

Jonsonian nerve, it has more of classical finish and choiceness than many pieces which we should recognize more easily as his. Jonson's warm and sincere friendships, untouched as they were by any hint of Platonic exaltation, were peculiarly favourable to these temperate, yet not tame or mediocre, regions of style. In this Horatian sphere he is hardly ever beneath comparison with Horace; whereas the themes and examples of a Catullus or a Pindar offered a seduction to which he rarely yielded without disaster and never without peril.

It was, however, to friendship—the friendship with a literary 'son'—that the most elaborately Pindaric of all his odes was devoted, that on the death of Morison. Jonson here sought to imitate not merely Pindar's rhythmical intricacy, as in the 'Desmond' and some other early odes, but the actual structure of the Pindaric ode, with its recurring groups of strophe, antistrophe, and epode. This had never before been attempted in England. At the very outset the bold mythic manner of Pindar beguiles him into bathos. It is hard to explain otherwise the tasteless opening stanza, based upon a serio-comic tradition of the siege of Saguntum. Jonson's literary tact, never impeccable, was habitually at fault when he was trying to reproduce antique effects in English. For some stanzas after this collapse the speech inclines to be either stilted or pedestrian, or both. Slowly, however, his weighty mind asserts itself, until at length the central thought finds clear and fine expression in the stanza which remains, with a few phrases from the memorial lines on Shakespeare, Jonson's sole legacy to the current 'winged words' of English-speaking peoples. 'It is not growing like a tree' does not, it is true, belong to the highest class even of Jonson's lyrics. The opening couplet states a truism with the emphasis only proper to an illuminating truth. But the 'lily' quatrain has true lyrical charm, and the closing couplet, if more proper for discourse than for song, is a dignified summing-up.

X

Of Jonson's translations in verse a few words only need be said. Among the qualifications of a successful translator he had only one,—complete mastery of the original. Some of his great qualities actually stood in his way. The powerful personality everywhere impressed upon his own work did not make for ready compliance with an alien manner; and nowhere is Jonson less plastic, more imperturbably and inflexibly his rugged self, than when he is professedly engaged in reproducing Horace or Martial. In the niceties of stylistic and metrical resource, which versifiers so much his inferior as Harington and Fairfax had at command in rendering Ariosto and Tasso, Jonson shows little skill; and their octave stanza taxed the translator more severely than any metre reproduced by him. Jonson, however, appears to have thought highly of his own performances. 'He read his translation of that Ode of Horace, Beatus ille qui procul negotiis, &c. and admired it', says Drummond;[1] and other pieces were apparently discussed by them. A translator so stubbornly individual as Jonson would have done best in the freest paraphrase. But this, by an unlucky conjunction, the pedant rather than the scholar in him forbade, devising for him and imposing on others the perverse doctrine that translation to be faithful must be rigidly literal. It would do wrong to scholarship to ascribe Jonson's relative failure solely to his greatness as a scholar; for to translate poetry like a scholar is to find language which satisfies scholar and poet at once; whereas Jonson, insisting on complete satisfaction for the scholar, and leaving to the poet such residual satisfaction as he could get on those terms, fails in reality to satisfy either. All that the verse, and in particular the rhyme, contribute to the effect is, as a rule, the qualified pleasure we experience in seeing a resolute but not agile or brilliant performer accomplish a difficult feat. The most important piece, the

---

[1] *Conversations*, v. 75-7.

De Arte Poetica, is that in which the literal theory of translation is most nearly justified. Horace's 'Epistle', richly stored as it is with felicitous sayings about poetry—the very mintage of the man of the world's notions of literature—is, of course, a didactic treatise—nay, a collection of apophthegms — not a poem. The real problem of the translator here is to match in his own tongue its incessant flow of significant and weighty epigram. If ever this was possible in English, it was possible to a contemporary of Shakespeare and of the Authorized Version of the Bible. Yet Jonson, certainly no mean master of phrase, fails signally,—nay, hardly seems to strive for success. He appears everywhere satisfied to convey the meaning accurately in terms however bald, clumsy, or commonplace, and that often for the sake of securing a rugged and mechanical verse, and a regular but rarely pleasing rhyme. Had he but turned Horace (as he turned Seneca or Scaliger) into the prose of the *Discoveries*! But even the praise of 'conveying the meaning' is not always deserved. Jonson, it must be owned, is often perfunctory, giving us vague phrases which may be said to contain Horace's sense, but only as a loose sleeve contains the arm. ''Tis hard, to speak things common, properly', for instance, is surely a 'fourth form' rendering of its famous and elusive original.

To the reader of Jonson's lyrics his renderings of the lyrics of Horace and Martial are still more disappointing. Here at least the delicate grace we know him to have been master of might have been expected. Inversions (to say nothing of bad rhyme) seldom more disastrously thwarted the lyric swing than in the crucial stanza of the ' Donec gratus eram tibi':

> But, say old Love returne should make,
> And us disioyn'd force to her brazen yoke,
> That I bright *Cloë* off should shake;
> And to left-*Lydia*, now the gate stood ope.[1]

[1] *Underwoods*, lxxxvii.

Happily, however, Jonson has given us a clue to the conditions of his real power even as a translator. When he is not trying to render completely, but is seeking, on his own terms, to choose and leave, refashion and recombine, Jonson is one of the great masters of this art in our literature. 'Drinke to me, onely, with thine eyes' more than atones for the *De Arte Poetica*. It would seem as if the semi-servile labour of fitting his mind implicitly to another's actually inhibited half its force; while the more inspiring call to educe the hidden, and collect the scattered, and exalt and glorify the inchoate and inexpressive, put him upon his mettle, and brought the energies of his intellect into full play.

XI

During his last years at least, Jonson was generally held by his contemporaries to be the first poet of the age. The judgement certainly took account of his great and splendid achievements in drama and in the Masque. But it is clear that his non-dramatic verse also, slight and occasional as it almost exclusively was, shared in the fame of his more imposing works, and contributed on something like equal terms to sustain his renown. The eulogists of *Jonsonus Virbius* do not always distinguish between the poet and the dramatist, but they often use terms which explicitly extol the verse. He was '*Prince* of *Numbers*', writes Mayne. Falkland's Dorus is 'fired' with 'the enchanting power' of his 'songs', and

speech exceeds not dumbenesse, nor verse *prose*,
More then His verse the low rough rimes of those

who 'possesst *Parnassus* ere his power appear'd'![1]

To the modern reader these eulogies appear imperfectly justified even by the lyrics of the Masques and the few songs in which to our ears he attains a genuine sweetness and grace. Jonson was far from standing alone, far from being even supreme, in these qualities; many of his contemporaries

---

[1] *Jonsonus Virbius*, p. 3.

and predecessors commanded them more easily, several in a higher degree, than he.

To explain Jonson's immense prestige as a poet, we must consent to descend from the high ground of absolute poetry,—the jewels, 'five words long', of immortal phrase,—to the table-land of qualities compatible with poetry and prose alike. This is not to represent him as a 'mediocre' poet, or to assign him to that neutral domain which Coleridge supposed Wordsworth to have in view when he identified the language of prose and verse. Daniel reigned in that region, and Jonson rightly (if arrogantly) refused to compare Daniel as a poet with himself. Jonson's case is somewhat like Dryden's. Dryden's position in English poetry is not inferior to Shelley's in the degree in which his poetry is at its highest reach less poetic. And Jonson too, as a poet, is not to be measured, and was not measured in his own day, by the degree in which his poetry at its highest reach is inferior to that of Herrick or Crashaw, Carew or Donne.

It is Donne, in particular, who helps us to measure both Jonson's inferiority in absolute poetry, and also the immense impression which it made on his own time, and the lessened but secure impression which it has made on critics since. The first is dangerously easy. The fiery and daring intellect of Donne, wrestling with passion or mastered and glorified by it, created marvels of strange and original song, where a tormented yet haunting music issues from the clash of contending, or the onrush of evolving, thought. Jonson's mind, more massive and coherent, if less nervous and high-strung, than Donne's, and shaken by no such tempests of the soul, moved in verse with more equable power, building up thought in orderly sequences and well-marked rhythm. The comparison, carried no farther than this, over-accentuates the difference between them, and suggests the conclusion that Jonson, as a poet, was simply a precursor of the Augustans, imperfectly grasping the ideals they were destined to achieve, and Donne the embodiment of everything that offended the 'correctness' that was so tardily to 'become their care'.

But it is plain that for their contemporaries the distinction between these two great men, however clear, was not antithetical at all. It was possible, as we have seen, for work of one to be ascribed to the other. Sharply as they might differ, and express their differences, an indefinable kinship united them. For the most rigid critic of his generation, Donne, however much he deserved hanging 'for not keeping of accent', was yet 'in some things the first poet in the world'. One had his disciples and the other his 'sons', and the sons were not always disciples; but within certain limits and in certain directions they co-operated, consciously or unconsciously, as moulding forces upon the poetry of the next generation.

In the first place, both stood with assured and peremptory convictions for a revolution in poetry. Both in different terms challenged the supreme poet of the previous generation, Spenser. Both stood for a masculine spirit in poetry, weighty, pregnant, concentrated, against a poetry of facile melody and melting phrase. Both sought to enlarge the intellectual compass of poetry, to charge it with more insistent thought, to bring it into more intimate relation with knowledge. The erudite temper of the Jacobeans is eloquent in both. No doubt the spheres of their erudition are widely different, like their uses of it. Donne's metaphysical wit haunts the crumbling but still imposing edifice of medieval scholasticism and the vast shadowy profiles of the new science. Jonson's wit, whatever its 'overplus', was not 'metaphysical' in any sense; but it commanded with secure mastery the whole field of classical learning, and had all the impetus and the ardour of the Renascence on its side. In this respect the religious poets, especially Herbert and Crashaw, stood nearer to Donne, but almost all the cavaliers had, like Jonson, cultivated the Latin lyrists.

Further, both Donne and Jonson helped poetry towards a

vital simplicity and directness of speech. Donne's passion preserves him from stylistic embroidery. All mere decoration shrivels up in his burning soul, and the thought stands out in its naked strength. This simplicity of Donne is disguised from us by the incomparable daring of his images. But his very daring makes him infallibly direct; he leaps to his goal, impatient of those stylistic *deversoria* which beguile less single-souled poets. Others may elaborate a comparison; Donne cries—

> She is all states; all princes I;
> Nothing else is;

or shatters at a stroke the whole delicate fabric of amatory compliment with his

> I wonder, by my troth, what thou and I
> Did, till we loved.

Jonson's simplicity is of a different order and of a different origin. It owes little to the purifying flame of passion, much to the winnowing and sifting hand of art. His training had steeped him in the classics, and his temperament drew him to the plainer and more direct varieties of classical style. The native vehemence which so often thrust ceremony aside and signed slave to no man emancipated him from affectations which beguile more patient men. In verse and prose alike, he sought brevity, terseness, emphasis; sentences not loosely connected or vaguely continuous, but sharply detached. 'Some', he told Drummond, 'loved running verses;

> plus mihi comma placet';

and if he has no definable position in what Mr. Saintsbury has called 'the battle' of the stopped and the enjambed couplet, it is because he uses with indiscriminate vigour the opportunities which both offered of the emphatic pause.[1]

---

[1] Cf. Professor Schelling, 'Jonson and the Classical School' (1898), who shows that his proportion of caesuraed verses is unusually large; and Jonson's remark ('A Fit of Rime against Rime', *Und.* xxix) that the modern languages, having to submit to rhymes, 'long since have refused other ceasure'.

Jonson's couplet-verse reflects his temperament too well to give him much chance of emulating the 'smoothness' of Waller. Its virtue lies not in music, but in its apt expression of the *ethos* of Jonson's character, his heroic ideal of manhood, his personal magnetism, his intellectual magnanimity.

But his lyrics have a higher virtue than this. Here his secure simplicity of style is wedded to a clear, succinct, and sometimes eloquent music; and both, if not inspired by passion, can convey it at moments with penetrating power. The divine unreason of the visionary or the prophet was not within Jonson's grasp. But his plain clear song, so classically rounded and complete, had scope and reach enough for imaginings which create out of the bones of antique traditions or forgotten folk-lore a population of splendid or awful shapes, such as animate *The Masque of Queens* or *The Golden Age Restored*; scope and reach, too, for the laconic grandeur of Epitaph, in the kind of which Callimachus and Landor are supreme masters,—monumental moments of poetry in which the vanished child or friend finds a human apotheosis, and where a fugitive sweetness comes out of the rugged strength of Ben.

INTRODUCTION TO
'THE ENGLISH GRAMMAR'

THE ENGLISH GRAMMAR

It is characteristic of Jonson, who had thought deeply on questions of style and language, that he turned his attention to grammar, and moreover to the grammar of his native tongue. Shirley and Milton, who composed Latin grammars, supply the nearest parallel among English men of letters. But Shirley's *The Way made plain to the Latin Tongue*, 1649, was the outcome of professional labours; he had been master of St. Albans Grammar School; and Milton's *Accedence Commenced Grammar*, 1669, with 'sufficient rules' for such as wanted to learn 'without more trouble than needs', was composed with an eye to his own pupils. Jonson voluntarily explored this by-path, into which his studies had conducted him. Once embarked upon it, he pursued the inquiry systematically. The version which has come down to us is a second attempt made late in life. It was printed, very incorrectly, in the Folio of 1640, with the title, *The English Grammar. Made by Ben. Iohnson. For the benefit of all Strangers, out of his observation of the English Language now spoken, and in use.*

Jonson had made an earlier attempt at a *Grammar*, but it perished in the fire of 1623. His ironic reference in the 'Execration upon Vulcan' to this work as designed

> To teach some that, their Nurses could not doe,
> The puritie of Language—[1]

shows that he did not write primarily to help foreigners. But in the extant version his tone is modest: 'it is the *lot* of my *age*, after thirty yeares conversation with men, to be *elementarius Senex*,' he writes.[2] In this touch of self-depreciation was he half-echoing Seneca's dictum?—'Turpis et ridicula res est elementarius senex; iuveni parandum, seni utendum est.'[3] He confesses to doubts and difficulties which he feels he has inadequately solved, even after 'pain-

---
[1] *Underwoods*, xliii. 91, 92.   [2] Book I, ch. vi.   [3] *Epistles*, xxxvi. 4.

full churning'; and his devoted follower, James Howell, in his own *New English Grammar*, 1662, gives us an interesting glimpse of these perplexities: 'Mr. Ben. *Johnson* a great Wit, who was as *patient* as he was *elaborat* in his re-serches and compositions, as he was framing an English *Syntaxis*, confess'd the further he proceeded, the more he was puzzled.'[1]

For part of the work he drew freely on earlier authorities, and we know, again from James Howell, that his library included a collection of grammars of various languages: Howell supplemented these with a Welsh grammar.[2] Jonson's chief predecessors were Sir Thomas Smith, whose *De recta & emendata Linguæ Anglicæ Scriptione, Dialogus* was published by Robert Estienne at Paris in 1568; John Hart, in *A Methode or comfortable beginning for all vnlearned*, published in 1570; Richard Mulcaster, in *The First Part of the Elementarie which entreateth chefelie of the right writing of our English tung*, printed by T. Vautroullier in 1582; William Bullokar, in *Bref Grammar for English*, 1586; P. Gr., conjectured to be P. Greenwood, in *The English Grammar called Grammatica Anglicana, a little epitome written according to the rules of art*, published at Cambridge in 1594; Alexander Gill, in *Logonomia Anglica, Qua Gentis Sermo facilius addiscitur*, printed by John Beale in 1619, and reissued in 1621 in a 'Secunda editio, paulo correctior, sed ad vsum communem accommodatior'; Charles Butler, in *The English Grammar, Or The Institution of Letters, Syllables, and Words, in the English Tongue*, published at Oxford in 1633; and to those may be added Simon Daines, schoolmaster of Hintlesham in Suffolk, in *Orthoepia Anglicana: Or, The First Principall Part of the English Grammar: Teaching The Art of right speaking and pronouncing English, With certaine exact rules of Orthography, and rules of spelling or combining of Syllables, and directions*

---

[1] Page 80; there is a similar statement in the address 'To the Reader', but this is vaguer, without the reference to the syntax. Compare Jonson's own statement in Book I, ch. xviii.

[2] See Appendix IV in vol. i, pp. 258-60, and the list of Jonson's grammars, ibid. p. 271.

for keeping of stops or points between sentence and sentence, which was 'Printed by Robert Young and Richard Badger, for the Company of Stationers, Anno Domini 1640' before the Jonson Folio containing the *Grammar* appeared. In the Commendatory verses 'T. B. Esquire' writes:

> *I've often heard an English Grammars name,*
> *That Forreign Countries might no more defame*
> *Our Tongue for being irregular; but till now*
> *Could never come to see one part: which thou*
> *Hast happily perform'd.* Ben Johnson *rail'd*
> *On* Vulcans *fury that had his entail'd.*

In addition to these more comprehensive studies there were limited works such as John Mercat's *A little brief of a sheet of paper, named a plain methode for speedy learning to reade,* Robert Robinson's *The Art of Pronunciation,* 1617, and *A Consolation for our Grammar Schools,* 1622.

Among the Sloane Manuscripts of the British Museum is a letter by John Webb to Jonson in 1628 on the subject,[1] an apologia for his 'little booke called, Entheatus Materialis primus', addressing Jonson as 'Dear Brother', and 'eldest sonne of our Brittaine muses', and stating 'Within ye circuite of my best acquaintance I find none of Apollo's Judges to grace more ye seate of his Justice either with gravity of person; multiplicitie of reading, or depht[2] of understanding, than you doe'. Unfortunately a letter of Jonson's replying to this effusion, which Webb evidently meant to publish, is lost.

One foreign authority counted for much with Jonson, Pierre de la Ramée. *P. Rami Grammatica. Parisiis, Apud Andream Wechelum, sub pegaso, in vico Bellovaco. Anno Salutis 1572* is a constant stand-by. Jonson also made some use of *P. Rami Scholae in Liberales Artes* (Basel, 1578), and J. C. Scaliger's *De Causis Linguae Latinae Libri Tredecim* (Lyon, 1540). In some points these authors proved dangerous guides.

Of the English authorities he used, and freely acknow-

---

[1] Sloane MS. 1466, folios 203–10.   [2] So in the manuscript.

ledged by reference and quotation, Sir Thomas Smith's work on the correct pronunciation of English. He used, equally freely, and without a word of acknowledgement, Mulcaster's *Elementarie*: his refusal to notice this native source of help is puzzling, when quotations from Smith and de la Ramée are given broadcast in his notes.

1. *Etymology and Syntax*

Jonson divides his grammar into two sections—etymology, which includes orthography as well as accidence, and secondly syntax. Most of the former is borrowed or adapted; the latter is mainly independent work, with slight help from de la Ramée. Full illustrations of Jonson's indebtedness must be reserved for the commentary; an example may be noted here. In describing the letter *r* Jonson deserts his usual authority, Smith, and writes:

> *R* is the *Dogs* Letter, and hurreth in the sound; the tongue striking the inner palate, with a trembling about the teeth. It is sounded firme in the beginning of the words, and more *liquid* in the middle, and ends: as in *rarer. riper*. And so in the *Latine*.

Yes, and so in the Latin of de la Ramée, who supplied Jonson with the illustrations he quotes from Terentianus Maurus, Persius, and Dionysius, and who describes the letter thus: 'R, mediocri sono, lingua interius palatum feriente, & circa dentes tremula, susurrat,' and 'literæ huius sonum firmiorem initio dictionis facimus, liquidiorem in medio & fine'. This borrowing illustrates two features of Jonson's work: first, his attention to phonetics, crude and elementary though his exposition of them may be. He is the first English grammarian who attempts to carry out this principle consistently. Secondly, the passage reveals the main weakness of this section of Jonson's *Grammar*. He had a fixed idea that the exposition of English usages must not only be illustrated from Latin, but must be based upon it: so he pressed home any and every analogy. It is noteworthy that he found this close parallel between the trilled *r* of the

Latins and of the Elizabethans, for there is some evidence that the sound of *r* was weakening in Jonson's day.[1] Yet he would hardly have written as he did if the statement had no foundation in contemporary use. But this type of comparison was an obsession with Jonson.

He has a curious theory about the subjunctive mood (II, ch. v). He appears to think that in the sentences 'It is preposterous to execute a man, before he have been condemned', 'Forsake sinne, ere sinne you forsake', 'Although a man be wise himselve', the verbs 'have', 'forsake', and 'be' are plural forms; he groups them with the use of a plural verb after a collective form. He did not know— probably no grammarian of that time could have known— that the form 'forsake', without inflexional *s* or *th*, for the second and third person singular of the present subjunctive, goes back to an Old English subjunctive. We should have expected that Greek and Latin usage would have led him to postulate a similar distinction between indicative and subjunctive in English too, but he ignores mood altogether both in the accidence and the syntax.

On the other hand, his scheme for the classification of verbs (I, ch. xvii–ch. xx) is, for the time at which he wrote, something of an achievement. It was drawn up in an age which had made no scientific study of comparative grammar, and he claims originality for it in the striking paragraph prefixed to his chapter on the second conjugation. He even invites criticism for it, 'hoping that I shall be thought sufficiently to have done my part, if in towling this Bell, I may draw others to a deeper consideration of the matter'.

Jonson in our day would have been a spelling reformer, within sober limits. The problem of securing an exact correspondence between the spoken and the written word

---

[1] See H. C. Wyld, *A History of Modern Colloquial English*, pp. 298–300. But Howell in his *New English Grammar*, 1662, p. 30, says, 'This letter sounds of a Dogs nostrill. The *French* women do oftentimes out of wantonnes leave it unpronounc'd at the end of words. In *English* tis pronounc'd as in other languages.'

exercised our early grammarians. By means of phonetic alphabets, by reviving obsolete letters, by inventing new ones, or by a lavish use of diacritical marks, they sought to teach the learner and succeeded in bewildering him. Quite early there was an outcry against retaining unsounded or 'superfluous' letters. As early as 1569 John Hart led the attack in *An Orthographie, conteyning the due order and reason, howe to write or painte thimage of mannes voice, most like to the life or nature.* He works out a phonetic system of spelling, enumerating its advantages: 'we should not neede to vse aboue the two thirdes or three quarters at most, of the letters which we are nowe constreyned to vse',[1] if we would adopt his scheme. His fifth chapter sets out 'The number of consonantes and breathes, which we vse in our speach, with the leauing of superfluous letters, and receyuing of such other as we neede: with example of their right vse.' Thus he would use *k* for the hard *c*, and *c* for *ch*, have *g* always hard, and revive ȝ for the soft *g*; and he would write uniformly 'war', not 'warre'. The fifth chapter of *Bullokars Booke at large, for the Amendment of Orthographie for English speech*, 1580, 'sheweth the superfluous letters not sounded, the misplaced, and some sounded not written, and how abbreuiations are allowed'. Bullokar had an elaborate system, but it included simple changes, such as the omission of *a* in 'heaven' and 'earth', of *g* in 'might', and *b* in 'doubt'. Mulcaster, two years later, was more conservative, but he proposed, for instance, to omit the *u* in 'guise', 'guide', 'guest', and 'beguile'. Jonson has similar criticisms, but no desire to push reform: '*C* is a letter, which our Fore-fathers might very well have spar'd in our tongue: but since it hath obtained place, both in our Writing, and Language, we are not now to quarrell *Orthographie*, or *Custome*; but to note the powers' (p. 43).[2] Custom—that is the determining factor. He was too sound a critic to fly

---

[1] Folio 5.
[2] References are to the pages of the text in the 1640 Folio.

in the face of it. 'Consuetudo', he quotes on his title-page from Quintilian, 'certissima loquendi magistra, utendumque plane sermone ut nummo cui publica forma est.'[1] He accepts that test even when he is dissatisfied with it. 'Mickle', 'pickle', 'trickle', 'sickle', would be 'better written without the *c.* if that which wee have received for *Orthographie*, would yet be contented to be altered. But that is an *emendation*, rather to be wished, then hoped for, after so long a raigne of *ill-custome* amongst us' (p. 44). '*Gh* is only a piece of ill writing with us : if we could obtaine of *Custome* to mend it, it were not the worse for our Language, or us: for the *g.* sounds just nothing in *trough, cough, might, night,* &c. Only, the writer was at leisure, to adde a superfluous Letter, as there are too many in our *Pseudographie*' (p. 51). *Th* with its 'double, and doubtfull sound' he regards as 'the greatest difficultie of our *Alphabet*, and true writing : since wee have lost the Saxon Characters ð and þ. . . .' But he makes no proposal to revive them. He is explicit on the point in discussing the plural suffix *en*, as in 'loven' and 'sayen', which lasted 'till about the reigne of King *Henry* the eighth. . . . But now (whatsoever is the cause) it hath quite growne out of use, and that other so generally prevailed, that I dare not presume to set this a-foot againe. Albeit, (to tell you my opinion) I am perswaded, that the lacke hereof well considered, will be found a great blemish to our tongue. For, seeing *time*, and *person* be, as it were, the right, and left hand of a *Verbe*; what can the mayming bring else, but a lamenesse to the whole body?'[2]

This freedom from pedantry is refreshing. It appears in another point. Jonson ends his chapter on the diphthongs (ch. v) by refusing to recognize triphthongs, though in chapter vi he so dubs 'yea', refusing, like Smith before him, to recognize the consonantal force of the *y*. 'The *Tripthong* is of a complexion, rather to be fear'd then lov'd : and would

---

[1] *Instit. Orat.* i. 6. 3. [2] Ch. xvi, p. 62.

fright the young *Grammarian* to see him. I therefore let him passe.'[1]

These faint gleams of humour flicker through the pages of the early grammars. Mulcaster writes that ' Z, is a consonant much heard amongst vs, and seldom sene. I think by reason it is not so redie to the pen as s, is, which is becom lieutenant generall to z, as gàse, amàse, ràsur, wher z, is heard, but, s, sene. It is not lightlie expressed in English, sauing in foren enfranchisments' (*Elementarie*, p. 123). And here is Sir Thomas Smith's sustained onslaught on *q*: ' Quid sibi velit hæc litera non possum intelligere: nam si accipimus *k* pro illo sono, qui adiunctus *a*, *ka* facit, & *u*, *ku*, quid agit, aut cui officio seruiet *q*? Si princeps essem Grammaticorum, ita vt leges æternas, & per omnem hunc Romanorum & Germanorum orbem valituras, ferendi haberem authoritatem, vt mendicam, supposititiam, & nulla necessitate veræ literæ locum iniuriosè occupantem expellerem, & longè hinc exulare iuberem: vt Sara facit Agar & Ismaelem, Isaacus postquam cœpit in robur crescere. Verè seruilis est *q*. manca & decrepita, & sine *u* tanquam bacillo nihil potest, et cum *u* nihil valet amplius quàm *k*.' (*De recta*, &c., p. 29). Jonson's resetting may be given as a pendant:—' Q is a Letter we might very well spare in our *Alphabet*, if we would but use the serviceable *k*. as he should be, and restore him to the right of reputation, he had with our Fore-fathers. For, the *English-Saxons* knew not this halting *Q*. with her waiting-woman *u*. after her, but exprest *quaile*, by *kuaile*.... Till *custome* under the excuse of expressing enfranchised words with us, intreated her into our Language, in *quality*, *quantity*, ... &c. And hath now given her the best of *k*^{s}. possessions.'

2. *The Text of 1692*

In 1692 Jonson's *Grammar* was carefully revised by some unknown authority, brought up to date, and—without any hint of the numerous changes which the text had under-

[1] But it is proper to note that Jonson had no clear idea of the diphthong; he confuses it with the digraph.

gone—inserted in the one-volume folio of Jonson's *Works*, issued in that year. Whalley in 1756, and Gifford in 1816, reprinted this transformed text in the belief that it reproduced the original text of 1640. Francis Cunningham, in the process of revising Gifford's edition for the Chiswick Press reissue of 1875, collated it with the text of 1640 and found out the discrepancies, but he credited Gifford with making the alterations himself. The confusion caused by this ignorance of the text of 1692 continues to this day. The only modern edition of the *Grammar*, that of Miss A. V. Waite in 1909, shows no knowledge of this phase of its history; and Sir Sidney Lee relies on a chapter as it was rewritten at the close of the seventeenth century, to prove, in the teeth of Elizabethan texts and Elizabethan printers, that the principles of punctuation in Jonson's day were essentially the same as they are in ours.[1]

The extent of the revision can only be shown by a full collation, which will be given in the text. The guiding principle of the reviser was to leave nothing which clashed with contemporary usage in 1692. He cut out obsolete spellings and words which would interfere with clearness of illustration. Thus in the examples of *o* 'in the long time' sounding 'sharp, and high', he omitted 'throte' (p. 39), because he spelt the word 'throat' with an additional vowel. When he feels that correction is needed, he rewrites. Jonson, discussing the conjugation of verbs (ch. xviii), classifies them according to vowel-changes; after instancing the changes of *i* into *a* and *o* (as in 'give' and 'win'), the 1640 text continues:

    Secondly, long *i*. into *e*.
    Pr. *reede*.
    Pa. *read*.
    Par. pa. *read*.

[1] *The Year's Work in English Studies, 1919-20*, pp. 66, 67; *Life of William Shakespeare*, 1922, preface, section 4. Sir Sidney's survey of the question is hasty and perfunctory; for example, he is ignorant of Mulcaster. An answer to his criticisms appears in the *Proceedings and Papers of the Oxford Bibliographical Society*, vol. i, part i, pp. 33-41.

'Long i' is a misprint for 'long e', and the spelling 'reede' was obsolete in 1692. The reviser substitutes—
    Secondly, *Verbs* that have *ee*, lose one; as,
        Pr. *Feed.*
        Past. *Fed.*
        Par. pa. *Fed.*

Similarly he modernizes in the text the spellings 'dipthong' 'syllabe', 'tyran', to 'diphthong', 'syllable', 'tyrant'. He omits obsolete or difficult words used in the examples. The first word to illustrate the 'Italian' sound of *g* in *gu* is 'guin' (p. 44): it is really 'Gwin', the proper name, which Jonson took over from Mulcaster. The reviser naturally failed to understand it, and omitted it. Similarly he dropped 'meece' and 'leece', the obsolete plurals of 'mouse' and 'louse' (p. 60).

He made many insertions. Sometimes they are slight, as when Jonson speaks of the use of *z* in 'indenison'd' words (p. 48), the reviser writes 'indenison'd, *i.e.* derived from the *Greek*, and commonly us'd as *English*'. More frequently the insertions aim at greater clearness. Jonson describes the 'weak' and 'hissing' sound of *c* before *e* and *i*, as in 'certain', and adds: 'Or, before the *Dipthongs*: as in *cease. deceive*' (p. 43). The reviser writes 'before *Diphthongs*, whose first *Vowel* is *e* or *i*', and adds 'ceiling' as a new illustration. Elsewhere, he deliberately corrects the text: when Jonson writes that 'rustick people' say '*zed, zay. zit. zo. zome*' for 'said', &c. (p. 48),—a pronunciation he had used for his own Middlesex clowns in *A Tale of a Tub*,—the reviser limits this use to 'West-Country People'. And similarly, when Jonson makes two declensions of nouns according as they form their plural in *s* or *n*, and concludes (p. 60), 'Some Nounes have the plurall of both Declensions:
as   *House. houses. housen.*
        Eye. eyes. eyen.
        Shoo. shooes. shooen.'
the reviser again limits the use to '*Nouns* (according to the different Dialects of several Parts of the Country).' The

The English Grammar 427

accounts of *z* and *h* are carefully retouched. Of *z* the 1640 text gives the following account (p. 48): 'Z, is a Letter often heard amongst us, but seldome seene: borrow'd of the *Greekes* at first, being the same with *ζ*. and soundeth a double *ss*. With us it hath obtained another sound; but in the end of words: as

Muse. maze. nose.
Hose. gaze. as.'

For the last sentence, the reviser substitutes 'tho' in the end of many *English* words (where 'tis only properly used) it seems to sound as *s*; as in *maze, gaze*; And on the contrary, words writ with *s* sound like *z*; as *Muse, nose, hose, as*'. In the account of *h*, the 1640 text has a glaring error, which pulled up the reviser—the remark about the phonetic value of *h* after *x*. The letter should be the Greek ρ, which the printer confused with the *x* of the English script written with a descending stroke curving sharply to the right. The reviser did not realize what had happened, but he saw that the text was nonsense; and in his rewriting he reintroduced *rh* in Greek derivatives. This is the 1640 text: 'Whether it be a Letter or no, hath beene much examined by the Ancients, and by some, too much, of the *Greeke* partie condemned, and throwne out of the *Alphabet*, as an *Aspirate* meerely, and in request only before *Vowells* in the beginning of words, and after *x*. where it added a strong spirit, which the *Welsh* retaine after many *Consonants*. But, be it a Letter, or Spirit, we have great use of it in our tongue, both before, and after *Vowells*. And though I dare not say, she is, (as I have heard one call her), the *Queene mother of Consonants*; yet she is the life, and quickening of them.' The 1692 text concludes the first sentence at 'the beginning of words', and continues 'The *Welsh* retain it still after many *Consonants*'. The concluding words run: 'Yet she is the life, and quickening of *c, g, p, s, t, w*; as also *r* when derived from the aspirate Greek *ῥ*; as *Cheat, Ghost, Alphabet, shape, that, what, Rhapsody*.'

Occasionally the corrections extend even to style. Jonson describes the *ll* of 'hell' or 'hill' as rare, 'but where the *Vowell* sounds hard upon it. ... And, even in these it is rather the haste, and superfluitie of the pen, that cannot stop it selfe upon the single *l.* then any necessitie we have to use it' (p. 47). The reviser repressed this whimsical flight of fancy as unbecoming in a grammarian : ' It 's always doubled, at the end of words of one Syllable ; . . . And, even in these Custom rather than Necessity obliges us to use a Double *l.*'

3. *Apostrophe and Elision*

Two subsidiary points which Jonson included in his treatment of syntax, apostrophe and punctuation, call for some notice because of their bearing on his own text and on Elizabethan writing generally.

Unfortunately the chapter '*Of Apostrophus*' (II, ch. i) is full of printers' errors, and most of the illustrative quotations contradict or stultify the text. In the first group of examples showing how a final vowel 'may be cast away', the printer retains it, giving 'ye' utter', 'thou' art', 'to' awake' with the vowels unelided. The last sentence of the chapter should have been printed in italic as a prose illustration to supplement the verse example from Gower with the elision ' privy to' t ' instead of ' privy to it '. By an appropriate irony Jonson's complaint that the mark of elision is ' many times . . . quite omitted ' ' through the negligence of Writers and Printers ' is amply confirmed by the printer's treatment of the immediate context.

Jonson distinguished two kinds of elision, ' the rejecting of a Vowell from the beginning, or ending of a Word '. The second class is exemplified in ' Th' outward man ' and ' is common with the *Greekes* '. The first is, he thinks, peculiar to English [1] and 'not usually express'd in writing or printing ', though ' in our common speech, nothing is more familiar : ' for example, ' there 's ' and ' to 't '. He states that this

---

[1] Jonson overlooked the reversed elision in Greek poetry of ἐγὼ 'δόκουν, λοισθία 'γώ.

elision takes place both after vowels and after consonants, but he forgot to add instances of elision after consonants, such as 'on't' and 'in't', which he used frequently himself. He also ignores the elision of consonants in such common examples as 'i' the', 'o' the' (or 'i' th'', 'o' th''), which contemporary writers and printers did not fail to indicate.

These positive statements are important in view of the doubts which have been cast on the correctness of the apostrophe in Elizabethan texts. It has even been suggested that this mark of punctuation is a form of shorthand, a scribe's convention: the Elizabethans wrote 'I'm sure on't', but they said 'I am sure of it',[1] and even though they saw these clipped forms written and printed they resisted the temptation to shorten them in pronunciation.

Jonson explicitly states the contrary. And when he himself wrote—

Two kindes of valour he doth shew, at ones;
Actiue in 's braine, and passiue in his bones.
Epigram lxviii (Folio, 1616, p. 787).

he certainly did not mean us to rattle off the second line in the form 'Active in his brain and passive in his bones'; or to convert the grave movement of the lines in *Catiline*,

Let 'hem call it mischiefe;
When it is past, and prosper'd, 'twill be vertue.
Th' are petty crimes are punish'd, great rewarded.
(Ibid. p. 718.)

to a loose rhythm more in the manner of Fletcher—

When it is past and prosper'd, it will be virtue;
They are petty crimes are punish'd, great rewarded.

But even in the text of the 1616 Folio peculiar rhythms caused by Jonson's use of elision are frequent. The result is more like assimilation than elision. What are we to say to such lines as the following, all of which are found in the opening pages of *The Alchemist*?

[1] See M. A. Bayfield, *Shakespeare's Versification*, especially the postscript on pages 244–313, in which he subjects the contracted forms of the 1616 Folio text of *Sejanus* to a close scrutiny.

Do you flie out, i' the *proiection*? (I. i. 79.)
For ne're a snarling dog-bolt o' you both. (Ibid. 121.)
Hee'll send such word, for ayring o' the house.
(Ibid. 186.)
Will take his oath, o' the *greeke* XENOPHON. (I. ii. 56.)
Hee'll winne vp all the money i' the towne. (Ibid. 77.)

These cannot be regarded as printers' errors; they occur too frequently for that in a text which underwent Jonson's personal supervision in the press. And the theory that the marks of elision are fictitious, that Jonson wrote 'i'' but pronounced 'in', is equally inadmissible in so exact and scrupulous a writer.[1] The explanation is given by Jonson himself in the last paragraph of this section of the *Grammar*. He is 'following Natures call' in using these elisions, 'considering that in our common speech, nothing is more familiar', although 'it bee not of any, that I know, either in Writing or Printing, usually express'd'. Such words must refer to a marked peculiarity. And the peculiarity is Jonson's use of these light syllables at points normally stressed in the scansion.

We may differentiate from normal elision another usage of Jonson's. He sometimes has apostrophe without elision.

If he be' at his booke, disturbe him not. BRA. Well sir.
E. M. I. H. I. i. 5.

Before our hands be' at worke. I can accuse . . .
Catiline, III. 587.
the same
They should for vertu' haue done, they'll doe for shame.
E. M. I. H. I. ii (ad fin.).

Ah, but what miserie' is it, to know this?
Ibid. II. iii. 69.

---

[1] Mr. Bayfield even credits him in the spelling 'tâne' with putting in the circumflex accent to 'indicate that what he wrote was merely a contraction of a word that was to be pronounced in full, "taken"' (*Shakespeare's Versification*, p. 302).

>   . . . we are mortall;
> And can but deedes of men: 'twere glory' inough,
> Could we be truely a prince.   *Sejanus*, I. 487-9.

Jonson used this device of the apostrophe between two unelided words to mark a kind of diphthong having the metrical value of one syllable.[1] His printers sometimes boggled at it. Thus the fourth example quoted above appears in the 1640 Folio as

> Ah, but what mis'rie is it, to know this?

And in *Sejanus*, v. 459, the Quarto of 1605 prints

> To beare thy'obsequious fatnesse, like thy *Peeres*.

but the Folio of 1616 has

> To beare thy obsequious fatnesse, like thy peeres.

Here it is clear that the later printer omitted the apostrophe, and that Jonson in reading the proofs overlooked the omission.

4. *Punctuation*.

The last chapter of the *Grammar* deals succinctly with punctuation, or, as Jonson, following Mulcaster and the Latin grammarians, calls it, 'the Distinction of Sentences'. The greater part of the chapter from the second paragraph to the definition of the 'period' is a close rendering from de la Ramée's *Grammatica*, 1572, iii, ch. 18, 'De Prosodia and orthographia orationis'. Jonson adds notes of interrogation and admiration, and sums up with a concluding comment, in which he notices the 'neglect' of the semicolon[2] in the lightly stopped sentences fashionable in his day. The semicolon is not recognized by Mulcaster and Hart; according to Ames,[3] it was introduced into England in 1569, but began to be used about 1580. When once it

---

[1] So did Donne. Compare with the preceding list, 'Like one who' in her third widdowhood doth professe' (*Poems*, ed. Grierson, i. 185), 'Betroth'd to no'one Art, be no' adulterie' (ibid.), 'Here's no more newes then vertue', I may as well' (ibid. 187), 'The story of beauty', in Twicknam is, and you' (ib. 193).

[2] Jonson calls this stop 'sub-distinction,' copying de la Ramée's 'ὑποστιγμή vel subdistinctio.'

[3] *Typographical Antiquities*, pp. 782, 858.

came into regular use, it brought a new element into punctuation. Comma, colon, and period were three defined time-values, invented, as Jonson says, 'as well for the speakers ease, as for the plainer deliverance of the things spoken'. The semicolon, bringing in a finer grading of the stops, started the logical system in use at the present day. It is characteristic of Jonson that he used it freely. Indeed his elaborate and overloaded system was ultra-logical. The actor who attempted to observe it faithfully in the plays would have been perpetually marking time. Mosca's eulogy on the parasite in *Volpone*, III. i, is an excellent example:

> O! Your Parasite
> Is a most precious thing, dropt from aboue,
> Not bred 'mong'st clods, and clot-poules, here on earth.
> I muse, the mysterie was not made a science,
> It is so liberally profest! almost 5
> All the wise world is little else, in nature,
> But Parasites, or Sub-parasites. And, yet,
> I meane not those, that haue your bare towne-arte,
> To know, who's fit to feede 'hem; haue no house,
> No family, no care, and therefore mould 10
> Tales for mens eares, to bait that sense; or get
> Kitchin-inuention, and some stale receipts
> To please the belly and the groine; nor those,
> With their court-dog-tricks, that can fawne, and fleere,
> Make their reuennue out of legs, and faces, 15
> Eccho my-Lord, and lick away a moath:
> But your fine, elegant rascall, that can rise,
> And stoope (almost together) like an arrow;
> Shoot through the aire, as nimbly as a starre;
> Turne short, as doth a swallow; and be here, 20
> And there, and here, and yonder, all at once;
> Present to any humour, all occasion;
> And change a visor, swifter, then a thought!
> This is the creature, had the art borne with him;
> Toiles not to learne it, but doth practise it 25
> Out of most excellent nature: and such sparkes,
> Are the true Parasites, others but their *Zani"s*.

Stops were invented, says Jonson, as a 'meanes, whereby men pausing a pretty while, the whole speech might never the worse be understood'. A minute examination of the words just quoted will show what he meant and how he applied his principles. The shades of distinction that lurk in pairs of words are indicated by using a comma with the first of the pair: as 'clods, and clot-poules' (l. 3), 'the belly, and the groine' (l. 13), 'fawne, and fleere' (l. 14), 'legs, and faces' (l. 15). Commas are used to give clearer definition or to mark off a qualifying phrase: as 'in nature' (l. 6), 'yet' (l. 7), 'Parasites, or Sub-parasites' (ibid.). But where there is a sharp antithesis, as in 'rise, And stoope' (ll. 17, 18), the qualifying phrase '(almost together)' is raised to the dignity of parenthesis. Commas again give emphasis to 'swifter' (l. 23) and 'sparkes' (l. 26).

These subtleties, it may be noted, are essentially points that meet the eye on the printed page; and it is suggestive that Bacon in the *Essays* of 1625 uses the same complicated system. The following passage from the opening essay, 'Of Truth' (pp. 3, 4), is a good example of the minute care which Bacon bestowed upon this feature of his text:

> The first Creature of God, in the workes of the Dayes, was the Light of the Sense; The last, was the Light of Reason; And his Sabbath Worke, euer since, is the Illumination of his Spirit. First he breathed Light, vpon the Face, of the Matter or Chaos; Then he breathed Light, into the Face of Man; and still he breatheth and inspireth Light, into the Face of his Chosen. The Poet, that beautified the Sect, that was otherwise inferiour to the rest, saith yet excellently well: *It is a pleasure to stand vpon the shore, and to see ships tost vpon the Sea: A pleasure to stand in the window of a Castle, and to see a Battaile, and the Aduentures thereof, below: But no pleasure is comparable, to the standing, vpon the vantage ground of Truth:* (A hill not to be commanded, and where the Ayre is alwaies cleare and serene;) *And to see the Errours and Wandrings, and Mists, and Tempests, in the vale below:* So alwaies, that this prospect, be with Pitty, and not with Swelling, or Pride. Certainly, it is Heauen vpon Earth, to haue a Mans Mind Moue in Charitie, Rest in Prouidence, and Turne vpon the Poles of *Truth*.

To get a clear view of the normal usage of contemporaries

we may set over against the passage from *Volpone* an extract from one of the 'good' Shakespeare quartos—that is to say, quartos in which the text is essentially sound and may be, probably is, printed from Shakespeare's autograph. In the first quarto of *Much Ado about Nothing* the following passage (III. iv. 65-84) is found on signature F 2 :

> *Mar.* Get you some of this distill'd *carduus benedictus*, and lay it to your heart, it is the onely thing for a qualme.
> *Hero.* There thou prickst her with a thissel.
> *Beat. Benedictus*, why *benedictus*? you haue some moral
> 5 in this *benedictus*.
> *Mar.* Morall? no by my troth I haue no morall meaning, I meant plaine holy thissel, you may thinke perchaunce that I think you are in loue, nay birlady I am not such a foole to think what I list, nor I list not to
> 10 thinke what I can, nor indeed I can not think, if I would thinke my heart out of thinking, that you are in loue, or that you will be in loue, or that you can be in loue : yet Benedicke was such another, and now he is become a man, he swore he would neuer marry, and yet now in dispight
> 15 of his heart he eates his meate without grudging, and how you may be conuerted I know not, but me thinkes you looke with your eies as other women do.
> *Beat.* What pace is this that thy tongue keepes?
> *Marg.* Not a false gallop.   *Enter Vrsula.*

Shakespeare's passage is expressly indicated in the concluding words as one designed for rapid delivery, and this is attained by its light stopping. It is a text for an actor, with only one well-defined and very emphatic pause at the crucial word 'love' in l. 12. Repunctuate it so as to bring it into line with the speech from *Volpone*, and the dramatic life and movement would evaporate from it. And this chiefly by the use of the semicolon, a stop which, Jonson says, was 'commonly neglected' in his day.

The chief authority for Elizabethan punctuation is Mulcaster in the twenty-first chapter of his *Elementarie* (1582, pp. 148-53). He defines the object of all his stops—his full list is ' *Comma, Colon, Period, Parenthesis, Interrogation, long time, shorte time, sharp accent, flat accent, streight accent*, *the seuerer* ' (i. e. diaeresis), '*the vniter* ' (i. e. hyphen for compound words), and '*the breaker* ' (i. e. the double hyphen to mark the division of syllables at the end of a line)—to be 'right and tunable vttering', not logical sequence or grammatical form. It is suggestive that in this section of his subject Jonson deserted Mulcaster and turned to de la Ramée.

INTRODUCTION TO
'THE DISCOVERIES'

THE DISCOVERIES

JONSON left behind him in manuscript a miscellaneous collection of notes, jottings, and miniature essays which were published in the 1640 Folio without any attempt to sort them out or group them. Commonplace books were a fashion in the seventeenth century, and a student turned them to good account. '*Adventure not all thy learning*', wrote Thomas Fuller, '*in one bottom, but divide it betwixt thy Memory and thy Note-books.* He that with Bias carries all his learning about him in his head will utterly be beggerd and bankrupt, if a violent disease, a mercilesse thief, should rob and strip him. I know some have a Common-place against Common-place-books, and yet perchance will privately make use of what publickly they declaim against. A Common-place-book contains many Notions in garison, whence the owner may draw out an army into the field on competent warning.'[1] The principle could hardly be better stated, and as a signal example of the practice we have Isaac Walton's record of Donne, that 'he left the resultance of 1400. Authors, most of them analyzed with his owne hand'.[2] Jonson must have been equally systematic, for there perished in the fire of 1623

> twice-twelve-yeares stor'd up humanitie,
> With humble Gleanings in Divinitie,

as he tells us himself in the 'Execration upon Vulcan'.[3] There is the corroborative testimony of Lord Falkland in *Jonsonus Virbius* (1638, p. 4):

> His *Learning* such, no *Author* old nor new,
> Escapt his reading that deserv'd his view,
> And such his *Iudgement,* so exact his *Test,*
> Of what was best in *Bookes,* as what *bookes* best,

---

[1] *The Holy State,* 1642, III. x, pp. 175–6.
[2] Life of Donne prefixed to the *LXXX Sermons,* 1640, sig. B 4 verso.
[3] *Underwoods,* xliii. 101, 102.

> That had he joyn'd those notes his Labours tooke,
> From each most prais'd and praise-deserving *Booke*,
> And could the world of that choise *Treasure* boast,
> It need not care though all the rest were lost:
> And such his Wit, He writ past what he quotes,
> And his *Productions* farre exceed his *Notes*.

Evidently the losses of the fire had been made good in Jonson's later years when Falkland knew him.

Before he died Jonson had planned to publish a selection from his note-books. In the 1640 Folio the collection is entitled *Timber: or, Discoveries; Made vpon Men and Matter: As they have flow'd out of his daily Readings; or had their refluxe to his peculiar Notion of the Times. By Ben: Iohnson. Tecum habita, ut noris quam sit tibi curta supellex. Pers. sat. 4. London, Printed M. DC. XLI.* This title must, substantially at least,[1] be Jonson's own. The explanatory description and the motto from Persius, 'Live at home in order to realize how scanty is your stock of furniture', are decisive on that point. The text is headed 'Explorata: or Discoveries', and the running-title is 'Discoveries'. In this alternative title Jonson was recalling the Senecan motto 'Tanquam explorator' which he inscribed on the books of his library.[2]

The signs of editorial preparation are evident in the care with which the selected extracts are translated, abridged, or adapted. After commenting on the vice of diffuseness—'a briefnesse of the parts sometimes, that makes the whole long,' —Jonson gives an example, and adds, 'This is the fault of some Latine Writers, within these last hundred years, of my reading, and perhaps *Seneca* may be appeacht of it; I accuse him not' (p. 123).[3] No, but it is instructive to watch that skilful hand pruning the redundancy. Seneca poses the question, 'Are we bound to be grateful to one who benefits us

---

[1] Professor Castelain in his valuable edition conjectures that *Timber* is a deliberate alteration of the editor to connect the title with those of *The Forest* and the *Underwoods*. The point will be discussed in the introduction to the text.

[2] See vol. i, Appendix I, p. 180, and Appendix IV, p. 261.

[3] References are to the paging of the 1640 Folio.

either unintentionally or ignorantly?' The case is stated with point, certainly, but also with some diffuseness: 'Et haec quaestio facile expedietur et si qua similis huic moveri potest si totiens illo cogitationem nostram converterimus beneficium nullum esse nisi quod ad nos primum aliqua cogitatio defert, deinde amica et benigna. Itaque nec fluminibus gratias agimus, quamvis aut magna navigia patiantur et ad subvehendas copias largo et perenni alveo currant aut piscosa et amoena pinguibus arvis interfluant. Nec quisquam Nilo beneficium debere se iudicat non magis quam odium si inmodicus superfluxit tardeque decessit. Nec ventus beneficium dat licet lenis et secundus aspiret, nec utilis et salubris cibus: nam qui beneficium mihi daturus est debet non tantum prodesse sed velle. Ideo nec mutis animalibus quicquam debetur: et quam multos e periculo velocitas equi rapuit? Nec arboribus: et quam multos aestu laborantes ramorum opacitas texit?' (*De Beneficiis*, vi. 7). Jonson gets the gist of this passage without a superfluous word: 'Nothing is a courtesie, unlesse it be meant us; and that friendly, and lovingly. Wee owe no thankes to Rivers, that they carry our boats; or Winds, that they be favouring, and fill our sayles; or Meats, that they be nourishing. For these are, what they are *necessarily*. Horses carry us, Trees shade us; but they know it not' (p. 94). This is not the mere transcript of a note-taker: the passage has been weighed and analysed.

Some of these siftings of Jonson's notes are significantly couched in the first person. The opening paragraph in the text begins: 'Ill *Fortune* never crush't that man, whom good *Fortune* deceived not. I therefore have counselled my friends, never to trust to her fairer side.... He knowes not his own strength, that hath not met Adversity.' A characteristic pronouncement on the value of the 'rules' also begins: 'I take this labour in teaching others, that they should not be always to bee taught; and I would bring my Precepts into practise' (p. 116). Still clearer is the personal note in the passage of militant apologia on p. 125, where Jonson at first quietly defends general and anonymous satire against the rebuke of contemporaries who see in it an attack on individuals: 'Whilst I name no persons, but deride follies; why should any man confesse, or betray himselfe?... The Person offended hath no reason to bee offended with the writer, but with him selfe.' For a time Jonson puts himself in the place of the unfortunate victim and argues temperately and disinterestedly, as if he wished to save him, not only from his slanderers, but from himself. Then, suddenly losing all self-control, he rounds off the defence with this terrific onslaught: 'It sufficeth I know, what kinde of persons I displease, men bred in the declining, and decay of vertue, betroth'd to their owne vices; that have abandoned, or prostituted their good names; hungry and ambitious of infamy, invested in all deformity, enthrall'd to ignorance and malice, of a hidden and conceal'd malignitie, and that hold a concomitancy with all evill.'[1]

The most vivid passage of autobiography in the *Discoveries* has a curious history. With slight modifications it is a transcript from the elder Seneca.[2] Jonson thus descants on memory: '*Memory* of all the *powers* of the mind, is the most *delicate*, and *fraile*: it is the first of our *faculties*, that Age invades. *Seneca*, the father, the *Rhetorician*, confesseth of himselfe, hee had a miraculous one; not only to receive, but to hold. I my selfe could in my youth, have repeated all, that ever I had made; and so continued, till I was past fortie: Since, it is much decay'd in me. Yet I can repeate whole books that I have read, and *Poems*, of some selected friends, which I have lik'd to charge my memory with. It was wont to be faithfull to me, but shaken with *age* now, and *sloath* (which weakens the strongest abilities) it may performe somewhat, but cannot promise much. By exercise it is to be made better, and serviceable. Whatsoever I pawn'd with it, while I was young, and a boy, it offers me

[1] The passage in the main is taken, as Professor Castelain pointed out, from Erasmus, but these concluding sentences are Jonson's own.
[2] M. Annaeus Seneca, *Controversiae*, i, §§ 2, 5.

readily, and without stops: but what I trust to it now, or have done of later yeares, it layes up more negligently, and often times loses; so that I receive mine owne (though frequently call'd for) as if it were new, and borrow'd. Nor doe I alwayes find presently from it, what I doe seek; but while I am doing another thing, that I labour'd for, will come: And what I sought with trouble, will offer it selfe, when I am quiet' (p. 95). In this detailed analysis only the passage 'I my selfe could in my youth . . . charge my memory with' is original. A personal note sounds throughout, but it is the echo of another man's experience. 'Nam quaecumque apud illam (i. e. memoriam) aut puer aut iuvenis deposui quasi recentia aut modo audita sine cunctatione profert: at si qua illi intra proximos annos commisi sic perdidit et amisit ut etiamsi saepius ingerantur totiens tamen tanquam nova audiam . . . Non enim dum quaero aliquid invenio semper: saepe quod quaerenti non comparuit aliud agenti praesto est; quaedam vero quae obversantia mihi et ex aliqua parte se ostendentia non possum occupare, eadem securo et reposito animo subito emergunt.' The sentences are adroitly culled and reset, and there is a significant change. The elder Seneca cites as examples of his portentous memory that he once repeated in correct order a list of two thousand names which he heard read aloud and more than two hundred separate lines quoted by individuals at a lecture. For this Jonson substitutes books he has read and the poems of his friends. When he stayed with Drummond, he repeated to him passages from *The Shepheardes Calender*, Chapman's *Iliad*, and Donne's poems, and Wotton's lyric, 'How happy is he born or taught'.[1]

One other passage derived from the same source is avowedly reminiscence, and gives the impression of being autobiography. '*Ease*, and relaxation', writes Jonson, 'are profitable to all studies. The mind is like a Bow, the stronger by being unbent. But the temper in Spirits is all, when to command, a man's wit; when to favour it.' So

[1] *Conversations*, vii. 117-20, 123-5, 129-30.

much by way of introduction. Then Jonson sketches a portrait: 'I have knowne a man vehement on both sides; that knew no meane, either to intermit his studies, or call upon them againe. When hee hath set himselfe to writing, hee would joyne night to day; presse upon himselfe without release, not minding it, till hee fainted: and when hee left off, resolve himselfe into all sports, and loosenesse againe; that it was almost a despaire to draw him to his booke: But once got to it, hee grew stronger, and more earnest by the ease. His whole Powers were renew'd: he would worke out of himselfe, what hee desired; but with such excesse, as his study could not bee rul'd: hee knew not how to dispose his owne Abilities, or husband them, hee was of that immoderate power against himselfe' (pp. 100, 101). This is Marcus Seneca's sketch of his friend and fellow-rhetorician, Porcius Latro.[1] Even the detail of the fainting is borrowed: 'Gravius sibi instabat nec desinebat nisi defecerat.'

Are such passages autobiography or only make-believe— just a plausible resetting of the ideas of others to give them the tone and colour of reality? This, it might be urged, would after all fulfil the purpose set forth on the title-page, to print extracts from the author's stores of reading and to modernize them from contemporaries. But to suggest this is to misread Jonson's habit of mind. His contempt for shallow writing and his belief in 'fundamental brain-work' as essential if a poem of lasting merit was to be produced—

I, that spend halfe my nights, and all my dayes,
Here in a cell, to get a darke, pale face,
To come forth worth the iuy, or the bayes— [2]

made him a profound student of all the literature within his reach. Above all, he turned to classical antiquity in a spirit not of blind adoration, but of keen and critical inquiry. What had it to teach his age? In a passage borrowed from Vives, which is the clue to his own outlook, he wrote: 'I know *Nothing* can conduce more to letters, then to

---

[1] M. Seneca, *Controversiae*, i, Praef. 15, §§ 13–24.
[2] *Poetaster*, 'Apologetical Dialogue', ll. 221–3.

examine the writings of the *Ancients*, and not to rest in their sole Authority, or take all upon trust from them; provided the plagues of *Iudging*, and *Pronouncing* against them, be away. . . . For to all the observations of the *Ancients*, wee have our own experience: which, if wee will use, and apply, wee have better meanes to pronounce. It is true they open'd the gates, and made the way that went before us; but as Guides, not Commanders: *Non Domini nostri, sed Duces fuére*. Truth lyes open to all; it is no mans *severall'* (p. 89). This is an attitude of reasoned faith, not of false worship. Jonson looked at older literature with a watchful eye for any guidance it could still give the moderns. As might be expected, he was keen in detecting analogies. If he found himself in Seneca, he similarly found Shakespeare and Bacon. The famous reference to the need for the dragchain is directly quoted; the praise of Bacon's oratory is adapted.[1] To study the ancients critically, with a view to extracting from them anything that threw light on the life or art of his own day, was the guiding principle of Jonson's reading.

The quest of knowledge he held to be essential. Plato, not content with the learning of Athens, went to Italy, and even to Egypt: 'Hee labour'd, so must wee' (p. 117). And the labourer needed guidance. Jonson noted shrewdly the weakness of the self-taught man: 'For hee that was onely taught by himselfe, had a foole to his Master' (p. 87). That is not mere epigram. It is a record of his own hard experience when his step-father took him away from the fourth form at Westminster to make a bricklayer of him. No doubt, if all help had failed him, he would have struggled manfully to continue his education himself, but he actually continued it under the scholarly guidance of Camden.

We can even trace in the *Discoveries* some steps of the

[1] For Shakespeare, see *Disc*. pp. 97, 98, and M. Seneca, *Controv.* iv, Praef. 7; for Bacon, *Disc.* pp. 101-2, and M. Seneca, *Controv.* iii, §§ 2-4. The latter passage includes such comments as 'Nemo non illo dicente timebat ne desineret', and 'quamdiu extra iocos se continebat, censoria oratio erat'.

educative process. 'For a man to write well, there are required three Necessaries. To reade the best Authors, observe the best Speakers: and much exercise of his owne style' (p. 115). Elaborate directions how to form a good English style are taken literally from Quintilian;[1] but it is Quintilian tested by Jonson's own experience. 'No matter how slow the style be at first, so it be labour'd, and accurate.' 'Repeat often, what wee have formerly written.' The best writers passed through a stage of experiments: 'they impos'd upon themselves care, and industry. They did nothing rashly.' As we read, we seem to hear Jonson communicating to us the secret of his own strong, compact, and masculine writing, in verse as well as in prose.

He even drew up a scheme for training poets.[2] 'First, wee require in our *Poet*, or maker, ... a goodnes of naturall wit' (p. 126). The postulate is his own, and he recurs to it. 'To this perfection of Nature in our *Poet*, wee require Exercise of those parts, and frequent.' The poet must train himself and not be in a hurry. 'There is no Statute *Law* of the Kingdome bidds you bee a Poet, against your will; or the first Quarter. If it come, in a yeare, or two, it is well.' There is a 'third requisite'—'*Imitation*, to bee able to convert the substance, or Riches of an other *Poet*, to his owne use'. The novice is to go a long way in the copying of his model—'to follow him, till he grow very *Hee*: or, so like him, as the Copie may be mistaken for the Principall'. Not that he is to be the 'sedulous ape' of a later seeker after style: Jonson specially disclaims that. It is to be a kinship of the spirit, such as Jonson himself exhibits at moments in his own work: a picture of old Rome in *Sejanus* drawn as by a seventeenth-century Juvenal or Tacitus, or the epigram of Martial revived, or the lyric of the Greek anthology. There is a further stage for the young poet, on which Jonson

[1] *De Institutione Oratoria*, x. 3. 4, 5.
[2] It works out a hint from Sidney, that 'Arte, Imitation, and Exercise' are the 'three wings' of the Daedalus who is to guide the high-flying wit of the poet (*Apology*, ed. Gregory Smith, p. 195). And Sidney postulates genius as a starting-point.

insists with emphasis: 'But, that, which wee especially require in him, is an exactnesse of Studie, and multiplicity of reading, which maketh a full man, not alone enabling him to know the *History*, or Argument of a *Poeme*, and to report it: but so to master the matter, and Stile, as to shew, hee knowes, how to handle, place or dispose of either, with *elegancie*, when need shall bee.' And finally, there is the crowning gift of Art: 'For to Nature, Exercise, Imitation, and Studie, *Art* must be added, to make all these perfect.'

The main idea underlying these astonishing suggestions for the training of a poet had been expressed by Jonson earlier in the tribute to Shakespeare which he prefixed to the First Folio. In stately ceremonial verse he had hailed Shakespeare as the 'Soule of the Age':

> Nature her selfe was proud of his designes,
> And ioy'd to weare the dressing of his lines!

Compared with him Aristophanes, Terence, and Plautus were antiquated.

> Yet must I not giue Nature all: Thy Art,
> My gentle *Shakespeare*, must enioy a part.
> For though the *Poets* matter, Nature be,
> His Art doth giue the fashion.

He 'must sweat', must 'torne' his lines 'vpon the *Muses* anuile':

> For a good *Poet's* made, as well as borne.

In effect, the qualifications of this praise in the *Discoveries*, where Jonson criticized Shakespeare's excessive facility—his refusal to 'torne' and reshape, in fact—and the abrupt statement to Drummond that Shakespeare 'wanted arte'—which unfortunately is reported without its context—are developments of the verse-tribute, not contradictions of it. How much 'Exercise, Imitation, and Studie' did Shakespeare practise? and without these essentials, how could he attain to 'perfection' in poetry?

The most finished section of the *Discoveries* is that which deals with literary criticism. It is also the part which later critics best appreciated. Dryden accepted as authoritative the final essay on the drama. He declared that 'in the precepts' which Jonson laid down in the *Discoveries*, 'we have as many and profitable rules for perfecting the stage, as any wherewith the French can furnish us'.[1] It is strange that Dryden did not know that the precepts were borrowed in the main from Heinsius.[2] In the eighteenth century Joseph Warton saved the *Discoveries* from complete oblivion by adding a selection from the work to his reprint of Sidney's *Apology* in 1757.[3]

Jonson's formulated rules are dead to-day, but his comments on style have still a vital meaning and interest as the utterance of a master of English. 'Pure and neat Language I love, yet plaine and customary. A barbarous Phrase hath often made mee out of love with a good sense; and doubtfull writing hath wrackt mee beyond my patience' (p. 118). In the autobiographical passage already quoted he writes with approval of an 'absolute *Speaker*, and *Writer*' whom he knew—'Hee never forc'd his language, nor went out of the high way of *speaking*; but for some great necessity, or apparent profit. For hee denied *Figures* to be invented for ornament, but for ayde; and still thought it an extreme madnesse to bend, or wrest that which ought to be right' (p. 101). With such views it was natural he should appreciate the clear thinking, close reasoning, and lucid expression of Bacon, and describe him as one 'who hath fill'd up all numbers, and perform'd that in our tongue, which may be compar'd, or preferr'd, either to insolent *Greece*, or haughty *Rome* . . . hee may be nam'd, and stand as the *marke*, and ἀκμὴ of our language' (p. 102).

The plain manner, then, appealed to Jonson. '*Custome*', he said after Quintilian, prefixing the words as a motto to his own *English Grammar*,—'*Custome* is the most certaine

[1] *Essay of Dramatic Poesy*, ed. Ker, p. 83.
[2] From the *De Tragoediae Constitutione Liber* and the *Ad Horatii de Plauto et Terentio judicium Dissertatio*.
[3] *Sir Philip Sidney's Defence of Poetry. And Observations on Poetry and Eloquence. From the Discoveries of Ben Jonson*.

Mistresse of Language, as the publicke stampe makes the current money' (p. 118). But he safeguarded himself carefully on this point: 'Yet when I name Custome, I understand not the vulgar Custome: For that were a precept no lesse dangerous to Language, then life, if wee should speake or live after the manners of the vulgar: But that I call Custome of speech, which is the consent of the Learned; as Custome of life, which is the consent of the good' (p. 119). 'The learned' he distinguished from other writers because they 'use ever election, and a meane' (p. 99). He relied, that is to say, on a selective process, the artist's instinct in the choice of words.

He had also the artist's sense of construction. He summed up his conception of this in words which Swinburne[1] justly praised as excellent: ' The congruent, and harmonious fitting of parts in a sentence, hath almost the fastning, and force of knitting, and connexion: As in stones well squar'd, which will rise strong a great way without mortar' (p. 119).

This ideal of ' election' and 'the mean', of careful and compact composition, is not the main characteristic of Elizabethan writing. Can we discern in Jonson's comments on style any reference to contemporaries—in his own words, the reflux of his criticism to his peculiar notion of the times? In the section headed ' Ingeniorum discrimina' (pp. 98–9)[2] he records some shrewd observations on the difference of wits, and there can be little doubt that he was weighing contemporaries in the balance. Writers who are ' ever more busie about the colours, and surface of a worke, then in the matter, and foundation' (p. 98), and who ' torture their writings, and go into councell for every word' (p. 95), are survivals of the school of Lyly. 'Others, that in composition are nothing, but what is rough, and broken: *Quæ per salebras altaque saxa cadunt*. And if it would come gently, they trouble it of purpose. They would not have it run without rubs'—this suggests John Marston before he was treated with the chastening emetic of *Poetaster*. ' Others

[1] *A Study of Ben Jonson*, p. 174.   [2] Based on Quintilian.

there are, that have no composition at all; but a kind of tuneing, and riming fall, in what they write. It runs and slides, and onely makes a sound. . . .

> They write a verse, as smooth, as soft, as creame;
> In which there is no torrent, nor scarce streame.'

That is a clear reference to Samuel Daniel, a verser, but no poet.[1] For the poet is a 'maker', and 'composes'. Lastly the strictures on those who 'speake all they can (how ever unfitly)' and 'are thought to have the greater copy' are pointed by a reference to the clanging verse of Marlowe's *Tamburlaine*. No doubt he included Shakespeare, who ought to have 'blotted' a thousand of his lines, in the same category of the over-copious.

Considering his views on art, his critical—not to say censorious—bent, and the new type he introduced in comedy, Jonson wrote surprisingly little criticism. What must have been his most striking contribution to it perished in his fire— the preface to his version of the *Ars Poetica* written in dialogue, with Donne for one of the speakers. It was a defence for a deviation from the norm of 'art'—his rough-and-tumble comedy of *Bartholomew Fair*. We may fairly assume that the part assigned to Donne in the discussion represented his views on poetry. Such an exposition would have been a memorable addition to English criticism. We are left with isolated comments in prefaces, such as the note on the essentials of tragedy in the Quarto of *Sejanus*, and the imperfectly edited *Discoveries*, which Sir Kenelm Digby probably saw through the press. But they are hints and sketches only. In criticism Jonson achieved no work worthy of his powers. The finest sayings of the *Discoveries* do not relate to books or theories of art. They deal with life and conduct, and they reflect Jonson's sterling honesty and fearlessness. '*Truth* is mans proper good; and the only *immortall* thing, was given to our mortality to use. No good *Christian*, or *Ethnick*, if he be honest, can misse it: no

---

[1] *Conversations*, iii. 23, 24.

States-man, or *Patriot* should.'—'*Language* most shewes a man: speake that I may see thee.'—'*Wisedome* without *Honesty* is meere craft, and coosinage. And therefore the reputation of *Honesty* must first be gotten; which cannot be, but by living well. A good life is a maine Argument.'— 'They say *Princes* learne no Art truly, but the Art of *Horse-manship*. The reason is, the brave beast is no flatterer. Hee will throw a *Prince*, as soone, as his Groome.'[1] The 'sentence' or moral maxim expressed with point and brevity was popular in Elizabethan writing; to achieve it with this searching insight and this fine economy of words is a signal revelation of a master mind.

[1] Pp. 95, 120, 88, 107.

INDEX

The main references are printed in thick type

LIST OF ABBREVIATIONS

Alch. = The Alchemist.
B. F. = Bartholomew Fair.
C. is A. = The Case is Altered.
Cat. = Catiline.
C. R. = Cynthia's Revels.
D. is A. = The Devil is an Ass.
Disc. = Timber, or Discoveries.
E. H. = Eastward Ho.
E. M. I. = Every Man in his Humour.
E. M. O. = Every Man out of his Humour.
Epig. = Epigrams.
G. A. R. = The Golden Age Restored.
G. M. = The Masque of the Metamorphosed Gipsies.
Gram. = The English Grammar.

L. T. = Love's Triumph through Callipolis.
L. W. = Love's Welcome at Bolsover.
M. L. = The Magnetic Lady.
N. I. = The New Inn.
P. R. V. = Pleasure Reconciled to Virtue.
Poet. = Poetaster.
S. of N. = Staple of News.
S. S. = The Sad Shepherd.
S. W. = Epicoene, or The Silent Woman.
T. of T. = A Tale of a Tub.
U. V. = Ungathered Verse.
Volp. = Volpone, or The Fox.

Abbreviations, colloquial, in Elizabethan English, ii. 284, 428–31.
Actors. See Companies.
ADDISON, Joseph, i. 85, 161.
AELIAN, i. 254, 265.
AESCHYLUS, *Persae*, ii. 116.
AGRIPPA, Cornelius, i. 253.
AIKINHEAD, David (Dean of Guild of the City of Edinburgh), i. 234.
ALENÇON, Francis, Duke of ('Monsieur'), i. 142, 167.
ALEXANDER, Walter (Gentleman usher to Prince Charles), i. 233, 235.
ALEXANDER, Sir William, Earl of Stirling, i. 77, 137, 160; his plays, ii. 114–15.
ALLEYN, Edward (actor), ii. 238.
ALLOT, Robert, publisher of *B. F.* and *D. is A.*, i. 211; ii. 131 n.
AMES, Joseph, *Typographical Antiquities*, ii. 431 n.
'ANACREON', ii. 358, 395–7.
Anagrams, Jonson's opinion of, i. 144, 170.
ANEAU, Barthélemi, i. 55 n, 167.
Annandale, i. 1, 139, 164, 174, 220.
ANNE, queen of James I, i. 36, 60, 160, 207; ii. 260, 265–6, 272, 275, 278, 281, 285.
ANNE, queen of Richard II, ii. 281.

Anthology, Greek, ii. 340, 446.
Antimasque, The, origin of, ii. 275; Jonson's use of, 275–334, *passim*; its later phase, 290.
Antiquarian Society, The, i. 35.
ANTONINUS PIUS, i. 147, 172.
APULEIUS, i. 252.
ARCERIUS, Sixtus, i. 254, 265.
ARGALL, Sir Reginald, i. 225, 226, 227.
ARGALL, Anne, Lady, i. 225, 226, 227.
ARIOSTO, L., translation of, i. 133, 153; *Negromante*, ii. 94.
ARISTOPHANES, i. 124; and *E.M.O.*, 376; and *C.R.*, 399; and *Poet.*, 424; his *Plutus* and *S. of N.*, ii. 177, 182–5; his *Vespae* and *S. of N.*, 184; his poetic burlesque, 279, 326; his poetic symbolism, i. 124; Jonson's copy of, 265.
ARISTOTLE, i. 337, 347; ii. 7–9, 181, 261–2, 339.
ARLOTTE, i. 147, 172.
ARNOLD, Matthew, ii. 267.
ARTHUR, Prince (son of Henry VII), ii. 252, 255.
Arthurian legend, i. 74, 136, 159; ii. 283–4.
ASHMOLE, Elias, his *Theatrum Chemicum*, ii. 93 n.

Index

ASPLEY, William, publisher of *E. H.*, ii. 31.
ASTLEY, Sir John, i. 87, 238, 239.
AUBIGNY, Esmé Stuart, Seigneur of (afterwards Duke of Lennox), i. 31, 36 n, 38, 56, 106, 110-11, 134, 139, 156, 164, 223; letter probably addressed to, 190, 198.
AUBIGNY, Katherine d', Lady, epistle to, ii. 370.
AUBREY, John, i. 5 n, 57, 103 n; *Notes on Jonson*, 178-184.
AUGUSTUS, the emperor, i. 419, 427, 431, 438; ii. 288.
AULUS GELLIUS, i. 179, 183.
AYSCOUGH, Samuel, i. 210.
AYTOUN, Sir Robert, i. 56-7, 76-7, 137, 160.

BACON, Antony ('A.B.'), i. 142, 167.
BACON, Sir Francis, Lord Verulam, his habit when speaking, i. 142, 167. Jonson's relations with, 77, 141, 166; ii. 445. On Bruno, ii. 95 n.; on the Cecils, 167. *Essays*, i. 9-10, 36; ii. 344, 433; Essex tourney, 256, 271; Jonson's copy of the *Novum Organum*, i. 267.
BADGER, Sir Thomas, i. 213.
BALL, W. W. R., and VENN, J. A., *Admissions to Trinity College, Cambridge*, i. 226 n.
Ballads, Jonson's opinion of, i. 145, 171, 354.
BALZAC, Honoré de, i. 279.
BANG, W., i. 188, 189, 385 n; ii. 402 n.
BAPTISTA MANTUANUS, ii. 219, 223.
BARCLAY, John, *Argenis*, i. 74-5, 87-8.
BARNES, Barnaby, i. 176-7; ii. 154, 276, 396.
BARNFIELD, Richard, *Encomium to the Lady Pecunia*, ii. 183.
BARON, Robert, *Pocula Castalia*, i. 189.
BASKERVILL, C., *English Elements in Jonson's Comedy*, i. 279 n, 291 n, 296 n, 298, 325 n, 339 n, 346 n, 352 n, 355 n, 376 n, 377, 389 n.
BASSE, William, ii. 378.

BASTARD, Thomas, his epigrams, ii. 345 n, 347 n.
BATHURST, Ralph (Dean of Wells), i. 178, 182.
BAYFIELD, M. A., *Shakespeare's Versification*, ii. 429 n, 430 n.
BAYLY, Lewis (Bishop of Bangor), *The Practise of Pietie*, i. 188.
BEALE, John, printer of *B. F.* and *D. is A.*, i. 211; ii. 418.
BEAUMONT, Francis, Jonson's relations with, i. 120, 136, 159; poems to, ii. 366; his death, i. 137, 161; Drummond's mistakes about, 47 n, 138, 164. *Elegy on the Countess of Rutland*, 138, 163. *Letters to Jonson*, **49-50**; ii. 366. *The Maid's Tragedy*, i. 155. *Masque of the Inner Temple, ib.*; ii. 291 n. *Philaster*, i. 182. Verses on *S. W.*, 46 n.
BEDFORD, Lucy Harington, Countess of, Jonson's relations with, i. 54, 419; his poems to, 130, 135, 156; ii. 346, 362, 367; 'Ethra' in *The May Lord*, i. 143. Patroness of Daniel, 152, 159; of Donne, 154, 204. Letter of Jonson perhaps addressed to her, 190, 197, 198.
BEECHING, H. C., i. 244-5.
Belvoir, masque at, i. 72; ii. 314.
BENN, Anthony (recorder of London), ii. 364.
BENSLEY, E., ii. 345 n.
BIRDE, William (actor), ii. 238.
BLACKWELL, George (archpriest), i. 203.
BOAS, F. S., i. 14 n; ii. 239-40.
BOCCACCIO, G., *Decamerone* and *D. is A.*, ii. 161.
BODENHAM, John, quotes *C. is A.* in *Belvedere*, i. 306 n.
BODIN, Jean, i. 253.
BOECKH, A., ii. 398.
BOILEAU, N., i. 108.
Bolsover, entertainment at, i. 101-2, 212 n; ii. 333-4.
BOLTON, Edmund, i. 86, 167; on Jonson's language, 124.
BOND, Thomas (? John), Jonson's letter to, i. 201.

BONNEFONS (Bonefonius), Jean, i. 134, 143, 156, 168.
BORLASE, Sir William ('painter'), i. 92.
BOSWELL, James, i. 80.
BOSWORTH, G. F., *The Manor of Higham Bensted*, i. 225 n.
BOWCHER (Burcheer), Paul, i. 225, 227.
BOWES, Sir Jerome, i. 148, 173.
BOYLE, Hon. Robert, i. 184.
BRANDT, Sebastian, *The Ship of Fools*, i. 341, 380.
BRETON, Nicholas, *No Whippinge*, i. 29 n; Jonson's poem to, ii. 393.
BRIDGEWATER, John Egerton, Earl of, and *Comus*, ii. 310.
BRIGGS, Henry, i. 216.
BRIGGS, Richard, i. 215, 216; ii. 348 n.
BRIGGS, W. D., i. 66 n, 114 n.
BRISSON, Barnabé, i. 252.
BROADUS, E. K., i. 232, 247, 248.
BROME, Richard, *The Lovesick Maid*, ii. 191; *The Northern Lass*, i. 105, 113.
BROOKE, Christopher, i. 22 n, 49 n, 257 n.
BROOKE, Ralph (herald), i. 262.
BROTANEK, R., *Die englischen Maskenspiele*, i. 62 n, 90 n; ii. 146, 249-334, *passim*.
BROWNE, Sir Thomas, ii. 208.
BROWNE, William (of Tavistock), i. 260; ii. 369; author of 'Underneath this sable hearse', 351, 381.
BROWNING, Robert, i. 80, 83; ii. 382.
BRUCE, John, i. 40 n.
BRUNO, Giordano, his *Candelaio* and *Alch.*, ii. **94-8**, 109-10.
BUC, Sir George (Master of the Revels), i. 87, 237-9.
BUCHANAN, G. (tutor to James I), i. 148; ii. 259, 262.
BUCKINGHAM, George Villiers, Marquess, afterwards Duke of, i. 87 n, 180; ii. 313. Jonson accused of writing a poem approving his murder, i. 94, 242-4.
BUCKLAND, F., i. 117 n.
BUDÉ, Guillaume, i. 252.

BULLOKAR, William (grammarian), ii. 418, 422.
BULSTRODE (Boulstred), Cecilia, the 'Court Pucell', i. 59, 135, 150; ii. 356.
BURBAGE, Richard (actor), i. 27 n.
BURGES, John, i. 236, 237.
BURGHLEY, William Cecil, Lord, i. 218; Jonson's epigram to, ii. 364.
Burley-on-the-Hill, masque at, i. 72; ii. 313.
BURNS, Robert, i. 57; ii. 315, 385.
BURRE, Walter, publisher of *C. R.*, i. 393 n.
BURTON, Robert, on Bruno, ii. 95 n; *Anatomy of Melancholy*, i. 35-6.
BUSH, Thomas (bell-ringer), i. 244, 245.
BUTLER, Charles (grammarian), ii. 418.
BUTLER, William (doctor), i. 145, 171.
BUTTER, Nathaniel (stationer), i. 89, 93, 100; ii. **172-5**, 203.
BYRD, William (musician), i. 60.

C., I. (? John Cleveland), *Ode to Jonson*, i. 97 n.
CAELIUS, Rhodiginus, i. 252.
CALLIMACHUS, ii. 359 n, 413.
CALVIN, John, i. 136, 158.
Cambridge:
  St. John's College, i. 4 n, 5 n, 56.
  Trinity College, i. 5 n, 178, 182.
CAMDEN, William, Jonson's schoolmaster, i. 3-4, 139, 143, 164; ii. 445; later relations with, i. 38, 65, 140, 165, 181, 184, 260; Jonson's epigram to, ii. 366; dedication of *E. M. I.*, i. 178; his scholarship, 35, 251; *Britannia*, 75, 149, 176; death, 91. Also i. 173, 249, 259, 262.
CAMPION, Thomas, his lyrics, ii. 387; his masques, i. 47, 70, 155, 213; ii. 272, 275, 281 n, 291, 302, 321; his verse theories, i. 32, 132, 152, 155; his epigram on Barnaby Barnes, 176-7.
CAPELL, Edward, *Notes on Shakespeare*, i. 186.

CARDANO, Girolamo, i. 147, 169, 172; ii. 273.
CAREW, Thomas, i. 95, 106 n, 111–12, 117; ii. 95 n, 192, 332, 410.
CARLETON, Sir Dudley (afterwards Viscount Dorchester), i. 75 n, 87; ii. 172 n, 175 n, 310 n, 330 n.
CARLYLE, Thomas, i. 412; ii. 358.
CARTWRIGHT, William, i. 113, 116.
CARY, Sir Robert, i. 232, 233, 235.
CASAUBON, Isaac, i. 52, 68, 146, 172; ii. 344.
CASTELAIN, Maurice, *La Vie et l'Œuvre de Ben Jonson*, i. 25 n, 34 n, 193, 322 n, 332; ii. 63 n; editor of *Disc.*, ii. 440 n, 442 n.
CASTIGLIONE, Balthazar, i. 385 n.
CATHARINE of Aragon, ii. 252.
CATILINA, ii. 113–28, *passim*.
CATO, the censor, in Martial and Jonson, ii. 349–50.
CATULLUS, i. 253, 279 n, 424; ii. 269, 349, 359, 386.
CAVENDISH, Charles, Entertainment at his christening, ii. 311.
CECIL, William, Lord Burghley, i. 218; ii. 364.
CERVANTES, M., *Don Quixote*, ii. 145; *Preciosa*, 315.
CHAMBERLAIN, John (letter-writer), i. 75 n, 90 n; ii. 172 n, 175 n, 288 n, 310 n, 320, 328 n, 330 n.
CHAMBERS, E. K., *Elizabethan Stage*, i. 12 n, 26 n, 155, 280 n, 333 n; ii. 249 n, 289 n; *Mediaeval Stage*, 249 n, 251 n, 254 n, 255 n.
CHAPMAN, George, Jonson's relations with, i. 137, 160, 420; Jonson's 'plot' handed over to him, 283; ii. 6; 'Virgil' in *Poet.*, i. 43–35; his collaboration in *Sej.*, 34; ii. 4–6; verses on *Sej.*, i. 36 n; his collaboration in *E. H.*, ii. 31–46; imprisonment with Jonson, i. 38–9, 190–3; letters from prison, *ib.* Masques, 47, 133, 155; ii. 291. *Invective against Jonson*, i. 83 n; death, 107.
Achilles' Shield, i. 435.
All Fools, i. 171; ii. 39, 41.

CHAPMAN, George (*cont.*)
Blind Beggar of Alexandria, ii. 39.
Gentleman Usher, ii. 5.
Hero and Leander, i. 420, 433.
Hesiod, i. 260.
Humorous Day's Mirth, and its relations to the Comedy of Humours, i. 343–7, 350, 355.
Iliad, i. 135, 153, 420, 433, 435; Jonson's copy of the *Seauen Bookes*, 263.
Musaeus, i. 138, 163.
Ovid's Banquet of Sense, i. 434 n.
'Character' sketches, i. 340–1, 374–5, 406; ii. 207.
CHARLES, Prince, afterwards Charles I, his character, i. 91; Platonism at his Court, ii. 197; Jonson's relations with, i. 145, 232, 233, 235, 241; ii. 361; his gifts to Jonson, ii. 95–6, 181, 183, 245–8; the translation of *Argenis*, 75 n, 173; *For the Honour of Wales*, ii. 309; the Spanish match, i. 90; ii. 183–4, 325–6; Masques performed before, 330–2; entertained at Blackfriars, 311; at Welbeck, i. 100; ii. 332–3; at Bolsover, i. 101; ii. 333–4; consults the Sortes Vergilianae, i. 436 n.
CHAUCER, Geoffrey, his alchemist, ii. 89, 97; *House of Fame*, 177, 281, 321; *Legend of Good Women*, 281; introduced in *G. A. R.*, 298; royal grant of wine to, i. 248; Jonson's copy of, 263.
CHESTER, Charles (buffoon), i. 383.
CHESTER, Robert, *Love's Martyr* and *The Phoenix and the Turtle*, i. 434, ii. 402–3.
CHETTLE, Henry, his *Catiline*, ii. 114.
CHETWOOD, W. R., *Memoirs of Ben Jonson*, i. 70 n.
CHILD, C. G., on *Alch.*, ii. 94.
Chorus, The, ii. 114–16.
CICERO, and *Catiline*, ii. 113–26, *passim*.
CLARENDON, Edward Hyde, Earl of, i. 91, 106.
CLARK, Andrew, i. 186, 224 n.
CLAUDIAN, ii. 125 n, 280.

Index

CLEVELAND, John, i. 95, 116 n.
CLIFFORD of Chudley, Thomas, Lord, i. 181.
CLUN, Walter, i. 180, 183.
COCKERELL, Sydney C., i. 255, 258.
COKE, Sir Edward, i. 172; ii. 160 n.
COLBY, epistle to, ii. 371–2, 397.
COLERIDGE, S. T., on the *Alch.*, ii. 109; his adaptation of *A Nymph's Passion*, 390; *The Ancient Mariner*, 281.
COLLIER, J. P., i. 157; *History of Dramatic Poetry*, ii. 253 n.
Common Conditions, i. 291.
Comoedia Vetus, i. e. old English comedy, i. 143, 169.
Companies of actors:—
  Admiral's men, i. 12.
  Chamberlain's men, i. 12, 18, 21, 22, 26, 331, 373, 415.
  Children of the Chapel, i. 12, 20, 21, 26, 305, 393, 415; ii. 31, 69.
  King's men, i. 21, 99; ii. 49, 87, 113, 151, 169, 203.
  Lady Elizabeth's servants, ii. 131.
  Queen Henrietta Maria's men, i. 275.
COOKE, Thomas (groom of the Prince's chamber), i. 235.
COPLEY, Antony, *Wits, Fits, and Fancies*, i. 172.
CORBET, Richard, i. 83–4.
CORBET, Vincent, i. 84; ii. 338.
CORNEILLE, Pierre, i. 123.
CORNWALLIS, Dorothy, ii. 264 n.
CORNWALLIS, Sir William, ii. 263.
CORYAT, Thomas, i. 49, 150, 177, 201; ii. 288 n.
COTTON, Sir Robert, i. 31–2, 33 n, 35, 49 n, 94, 107, 139, 164, 242, 243; letter of Jonson to, 215.
Couplet, the heroic, Jonson's advocacy of, i. 32, 130, 132, 152, 153; ii. 412.
COX, Captain, of Kenilworth, ii. 330.
CRASHAW, Richard, ii. 410, 411.
CRAWFORD, C., i. 306 n.
CUMBERLAND, Richard, on *Volp.*, ii. 59.
CUNNINGHAM, Francis, editor of Jonson, ii. 425.

DAINES, Simon (grammarian), ii. 418.
DANIEL, Samuel, his relations with Jonson, i. 39, 136, 159; ii. 136, 147–8, 270–1; 'no poet', i. 132, 152, 351 n; ii. 450. *Cleopatra* and *Philotas*, ii. 114. *Civil Wars*, i. 138, 163; Jonson's copy of, 253, 263. *Defence of Ryme*, i. 32, 132, 152. *Queen's Arcadia*, ii. 221. *Tethys' Festival*, i. 61, 276 n. *Vision of the Twelve Goddesses*, i. 159; ii. 147–8, 264–5, 270–1. Also i. 79, 155, 173, 428 n, 430; ii. 382, 410.
DANTE ALIGHIERI, i. 120; ii. 366.
Darlington (Darnton), Jonson at, i. 77, 150, 177.
DASENT, J. R., *Acts of the Privy Council*, i. 218.
DAVENANT, Sir William, *News from Plymouth*, ii. 178.
DAVIES, John, of Hereford, ii. 345 n, 397.
DAVIES, Sir John, i. 130, 143, 168, 378. *Epigrams*, 137, 150, 162, 177, 345–6; ii. 147, 345 n, 346, 350–1. *Orchestra*, i. 143, 147, 168, 170.
DAVIS (Davies), John (grammarian), i. 105, 258–61.
DAVISON, Francis, his Court masques, ii. 257–8.
DAY, John, Jonson's opinion of, i. 133, 137, 154, 160.
'Decorum', i. 132, 134, 149, 152, 337, 339, 343; ii. 109, 133.
DEE, John (alchemist), ii. 93.
DEKKER, Thomas, satirizes Jonson, i. 13, 28; a 'rogue', 133; not attacked in *E. M. O.*, 382; nor portrayed in *C. R.*, 406–10; 'Demetrius' in *Poet.*, 423–5. *Coronation Entertainment*, his part in, 40; ii. 261. *The Honest Whore*, i. 172; ii. 180. *If it be not good*, ii. 154, 156–60. *Page of Plymouth*, i. 20; ii. 5. *Patient Grissel*, i. 383. *Satiro-mastix*, 13, 14 n, 19 n, 28–9, 164, 174, 239, 339 n, 347 n, 407, 416, 423–5. *The Shoemakers' Holiday*, 325; ii. 33.
DELACOURT, Raymond, i. 203.

DELONEY, Thomas, i. 325.
DELRIO, Martinus, i. 253.
DEMOCRITUS, i. 145, 171.
DESMOND, James Fitzgerald, Earl of, ii. 399 n.
DE SPINA, Bartholomaeus, i. 252.
DEVEREUX, Walter, i. 148, 173.
DEVONSHIRE, Charles Blount, Lord Mountjoy, Earl of, i. 224.
Dialect, Jonson's use of, i. 180, 183, 277, 286 n ; ii. 293, 315.
DICKENS, Charles, i. 357 n.
DIGBY, Sir Kenelm, i. 106 n, **110**, 260; editor of the 1640 Folio, ii. 213, 337, 450; gives Jonson a Savonarola, i. 268-9.
DIGBY, Lady Venetia, i. 63, 110; ii. 214, **382-3**.
DIGGES, Leonard, ii. 27 n.
DION CASSIUS, ii. 11-16.
DIXE, John, i. 221, 223.
DOBELL, Bertram, i. 190.
DOBELL, Percy J., i. 113 n.
DOD, John, i. 146, 172.
DOMITIAN, the Emperor, and Martial, ii. 348, 361.
DONNE, John, his relations with Jonson, i. 22 n, 49 n, 51, 56, 420; ii. 410-11 ; Jonson's opinion of him, i. 133, 135, 138, 154; 'Criticus' in Jonson's *A. P.*, 134, 144 ; ii. 450 ; poems repeated by Jonson, 135, 150, 177 ; ii. 443 ; letter of Jonson to, i. 51, 54 n, 203-4; his reading, ii. 439; his wit, 344; his directness, 411-12; his elegiac temper, 360, **383-4**, 388 ; metrical apostrophe in, 431 n ; death, i. 107. Also i. 45 n, 52 n, 79, 137, 257. *Anniversary,* 133, 149, 154, 176 ; *Epistle to Goodyere,* ii. 372 n ; *Epitaph on Prince Henry,* i. 136, 157; *Epitaph on Mrs. Bulstrode,* 135; ii. 356; *Metempsychosis,* i. 136, 158.
DONNE, John, the younger, i. 204.
DORSET, Sir Edward Sackville, Earl of, epistle to, ii. 371.
DORSET, Thomas, Earl of, and Baron Buckhurst, i. 189, 218.
DRAYTON, Michael, Jonson's relations with, i. 85, 136, 159;

DRAYTON, Michael (*cont.*) ii. **375-7**, 393 n, 396-7 ; friend of Drummond and Alexander, i. 77, 128, 160; epigram on, 137, 162; death, 107; epitaph of, ii. 381 ; Elegies, 360 ; Epistles, 338 ; Fairy poetry, 285. *Mortimeriados,* i. 137, 161-2. *Odes,* ii. **396-7**. Pastoral poetry, 219-20, 229-30. *Polyolbion,* i. 132-3, 153, 159; ii. 339.
DRINKWATER, John, i. 116 n.
DRUMMOND, William, of Hawthornden, Jonson's visit to, i. **79-83**; letters to Jonson, 204-6, 208-10 ; Jonson's letter to, 207 ; his opinion of Jonson, 151 ; Jonson's opinion of him, 148, and of his verses, 135, 152 ; gift of a book to Jonson, 260, 267. Collected *Works,* 128.
Characters of Authors, i. 79.
Conversations, text of, i. **128-51**; commentary on, 152-178 ; quotations from, 1, 2, 3 n, 4, 5 n, 6 n, 8, 9 n, 18, 19, 23, 25 n, 26 n, 31 n, 32 n, 37, 38, 45 n, 47, 49, 52 n, 54 n, 55 n, 57, 69, 70 n, 72, 73, 74, 77, 82, 103, 183, 187, 191, 193, 200, 207, 223, 224 n, 251, 261, 282, 283, 305, 376 n ; ii. 4, 70, 95, 134 n, 142 n, 151, 153, 206, 216, 226, 339, 345 n, 347 n, 348, 351, 356 n, 362, 366, 374 n, 376 n, 388, 389 n, 390, 392, 393 n, 407, 411, 412, 443 n, 447; errors in reporting, i. 47, 152, 153, 155, 156, 158, 159, 162, 164, 168, 170, 174, 176, 191.
Democritie, i. 170, 173, 177, 178.
Forth Feasting, i. 79, 135, 156.
Poems, i. 79.
Tears on the Death of Meliades, i. 79 ; ii. 283.
DRUMMOND, Sir William, i. 130.
DRYDEN, John, disparages Chapman and revenges Jonson, i. 435 n ; on *Alch.,* ii. 96 n ; on *Cat.,* 126-7 ; on *Disc.,* 448 ; on *Sej.,* 20; on *S. W.,* 70, 79; on Jonson's 'dotages', i. 278. Also i. 126 n, 182, 189; ii. 127 n, 410.

Index

DRYSDALE (Scottish herald), i. 205, 206.
DU BARTAS, Guillaume, i. 133, 153.
DU BELLAY, J., ii. 394.
DUPERRON, Jacques Davy (Cardinal), i. 67-9, 134, 156.
DUPPA, Brian (Dean of Christ Church), editor of *Jonsonus Virbius*, i. 116, 235.
Durance, i. 55; ii. 371.
DÜRER, A., ii. 196.
DYER, Sir Edward, i. 138.

EARLE, John, *Microcosmographie*, ii. 207.
ECKERMANN, J. P., i. 80.
Edinburgh, i. 76-8, 81, 143, 150, 169, 177, 207, 208.
EDMONDES, Clement, i. 260, 263.
EDWARD THE SIXTH, King of England, i. 280.
EDWARD THE THIRD, King of England, in a Court 'disguise', ii. 255.
EDWARDES, Richard, *Damon and Pithias*, i. 339.
ELLESMERE, Sir Thomas Egerton, Lord, i. 180, 201.
ELICH, Philippus Ludwigus, i. 253.
ELIZABETH, Princess (daughter of James I, Queen of Bohemia), i. 52 n, 64; ii. 291.
ELIZABETH, Queen, i. 138, 139, 141, 142, 148, 158, 162, 165, 166, 167, 209, 217, 219, 280; ii. 259; introduced into the original version of *E. M. O.*, i. 374; addressed in *C. R.*, 393-6, 401-5; her Court masques, ii. 254-8, 260, 265.
ELLIS, C. F. Corbould, i. 237.
ELTON, O., ii. 95 n, 397.
Emblems, i. 82, 208-10, 427; ii. 344.
England's Parnassus, i. 434; ii. 402 n.
Epigram, Jonson's treatment of the, ii. 339-40, **342-68**, 374-5, 379; his criticism of other epigrammatists, i. 133, 138, 143; the epigram in Jonson's time, 345-6.
Epistle, Jonson's treatment of the, ii. 338.
ERASMUS, Desiderius, ii. 442 n; *De Alcumista*, 98-9; Jonson's copy of the *Colloquia*, i. 268.

ESSEX, Lady Frances Howard, Countess of. ? *See* Somerset, Countess of.
ESSEX, Robert Devereux, 2nd Earl of, and Elizabeth, i. 28, 158, 394-6; as author, 142, 167; patron of Spenser, 137, 161; his impresas, 148, 173.
ESSEX, Robert Devereux, 3rd Earl of, i. 143, 169; ii. 268.
EUPOLIS, ii. 61 n.
EURIPIDES, i. 107; ii. 8.
EUSEBIUS, i. 252.
Every Woman in her Humour, i. 349.

FAIRFAX, Edward, i. 133, 153; ii. 407.
FALKLAND, Lucius Cary, Lord, i. 106, 109, 114, 116, 210, 436 n; ii. 214, 367, 439-40.
FARNABY, Thomas (classical scholar), i. 215, 216; ii. 348.
FEATLEY, D. (Protestant minister), i. 65-7.
FELTHAM, Owen, i. 95.
FELTON, John, assassin of the Duke of Buckingham, i. 90, 94, 243-4.
FENNOR, William, i. 36 n.
FENTON, John, i. 78, 205, 206, 207.
FERRABOSCO, Alphonso (musician), i. 60-1, 131; ii. 274 n.
FESTUS, Pompeius, i. 252.
FEUILLERAT, A., ii. 265 n.
FIELD, Nathan, i. 26, 137, 160; ii. 348 n.
FIELDING, Henry, *Tom Jones*, ii. 109.
FINCHAM, F. W. X., i. 43 n, 223.
FIRTH, Sir C. H., i. 49 n, 162.
FLASKET, John (publisher), i. 29 n.
FLEAY, F. G., *Biographical Chronicle of the English Drama*, i. 6 n, 14 n. 17 n, 20 n, 26 n, 28 n, 43 n, 50 n, 55 n, 166, 279, 332, 351 n, 381, 383, 394 n, 407 n, 428 n, 432; ii. 69 n, 71, 132 n, 146-7, 160 n, 169 n, 185 n, 190, 191 n, 216-17.
FLETCHER, Giles, D.C.L., i. 217, 218.
FLETCHER, Giles (poet), i. 218.
FLETCHER, John, loved by Jonson, i. 137, 161; Jonson's poem to, 164; ii. 366; his loose rhythm, 429. *The Bloody Brother*, i.

FLETCHER, John (*cont.*)
170. *The Chances*, ii. 155.
The Faithful Shepherdess, i.
31 n, 138, 164, 260; ii. 221,
227, 229. *Masques*, i. 47, 133,
155. *Love's Pilgrimage* and
N. I., ii. 193 n, **198–200**. *The
Tamer Tamed*, i. 375.
FLETCHER, Phineas, i. 161, 218.
FLORIO, John, ii. 95, and vol. i,
illustration, p. 56.
Flowers, The Masque of, i. 71.
FORMAN, Simon (alchemist), ii. 98.
FORTESCUE, Sir John, i. 218.
FOSTER, Joseph, *Alumni Oxonienses*, i. 226 n.
FOWLER, Eliza, i. 208.
FRANCIS THE FIRST, King of France, i. 208.
FRANZ, W., *Shakespeare-Grammatik*, i. 362 n.
FRAUNCE, Abraham, i. 133, 154, 155.
FREYTAG, G., i. 89.
FULLER, Thomas, i. 2 n, 3, 4 n, 5 n, 50; ii. 439.

GAINSFORD (Gainford), Thomas (captain and news-purveyor), ii. 173–5.
GALLUS, i. 419 n.
Gammer Gurton's Needle, i. 290, 296.
GARLAND, Walter, i. 223–31.
GASCOIGNE, George, i. 7; ii. 32, 34, 179, 254.
GAYTON, Edmund, i. 46 n.
Gesta Grayorum, ii. 257.
GIFFORD, William, editor of Jonson, i. 40, 71 n, 183, 190, 205, 227 n, 403, 432, 436; ii. 4, 69 n, 70, 100 n, 146, 189 n, 194, 195 n, 215, 263 n, 291, 294, 324 n, 389, 425.
GILES, Thomas, i. 60.
GILL, Alexander, the elder, *Logonomia Anglica*, ii. 322, 418.
GILL, Alexander, the younger, i. 100, 243.
GODELMANNUS, Johannes Georgius, i. 253.
GODOLPHIN, Sidney, i. 116.
GOETHE, J. W. von, i. 120–1; ii. 271, 288, 299; *Epigrams*, 342–3; *Faust*, 155 n, 157; *Lyrics*, 385; *Philine*, 35.

GOFFE, T., i. 185; *The Careless Shepherdess*, ii. 215–16.
GOODWIN, Gordon, i. 249.
GOODWIN, R., i. 210.
GOODWIN, William (Dean of Christ Church), i. 235.
Gorboduc, ii. 8, 114.
GOSSE, Sir Edmund, i. 204.
GOSSON, Stephen, *Catilines Conspiracie*, ii. 114.
GOW, James, i. 3 n.
GOWER, John, a character in *G. A. R.*, ii. 298.
GRABAU, W., i. 358 n.
GRAY, T., *Odes*, ii. 398.
GRAY, W., *Chorographia*, i. 77 n.
GREENE, Robert, i. 11, 389 n; *Friar Bacon and Friar Bungay*, i. 281 n.
GREENSTREET, James, i. 26 n.
GREENWOOD, P. (grammarian), ii. 418.
GREG, W. W., ii. 6 n, 189, **213–17**, 249.
GRENEWEY, Richard, i. 167, 174.
GREVILLE, Fulke, performer in a 'triumph', ii. 255.
GRIERSON, H. J. C., editor of Donne's *Poems*, i. 157, 158, 159, 163, 224.
GRIMM, Jakob, on the 'Stupid Devil', ii. 155 n.
GRYSE (Le Grys), Robert, i. 75 n, 148, 173.
GUARINI, G. B., *Pastor Fido*, i. 134, 149, 152, 155, 176; ii. 95 n, 220, 226, 229, 271 n.
GUILPIN, Edward, *Skialetheia*, i. 346, 425 n; ii. 345 n, 346.
GYRALDUS, Lilius Gregorius, i. 252, 253.

HADDINGTON, James Ramsay, Viscount (afterwards Earl of Holderness), his wedding masque, i. 53; ii. 272, 274 n, 276–7.
HALL, Arthur (translator of Homer), i. 435.
HALL, E. (chronicler), ii. 255 n, 271.
HALL, Joseph (Bishop of Norwich), the 'harbinger' to Donne's *Anniversary*, i. 149, 176. *Characters of Virtues and Vices*, ii. 207. *Satires*, i. 378; ii. 345.

Index

HALLIWELL-PHILLIPPS, J. O., i. 186.
HAMERSLEY, Sir Hugh (Lord Mayor of London), i. 240, 241.
HAMMOND, Eleanor P., ii. 254 n.
HANDCLER (Handser?), John, i. 221, 223.
HANNAM, Captain, possible original of Tucca in *Poet.*, i. 425.
HARINGTON, Sir John, and 'Daw', ii. 71. *Apologie for Poetrie*, 71 n. *Ariosto*, i. 133, 153; ii. 407. *Epigrams*, i. 133, 153, 163, 398; ii. 147, 345 n, 351.
HARRIS, M. A., i. 339 n.
HARRISON, G. B., editor of the *Conversations*, i. 131.
HARRISON, Stephen (architect), ii. 262 n.
HART, H. C., i. 325 n.
HART, John (grammarian), ii. 418, 422, 431.
HATHAWAY, C. M., editor of *Alch.*, ii. 88 n.
HATTON, Lady Elizabeth, ii. 190.
HAUGHTON, William, *The Devil and his Dame*, ii. **154-9**; *Englishmen for my Money*, i. 291.
HAYES (Hay), James, Lord, his wedding-masque, i. 213; ii. 302.
HAYMAN, Robert, *Quodlibets*, i. 187.
HAZLITT, William, on *Sej.*, ii. 11, 25.
HAZLITT, W. C., on Jonson's library, i. 251 n.
HEATH, John, *Epigrams*, ii. 345 n.
HEATH, Sir Robert, i. 94, 242, 247, 248.
HEINSIUS, Daniel, i. 104, 336; ii. 448.
HENN, Thomas (groom of the Prince's chamber), i. 233.
HENRIETTA MARIA, queen of Charles I, i. **90-1**; ii. 197, 328, 330-1, 361.
HENRY THE EIGHTH, King of England, i. 1, 2, 209, 281; ii. 293 n, 423.
HENRY THE FIFTH, King of England, Jonson's lost work on, i. 73.
HENRY THE FOURTH, King of France, i. 67, 144.
HENRY THE SECOND, King of France, i. 208.
HENRY THE THIRD, King of France, i. 67.
HENRY, Prince of Wales (son of James I), i. 47, 64, 83, 135, 136, 146, 148, 156, 157, 164, 174, 252; ii. 258, **282-4**.
HENRY, Aurelia, editor of *S. W.*, ii. 72 n.
HENSHAW, Samuel (deputy Teller of the Exchequer), i. 236, 237.
HENSHAWE, Thomas (scientist), i. 181, 184.
HENSLOWE, Philip, i. 6, **13-14**, 15 n, 16 n, 17 n, 18 n, 21, 33, 343, 426 n; ii. 237-9, 241, **245**.
HERBERT of Cherbury, Edward, Lord, epigram to Jonson, i. 134; ii. 347 n; his obscurity, i. 136, 157; gift of a book to Jonson, 260, 270.
HERBERT, George, ii. 391, 411.
HERBERT, Sir Henry (Master of the Revels), records from his office-book of plays at Court, i. 275; ii. 203.
HERRICK, Robert, i. 46, 50, 86, 111-12, 117; poems to Jonson, 1 n, 46.
HESIOD, ii. 299.
HEYWARD, Edward, i. 87 n, 149, 175.
HEYWOOD, John, i. 137, 148; ii. 344.
HEYWOOD, Thomas, i. 187.
HILL, Nicholas, i. 145, 171.
HIPPOCRATES, i. 136, 158.
HOBBES, Thomas, i. 57 n, 213.
HOFFSCHÜLTE, H., *Über Jonson's ältere Lustspiele*, i. 394 n.
HOLLAND, Hugh, i. 32-3 n, 36 n, 204; ii. 403.
HOLME, William, publisher of *E. M. O.*, i. 373.
HOLT, L. H., ii. 49 n.
HOLYDAY, Barten, i. 251.
HOMER, quoted by Jonson while bricklaying, i. 178. *Iliad*, imitated in *Poet.*, 438 n; Chapman's translation, 133, 138, 153, 163; Hall's, 153. *Odyssey*, ii. 267, 272-3.
HOOKER, Richard, i. 136, **159**.

Index

HORACE, praised by Jonson, i. 132, 136; *Satires* read with Field, 137; impersonated in *Poet.*, 418-28, 436-41; Jonson's manuscript of the *Ars Poetica*, 251, 262-3; his translation of it, 134, 144, 156, 169; ii. 134, **408-9**; of two odes, i. 134, 156; ii. 407-8. His critical laws, i. 337; ii. 14, 114; his lyrics, ii. 364, **369-70**, 394, 398; his *Epistles*, 363-4, 368. Jonson's *Speech according to Horace*, 397.
HOSKINS, Sir John, i. 3 n, 22 n, 164, 179.
HOWELL, James, a 'son' of Ben, i. 111; helps to put out his fire, 261; on *M. L.*, 99; ii. 203-4; on Jonson's *Grammar*, 418, 421 n; *New English Grammar*, *ib.*; gives a Welsh grammar to Jonson, i. 103, 105, **258-60**; *Letters*, 112 n, 227 n; on the Court of Charles I, ii. 197.
HUGHSON, David (Edward Pugh), i. 188, 189.
HULL, John, deed of assignment to, i. 236.
HUNSDON, George, second Lord, i. 218.

I. (Ingram ?), W., on Jonson, i. 29 n, 357.
IBSEN, Henrik, and Jonson, i. 89; as satirists in drama, 377; as tragic poets, ii. 27.
Impresas, i. 82-3, 148, 173, 208, 209, 427 n.
INGELAND, Thomas, *The Disobedient Child*, ii. 32-3, 179.
Irish in Court masques, ii. 292-4.

JAMES THE FIRST, King of England, i. 35, *et passim*; his 'Academ Roial', 86; *E. H.*, 38, 190-200; Jonson's *Coronation Entertainment*, ii. 261; Jonson's *Masques*, 258-324, *passim*; his appreciation of Jonson, i. 205, 207; his grants to Jonson, 231-2, 237-9, 245-8; Jonson's frankness to, 141, 148, 173,

JAMES THE FIRST (*cont.*) 181; Jonson's epigrams to, ii. 361; Jonson's grace before, i. 180; Jonson's copy of *His Majesty's Poetical Exercises*, 264; *Demonologia*, quoted by Jonson, 253; his examination of the boy Smith, ii. 163 n; Barclay, i. 74-5; Duperron, 68; Selden, 87; Sidney and John Taylor, 142, 168; the Puritans, 180; death, 90.
JEAFFRESON, J. C., i. 18 n, 219, 220.
JENKINSON, Hilary, i. 223 n.
JEPHSON, Sir William, epigram to, ii. 363.
JODELLE, Étienne, *Cléopâtre*, ii. 8.
JOHNSON, Dr. Samuel, i. 58, 63, 120, 127.
JOHNSON, W. S., editor of *D. is A.*, ii. 160 n.
JONES, Inigo, at the Mermaid, i. 49 n; at Lord Salisbury's, 141. Masque-producer, **60-2**, 90, 97-8; ii. 268, 273, 317, 318 n, 330-1; Masque designs at Chatsworth, 266 n, 282 n, 318 n, 331; satirized in *B. F.*, 136, **146-8**; in *L. W.*, i. 101; ii. 334; in *T. of T.*, i. 101, 276-8, 286; quarrel over *L. T.*, 97; ii. 331. Jonson's 'Expostulation' with, i. 98; ii. 356-7; Jonson's epigrams on, i. 61, 98; ii. 356; 'greatest villain in the world', i. 145; 'Iniquity Jones', 171; 'Jackanapes', 184; his verses on Jonson, 82 n, 86 n; sees the *M. L.*, ii. 203; final rupture with Jonson, 332.
JONSON, Benjamin. Date and place of birth, i. 1. His ancestry, *ib.*, 139. His grandfather, *ib.* His family arms, 1 n, 148, 174. His father, mother, and stepfather, 2, 5, 38-9. His childhood, 2, 3, 139. Sent to Westminster School by a friend, 3, 139. Identity of the friend, 3, 164, 179. Relations with Camden, 3, 4, 139. Put to bricklaying, 4, 5, 139, 164. Throws it up, 6, 139. His adventure in Flan-

Index 463

JONSON, Benjamin (*cont.*)
ders, 6, 139. Soldiership and letters among the Elizabethans, 7. Marriage, 8. His wife, 8, 9, 139. Their children, 9, 139. Life in London; literature of the nineties; Jonson's literary tastes, 10. Antagonism to Spenser, *ib.* Attitude to Shakespeare, 11. Tendencies congenial to him, 11. Jonson on the stage, 12. London theatres in 1596; plays in *The Spanish Tragedy*, 13. Relations with Henslowe, 13-17. Finishes Nashe's *Isle of Dogs*, 15, 196, 217-18. Imprisonment and release, 15-16, 196, 217-18. Jonson employed by Henslowe to write for his stage, 17. Mention of him as author of tragedies by Meres, *ib.* Kills Gabriel Spencer, 18; trial and imprisonment, 18-19, 139, 219-20. *Every Man in His Humour* performed, 18. Becomes a Catholic, 19, 139. *The Case is Altered* performed, 20. *Every Man out of His Humour* performed, 22. Jonson's relations with the Inns of Court, *ib.* Relations with his fellow-playwrights, 23. The Stage Quarrel, 24 ff. Relations with Marston, 24-9, 136, 140; and Dekker, 27-9. The Children of the Chapel, 26-7. Performance of *Poetaster*, 28-30. Threatened prosecution, 30. Withdraws from the stage, *ib.* Relations with Townshend, 30-1. Five years' residence with Lord d'Aubigny, 31, 139. Friendship with Sir Robert Cotton, 31. Controversy with Campion and Daniel, 32. Translation of Horace's *Art of Poetry*, *ib.* Returns to tragedy: *Sejanus*, 33-8. Death of Elizabeth; character of James; growth of the prestige of scholarship and of the zest of learning in the new reign, 35-6. Jonson called in to provide entertain-

JONSON, Benjamin (*cont.*)
ments for the Court, 36. Performance of *Sejanus*, *ib.* Summoned before the Council on its account, 37. Expulsion with Roe from Whitehall, 39. Relations with the earl of Northampton; joint-author with Chapman and Marston of *Eastward Ho*, 38, 140. Voluntary imprisonment, and release, *ib.* Letters written by Jonson and Chapman from prison, 39, 190-200. Employed to search for Gunpowder Plot conspirators, 40, 202. Summoned, with his wife, before the London Consistory Court, 42-3, 220-3. Performance of *Volpone*; rapid growth of Jonson's prestige, 43-4. *Volpone* performed before the two universities, *ib.* His dedicatory address to them, 44, 83. Performance of *The Silent Woman*, 45; *The Alchemist*, 45-6; and *Catiline*, 46. Its failure followed by three years' withdrawal from the stage, 47. Jonson's private life between 1603 and 1612, 48-9. Relations with Selden, and Ralegh, *ib.* The Mermaid meetings, 49-50. Relations with Beaumont, *ib.* Shakespeare, 50-1. Donne, 51. The Roe family, 51-2. Relations with the Court; his person and presence at this date, 53. Friendships with women of rank: 'Charis,' *ib.* Lady Bedford, 54. Lady Rutland, *ib.* Lady Wroth, 54-5. Sir R. Wroth, *ib.* Sir R. Sidney, 55. The Earl of Pembroke, *ib.*, 141. Sir H. Goodyere, 56. Lady d'Aubigny, *ib.* Relations with the Universities before 1619, *ib.* Scottish friends at Court, 57. Jonson's demeanour at Court, 57-8. His occasional rebuffs, *ib.* Satire on Cecily Bulstrode, 59. Jonson's Court masques of this period, 59-61. Relations with fellow-artists:

464   *Index*

JONSON, Benjamin (*cont.*) T. Giles, Ferrabosco, 60; Inigo Jones, 60-2. The Folio edition of Jonson's Works, 64. Reasons for delay in publication, *ib.* Jonson's visit to France as tutor to young Ralegh, 64-9, 140, 165. Present at a 'Conference touching the Real Presence', 65-6. Gives a certificate of the accuracy of the Report, 66-7. Interview with Cardinal Duperron, 67. Duperron and James I, 68. Jonson's return to London, 69. *Bartholomew Fair*, 69-70. *The Devil is an Ass*, 70. Jonson's nine years' absence from the stage, 72. Evidence of decline of Jonson's interest in drama, 73. Epic plans, 73-4. Works destroyed by the fire in his library, *ib.* Translation of *Argenis*, 74, 88. Journey to Scotland, 75-7. Reception at Edinburgh, 77-9. Private and public festivities, *ib.* Entertained by W. Drummond, 79-82. Drummond's character and qualifications, *ib.*, 151. Jonson's departure, 81, 150; correspondence with Drummond, 81-2. Return to London, 82. Visit to Oxford: receives M.A. degree, 83, 234-5. Relations with Richard and Vincent Corbet, 83-4. Jonson the head of English letters, 84-6. Meetings in the 'Old Devil' and other taverns, 85. The 'Apollo' chamber, *ib. Leges Convivales*, 85-6. Marks of the king's favour; his pension, 86. Intervenes on behalf of Selden, 87. Narrowly escapes a knighthood, *ib.* Granted reversion to Mastership of the Revels, *ib.* Return to the stage: *The Staple of News*, 88. Death of James, 90. Less favourable atmosphere of the new Court, *ib.* Characters of Charles and the queen, 90-1. Death of friends, 91. Advanc-

JONSON, Benjamin (*cont.*) ing age; paralytic stroke, 91-2. Growing poverty and neglect, 93. Appointed City Chronologer, *ib. The New Inn, ib.* Charged with implication in assassination of Buckingham, 94. Disastrous failure of *The New Inn, ib.* Second 'Ode to Himself', 95. Simultaneous gift from the Chapter of Westminster, *ib.* Further gifts from the king, 96. Again called upon for a Court masque: *Love's Triumph through Callipolis, ib. Chloridia, ib.* Renewed dissensions with Inigo Jones, 97. 'Expostulation with Inigo Jones', 98. 'Mendicant Epistle' to the Treasurer, *ib.* His salary as Chronologer stopped, *ib.* Begins to print second volume of his Works, 99. *The Magnetic Lady, ib.* Revives the *Tale of a Tub*, with inserted satire upon Jones, 100-1. Commissioned by the Earl of Newcastle to prepare *The King's Entertainment at Welbeck*, 101; and *Love's Welcome at Bolsover, ib.* Jonson's last years; his sick chamber a focus of the learning and letters of London, 103-4. The *Discoveries*, 104-5. *The English Grammar*, 105. *The Sad Shepherd, ib.*, 115. Friends: Howell, 105-6, 111; Hyde, Falkland, 106. Death of his early friends, 107. His 'sons', 108-9. The Earl of Newcastle, 109. Sir Kenelm Digby, 110. The Westons, *ib.* Carew, 111-12. Herrick, *ib.* Young dramatists influenced by Jonson, 113. Cartwright, Brome, *ib.* Obscurer acquaintanceships, *ib.* Oldisworth's notice of Jonson, *ib.* n. Dedications; J. Webbe, 114. Morley's account of Jonson's last months, 115, 181-2. His death, 115. Funeral, 115-16. *Jonsonus Virbius*, 116. Poets

JONSON, Benjamin (*cont.*)
who did not contribute, 117. 'O rare Ben Jonson', 117-18. His personal appearance, 14, 53, 76, 81, 97, 149, 151, 174, 185; ii. 390. Final appreciation, i. 119-27. The 'rareness', and the commonness, of Jonson, *ib.* Continuity of his personal note, 120. Kinship with his time, 121-2. Limitations of his 'classicism', *ib.* Predominantly English form and substance of his Comedy, 122. His distinctive treatment of this form and substance, *ib.* Bias of the scholar, 123-4. Bias of the satirist, 124-5. His limitations as a poet, 125-6. His reputation abroad and at home, 126-7. Jonson, like Bacon, mediates between the Elizabethan and the coming age, 127.

Plays.
The Alchemist. Circumstances of production, ii. 87; highest achievement of Jonson's comic art, 88; relation to *Volpone* and *Epicoene, ib.*; position of alchemy in Jonson's Europe, 89 ff.; favouring conditions, *ib.*; Elizabeth's dealings with 'goldmakers', 91; alchemy in sixteenth-century literature, 93-5; alleged derivation of the plot from earlier alchemy plays, 94-8; comparison of Bruno's *Candelaio*, 96-8; comparison with *Volpone*: insistent realism, 100; Volpone and Subtle, 100-1; Mosca and Face, 101-2; Dol Common, 102; the dupes, 103-5; Sir Epicure, 105; Dame Pliant, Surly, 106; Lovewit, 107; the denouement, 107-9. Also i. 9, 21, 45-6, 70, 198, 256, 257, 262, 288, 292, 295, 333 ff., 365, 384; ii. 17, 153, 203.

Bartholomew Fair. Circumstances of production, ii. 131-2. Jonson's renewed geniality, 132-3; the Induction, 133-5; its satirical allusions, 134-6; relation of the play to Jonson's

JONSON, Benjamin (*cont.*)
previous comedies, 136-7; its true subject the Fair, 137-9; the visitors to the Fair, 140-3; Cokes and Waspe, 140-2; Grace, 142-3; the Puritans, 143-4; Jonson and Puritanism, 145. Also i. 10, 27, 64, 69-70, 99, 211, 257, 287, 289, 294-5, 384; ii. 104, 151 n, 239.

The Case is Altered. Circumstances of production, i. 305-6. The satire on Munday, *ib.* Plautus's *Captivi* and *Aulularia*, 307-9. Relation of this play to them, 310-11. Romantic treatment of Plautine theme, 312-13. Separation and recovery of kindred, 313. Mistaken identity, 315. Ready forgiveness, 316. Love-interest, 317. The *Aulularia* story, 321. Treatment of the miser-theme, 321-3. The comic slave, 323. The cobbler-type in Elizabethan comedy, 324-5. Problem of authorship, 325-7. Motives repeated in Jonson's later plays, 327 n. Also i. 20-1, 23, 288, 299, 354; ii. **241-2**.

Catiline. Circumstances of production, ii. 113; Jonson's appeal from the audience to the reader, *ib.*; previous *Catiline* plays, 113-14; *Catiline* and *Sejanus*, 114-16, 122; reverts to classical technique in (1) chorus, 114-16; (2) Prologue, 116; sources of the play, 117-20; Jonson's independent handling of them, 118-20. Characters: Catiline, not tragic, 123-5; Cicero, 124-5; Fulvia and Sempronia, 126-7. Also i. 46, 64, 188, 312, 333; ii. 132.

Cynthia's Revels. Circumstances of production and publication, i. 393. Addressed to the Queen; reasons for her indifference, 394-6. Essex-Actaeon, 395-6. Technique of the play; drama subordinate to satire and allegory, 396-9; presentation of persons, 398-9;

JONSON, Benjamin. **Plays** (*cont.*)
the Fountain of Self-Love, *ib.*;
relation to later satiric devices,
399; the Court masque, 400 ff.;
allegory and realism, 402;
conflict of good and evil types,
404–6; Hedon and Anaides,
relation to Marston, Dekker,
406-10; relation of his play to
the earlier and later Humour
plays, 411–12. Also i. 21, 26–7,
70, 290, 334, 339–40, 365, 374 n,
375, 384, 418, 438; ii. 20,
171, 179, 239.
The Devil is an Ass. Circumstances of production, ii. 151–3;
hints of difficulties with James, i.
143–4, 169; ii. 151–3; the 'duke of Drownland' and contemporary drainage schemes, 151, 152 n; the 'projector', 152–3. The devil-drama: its antecedents, 153–60. Blend of Christian and Germanic myth, 155; Jonson's treatment of the stupid devil theme, 158–60. The true comic hero Fitzdottrel, 160–1; Meercraft, 162; 'possession-feigning', 163. Mrs. Fitzdottrel, 164–5. Signs of incipient decadence, 165. Also i. 53, 70, 72, 99, 143, 189, 211, 399; ii. 387.
Eastward Ho. Grounds for inclusion among Jonson's works, ii. 31. Circumstances of production, *ib.* The Prodigal Son motive in Elizabethan drama, 32–5; transfer from academic to bourgeois *milieu*, 33. Dekker's Simon Eyre and Touchstone, 33–4; the apprentices and daughters, good and bad, 34–5. Discrimination of the shares of Chapman, Marston, and Jonson in the play, 37–46; plot elements, 41–3; characters, style, 43–5; excellence of the play as a whole, 45–6. Also i. 38, 140.
Every Man In His Humour. Circumstances of production and publication, i. 331–2; the Quarto and Folio texts: date of the revision, 332–3; and of the

JONSON, Benjamin. **Plays** (*cont.*)
Prologue, 333. Technique based on Sidney's *Apology*, 335–9. Treatment of the Unities, *ib.* His demand for unity of tone, 336–7. 'Truth to life' sought but imperfectly achieved, 337–8. Tendencies of Elizabethan characterization related to the 'Humour', 339–40. Origin and varied usage of this term, 340–1; Jonson's satire on its abuse, 342. Humour comedy before Jonson: Chapman's *An Humorous Day's Mirth*, 343–7. Jonson's handling of 'Humours' in this play, 347–8. Characters without 'humorous' traits, 349. The Gulls, 350–3. Downright, Cob, Clement, 354–5. Comparison with Jonson's later comedies, 355–6. After-repute, 357. Appendix: Comparison of Quarto and Folio texts, 358–70. External changes, 358–9; style and language, 361–9; structural changes, 369–70. Also i. 6, 10, 18–20, 30, 283–4, 288, 290–1, 305, 312, 379, 397, 429; ii. 17, 33, 54, 65, 74.
Every Man Out of His Humour. Circumstances of performance and publication, i. 373–4. Deletion of the original conclusion, 374; preliminary 'character of the persons', *ib.*; relation to the previous play: a more satirical rehandling of the same theme, 375–6; Jonson's defence of it as 'like Vetus Comoedia', 376; effect on the technique of the play, 378–81; an 'anatomy' of society, *ib.*; relation of the persons to Brandt's 'Fools' and Thackeray's 'Snobs', 380; question of their relation to living originals, 382–4. The plot a congeries of miniature plots, 384–5; comparison of the several 'catastrophes', 385–6. The chastisers: ambiguous character of Buffone and Macilente, 387. Asper, Jonson's mouthpiece, 388. Also i. 11–12,

Index 467

JONSON, Benjamin. **Plays** (*cont.*) 20, 22–4, 70, 290–1, 312, 334, 397; ii. 20, 74, 136 n, 137, 355.
The Magnetic Lady. Circumstances of production, ii. 203; reversion to methods of Humour plays, 204–5; but with new devices, 205–6; love-intrigue now the central motive, 206–7; the characters, 207–8; professional types, *ib.*; the women, 208–9; Polish and Shakespeare's 'Nurse', 209; Jonson's interventions, 209–10; the Boy, *ib.* Also i. 92, 94, 99, 103 n, 243, 288, 290, 292, 296.
The New Inn. Circumstances of production, ii. 189–90; causes of its rejection, 190–1; the 'Ode to Himself', 192, **401**; the play published with a commentary, 192. Its inequality, *ib.*; dregs of Humour comedy, 192–3; but with redeeming excellences, 195–6. Lovel and the Host, 196–7; Platonism at the English Court, 197–8; Lovel's speeches; the 'Court of Love', *ib.* Also, i. 93–5, 262, 288, 290, 292. 'Ode to Himself', i. 195.
Poetaster. Circumstances of production, performance and publication, i. 415; anticipates an attack by Dekker and Marston, *ib.*; stormy reception, 416; the 'Apologetical Dialogue', 417; representation of Augustan Rome, 418 ff.; comparison of Horace's situation with Jonson's, 419–20; resemblance only in number of literary enemies, 420–1; the 'Horace' of the play, 422; 'Crispinus' and 'Demetrius', 423–5. Larger purpose of the play: the 'master-spirits', 427 ff. 'Ovid', 428–31; 'Virgil', 429–32; problem of identification, 432–7. Motives from the earlier Humour plays, 438–40. The temper of Comedy on the whole preserved, 440–1. Also i. 27–30, 140, 196, 255, 275, 290, 318, 327 n, 373, 382; ii. 3, 54, 74, 449.

JONSON, Benjamin. **Plays** (*cont.*)
The Sad Shepherd. Circumstances of publication, ii. 213; the problem of its date, 214 ff.; relation to *The May Lord*, 216–17; an attempt to create Pastoral at once Theocritean and English, 218–19; compared with previous Pastoral literature, 219–22; Jonson's independence, 222–3; his Theocritean realism, 223; from exotic pastoralism to the English greenwood poetry, 223–4; the two traditions harmonized, 225–7; the lyric poetry, 227; the malign characters, 228–34. Also i. 93, 105, 251, 282, 284; ii. 244.
Sejanus. Circumstances of production, ii. 3. The 'second pen', 3–5; case for Chapman, 4–5. Ignores antique Tragedy for the sake of historic truth, 6–8; and *Julius Caesar*, 9–10. Sources of the play, 11–16. Jonson's modifications of the historic record, 12–13; additions to it, 13–15; Jonson's Arruntius, 13; the play thoroughly Jonsonian, 16–19; the situation of *Volpone* and the *Alch.* anticipated, 17–19; the characters, 19 ff.; Eudemus and Livia, 20; Sejanus, 21–4. Tiberius, 24–7; later fortunes of the play, 27. Also i. 33–4, 36–7, 288, 312, 434; ii. 60, 114, 122.
The Silent Woman. Circumstances of production, ii. 69–71; question of personal satire, 70–1; severe technique of the play, 71–2; comparison with the Humour plays, 72–5; growth in geniality, Morose and Malvolio, 75; plot combines two Greek jests, 75–9; character of Morose, 76–7; the agents in the device, 81–2; the Collegiate ladies, *ib.*; farce and comedy, Jonson and Molière, 83–4. Also i. 45–6, 123, 151, 188, 288, 292, 334; ii. 99, 185.

H h 2

JONSON, Benjamin. **Plays** (*cont.*)
The Staple of News. Circumstances of production, ii. 169; renewal of Jonson's poverty, 170; the subject foreshadowed in *News from the New World*, 170-1; news-mongering, unlike alchemy, a new activity in London, 171; stimulated by the war, *ib.*; the first newspapers, 172; stationers and editors: Butter and Gainsford, 173-5; Jonson's 'Captain', 175-6; the 'Staple of News' as a comic device, 177; the financial satire, 178; Peniboy and Pecunia, 179-82; relations to the *Plutus*, 182-4; recurrence of Humour types, 185; and of critical comment between the acts: 'Intermeans', 186. Also i. 72, 85, 86, 99, 288, 290, 292, 296, 399; ii. 155 n., 312.
A Tale of a Tub. Circumstances of production, i. 275. The satire on Jones, *ib.* Inserted in a play preceding *Every Man in His Humour*, 276-8. Characteristics of the original play, 281-2. Comparison in subject-matter and technique with Jonson's Comedies from 1598 to 1616, *ib.*; Jonson's earlier and later blank verse, 284; and plot-structure, 289. Qualified observance of the unities, 291-3. Traces of pre-Jonsonian technique, 293-4. But little of Jonson's later virtuosity in characterization, 294-5. Contrasted in technique with the other 'dotages', 296-7. Puppy the only clown-jester surviving in Jonson's comedy, 298. Anti-romantic treatment of love: Awdrey, 299-301. Also i. 100-1, 180, 183, 189.
Volpone. Circumstances of production, ii. 49; return to Comedy, *ib.*; relation to *Sejanus*, 50, 56, 60; motive of legacy-hunting, 50; Lucian's *Dialogues of the Dead*, Petronius's *Satiricon*, 51-3; slight relation to

JONSON, Benjamin. **Plays** (*cont.*)
London life, 53-4; Jonson's Venice, 54; general baseness of the characters, 55. Jonson's poetry of indignation, 56; character of Volpone, 57-9; Mosca, 60-3; the three dupes, 63-4; the 'good' characters', *ib.*; the by-plot: Sir Politick Would-be, 64-5. Also i. 21, 31 n., 43-4, 70, 115, 123-4, 188, 196, 288-9, 292, 322, 336-7, 365; ii. 17, 73, 75 n, 97, 107, 132.
Fragment: *Mortimer, The Fall of*, i. 17 n; ii. 6, 214.
Lost Plays.
Page of Plymouth, i. 20; ii. 5.
Robert II, i. 20; ii. 6.
Richard Crookback, i. 21, 33; ii. 6.
Ascribed to Jonson: Additions to *The Spanish Tragedy*, i. 21, 33; ii. 6, **235-451**.
May Lord, The, i. 143, 168, 282; ii. **214-17**.
Masques.
Althorpe, Entertainment at, i. 36; ii. **260**.
Augurs, The Masque of, ii. **316-19**.
Beauty, The Masque of, i. 45; ii. 267, **272-4**.
Blackfriars, Entertainment at, ii. 311.
Blackness, The Masque of, i. 40, 45, 61 n; ii. **265-7**.
Challenge at Tilt, A, i. 64, 71; ii. 132, **291-2**, 334.
Chloridia, i. 96; ii. **331-2**.
Christmas his Masque, ii. **300-1**.
Coronation Entertainment, i. 40, 260 n; ii. **261-3**.
Fortunate Isles, The, i. 72; ii. **328-30**.
Golden Age Restored, The, i. 47, 71, 74; ii. **297-300**; veiled personal allusions, 298.
Gypsies, The Metamorphosed, i. 72, 188, 282; ii. **313-16**.
Haddington, Lord, Masque at wedding of, i. 45; ii. **276-7**.
Henry's Barriers, Prince, i. 74, 213 n; ii. **282-4**.
Highgate, Entertainment at, i. 40; ii. **263-4**.

Index 469

JONSON, Benjamin. **Masques** (*cont.*)
Hymenaei, i. 39, 45, 61, 143, 169; ii. 147, **267–71**. Jonson's Introduction to the printed text, 269, 349 n. The Barriers, 271–2.
Irish Masque, The, i. 71; ii. 132, 291, **292-4**, 297, 312, 315.
King's Entertainment at Welbeck, The, i. 101, 105, 212; ii. **332-3**.
Love Freed from Ignorance and Folly, i. 47, 61; ii. 285, **286-8**.
Love Restored, i. 47, 64; ii. **288-91**, 312.
Lovers made Men, i. 71; ii. 258, **301-3**, 314.
Love's Triumph through Callipolis, i. 96, 275; ii. **330-1**.
Love's Welcome at Bolsover, i. 101, 282; ii. **333-4**.
Mercury Vindicated, i. 47, 71; ii. **294-7**, 312.
Neptune's Triumph, i. 72; ii. 317, **325-8**.
News from the New World, i. 72; ii. 310, **311-13**.
Oberon, The Masque of, i. 47, 61; ii. **284-6**.
Owls, The Masque of, ii. **330**.
Pan's Anniversary, ii. **323-5**.
Panegyre, A, i. 40, 107.
Pleasure Reconciled to Virtue, i. 71; ii. **304-9**, 321, 323. Relation to Milton's *Comus*, **307-9**.
Queens, The Masque of, i. 45, 47, 60 n; ii. 275, **277-82**, 321.
Theobalds, Entertainment of the two Kings at, i. 58 n; ii. 264.
Theobalds, Entertainment of the King and Queen at, i. 58 n; ii. 264.
Time Vindicated, i. 72; ii. **319-23**.
Vision of Delight, The, i. 71; ii. **303-4**.
Wales, For the Honour of, ii. **309-10**, 312, 315.
Poems.
 Epigrams, publication of, i. 333; dedication to Pembroke, 200; ii. 343, 361.
  xii. On Lieutenant Shift, i. 381; ii. 353, 355.

JONSON, Benjamin. **Poems** (*cont.*)
 Epigrams (*cont.*)—
  xiv. To William Camden, i. 4, 260 n; ii. 336.
  xvi. To Brainhardy, ii. 352.
  xviii. To my Mere English Censurer, ii. 346-7.
  xxii. On my first Daughter, i. 9; ii. 346, 380.
  xxiii. To John Donne, ii. 366.
  xxv. On Sir Voluptuous Beast, ii. 355.
  xxvii. On Sir John Roe, i. 224; ii. 366.
  xxviii. On Don Surly, ii. 346-7, 353, 355.
  xxxii. On Sir John Roe, i. 52; ii. 336.
  xxxiii. To the Same, i. 224; ii. 366, 381.
  xxxvi. To the Ghost of Martial, ii. 361.
  xxxvii. On Chev'rill the lawyer, ii. 352.
  xl. On Margaret Ratcliffe, ii. 381.
  xlii. On Giles and Joan, ii. 352.
  xliii. To Robert, Earl of Salisbury, i. 57.
  xlv. On my first Son, i. 9, 179, 183; ii. 346, 380.
  xlix. To Playwright, ii. 346.
  lv. To Francis Beaumont, ii. 366.
  lvi. On Poet-ape, ii. 353, 355.
  lix. On Spies, i. 139; ii. 347 n.
  lx. To William, Lord Monteagle, i. 41.
  lxiii. To Robert, Earl of Salisbury, i. 57.
  lxiv. To the Same, i. 57; ii. 365.
  lxv. To my Muse, ii. **365**.
  lxvii. To Thomas, Earl of Suffolk, i. 57.
  lxx. To William Roe, i. 230; ii. 366.
  lxxi. On Court Parrot, i. 58.
  lxxii. To Courtling, i. 58.
  lxxiv. To Thomas, Lord Egerton, Chancellor, i. 180, 183; ii. 364.
  lxxvi. On Lucy, Countess of Bedford, i. 54, 197-8; ii. 346, **367-8**.
  lxxix. To Elizabeth, Countess of Rutland, i. 54, 198; ii. 368.

H h 3

JONSON, Benjamin. **Poems** (*cont.*)
Epigrams (*cont.*)
lxxxiv. To Lucy, Countess of Bedford, i. 54, 135, 198; ii. 362.
lxxxv. To Sir Henry Goodyere, i. 56.
lxxxviii. On English Monsieur, ii. 354.
xcii. The New Cry, i. 254; ii. 355.
xciii. To Sir John Radcliffe, i. 263; ii. 364.
xciv. To Lucy, Countess of Bedford, with Master Donne's satires, i. 198; ii. 346.
xcv. To Sir Henry Savile, i. 56; ii. 341, 364.
xcvi. To John Donne, i. 51; ii. 366 n.
xcviii. To Sir Thomas Roe, i. 224; ii. 375.
xcix. To the Same, *ib.*
cvii. To Captain Hungry, i. 7.
cviii. To True Soldiers, i. 8; ii. 284, 353.
cxii. To a Weak Gamester in Poetry, ii. 339 n, 355.
cxv. On the Town's Honest Man, i. 61; ii. 355, 374.
cxvi. To Sir William Jephson, ii. 363.
cxviii. On Gut, i. 135; ii. 341.
cxx. An Epitaph on Salathiel Pavy, i. 20; ii. 341, **379-80**.
cxxii. To Benjamin Rudyerd, ii. 364.
cxxiv. Epitaph on Elizabeth, L. H., ii. 380-1.
cxxv. To Sir William Uvedale, ii. 363.
cxxvi. To his Lady, then Mistress Cary, ii. 368.
cxxviii. To William Roe, i. 51-2, 231; ii. 366.
cxxix. To Mime, i. 61; ii. 354.
cxxx. To Alphonso Ferrabosco, on his Book, i. 60 n.
cxxxi. To the Same, i. 60 n.
cxxxiii. On the Famous Voyage, i. 63; ii. 339, 341.
Forest, The.
i. Why I write not of Love, ii. **385.**

JONSON, Benjamin. **Poems** (*cont.*)
Forest, The (*cont.*)
ii. To Penshurst, i. 55; ii. **369.**
iii. To Sir Robert Wroth, i. 55; ii. **369.**
iv. To the World, A Farewell, ii. 389.
v. Song, to Celia, ii. **386-7.**
vii. Song, that Women are Men's Shadows, i. 55, 142, 167; ii. 389.
ix. Song, to Celia, 'Drink to me', i. 135; ii. **385-7.**
x. Praeludium, ii. 402.
xi. Epode, ii. **402-3.**
xii. Epistle to Elizabeth, Countess of Rutland, i. 198; ii. **370.**
xiii. Epistle to Katharine, Lady d'Aubigny, i. 56; ii. **370.**
xiv. Ode to Sir William Sidney, ii. 399, **404.**
xv. To Heaven, ii. 391-2.
Underwoods.
i. Poems of Devotion (1-3), ii. 392.
ii. Charis (1-10), i. 53, 135, 156; ii. **387-9.**
iii. Musical Strife, i. 134, 156; ii. 389.
iv. A Song, ii. 389.
vii. A Nymph's Passion, ii. 390.
viii. The Hour-glass, i. 71 n, 150-1, 177-8; ii. 390.
ix. My Picture left in Scotland, i. 1 n, 150-1, 177-8; ii. 390.
x. Against Jealousy, ii. 390.
xi. The Dream, ii. 390-1.
xii. An Epitaph on Master Vincent Corbet, i. 84; ii. 381.
xiii. An Epistle to Sir E. Sackville, ii. **371.**
xiv. An Epistle to Master John Selden, ii. 365, **372-3.**
xv. An Epistle to a Friend (Colby), ii. **371-2**, 397.
xviii. An Elegy ('Can Beauty'), ii. **388.**
xix. An Elegy ('By those bright Eyes'), ii. **388.**

Index 471

JONSON, Benjamin. **Poems** (*cont.*)
Underwoods (*cont.*)
- xxii. An Elegy ('Though Beauty'), ii. 388.
- xxiii. Ode to Himself, ii. **399–401**.
- xxiv. The Mind of the Frontispiece (Ralegh's *History of the World*), i. 162.
- xxv. An Ode to James, Earl of Desmond, ii. 396, **399–400**.
- xxvi. An Ode ('High-spirited Friend'), ii. 399.
- xxvii. An Ode ('Helen'), ii. **387**, 399.
- xxviii. A Sonnet to Lady Wroth, i. 54–5, 198 : ii. 393.
- xxix. A Fit of Rime against Rime, ii. 412 n.
- xxx. An Epigram on William, Lord Burleigh, ii. 364.
- xxxi. An Epigram to Thomas, Lord Ellesmere, i. 180, 183, 201.
- xxxii. Another to him, *ib.*
- xxxiii. An Epigram to the Counsellor that pleaded the case, ii. 364.
- xxxviii. An Elegy ('Tis true, I'm broke'), ii. **383-4**.
- xxxix. An Elegy ('To make the doubt'), *ib.*
- xl. An Elegy ('That love's a bitterness'), *ib.*
- xli. An Elegy ('Since you must go'), *ib.*
- xlii. An Elegy ('Let me be what I am'), i. 59, 401 ; ii. **358**, 360.
- xliii. An Execration upon Vulcan, i. 4, 19 n, 32 n, 67, 69 n, 72, **73-4**, 74 n, 261 n ; ii. 7, 172, 174, 339, 357, 439.
- xliv. A Speech according to Horace, i. 241 ; ii. 397–8.
- xlv. An Epistle to Master Arthur Squib, ii. 375.
- xlvi. An Epigram on Sir E. Coke, ii. 160 n.
- xlvii. An Epistle answering one that asked to be Sealed of the Tribe of Ben, i. 90 ; ii. **373-5**.

JONSON, Benjamin. **Poems** (*cont.*)
Underwoods (*cont.*)
- xlix. An Epigram on the Court Pucell, i. 59, 135, 150, 156 ; ii. 356.
- l. An Epigram to the Countess of [Rutland], i. 163, 198.
- lii. The Poet to the Painter, i. 92.
- liii. An Epigram to William, Earl of Newcastle, i. 109.
- liv. Epistle to Master Arthur Squib, ii. 375.
- lix. An Epigram to the Earl of Newcastle, i. 109.
- lxi. An Epigram to the Lord Keeper, i. 245.
- lxii. An Epigram to King Charles, i. 96 ; ii. 361.
- lxiii. To King Charles and Queen Mary, ii. 361.
- lxvi. An Epigram to the Queen lying-in, ii. 361.
- lxviii. An Epigram to the Household, i. 96 ; ii. 356.
- lxix. An Epigram to a Friend and Son, ii. 367.
- lxx. A Pindaric Ode on the death of Sir H. Morison, i. 109 ; ii. 381, 398, 399, 404, **406**.
- lxxi. To the Lord High Treasurer, an Epistle Mendicant, i. 92, 98, 110 ; ii. 371.
- lxxiii. To Lord Weston, i. 110.
- lxxiv. To Hierome, Lord Weston, ii. 399, 404-6.
- lxxv. Epithalamion ... to Master H. Weston, ii. **404-5**.
- lxxvi. The Humble Petition of poor Ben to ... King Charles, i. 248.
- lxxvii. To the Lord Treasurer ('If to my mind'), i. 110.
- lxxviii. An Epigram to my Muse, the Lady Digby, i. 1 n, 110 ; ii. 382.
- lxxxiii. An Elegy on the Lady Jane Pawlet, ii. 381-2.
- lxxxiv. Eupheme (1–9), i. 110 ; ii. 214, **382-3**.

Index

JONSON, Benjamin. **Poems** (*cont.*)
Underwoods (*cont.*)
lxxxv. Horace, *Epode* ii, i. 134, 156; ii. 407.
lxxxvi. Horace, *Odes*, iv. 1, ii. 408.
lxxxvii. Horace, *Odes*, iii. 9, ii. 408.
lxxxviii. Fragment of Petronius, i. 134, 156.
lxxxix. Martial, viii. 77, ii. 408.
Ungathered Verse.
  ii. Breton's *Melancholic Humours*, ii. 393.
  v. Chester's Ode 'Ενθουσιαστική, ii. 403.
  vi. Holland's *Pancharis*, i. 32 n; ii. 399, **403–4**.
  vii. Wright's *Passions of the Mind*, ii. 393.
  ix. Epitaph on Cicely Boulstred, ii. 356.
  xxvi. Shakespeare ('To draw no envy'), ii. **376–8**, 447.
  xxx. Drayton's *Battle of Agincourt*, ii. 339, **375–6**.
  xxxiv. Expostulation with Inigo Jones, i. 98; ii. 146, 356.
  xxxv. To Inigo Marquis Wouldbe, i. 98.
  xxxvi. An Epigram of Inigo Jones, i. 98; ii. 356.
  xlvii. Extempore Grace before King James, i. 180, 183, 189.
  l. Martial, x. 47 ('The things that make'), i. 132, 135; ii. 408.
Translation of Horace's *De Arte Poetica*, i. 134, 144, 156; ii. 407–8.
Works planned, but either not written or lost.
Amphitryo (a play), i. 73, 145.
Anne, Queen, poem on the death of, i. 207.
Argenis, translation of, i. 74–5, 87–8.
Fisher play, A (the scene Loch Lomond), i. 73, 143.
'Discourse of Poesy' (against Campion and Daniel), i. 132.
Discovery, A, describing the Scottish journey, i. 73–4, 143, 169; ii. 339.
Henry V, A History of, i. 73–4.

JONSON, Benjamin (*cont.*)
Works planned (*cont.*)
Heroologia, i. 73–4, 132, 152; ii. 339.
'Observations upon Horace's *Art of Poetry*' (including an 'Apology for *Bartholomew Fair*'), i. 48, 70 n, 134, 144, 156; ii. 134, 450.
'Parabostes Pariane with his letter', i. 131, 135, 156.
Proserpine, an epic on, i. 73; ii. 339.
Satires on 'abuses' and on a lady, i. 135.
Vigilium Veneris, A (after Bonnefons), i. 143.
Prose Works.
The Discoveries. Commonplacebooks in the seventeenth century, ii. 339. Donne's practice, and Jonson's, *ib.* The publication of the *Discoveries*, 440. The autobiographical element in them, 441–4, 448. Jonson's study of the classics, 444–5. Knowledge and self-education, 445–6. The training of a poet, 446–7. Criticism of Shakespeare, 447. Comments on style, 448–9. Construction, 449. Criticism of contemporaries, 449–50. On life and conduct, 450–1. Also i. 104–5, 123, 336 n, 376–7, 433; ii. 9, 343 n, 345 n, 408.
The English Grammar. Jonson's two attempts, ii. 418. His predecessors, 418–20. Etymology and syntax, 420–4. Attention to phonetics, 420. Latin analogies overdone, 420–1. Spelling reform, 421–3. The revised text of 1692, 424–8. Apostrophe and elision, 428–31. Punctuation, 431–5. Also i. 73, 105.
Leges Convivales, i. 85–6; ii. 373 n.
JONSON'S FAMILY:—
Grandfather, i. 1, 139.
Father, i. 2, 139, 178.
Mother, i. 2, 38–9, **140**, 178.
Wife, i. 8–9, 139–40, **220–3**.

Index 473

JONSON'S FAMILY (*cont.*)
  Son, eldest (Benjamin), i. 9, 32, 139-40, 164, 183; ii. 241-2, 282, 380.
  Son, second (Benjamin), i. 9.
  Daughter (Mary), i. 9, ii, 380.
Jonsonus Virbius, i. 116-17; quoted, 43 n, 50 n, 106 n, 107 n, 186; ii. 214, 409, 439-40.
JORDAN, Thomas, *Fancy's Festivals*, ii. 304; *Jewels of Ingenuity*, i. 187.
JOSEPHUS, i. 252.
JUVENAL, i. 59, 132, 136, 156, 160, 176, 181, 216, 251; and *Sej.*, ii. 11, 15, 19, 446; Jonson's copy of, i. 266; Jonson's manuscript of, 251, 262-3.

KARL AUGUST, Grand Duke of Weimar, ii. 288.
KASTNER, L. E., editor of Drummond, i. 79 n.
KEATS, John, ii. 304.
KELLY, Edward (alchemist), ii. 93.
KEMPE, William (actor), i. 28 n, 416 n.
KING, Edward, ii. 338.
KITTREDGE, G. L., on *D. is A.*, ii. 151 n, 163 n.
KNEVET, Master, disputation in his house at Paris, i. 65-7.
KNOLLYS, Sir William, i. 218.
KNOX, John, i. 59; ii. 262.
KNYVETT, Thomas, i. 232.
KOEPPEL, E., ii. 75 n, 178 n.
KYD, Thomas, i. 17, 356; ii. 55. *Soliman and Perseda*, i. 352. *The Spanish Tragedy*, 13, 354, 426; ii. 135; Jonson's 'Additions' to, i. 21, 33; ii. 237-45.

LACY, John (actor), i. 179, 180, 183.
LAING, David, editor of the *Conversations*, i. 129, 130, 170, 173, 234.
LAMB, Charles, i. 94.
LANDOR, W. S., ii. 343, 385, 413.
LANGBAINE, Gerard, i. 1 n, 5 n; on *Cat.*, ii. 113; on *M. L.*, 204.
LANGLAND, William, his 'Lady Mead', ii. 183 n.
LANIER, Nicholas (musician), ii. 301.

LAUD, William (Archbishop of Canterbury), i. 245.
LEE, Sir Sidney, i. 155; ii. 173 n, 425.
LEECH, John, Jonson's letter to, i. 200.
LEICESTER, Robert Dudley, Earl of, i. 142, 167.
LEICESTER, Robert Sidney, Viscount Lisle, Earl of, i. 139, 164.
Leigh, Swain's Farm at, ii. 368 n.
LESSING, G. E., on the epigram, ii. 345 n, 351-2.
L'ESTRANGE, Sir Nicholas, anecdote of Shakespeare and Jonson, i. 186.
LIBANIUS and *S. W.*, ii. 75.
LING, Nicholas, publisher of *E. M. O.*, i. 373.
LOCRINE, i. 325.
LODGE, Thomas, i. 340; his satires, 378, 397-8; ii. 345.
Lomond, Loch, i. 73, 74, 143, 150, 168, 169, 177, 207, 208.
London in Jonson's day, i. 9-12; on the stage, ii. 33.
  Artillery Garden, The, i. 359.
  Bankside, The, i. 12, 15; ii. 131.
  Bartholomew Fair, ii. 131-145.
  Blackfriars, Earl of Newcastle's house in, ii. 311.
  Blackfriars, Jonson's house in, i. 31 n, 56, 228, 232-3; ii. 50.
  Blackfriars Theatre, i. 91 n, 99, 100, 275, 393; ii. 31, 151, 191, 203.
  Bunhill, i. 178 n, 241.
  Coleman Street, i. 359.
  Consistory Court of, i. 8, 42-3, 220-3.
  Counter, The, ii. 41.
  Curriers' Hall, ii. 300, 301.
  Curtain Theatre, The, i. 12, 18, 179, 182.
  Devil tavern, i. 85-6, 104, 188-9.
  Dog tavern, i. 85, 112.
  Exchange, The, i. 9, 358.
  Finsbury, i. 276, 359.
  Fleet bridge, i. 358.
  Fleet Street, i. 359.
  Globe Theatre, The, i. 67, 69, 373; ii. 49, 261.
  Hartshorn Lane, i. 1 n.

London in Jonson's day (*cont.*)
 Hope Theatre, The, ii. 131.
 Houndsditch, i. 359.
 Hoxton (Hogsden), i. 18, 359.
 Inns of Court, i. 12, 22-3, 358; Gray's Inn, i. 47, 70; ii. 257, 291 n; Inner Temple, i. 47, 291 n; Middle Temple, *ib.*
 Islington ponds, i. 356.
 Jewry, The Old, i. 359.
 Kentish Town, i. 292.
 Love Lane, ii. 300.
 Marshalsea, The, i. 15.
 Marylebone (Maribone), i. 292.
 Mermaid tavern, i. 49-51, 58, 120.
 Mitre tavern, i. 257 n.
 Moorgate, i. 359.
 Newington Butts Theatre, i. 12.
 Old Bailey, The, i. 18.
 Paris Garden, i. 12, 13, 14.
 Pudding Lane, ii. 300.
 Rose Theatre, The, i. 12.
 St. Pancras, i. 285, 292.
 St. Paul's Cathedral, i. 10, 358; ii. 177.
 St. Paul's School, i. 26; ii. 322 n.
 Shoreditch, i. 18, 219, 359.
 Smithfield, ii. 133, 134, 255.
 Somerset House, ii. 91.
 Star Chamber, The, i. 358.
 Sun tavern, i. 85.
 Swan tavern, i. 180.
 Swan Theatre, i. 12.
 Thames Street, i. 359.
 Theatre, The, i. 12.
 Totten Court, i. 285, 292.
 Tower, The, i. 358; ii. 49 n, 91.
 Triple Tun tavern, i. 85, 112.
 Westminster, i. 2, 103, 113 n, 242; ii. 177; Jonson's house in, i. 98, 103, 113 n, 115, 179.
 Westminster Abbey, Jonson's grave in, i. 115, 117, 179-80.
 Westminster, Dean and Chapter of, i. 95, 114 n, 115 n, 244-5.
 Westminster School, i. 3-4, 178, 245; ii. 445.
 Whitechapel, i. 359.
 Whitefriars, ii. 69.
 Whitehall, i. 26, 69, 96-7; ii. 261, 265, 278, 295, 302 n, 317, 320-1, 326.
London Prodigal, The, ii. 180.

LUCAN, i. 130, 134, 152, 155, 156, 168, 176, 252.
LUCIAN, used in *Poet.*, i. 440 n; in *Volp.*, i. 43; ii. 51-3; Jonson's copy of, i. 266.
LUCRETIUS, Jonson's copy of, i. 255-7, 266.
LUTHER, Martin, ii. 90.
LYDGATE, John, his disguisings, ii. 254; in *G. A. R.*, 298-9.
LYLY, John, i. 214, 298, 300. *Endimion* and *C. R.*, 403-4. *Gallathea* and *Alch.*, ii. 94. Lyly and Guarini, 221.

MABBE, James, i. 260, 264.
MACHIAVELLI, N., *Belphegor*, ii. 154.
MCKERROW, R. B., i. 16 n.
Malleus Maleficarum, i. 252.
MALONE, Edmond, *Variorum Shakespeare*, i. 239; ii. 189 n, 191 n, 321 n.
MANNING, O., and BRAY, W., *History of Surrey*, ii. 368 n.
MANNINGHAM, John, *Diary*, i. 30, 31 n; ii. 3.
'Marforio', i. 144, 170; ii. 345.
MARIUS, Hadrianus, his gift of a book to Jonson, i. 260, 270.
MARKHAM, Gervase, i. 137, 160, 251.
MARLOWE, Christopher, i. 178 n, 339, 356; ii. 21-2, 294, 397. *Doctor Faustus*, i. 10, 280 n, 281 n; ii. 154, 157, 237. *Elegy* I. xv quoted in *Poet.*, i. 431. *Hero and Leander*, 420. *The Jew of Malta*, 321-2; ii. 21-2. *Tamburlaine*, i. 10; ii. 450.
MARMION, Shackerley, i. 86 n.
MAROT, Clement, his pastoralism, ii. 223.
MARSTON, John, Jonson's relations with, i. 24-7, 131, 136, 140, 159; Jonson's quip on his comedies, 138, 163; Jonson's copy of *Tragedies and Comedies*, 264; attacked in *The Whipping of the Satyre*, 29; not attacked in *E. M. O.*, 382; nor portrayed in *C. R.*, 406-10; 'Crispinus' in *Poet.*, 423-6, 438-40; ii. 449; his verses on *Sej.*, i. 36 n. *Dutch Courtesan*, ii. 39. *East-*

Index

MARSTON, John (*cont.*)
   ward Ho, i. 140, 164-5, 190-3.
   Histriomastix, 24-5, 373, 382; ii. 347. *Jack Drum's Entertainment*, i. 24, 407. Poem in *Love's Martyr*, 434. *The Malcontent*, 192. *Parasitaster*, 192; ii. 180. *Satires*, i. 29, 378, 382. *Sophonisba*, 192. *What you Will*, 27, 407.
MARTIAL, his epigrams, i. 23, 26, 131, 132, 135, 136, 137, 156, 166, 170, 176, 196, 375; ii. 340, **342-57**; Jonson's copy of, i. 253-4, 266; gives a copy of Farnaby's edition, 215-16.
MARTIN, Sir Richard, i. 22 n, 30, 49 n.
MARY, Queen of England, i. 2, 139, 148, 280 n.
MARY, Queen of Scotland, i. 59, 82, 137, 161, 166, 208-9; ii. 262.
MARY of Lorraine (queen of James V of Scotland), i. 208.
Masque, The, nature and conditions of, ii. 249-50; early history of in England, 250-8; essential features of, 251-4.
MASSINGER, Philip, i. 73, 199; 'Sir Giles Overreach', ii. 57.
MASSON, David, i. 78 n, 206, 207-8.
MATTHEW, Sir Tobie, i. 18 n, 204, 331.
MAY, Thomas, i. 75 n.
MAYNE, Jasper, i. 116; on *Volp.*, 43 n; on Jonson's critics, 50 n; on his slowness in composing, 186; on his verse, ii. 409.
MEAD, Joseph (letter-writer), i. 87 n, 90 n.
MEIGHEN, Richard (publisher), ii. 131 n.
MELLIN de Saint-Gelais, ii. 395.
MENANDER, Jonson compared to, i. 97 n; and the Old Comedy, 376.
MERCAT, John (grammarian), ii. 419.
MEREDITH, George, ii. 364; and the Comic Spirit, 83.
MERES, Francis, *Palladis Tamia*, i. 17, 283, 305-6, 331; ii. 240-1.

Merry Devil of Edmonton, The, ii. 154.
MEYNELL, Alice, ii. 390.
MIDDLETON, Thomas, Jonson's opinion of, i. 73, 137, 160; City Chronologer, 93, 240, 241. *Blurt Master Constable*, 297. *A Game of Chess*, ii. 325. *The Widow*, 195 n.
MILDMAY, Sir Walter, i. 218.
MILTON, John, *Comus*, i. 108, 320; ii. 250, 274, **307-9**. *Il Penseroso*, i. 320; ii. 145. *Lycidas*, i. 117; ii. 281, 325, 338, 383. *Sonnets*, 363. Elegy on Lady J. Pawlett, i. 111. Latin grammar, ii. 417.
MINSHEU, John, Jonson's opinion of, i. 133, 154, 172.
Mirror for Magistrates, The, ii. 24.
MOLIÈRE, J.-B., i. 108, 125, 126; his plot structure, 307; treatment of the miser-type, 321-2; comedy and farce, ii. **82-4**. *Georges Dandin*, 108. *Malade Imaginaire*, 83. *Misanthrope*, i. 388-9; ii. 83, 145. *Tartuffe*, i. 351.
MOLIN, Nicolò (Venetian ambassador), i. 203.
MONSON, Sir Thomas, i. 254.
MONTEAGLE, William, Lord, epigram to, i. 41.
MONTGOMERY, Philip Herbert, Lord, Jonson's letter to, i. 190, 199.
MORANT, Philip, *History of Essex*, i. 225 n.
MORE, John (letter-writer), ii. 286 n.
MORE, Sir Thomas, the play of, i. 355.
MORISON, Sir Henry, ode on, i. 109; ii. 381, 398, 404, 406.
MORLEY, George (Bishop of Winchester), i. 5 n, 115, 181, 184.
MORYSON, Fynes, i. 75-6.
MOSCHUS, his idyll of 'runaway Cupid', ii. 276.
MOSELEY, Humphrey (publisher), ii. 213 n.
MOUNTFORDE, Thomas, i. 221, 223.
Mucedorus, i. 291, 296-8, 300.
MULCASTER, Richard, i. 26; *Elementarie*, ii. 418, 420, 422, 424, 426, 431, 434-5.

476 Index

MUNDAY, Anthony, satirized in *C. is A.*, i. 20, 305-7. *Downfall and Death of Robert, Earl of Huntingdon*, ii. 224. *John a Kent and John a Cumber*, i. 296. *The Two Italian Gentlemen*, 352.
MURETUS, M. A., i. 253.
MURRAY, Sir James, and E. H., i. 140, 164, 191.
MYERS, F. W., i. 436.

NAPIER, John, his invention of logarithms, ii. 207.
NASHE, Thomas, i. 11, 122, 340, 389 n. *Christ's Tears*, ii. 82 n. *Have with you to Saffron-Walden*, i. 177. *Isle of Dogs*, **15-16, 217-18**. Notices *C. is A.* in *Lenten Stuffe*, 16, 306.
NEWCASTLE, Elizabeth Barret, Countess of, i. 211.
NEWCASTLE, Margaret Cavendish, Countess, afterwards Duchess of, on Jonson's masques, ii. 332-3.
NEWCASTLE, William Cavendish, Earl, afterwards Duke of, i. 109-10, 181; Jonson's letters to, 98 n, 210-14, 241; Entertainments for, ii. 311, 332-4.
NEWTON, Adam, i. 232, 233, 235.
NICHOLS, John, *Progresses of Queen Elizabeth*, ii. 255 n, 256 n, 257 n, 260 n; *Progresses of King James*, 271 n, 274 n, 328 n.
NICHOLSON, Brinsley, i. 34 n, 332.
NIDER, Johannes, i. 252.
NISBET, James (baillie of Edinburgh), i. 207.
NISBET, Sir William (Lord Provost of Edinburgh, i. 207, 234.
NOBLE, T. C., *Memorials of Old Temple Bar*, i. 235.
NORTHAMPTON, Henry Howard, Earl of, Jonson's enemy, i. 37, 141, 166, 193; ii. 4.
NORTHUMBERLAND, Henry Percy, Earl of, i. 144, 171.
NOTTINGHAM, Charles Howard, Earl of, i. 218.
NOYE, Sir William (attorney-general), i. 185, 187.

OLDISWORTH, Michael, his visit to Jonson, i. 113 n.
OLDISWORTH, Nicholas, i. 210.
OLDYS, William, i. 5 n. 165, 183.
OSBALSTON, Lambert, i. 244, 245.
OVERALL, John (Dean of St. Paul's), i. 223.
OVERBURY, Sir Thomas, Jonson's relations with, i. 54, 137, 138, 161; Jonson's epigram to, 161; ii. 366; 'Mogibell' in *The May Lord*, i. 143; Characters attributed to, ii. 207; *The Wife*, i. 54, 138, 163; murder, 254.
OVID, his story of Narcissus and *C. R.*, i. 399; a character in *Poet.*, 29, 417-19, 428-31, 436, 438; ii. 74, 207. Also i. 252; ii. 204.
OWEN, John (epigrammatist), i. 138, 154, 163; ii. 345 n, 351.
Oxford, Jonson at, i. 56, 83-4, 234-5.
OXFORD, Henry de Vere, Earl of, i. 260, 266.

PALISSY, Bernard, his alchemic experiments, ii. 91.
PALSGRAVE, John, *Acolastus*, ii. 32.
PANVINIUS, Onuphrius, i. 252.
PARABOSCO, Girolamo, i. 131, 135, 156; ii. 95.
PARACELSUS, i. 253; ii. 92-3, 295.
Paris, Jonson in, i. 64-9; ii. 142.
PARTENIO, Bernardino, i. 254.
PASFIELD, Zacharias, i. 221, 223.
'Pasquil', assumed name of satirists at Rome, i. 144, 170; ii. 345.
PATERSON, Alexander, i. 234.
PATTERSON, R. F., editor of the *Conversations*, i. 130-1, 149 n, 176.
PAVY, Salathiel (child-actor), epitaph of, ii. 341, **379**.
PAWLET. See Winchester.
PAYNE, Robert, i. 212, 213.
PEACHAM, Henry, i. 60 n.
PECK, H. W., editor of *M. L.*, ii. 204.
PEELE, George, and Jonson's Inductions, i. 389 n. *Arraignment of Paris*, ii. 221.

Index

PEMBROKE, Mary (Sidney), Countess of, translator of the Psalms, i. 138.
PEMBROKE, Mary (Talbot), Countess of, i. 55, 142; ii. 389.
PEMBROKE, William Herbert, Earl of, Jonson's relations with, i. 55, 141, 142, 200, 250; procures Jonson an honorary degree at Oxford, 83, 234-5; Jonson's letter to, 190, 199-200; *Cat.* and *Epigr.* dedicated to him, 46-7, 165; ii. 113, 343, 361; on Inigo Jones, i. 171.
PENNIMAN, J. H., *The War of the Theatres*, i. 25 n, 131, 140 n, 165, 351 n. Also i. 339 n.
Penshurst, i. 55, 57; ii. 369, 371.
PEPYS, Samuel, i. 260; ii. 79 n.
PERCY, Sir Jocelyn, i. 148, 173.
PERSIUS, i. 52, 136, 216, 251, 434; ii. 440.
PETRARCH, Drummond on, i. 79; Jonson on, 79, 133; ii. 95 n, 392.
PETRONIUS, his *Satiricon* and *Volp.*, i. 43; ii. 51-5, 60; spurious epigram of, i. 134, 136, 156.
PHAER, Thomas, i. 153.
PHILIP THE SECOND, King of Spain, i. 142.
PHILLIPS, Edward, i. 183.
PHILOSTRATUS, i. 251, 252; ii. 386.
PINDAR, to be read 'for delight', i. 136, 158; the 'Pindaric' ode, ii. 340, 394-401.
PLATO, ii. 268, 331, 342, 445; his idealization of friendship, 197-8, 376; *Symposium*, 198.
PLAUTUS, i. 122, 338, 347, 349, 352, 376; ii. 137. *Amphitryo*, i. 144. *Aulularia*, 307-10, 321-4. *Captivi*, 307-10, 315-17. *Casina*, ii. 76, 78. *Cistellaria*, i. 385 n. *Mostellaria*, ii. 98, 100 n. *Poenulus*, 100 n.
PLINY, the Elder, ii. 262, 273.
PLINY, the Younger, i. 104, 132, 136, 149, 170, 176; ii. 296.
PLUME, Thomas (Archdeacon of Rochester), notes on Jonson, i. 184-188.

Polesworth, i. 56.
POLITIANUS, Angelus, i. 252.
POPE, Alexander, i. 58, 59, 85; ii. 279, 381.
PORPHYRIUS of Tyre, i. 253.
PORTA, Johannes Baptista, i. 253.
PORTAL, E. M., i. 86 n.
PORTER, Henry, *The Two Angry Women of Abingdon*, i. 300, 344 n.
PORTLAND, Richard, Lord Weston, Earl of, i. 110.
PORY, Sir John (letter-writer), i. 66, 92 n; ii. 203 n.
PRICE, Theodore (sub-dean of Westminster), i. 244.
PROPERTIUS, his Elegies, ii. 358-60; undervalued in Jonson's time, i. 428-9; his relations with Ovid and Horace, 419.
PSELLUS, Michael, i. 253.
PUCKERING, Sir Thomas, i. 92 n; ii. 203 n.
PULTAN, Ferdinando, i. 223.
Punctuation, Elizabethan, ii. 431-5.
PURBECK, Frances, Lady, ii. 190.
PURBECK, John Villiers, Viscount, in *G. M.*, ii. 314.
Puritans, satire on the, i. 180, 256-7; ii. 104-5, 132, 139, 140, 143-5, 320-1; 'The Blatant Beast', i. 137, 161.
PUTTENHAM, *Art of English Poesie*, i. 144, 169; ii. 345, 396; Jonson's copy of, i. 169, 262, 264.

QUINTILIAN, i. 104, 132, 136, 155, 156, 251; ii. 446, 448.

RABELAIS, François, ii. 110, 195.
RACINE, Jean, i. 108, 307.
RADCLIFFE, Sir John, his gift of a manuscript and a book to Jonson, i. 260, 263, 265; Jonson's epigram to, ii. 364.
RAE, William (treasurer of the City of Edinburgh), i. 234.
RAITH, James. *See* Writh.
RALEGH, Sir Walter, i. 37, 64, 140, 165, 383; ii. 142 n, 284; Jonson's contribution to his *History of the World*, i. 49, 65, 138, 162, 165; and Spenser, 132, 137, 152.

478   Index

RALEGH, Walter, the younger, i. 65, 67, 140, 165, 181, 185; ii. 141-2.
'Ralph', a drawer at the Swan tavern, i. 180, 189.
RAMÉE, Pierre de la (grammarian), ii. 419, 420, 431, 435.
RAMSEY, Robert W., on Jonson's library, i. 251 n.
RANDOLPH, Thomas, i. 95, 113; *Amyntas*, ii. 215 n.
RATCLIFFE, Margaret, epitaph of, ii. 381.
REMY, Nicholas, i. 253.
Return from Parnassus, The, i. 5 n, 6 n, 28 n, 416 n.
REYHER, Paul, *Les Masques Anglais*, ii. 249, 251, 257, 276.
RICH, Barnaby, i. 11.
RICHARD THE SECOND, King of England, as prince receives a Court pageant, ii. 251.
RIGAL, E., on Molière, ii. 83.
ROBINSON, Robert (grammarian), ii. 419.
RODMAN, G. H., *A Calendar of Grants of Probate ... of the Commissary Court of Westminster*, i. 249.
ROE, Cheney, i. 225, 226, 227.
ROE, Sir John, i. 39, **51-52**, 136, 137, 159, **224**; Jonson's epigrams to, 230; ii. 366.
ROE, Sir Thomas, i. 45 n, 52 n, 224.
ROE, Thomas, the younger, i. 226.
ROE (ROWE), Sir William, plaintiff in a Chancery suit, i. 1 n, **51-2**, 223-31; Jonson's epigrams to, 230-1; ii. 366.
RONSARD, Pierre, i. 67, 134, 173; ii. 394-6, 398.
ROS, Robertus de, i. 179, 180.
Rosicrucians, the, ii. 329.
ROSINUS, Johannes, i. 252.
ROSSETTI, D. G., ii. 405.
ROUTH, H. V., i. 11 n, 346 n.
ROWE, Nicholas, on Shakespeare and *E. M. I.*, i. 18 n.
RUDDIMAN, Thomas, editor of Drummond, i. 128.
RUDOLF THE SECOND, Emperor of Germany, ii. 90 n.
RUDYARD, Sir Benjamin, epigram to, ii. 364.

RUGGLE, George, i. 268.
RUTLAND, Elizabeth (Sidney), Countess of, Jonson's relations with, i. 54, 138, 142, 419; his poems to, 54, 163, 198; ii. 368, 370; a character in *The May Lord*, i. 143; ii. 216-17.
RUTTER, Joseph, i. 113.
RYMER, Thomas, *Foedera*, ii. 320 n.

SACKVILLE. *See* Dorset.
SAGE, John, editor of Drummond, i. 128, 130.
SAINT-AMANT, i. 107.
St. Andrews, students of, i. 207.
SAINT-ÉVREMOND, i. 126.
SAINTE-BEUVE, C. A., ii. 395.
SAINTSBURY, George, ii. 412.
SALISBURY, Sir Robert Cecil, Earl of, Jonson's relations with, i. 57-8, 141, 142, 167, 170; ii. 362; and *The Isle of Dogs*, i. 196, 218; *E. H.*, 39, 190; ii. 349 n; Gunpowder Plot, i. 40-1; Jonson's letters to, 41, 194-6, 202-3; Jonson's epigram to, ii. 365; Entertainments at Theobalds, i. 58 n; ii. 264.
SALLUST, and *Cat.*, ii. **117-21**, 123; Jonson's copy of, i. 254, 267.
SANDYS, Sir George, ii. 255.
SANNAZZARO, G., his *Arcadia*, ii. 219.
SAVILE, Sir Henry, i. 56, 235; Jonson's epigram to, 56, 107; ii. 341, 346, 364; his translation of Tacitus, ii. 167.
Savoy, Duke of, i. 209.
SCALIGER, Joseph, i. 146, 172, 176.
SCALIGER, J. C., ii. 343, 408, 419; on epigram, 351.
SCHELLING, Felix, i. 198; ii. 98, 412 n.
SCHILDERS (Puritan controversialist), i. 357.
SCHILLER, F., on the drama, ii. 249; his epigrams, 343.
SCHMIEDER, K., *Geschichte der Alchemie*, ii. 90.
SCOT, Sir John, of Scotstarvet, i. 78, 207.
SCOTT, Sir Walter, i. 436.
SCRIVERIUS, Petrus, Jonson's copy of his *Martial*, i. 253-4; ii. 348 n.

Index

SELDEN, John, i. 35, 105, 106 n, 251; and James I, **86-7**; on Jonson's library and learning, 48, 103, 250; on *B. F.*, ii. 146; Jonson's epistle to, 367, **372-3**. *De Diis Syris*, i. 136, 159, and Jonson's copy of, 270. *De Successionibus in Bona Defuncti*, 176. *Jani Anglorum Facies Altera*, Jonson's copy of, 270. *Titles of Honor*, 136, 149, 159, 250, and Jonson's copy of, 264.

Selimus, i. 297.

SENECA, L. Annaeus (tragedian and philosopher), i. 252; ii. 408. *Tragedies*, i. 216; ii. 8, 114-16. *Epistles*, i. 180, 183, 261; ii. 417, 440. *De Beneficiis*, 441. *De Tranquillitate*, 11.

SENECA, M. Annaeus (rhetorician), ii. 442-3, 444-5.

SETON, Alexander (alchemist), ii. 92.

SHAA, Robert (actor), i. 16, 218.

SHADWELL, Thomas, i. 126 n, 181; and *S. W.*, ii. 79.

SHAKESPEARE, William, with Jonson at the Mermaid, i. 49-51; at a christening, 184-5, 186-7; takes part in the Stage Quarrel, 357, 416; his alleged epitaph on Jonson, 184, 186; with Jonson at Stratford, 85; and Jonson's début, 10, 11, 311-12; and *E. M. I.*, 18, 331; as 'Virgil' in *Poet.*, 432-3, 437; and *Sej.*, ii. 4; reminiscences of in *C.R.*, i. 410; in *S. W.*, ii. 73-4; Kitely and King John, i. 348; Prospero and Subtle, ii. 94; Jonson to Drummond on, i. 73; Jonson's criticism of, 185; ii. **376-8**, 447; 'wanted art', i. 73, 129, 133, 154, 430; ii. 447; 'sufflaminandus erat', 445, 450; on *The Tempest*, 135; on *The Winter's Tale*, i. 129, 138, 163, 185, 187; ii. 135.

Titles of his comedies, i. 280; his description of the aims of drama, 378-9; on 'secrets' kept from the audience, ii. 79-80; clowns and jesters, i. 297-8; mingling of wit and

SHAKESPEARE, William (*cont.*) passion, 300; of comedy and tragedy, 313; poetic use of farce, ii. 83; psychology of character, i. 339; use of the motive of forgiveness, 316; his 'repentances', ii. 36; his satire on gravity, i. 320; on academies, ii. 104; his citizens, 33-4; his Histories, 9; his reticence, 18-19; his criminals and Jonson's, 20-2, 127; his Tragedy and Jonson's, 127; his Chorus and Jonson's, 115-16; his later Romantic plays, 135; his Venice, 57; his Pastoralism, 221-2; and Lyly, i. 403; and Puritanism, ii. 145; friend of Florio, 95.

Antony and Cleopatra, i. 438; ii. 7.

As You Like It, i. 28 n, 280, 298, 300, 314, 317, 319, 401, 410; ii. 218, 221.

Comedy of Errors, i. 290, 311, 313.

Coriolanus, i. 284; ii. 16.

Cymbeline, i. 316.

Hamlet, i. 11, 315, 378; ii. 115, 180, 237, 244; and the 'Children', i. 415-16; and Marston, ii. 40.

Henry IV, ii. 141.

Henry V, i. 311; ii. 115, 180, 293.

Henry VI, ii. 237.

Henry VIII, i. 69.

John, King, i. 348.

Julius Caesar, i. 185, 340; ii. **9-10**, 16, **26**, 122-4.

Lear, King, i. 11; ii. 20, 127-8, 244, 324 n.

Love's Labour's Lost, i. 296-7, 317, 326, 341, 375; ii. 104, 209-10.

Love's Labour's Won, ii. 375.

Macbeth, ii. 20-2, 56, 232-3; and *M. of Q.*, 279.

Measure for Measure, i. 316; ii. 180.

Merchant of Venice, The, i. 299, 307, 311, 315-16, 318, 326, 410 n.

Merry Wives of Windsor, The, i. 291; ii. 33, 293; and Jonson's comedy, 73.

Midsummer Night's Dream, A, i. 296, 307, 400-1; ii. 225, 233, 290.

SHAKESPEARE, William (cont.)
  Much Ado about Nothing, i. 297,
    320, 325, 386; ii. 293.
  Othello, ii. 16, 27, 63, 128, 265 n.
  Richard III, i. 11; ii. 22, 63.
  Romeo and Juliet, i. 11; ii. 209;
    and Poet., i. 430.
  Taming of the Shrew, The, i. 375.
  Tempest, The, i. 154, 316, 440; ii.
    94, 135.
  Timon of Athens, ii. 83, 182
  Titus Andronicus. See under
    separate heading.
  Troilus and Cressida, i. 28 n.
  Twelfth Night, i. 280, 298, 320,
    386; ii. 78, 141, 145, 196.
  Two Gentlemen of Verona, The,
    i. 298, 316, 318, 326.
  Winter's Tale, The, i. 154, 167,
    284, 311; ii. 79-80, 135, 221.
  Sonnets, ii. 376, 393 n, 403.
SHARPHAM, Edward, Jonson's
  opinion of, i. 133, 154.
SHAW, G. Bernard, i. 89.
SHAW, W. A., The Knights of England, i. 183.
SHELLEY, P.B., ii. 233, 271, 340-2, 410.
SHEPPARD, Samuel, and Sej., i. 34 n.
SHERBURN, Sir Edward, on P.R.V.,
  ii. 309.
SHERIDAN, R. B., i. 89.
SHIRLEY, James, his Latin Grammar, ii. 417; Triumph of
  Peace, 304, 332.
SIBBALD, Sir Robert, his transcript of Drummond's manuscript of the Conversations, i.
  129, 130, 176.
SIDNEY, Mary (Dudley), Lady, i.
  142, 167.
SIDNEY, Sir Philip, i. 79, 116; ii.
  382; his mother, i. 142, 167;
  his personal appearance, 138-9,
  164; performs in a 'Triumph',
  ii. 255; King James on, i. 142,
  168; and Bruno, ii. 95 n; his
  failure in 'decorum', i. 132, 149,
  152, 176; ii. 223, 226. Apology
  for Poetry, i. 10-11, 291, 311,
  335, 338-9, 342; ii. 446 n, 448.
  Arcadia, i. 10, 136, 137, 162; ii.
  220, 222. Lady of May,
  221, 256-7, 260. Translation of
  the Psalms, i. 138, 162.

SIDNEY, Philip, editor of the Conversations, i. 130.
SIDNEY, Sir William, ii. 399, 404.
SKELTON, John, i. 249, 286, 405-6; ii. 329-30.
SKINNER, Robert (Bishop of Oxford), i. 179.
SMALL, R. A., The Stage Quarrel,
  i. 14 n, 24 n, 25 n, 27 n, 33 n,
  279 n, 373 n, 382, 394 n, 407 n,
  428 n; ii. 147.
SMITH, Gregory, Ben Jonson, i.
  71, 171; Elizabethan Critical
  Essays, ii. 71, 446 n.
SMITH, L. Pearsall, Life of Sir H.
  Wotton, i. 172, 201; ii. 403 n.
SMITH, Richard (Bishop of Chalcedon), i. 66.
SMITH, Sir Thomas (grammarian),
  ii. 418, 420, 424.
SNELL, Florence, editor of T. of T.,
  i. 279 n, 284 n.
SOMERSET, Lady Frances Howard,
  Countess of (formerly Countess of Essex), her first marriage, i. 39, 69, 143; ii. 268; her
  second marriage, i. 70-1, 163; ii.
  291; a character in The May
  Lord, i. 143; her trial, 298.
Sonnet, Jonson on the, i. 133-4,
  155; ii. 392-3.
SOOTHERN, J., ii. 396.
SOPHOCLES, Oedipus, ii. 109.
SOUTHWELL, Robert, The Burning
  Babe, i. 137, 161; ii. 391-2.
SPEED, John, i. 35.
SPEGHT, Thomas, editor of Chaucer,
  i. 248; Jonson's copy of, 263.
SPENCER, Gabriel (actor), killed by
  Jonson), i. 16, 18-19, 218, 219.
SPENSER, Edmund, Jonson's
  opinion of, i. 10, 132, 152; Jonson's literary relation to, ii.
  411; his 'Cynthia' symbolism,
  i. 401; his enchanter, ii. 94; a
  character in G. A. R., i. 74; ii.
  298; said to have died in poverty, i. 137, 161. The Faerie
  Queene, 132, 137, 152, 161;
  ii. 233, 376. The Shepheards
  Calendar, i. 136; ii. 218, 220,
  276.
SPINGARN, J. E., i. 339 n, 342-3.
SPRENGER, Jacobus, i. 252.

Index

SQUIB, Arthur, epistles to, ii. 375.
STEELE, Sir Richard, ii. 177.
STOW, John, *Annals*, i. 149, 174; ii. 49 n.
STANHOPE, Edward, i. 223.
STANLEY, A. P., on Jonson's grave, i. 117 n.
STESICHORUS, ii. 219, 328.
STOLL, E. E. i. 325 n.
STRANGE, Thomas, gave Jonson a Statius MS. and a Bible, i. 262, 263.
Stratford-on-Avon, Jonson at, i. 85.
STUART, Sir Francis, *S. W.* dedicated to, i. 45 n; ii. 70.
STUART, John (of Leith), i. 78.
STUCKIUS, Johannes Gulielmus, i. 252.
STUTEVILE, Sir Martin, i. 87 n.
SUCKLING, Sir John, *A Session of the Poets*, i. 108; *Last Remains*, ii. 213 n.
SUETONIUS, i. 136; and *Sej.*, ii. 13, 21, 25.
SUFFOLK, Catherine Knyvet, Countess of, an enchantress in *The May Lord*, i. 143.
SUFFOLK, Thomas Howard, Earl of, and *E. H.*, i. 38-9, 159, 195 n; letter of Jonson probably addressed to him, 190, 193, 194; ii. 5; Jonson's epigram to, i. 159; his daughter's marriage, 39 (*see* Somerset, Countess of).
SURREY, Henry Howard, Earl of, ii. 382.
SUTCLIFFE, Matthew, i. 50 n.
SUTTON, Christopher, i. 244, 245.
SWIFT, Jonathan, ii. 305, 358.
SWINBURNE, A. C., *George Chapman*, ii. 5. *A Study of Ben Jonson*, i. 430 n; ii. 122 n, 204, 391 n, 449.
SYLVESTER, Joshua, i. 133, 153, 157.
SYMONDS, John Addington, *Ben Jonson*, i. 426 n, 432; ii. 62, 237.

TACITUS, and *Sej.*, i. 149, 162, 174; ii. **11-26**, 446; Jonson's praise of, i. 74, 136; Jonson's text of, 252; Grenewey's translation, 149, 167, 174; Savile's, 167.
Taming of a Shrew, The, i. 291.

TASSO, Torquato, ii. 94, 407; his pastoral poetry, 220-1, 227,229.
TAYLOR, John (the 'Water-poet' or 'Sculler'), i. 76-8, 142, 149, 168, 175, 206; ii. 397.
TENNANT, G. B., editor of *N. I.*, ii. 189 n, 191 n, 200.
TERENCE, ii. 210; Jonson's mn uscript of, i. 263.
TERRELL, Sir Robert, i. 229, 231.
THACKERAY, W. M., his 'Snobs', i. 341, 380.
Theobalds, i. 58 n, 87 n; ii. 264.
THEOCRITUS, ii. **218-19**, 223-5, **231-2**.
THEOPHRASTUS, *Characters*, i. 23, 340-1, 374-5; ii. 344.
THORNDIKE, A. H., i. 20 n, 394 n; ii. 69 n.
THROCKMORTON, Sir J., i. 224.
THUCYDIDES, ii. 117 n.
TIBULLUS, i. 419 n, 436; ii. 359.
Titus Andronicus, ii. 135, 239.
TOLSTOY, L., i. 279.
TOMKIS, Thomas, his *Albumazar*, ii. 96 n.
TOOKE, Horne, ii. 372.
TOPCLIFFE, Richard, i. 217, 218.
TOWNLEY, Zouch, i. 94, 242, 243, 244.
TOWNSHEND, Aurelian, i. 30 n, 98; ii. 332.
TOWNSHEND, Sir Robert, i. 30 n, 31 n; ii. 3.
TRISSINO, G. G., his *Sophonisba*, ii. 8.
TURBERVILE, George, i. 251.
TURNEBUS, Adrianus, i. 252, 270.

UBERTUS, Stephanus, i. 172.
UDALL, Nicholas, *Ralph Royster Doyster*, i. 290, 352.
UNWIN, G., *Industrial Organization in the Sixteenth and Seventeenth Centuries*, ii. 152 n.
UVEDALE, Sir William, epigram to, ii. 363.

VERE, Sir Edward, i. 255.
VERGIL, in *Poet.*, i. 418-20, 424, **427-37**; *Aeneid*, 431-6; ii. 280; *Eclogues*, 219, 286, 299, 364; translated by Duperron, i. 68-9, 134; by Phaer and Twyne, 133, 153.

Index

Vice, The, in the interludes, i. 144, 169.
VINCENT, Augustine (herald), i. 262.
VIVES, Juan Luis, ii. 444; Jonson's copy of his works, i. 269.

WADLOE, Simon (host of the 'Old Devil'), i. 85.
WAITE, A. V., editor of Jonson's *Grammar*, ii. 425.
WALKER, Sir Edward, i. 115 n.
WALLACE, C. W., i. 223 n.
WALLER, Edmund, ii. 413.
WALPOLE, Horace, i. 204.
Walpole Society, Catalogue of Inigo Jones's designs, ii. 266 n, 282 n, 318 n, 331 n.
WALSINGHAM, Sir Francis, i. 148.
WALTON, Izaak, his recollections of Jonson, i. 5 n, 69, 115, 181-182, 184; on Donne's reading, ii. 439.
WARD, Sir A. W., *History of English Dramatic Literature*, i. 394 n; ii. 122 n, 189 n.
WARD, John, i. 85 n.
WARNER, William, *Albion's England*, i. 133, 154.
WEBB, Joseph (grammarian), i. 114; ii. 419.
WEBSTER, John, i. 73.
WEEVER, John, *Epigrams*, ii. 345-7.
Welbeck, entertainment at, i. 100-1, 105, 212; ii. 332-3.
WELSFORD, Enid, ii. 265 n, 278 n.
WEST, Richard, i. 107 n.
WESTON, Hierome (afterwards Earl of Portland), i. 110; ii. 338, 404-5.
WESTON, Richard, Lord. See Portland, Earl of.
WEVER, R., *Lusty Juventus*, ii. 179.
WHALLEY, Peter, editor of Jonson, ii. 69 n, 425.
WHETSTONE, George, *Promos and Cassandra*, i. 339.
Whipper of the Satyre, The, i. 29 n.
Whipping of the Satyre, The (by 'W. I.'), i. 29, 357.
WHITE, William Augustus, i. 190.
WHYTE, Rowland (letter-writer), ii. 274 n.
WHYTE, Thomas, i. 235.

WILBRAHAM, Roger, i. 217, 218.
WILLIAMS, John, Bishop of Lincoln, i. 244, 245.
WILSON, John, *Belphegor*, ii. 154.
WILSON, Robert (dramatist), *Cobbler's Prophesie*, i. 324. *The Three Lords and the Three Ladies of London*, 406.
WILSON, Robert (inn-keeper), Jonson's chair at his inn in the Strand, i. 183.
Wily Beguiled, i. 291.
WINCHESTER, Lady Jane Pawlet, Marchioness of, i. 111; ii. 381.
Windsor, masque at, i. 72; ii. 314.
WINSTANLEY, William, i. 1 n.
WINTER, De, editor of *S. of N.*, ii. 181 n, 185 n.
WINWOOD, Sir Ralph, i. 224; ii. 286 n.
WISE, T. J., i. 30 n.
WISEMAN, Sir W., i. 181, 183.
WITHER, George, ii. 369; not 'Madrigal' in *S. of N.*, 185 n; 'Chronomastix' in *Time Vindicated*, i. 72, ii. **320-3**.
WOOD, Anthony à, i. 179 n.
WOOD, George (printer), ii. 322 n.
WORDSWORTH, William, i. 74; ii. 218, 372.
WOTTON, Sir Henry, i. 130, 146, 171-2, 201; ii. 347 n; his 'verses of a happy life', i. 73, 135, **157**; ii. 443.
WREN, Christopher (proctor of Oxford University), i. 235.
WREN, Sir Christopher, i. 311.
WRIGHT, T., poem to, ii. 393.
WRITH (RAITH), James (Edinburgh advocate), i. 78, 207-8.
WROTH, Mary, Lady, i. 54, 142, 167, 198; ii. 393; a character in *The May Lord*, i. 143.
WROTH, Sir Robert, i. **54-5**, 142, 167; ii. 369.
WYAT, Sir Thomas, ii. 344, 382, 395.
WYLD, H. C., ii. 421 n.

YOUNG, Sir John, i. 117, 179, 183.

ZACHAIRE, Denys (alchemist), ii. 91.
'Zulziman', i. 13-14.

PRINTED IN
GREAT BRITAIN
AT THE
UNIVERSITY PRESS
OXFORD
BY
CHARLES BATEY
PRINTER
TO THE
UNIVERSITY